New Interpretations
in Naval History

New Interpretations in Naval History

⚓

Selected Papers from the
Fourteenth Naval History Symposium

Held at Annapolis, Maryland
23–25 September 1999

Edited by
Randy Carol Balano
and
Craig L. Symonds

NAVAL INSTITUTE PRESS
Annapolis, Maryland

Naval Institute Press
291 Wood Road
Annapolis, MD 21402

© 2001 by the U.S. Naval Institute, Annapolis, Maryland

All rights reserved. No part of this book may be reproduced or utilized in any form or by any means, electronic or mechanical, including photocopying and recording, or by any information storage and retrieval system, without written permission from the publisher.

Library of Congress Cataloging-in-Publication Data

United States Naval Academy History Symposium (14th: 1999)
    New interpretations in naval history: selected papers from the Fourteenth Naval History Symposium, held at Annapolis, Maryland, 23ƒ25 September 1999 / edited by Randy Carol Balano and Craig L. Symonds.
    p. cm.
    ISBN 1-55750-498-9 (alk. paper)
    Includes bibliographical references.
    1. Naval history, Modern-18 th century-Congresses. 2. Naval history, Modern-19 th century-Congresses. 3. Naval history, Modern-20 th century-Congresses. I. Balano, Randy Carol, 1959ƒ II. Symonds, Craig L. III. Title.

V47.U55 2001
359'.009'03—dc21   2001042746

Printed in the United States of America on acid-free paper ∞

08 07 06 05 04 03 02 01   9 8 7 6 5 4 3 2

First printing

This volume is dedicated to:

⚓

John Gage Balano
for his unconditional support and infinite patience

⚓

and to the memory of
William J. Clipson
(1930–2000)
graphic artist, cartographer, and friend.

Contents

Preface   xi

Part I   British Naval History and Historiography

    The Use of Intelligence in Royal Navy Amphibious   3
        Operations, 1739–1783
            Richard H. Harding

    "Too Much Mixed in This Affair": The Impact of   21
        Ministerial Politics in the Eighteenth-Century
        Royal Navy
            Daniel A. Baugh

    In the Shadow of Marder: A New Perspective of   44
        British Naval Administration and the Naval Defense
        Act of 1889
            Robert E. Mullins

    Holding the Ring: The Royal Navy's Palestine   82
        Patrol, 1945–1948
            Ninian L. Stewart

Part II   French Naval History and Historiography

    Marines and Martial Races: The Recruitment of the   97
        Tirailleurs Sénégalais in French West Africa, 1857–1914
            Bruce Vandervort

    Officers in Charge of the French Navy Department   110
        during the Third Republic, 1870–1940
            Jean Martinant de Préneuf

Colbert's Legacy: The French Navy and Her Inheritors   123
in the Early 20th Century
R. Chalmers Hood with Phillippe Vial

Part III   The 19th Century U.S. Navy

"To Strike a Blow in the World that Shall Resound   131
through the Universe": American Naval Operations
and Options at the Start of the War of 1812
Jeff Seiken

"Concessions Where Concessions Could Be Made":   147
The Naval Efficiency Boards of 1855–1857
Kenneth J. Blume

"The Sudden Destruction of Bright Hopes":   160
Union Shipbuilding Management, 1862–1865
William H. Roberts

Mahan *versus* the Pacifists   189
Suzanne Geissler

Part IV   Naval Forces in World War II

Breaking out of Prison: Italian Naval Policy and   203
Operational Planning, 1935–1938
Robert Mallett

Doyle's Dauntless Dory: USS *Nassau* and the   217
Evolution of Carrier-Based Close Air Support
Hill Goodspeed

Military Missionary: The Riddle Wrapped in a   251
Mystery inside an Enigma that Was Evans F. Carlson
Phyllis A. Zimmerman

Admiral Henry Kent Hewitt: The Powerless Expert   265
    Adrian Lewis

Intelligence Test: Evaluating Ultra in the Battle of the Atlantic   280
    W. J. R. Gardner

F-21 and F-211: A Fresh Look into the "Secret Room"   298
    David Kohnen

Part V   The U.S. Navy Since World War II

A New Cold War: U.S. Marines in Norway and the Search for a New Mission in NATO   343
    David B. Crist

"Boulder Boys": Naval Japanese Language School Graduates   366
    Pedro Loureiro

Protested Presence: The Nuclear Navy Comes to Japan, 1961–1968   389
    Roger Dingman

After the Gulf War: Operational History for the 21st Century   424
    Charles D. Melson

Preface

The Fourteenth Naval History Symposium took place on the grounds of the U.S. Naval Academy in Annapolis, Maryland from 23-25 September 1999. The Naval Academy has hosted this biennial event in the fall of each odd-numbered year since 1971. The purpose of the meeting, which has become international in scope, is to provide a forum for the leading scholars in naval history to present the products of their research and to engage in conversations with each other as well as with the practitioners of naval warfare from the United States Navy and other navies around the world.

Some 250 individuals from fourteen countries attended the event in 1999. A total of eighty-three individuals made presentations, and after a difficult process, the editors selected twenty-one of those papers for inclusion in this volume. The symposium format in which two or three papers are presented in an hour-and-a-half session, necessarily meant that the oral versions of the papers had to be limited in length. This volume, however, contains the full-length versions of these papers, including endnotes.

The editors have grouped the papers selected for publication into five sections so that they are not necessarily matched up with the papers that comprised the original panel sessions. Nevertheless, the work published herein provides a sweeping *tour d'horizon* of the latest and most important work being done in the field of naval history.

The editors are grateful to the men and women who agreed to serve as session chairs and commentators at the Fourteenth Naval History Symposium, and who helped in the difficult process by which the papers included herein were selected. In recognition of their service, we list them here: Dean Allard, Former Director, Naval Historical Center (U.S.); John Beeler, University of Alabama; David Brown, Naval Historical Branch, Ministry of Defence (U.K.); William B. Cogar, The Mariner's Museum; B. Frank Cooling, National Defense University, (U.S.); Harry W. Dickinson, Britannia Royal Naval College (U.K.); W. J. R. Gardner, Naval Historical Branch (U.K.); Frank Gibney, Pacific Basin Institute, Pomona College; William H. Garzke, Jr., Gibbs and Cox, Inc.; William Glover, National Defense Headquarters, Canada; Barry Gough,

Wilfred Laurier University; John B. Hattendorf, U.S. Naval War College; Chalmers Hood, Independent Scholar; Capt. Peter Hore, Head, Defense Studies, Royal Navy; Harold D. Langley, The Catholic University of America; William McBride, U.S. Naval Academy; Christopher McKee, Grinnell College; John Miller, U.S. Naval Institute; Allan Millett, The Ohio State University; G. J. Montenegro, Escuela de la Guerra Naval, Argentine Navy; John Prados, Independent Scholar; Capt. Werner Rahn, German Navy (Ret.); James Reckner, Texas Tech University; Tim Runyan, East Carolina University; Brig. Gen. Edwin H. Simmons, History and Museum Division, USMC (Ret.); David Skaggs, Bowling Green State University (Emeritus); Ronald Spector, George Washington University; David Syrett, Queens College, City University of New York; Phillippe Vial, Service Historique de la Marine; Gary Weir, Naval Historical Center (U.S.); Richard Werking, Director, Nimitz Library, U.S. Naval Academy; Kathleen Broome Williams, Bronx Community College, City University of New York; David F. Winkler, Naval Historical Center (U.S.); Maochun Yu, U.S. Naval Academy.

Finally, the editors wish to thank their colleagues in the History Department who helped with the symposium administration, especially Capt. Wesley Feight, USMC; Maj. Vince Droddy, USAF; Lt. Comdr. Scott Granger, USNR, and Capt. Mark Lwin, USMC. To them, and to the rest of our colleagues in the History Department, we offer thanks not only for their assistance with the symposium, but for the stimulating environment they provide day to day throughout the year.

Randy Carol Balano
Craig L. Symonds

Part I

British Naval History and Historiography

New Interpretations in Naval History

The Use of Intelligence in Royal Navy Amphibious Operations, 1739-1783

Richard H. Harding

Intelligence is a crucial factor in warfare—including (maybe even especially) naval warfare. Yet in the Age of Sail, efforts to accumulate useful intelligence for fleet operations was generally haphazard and hampered by both slow communications and by the absence of an established system to gather and evaluate intelligence data. In this essay, Richard Harding evaluates several British efforts to use military intelligence during the Seven Years War, and concludes that despite significant gains in the accumulation of military intelligence—especially the mapping of North America—intelligence was not a key factor in the British war effort. Instead, politics, opportunism, and a blind faith in the superiority of British arms dominated strategic decision making in Whitehall. Worse, the failure to establish a system for the evaluation of military intelligence left the Royal Navy, and particularly the British Army, poorly prepared to fight the War of the American Revolution.

The study of military and naval intelligence has concentrated largely on the period after 1880 when both popular literature and the records of specific bureaucratic organizations demonstrate the existence of identifiable intelligence-related activities. The role of intelligence in eighteenth-century warfare has attracted less attention. There are good reasons for this. Espionage and counterespionage formed an integral part of military activities. They were not differentiated by specialisms nor recorded in a manner that emphasized any special role. Intelligence activities have always been recognized. There were *causes célèbre*, such as the treason of Benedict Arnold and the execution of Major André in 1780, and innumerable *ruses de guerre* which are the very stuff of military and naval history. There are the stories of cloak-and-dagger high politics, and of spymasters like Walsingham, which

---

Richard H. Harding is Professor of Organizational History at the University of Westminster in England.

punctuate most national histories. On the other hand, very little attention has been paid to how the generation and possession of intelligence influenced the military decisions and activities of a country. An examination of this process might throw some light on the conduct of British amphibious operations in the middle of the eighteenth century. During the period 1739-83, British forces conducted extensive amphibious operations in all kinds of conditions across the globe. They ranged from the spectacularly successful to the disappointing and downright disastrous. For the period as a whole, the experience and expertise of the British in these operations developed into a massive global capability unmatched by any other power. Some of the reasons for this have been examined elsewhere, but the system for gathering and analysing intelligence has not been one of them.[1]

Of particular interest is the role that intelligence may have played in the Seven Years War. The figure of William Pitt dominates the conduct of the war. At the beginning of this century Pitt was credited with having the exceptional strategic vision and organizational capability that fashioned victory from the chaos of 1755-56. His qualities include the vision of the eccentric attacks that secured North America.[2] He possessed the ability to make the vital changes to the military and naval organization that enhanced operational capability.[3] In recent years, the Pitt Legend has been increasingly questioned and his contribution to the victory has been put much more firmly in the military context of the time. While he possessed extraordinary political skills, which were the foundation of his power, his organizational skills are now not considered so exceptional.[4] One aspect of Pitt's performance as a war minister which deserves some attention is his planning and use of intelligence. In 1922 Captain Herbert Richmond reflected the popular view of the time when he compared the 1746 expedition to Lorient to Pitt's later expeditions. In Richmond's view of that undertaking, the former was poorly organized. He contrasted what he believed was the slipshod planning with "the infinite care taken by Pitt in his painstaking and thorough consideration of every detail for the expeditions under his direction."[5] How accurate is this assessment in relation to the intelligence processes of the time? Did Pitt have a particularly careful approach to the use of intelligence, and can this be used to explain the comparative success of the Seven Years War compared to the wars of 1739–48 and 1775–83?

The major trans-oceanic expedition to the West Indies in 1740 illustrates some of the essential features of the mid-eighteenth-century intelligence process. It was the largest and most complex trans-Atlantic expedition up to that point employing 8,000 British troops which had to be sent from Europe. They had to avoid the usual watering stop in the Azores and unite at Kingston, Jamaica, with about 3,000 American troops who had sailed from Virginia and New York. It was perceived as Britain's one and only chance of achieving a decisive result in the war with Spain.

The dispute with Spain was long standing and the Secretary of State for the Southern Department, the Duke of Newcastle, received periodic proposals from colonial officials, merchants and entrepreneurs for offensive operations against the Spanish Colonies which were retained for future use.[6] His office also contained some documents about expeditions in previous wars, although these were not systematically retained or recorded. The distinction between private and official papers was unclear at this time and secretaries of state, including Newcastle, removed some papers as if they were personal property.[7] Other ministers might also have information passed on to them in an *ad hoc* fashion, although so far as the 1740 expedition is concerned, it is known only that the Prime Minister, Sir Robert Walpole, and the First Lord of the Admiralty, Sir Charles Wager, had information to assist the planning process. To assist the decision-making process, maps could be called upon from the storeroom (the old chapel) at the Tower of London. These maps were acquired on an *ad hoc* basis, so finding any of value was a matter of serendipity.

The actual decision to undertake a particular operation rested, formally, with the King. He, in turn, would expect advice from his Cabinet Council. In practice, a small inner cabinet gave this advice. In 1739 even this group of politicians found advising on such a complex operation beyond their competence, and the collected information was handed over to Sir Charles Wager and the Admiral of the Fleet, Sir John Norris, for consideration. Their job was to assess the force required to attack positions in the Spanish Empire. The documents were supplemented by interviews with interested individuals. Armed with these descriptions of the target area, the admirals made some judgments.

Between them, Wager and Norris had a great deal of knowledge about the capability of the navy. They had also read history and knew what had happened in the past, but they knew little about the requirements of the army. For this they were assisted by General George Wade. So far as is possible to establish, Wade had no particular knowledge and based his judgment on the documents provided to the admirals. As the plan took shape in the autumn of 1739, Colonel Martin Bladen, an extremely active commissioner of the Board of Trade, provided additional expertise. The Board had been collating detailed descriptions of the British colonies in America since 1721 and Bladen was a conscientious board member who advised on the practicability of raising troops in America. As the plans were being laid, additional information about the Spanish reactions to the crisis were being relayed from Benjamin Keene, the ambassador at Madrid, and consuls in the Spanish ports. French reactions at court and activity in the ports, were sent by the ambassador in Paris, the Earl of Waldegrave.

The plan that emerged was as good as could have been expected under the circumstances. It could not, however, pretend to determine where best to undertake the initial landing in the Spanish colonies. Havana was the greatest prize, but Cartagena de las Indias was the weaker position. In conformance with precedent, this decision was left to the commanders on the spot, Major General Lord Cathcart and Vice Admiral Edward Vernon.

Once in the West Indies, there were two chief sources of intelligence. The Governor of Jamaica, Edward Trelawney, had merchant contacts, and Vice Admiral Vernon had information coming from his cruisers. Cathcart died on 20th December at Dominica, but his successor, Major General Thomas Wentworth, possessed no independent sources of intelligence and relied almost entirely upon

Vernon. He even deferred to him in matters that a more confident army commander would never have permitted. It was only after the disaster at Cartagena and particularly after the occupation of Guantánamo Bay between June and October 1741, that Wentworth realized how Vernon was manipulating the flow of information. Wentworth was never able to develop his own information system, but he profited from Trelawney's growing estrangement from Vernon in the early part of 1742. The result was another disaster at Panama in March and the gradual collapse of the expedition into inactivity until recalled in August.

If this expedition were typical of the mid-eighteenth-century planning process, then it would be possible to identify some of its principal features. Unsurprisingly, the king's ministers determined the policy and objectives that led to the plan. The information upon which detailed planning was based came from accumulated sources in departments and interested individuals. Professional naval and military men, basing their judgments upon experience but little direct knowledge of the situation, conducted the detailed planning. Their conclusions had to be agreed to by the king and inner cabinet. The result was an agreement on the resources to be employed and the production of instructions that outlined the general objectives and conduct, but which left the final decisions to the commanders on the spot. Once embarked on the operation, commanders' decisions were based upon the best information that could be gleaned locally: from naval vessels and, if a trans-oceanic operation, from the colonial or company officials. While this can be broadly described as the process, how far was this typical of the intelligence and decision processes of the British government and what variations or deviations occurred?

The only other major operation carried out during the war, the expedition to Lorient of September 1746, conformed to this model. The original plan was to send an expedition to Québec. This was consistent with the political objectives of the Bedford Whigs, new partners in the administration, but it was first suggested by Commodore Peter Warren, who had commanded the naval forces at the capture of Louisbourg in August 1745.[8] The plan was considered by Bedford, who was Secretary of State for the Southern

Department, Field Marshal Wade, the Lieutenant General of the Ordnance, the Duke of Montagu, and Lieutenant General St Clair, lately Quarter Master General of the British forces in Flanders.[9] Bedford had prepared for the meeting by copying papers related to an earlier attempt on Québec in 1711. The conclusions that they reached formed the basis of the plan of campaign.[10]

Events were to prevent the expeditionary force going to Canada. However, political and diplomatic pressures made it essential that the expeditionary force be seen to do *something* and the ministry seized upon a "random" suggestion from St Clair that they might attack Lorient.[11] There is no evidence of careful reconsideration of the information in front of them, but few thought the dangers significant. The expedition was not a military success. The town was found to be too well defended to make a siege practicable. Yet it achieved its immediate political objective and demonstrated the vulnerability of the French coast. In this respect it provided an informative backdrop to Pitt's later operations.[12]

The war also generated other developments. The most significant was the growing intelligence capability of the Royal Navy. The Lord High Admiral or the Admiralty Commissioners had long acted as a conduit for intelligence. Their ships received information from merchant and naval vessels on the high seas that enabled captains to report the movements of enemy squadrons, information that formed the basis for both political and military decision-making.[13] Although a great deal of intelligence came directly through the offices of the Secretaries of State, the Admiralty maintained an important intelligence service with the Secretaries of State at Rotterdam. During the War of Austrian Succession, Richard Wolters was partly responsible for the management of shipping and information between Britain and the United Provinces. During the Seven Years War, Wolters worked from Rotterdam, exploiting the neutrality of the United Provinces to provide the Admiralty with intelligence from sub-agencies in France and Spain. Much of the transcription and translation work was carried out at Rotterdam, but from 1755 it was usual for the Admiralty to employ an Extra Clerk as a French and Spanish translator.[14] After Wolters' death in 1770, his wife Margaret kept the business going, channelling information to the Admiralty. The results appear to have been some excellent political intelligence. The Wolterses managed to infiltrate to the very heart of the French ministries and had impressive information from the Spanish court. The outbreak of war between the United Provinces and Great Britain in 1781 compelled Margaret Wolters to move a substantial portion of the operation to Ostend in the Austrian Netherlands, but the service continued to provide good quality information.[15]

At a strategic level this information was matched by improvements in the operational information of the navy. The period 1739-47 was very difficult for the navy. The political expectations, which had been so high in 1739, were deflated by a series of disappointments. The indecisive Battle off Toulon in February 1744 and a number of inconclusive actions against French ships led to what amounts to a crisis of confidence both within Parliament and the navy during 1745-46. The two victories off Finisterre in May and October 1747 did a great deal to restore the navy's prestige, but other factors also played an important role in strengthening its operational capability. Just before the expeditionary force sailed for Lorient, Lord Chancellor Hardwicke professed himself shocked to hear "that our Sea Officers in general should know so little, with any correctness, of the coast of France . . . especially since it is known that the French have been sounding and surveying our coasts for several years."[16]

By 1748 this position had been rectified. During the expedition to Lorient, British warships had taken the islands of Hodic and Houat. They knew the waters around Belle Isle. They had sheltered in Quiberon Bay and taken soundings. The earlier blockade of the Channel ports during the Jacobite Rebellion had provided additional information about the treacherous shallows. In the West Indies, substantial operations against the Spanish Main early in the war, and the blockade of Martinique later, provided the British with topographical intelligence and operational experience in these waters. There were fewer operations in North America, but the capture of Louisbourg in 1745 and its retention until the peace in 1748 gave officers a chance to understand the waters and strategic possibilities of the region. In the East Indies, a similar familiarization was underway. Yet none of this experience had been translated into decisive advantages by 1748. Nor is it yet possible to track the way in which this expertise and intelligence was disseminated or internalized. Nonetheless, the navy had gone through a major learning experience and emerged with some important additional qualities.

These changes which marked significant improvements in the operational capability of the Royal Navy were not matched by changes in the army. The army had undertaken a major operation against the Spanish colonies between 1741–42 during which it had been dependent upon the navy and the colonial government for intelligence. After 1743 the army was drawn into a major campaign in Germany and Flanders where it relied upon the traditional sources of intelligence. In the 1746 expedition, the army commander, Lieutenant General St Clair, had no particular knowledge of the area around Lorient, but embarked on the campaign in the hope that speed would enable him to maneuver without danger. In the event, he was right. However, the timely decision to withdraw, and the courage of the naval commander, Vice Admiral Richard Lestock, meant that he did not have to execute a highly speculative march around the town to meet the fleet in Quiberon Bay. For the rest of the war the field army continued to campaign as part of a coalition army. It had performed well enough against the Jacobite rebels, 1745–46, but the war ended with further defeats at Laffeldt and Roucoux. By 1748, the army had experienced neither the crisis of political expectations nor the development of its operational expertise. Its ability to contribute to the decision-making process regarding amphibious operations was, therefore, little more advanced than in 1739.

Two other sources of information saw a little development. In 1739 the involvement of the East India Company in plans to attack Manila were largely accidental insofar as the principal source of the scheme was a personal contact of Sir Robert Walpole, James Naish.[17] Although these personal contacts remained highly important for financial planning, there seems to have been a shift to consult more formally with the Company's Secret Committee over military matters after 1744.[18] The other source was the colonial governments. Since the establishment of colonial government, royal governors and assembly agents had represented colonial defense needs to London. After 1696 the Board of Trade provided a powerful addition to this informed lobbying.[19] This power extended further after 1748 when the Duke of Bedford became Secretary of State for the Southern Department. His willingness to allow the Board to develop under the Earl of Halifax gave the Board greater colonial power and metropolitan influence.[20] The overall effect appears to have been that the administrative machinery for receiving and using information became rather more formalized and receptive. The intelligence had always been there, but it had not been received quite as clearly before mid-century. The government was better equipped with intelligence than during the previous half century, but did it make any difference to operations?

When war broke out between Britain and France in May 1756, it occurred after a long period of tension and it was accompanied by the usual British floundering at the beginning of a conflict. The disaster on the Monongahela, fears of invasion, and the loss of Minorca all suggest that the intelligence and decision-making processes were no better than they had been before. Pitt's championing of the war in the Americas, East Indies and Africa had created an expectation that measures would be taken and, more importantly that they would be successful because of Britain's naval superiority. Although this superiority had not been demonstrated by mid-1757, public expectations that it could easily be asserted were instrumental in Admiral Byng's execution and the political eclipse of Admiral Lord George Anson, who up until that time had personified the British naval recovery since 1745. Although Anson's eclipse was temporary, these events were a sharp reminder of the political sensitivity of the navy.[21]

Pitt's political technique depended upon creating expectations of military success. It was environment that demanded activity, although the translation of this activity into effective action depended upon other variables. In mid-1757 Pitt was anxious to demonstrate success against the French and supported an attack upon Rochefort. The information about Rochefort came from an officer, Robert Clerk, who had been on the Lorient expedition and who had taken the opportunity to view the defenses of Rochefort while on his way back from Gibraltar in 1754. His information was supplemented by a French Protestant pilot, Joseph Thierry. As with earlier expeditions, this initial intelligence was interrogated by politicians, and by senior officers such as Field Marshal Ligonier and Admiral Lord Anson. The decision to proceed was based on Clerk and Thierry's account of the defences at Rochefort.

As with previous expeditions, the commanders of this operation, Vice Admiral Edward Hawke and Lieutenant General Sir John Mordaunt, had discretion in their orders to act as the local conditions demanded. By the time the expedition reached the Aix Roads at the mouth of the Charente River, the French had been alerted and Mordaunt was reluctant to land without more information about the town. At this point it was discovered that the town defences were far more formidable than Thierry had asserted. Since taking the town by surprise was now out of the question, and since a regular attack would take far longer than initially expected, the council of war decided that the expedition should return home. Pitt and George II were furious, but, as the subsequent Board of Enquiry and court martial confirmed, Mordaunt was acting within his instructions. Even before the news had reached London, Hawke had distanced himself from the council of war's decision. Indeed, he was responsible for the way the news was reported in London. It had been agreed that minutes of the council would not be taken, but Hawke took his own minutes and forwarded them to Pitt at the first opportunity.[22] Here was a clear lesson for the army that in this charged environment—the political expectations of action were as important as the military expectations of success.

In the following year, two other expeditionary force commanders showed they had learned this lesson. The Duke of Marlborough was instructed to attack the French coast. Marlborough and his second in command, Lord George Sackville, had been on the Board of Enquiry that considered Mordaunt's behavior. Together with the commander-in-chief, Lord Ligonier, they had learned that action was vital regardless of the state of the intelligence they possessed. They had very little good intelligence, but nevertheless stated their intention to attack St Malo. They would land and stay ashore until French forces threatened them, even if St Malo could not be taken.[23] They landed at Cancale Bay and managed to burn some shipping in the Rance River, but Marlborough did not have adequate artillery to assault the town. He therefore fell back on Cancale Bay to re-embark as French forces advanced.[24]

Marlborough's successor, Lieutenant General Thomas Bligh, continued the raids. He appears to have had no more intelligence than Marlborough, but recognized the imperative of landing.[25] He did have the advice of Captain Richard Howe, who had commanded the close naval support to Marlborough and had seen the French coast in some detail during the cruise in June. It may have been Howe who encouraged Bligh to attack Cherbourg, which was captured and burned in August. In September Bligh landed his force at St Lunaire Bay to attack St Malo, but like Marlborough found the defences too strong. As he retreated to meet the transports in St Cast bay, his force was caught on the beach and sustained over eight hundred casualties. For the army, these coastal raids took place in an intelligence vacuum. The army had to operate in the expectation that their transports gave them greater mobility than their enemy ashore.

For its part the navy had access to good operational intelligence. Its ships could patrol the French coast with relative impunity. Intelligence of the weather would have been just as important, but was not available. The naval commanding officers reserved the right to draw away from the beachhead if threatened by adverse weather. While this was entirely reasonable, it was this prerogative that led to the disaster at Saint Cast Bay. In 1761, when the coastal raiding was resumed, this time against Belle Isle, the situation was the same. The navy was strongly positioned to alert itself to any enemy activity along the Biscay coast. General Hodgson's army had very little intelligence of enemy forces ashore, but was able to use superior mobility to effect a landing even against defenders operating on interior lines.

Colonial expeditions suffered from the same intelligence problems. This is particularly true of West Indian operations. In most operations it is not known what information the commanding officers had at their disposal at the planning stages of their commands. This is particularly true of the army officers. The official machinery for providing information was limited in the extreme. While the Admiralty and the Board of Ordnance may have had some information, the War Office appears not to have maintained an intelligence system at all and unlike ships, regiments did not regularly turn over on tours of duty. As a result, Army officers seldom had a variety of operational experiences. Some officers went out of their way to secure information from booksellers and cartographers in London. There are hints that Wolfe, for example, collected information about the St Lawrence during his stay in England over the winter of 1758-59. But for other officers, the need to gather such information did not become a priority until their destination was known.

It is not known what information Major General Peregrine Hopson had with him when he sailed for the West Indies in October 1758 with orders to take Martinique. Pressure to take Martinique came from the City, and Pitt concerted plans with the Admiralty secretary, Thomas Clevland. It does not appear that any others were involved in the decision, either by providing intelligence or advice, though there was a general consensus that it was both practicable and desirable.[26] It is possible that Pitt was receiving professional advice from Admiral Charles Knowles.[27] Whatever the source of Pitt's intelligence, Hopson appears to have sailed with very little specific information, and when he landed at Point Negro west of Fort Royal, the topography of the island was a shock to him. He "never saw such a country, the Highlands of Scotland, for woods, mountains, caves and continual ravines is nothing to it."[28] The plan to march on Fort Royal with artillery proved completely impracticable. A subsequent plan to land at Saint Pierre was likewise aborted after Commodore Moore feared that his ships might suffer crippling damage in the attack. It was agreed by council of war to abandon the attempt and try instead to capture Basseterre, Guadeloupe. Here they had no more intelligence, except for the quality of the harbor at Basseterre. They relied on local intelligence gathered immediately as the operation unfolded. In the event, the ability of the Royal Navy guns to silence the fort and the capture of Basseterre itself provided the base for the reduction of the island. As with previous operations, Pitt's West Indian operation was driven by the fact that the political imperative of action outweighed the possible risks from inadequate intelligence. It was a risk that strained Pitt's political credibility in the summer of 1759 as the nation waited impatiently for good news. It was a similar story at the end of 1761 during a renewed attempt to take Martinique, but the situation was better in North America.[29] Louisbourg had fallen to New Englanders in 1745 and that experience helped to inform the landings at Gabarus Bay. The advance up the Hudson towards Lake Champlain was a well-trodden path for forces from the Middle Colonies. Perhaps the greatest single prize of the war, Havana, fell in August 1762. Before Lord Albemarle sailed in March 1762, Admiral Charles Knowles gave him detailed information about the city.[30] Likewise, the expedition to Manila was based upon information from Colonel William Draper. Admittedly this information was inadequate for the execution of the plans, but was a great help in the initial phases.

While it must be admitted that the evidence available is incomplete, the overall impression is that the successes of the Seven Years War were not based upon better or more carefully analyzed intelligence and decision-making processes at the ministerial level. Despite the claims of Pitt's champions, the type of information and the use to which it was put was much the same during Pitt's ministry as it was during the earlier ministries. His ministry's decisions were not based on any particularly sound information or analytical processes, but on the same faith that the operation ought to succeed in the general context of the military situation. A modicum of surprise, general naval superiority and a relatively large amphibious army with a local supporting infrastructure was the formula for Walpole, Newcastle, and for Pitt. Louisbourg and Québec were long-standing objectives of British policy and there was a considerable amount of intelligence in North America to draw upon. Rochefort had some specific planning, but was based on faulty intelligence and a degree of wishful thinking. St Malo, Cherbourg and St Cast were all opportunistic targets. The expedition to the West Indies in 1758 was powerfully influenced by pressure from the City and the capture of Guadeloupe was a consolation for the failure at Martinique. Operations against neither island seem to have been planned with any significant recent intelligence. Gorée was also captured as the result of private lobbying and with little examination of the situation on the West African coast by ministers.[31] The capture of Dominica, Saint Lucia and Martinique in 1761 were further opportunistic operations undertaken in response to the collapse of the French position in Canada during 1760.[32]

After Pitt fell and the nation faced the novel situation of war with Spain, there appears to have been more discussion of objectives in London. The Ministry took advice and held formal meetings on expeditions to both Havana and Manila. It was not particularly high quality advice, and whether the operations were influenced by it is an open question. It is possible that Bute's ministry was just continuing where Pitt had left off.[33] It might be assumed that the Royal Navy benefited from both the general improvements in understanding of its officers of the waters off France and Spain, gathered during the War of Austrian Succession. It also benefited from the ability of these officers to apply this knowledge to inshore work in the Seven Years War, which provided the Admiralty with better specific intelligence about the Bourbon navies. The army had not benefited in the same way, but in 1757 the soldiers recognized the political necessity of acting despite their relative lack of intelligence. The results were that at a local level commanders applied their forces to the tasks given them and on the whole they were successful. This was not the result of better planning or insight, but the exploitation of professional expertise in an environment that was, for the most part, supportive of British offensive operations.

A number of small changes occurred in relation to the acquisition and use of intelligence in the period 1739–63. In the early years, information from the secretaries' offices, supplemented by personal contacts with interested parties, provided the basic information for planning. This information was submitted to naval and military officers for comment and development into operational instructions. These officers then discussed their conclusions with their political masters. The Royal Navy gained vital information for effective operations off the coasts of Europe and the Americas. The navy also learned a vital political lesson: while the nation expected success, it could tolerate failure, but not inaction. The actions it took in 1746–47 secured its political stability and gave it good information for future operations. This situation continued throughout 1757. By the beginning of 1758 the army had learned the political imperative of action as a result of Rochefort. The political situation in Britain favoured an ideology of the offensive. In the absence of good intelligence this could have been disastrous. A number of the results were disappointing, but in the long run the weight of Britain's material resources at sea and in North America proved decisive. By the end of 1760 the weight of resources was such that up-to-date local intelligence was unnecessary. The margins for victory at Dominica, St Lucia and Martinique were so large as to overwhelm any surprises the enemy might have. The same was true at Manila. At Havana this was not the case and the wisdom of better planning and preparation paid off. However, this was a unique situation—an attack upon the best-fortified and defended point in the Caribbean.[34]

Britain emerged from the Seven Years War with more knowledge of her strategic environment than ever before. Her seamen and soldiers had navigated seaways and rivers, conquered territories and mapped them. The expertise gained here provided unprecedented capability for gathering information, which was utilized in the exploration of the Pacific over the next fifteen years. However, an important question remains—did the successes of the Seven Years War actually lead to a reduction in the analysis of information by government and thereby store up problems for the future? In 1775, the loss of a substantial part of the local infrastructure in North America was critical. However, the inability to produce a coherent strategy was also vital. The formal structures of government and decision-making remained unchanged, yet the ability of the North ministry to cope with the American rebellion was remarkably weak. Personalities played a part. Anson, Saunders, and Ligonier were dead. Hawke was in retirement and Amherst was reluctant. Information came through the same channels—colonial governors, military officers, the East India Company. The analysis of information does not appear to have been as thorough as might have been the case in the 1740s. The Germain papers do not reveal the same level of consultation and discussion of earlier years.[35]

From the initial plans to reinforce Gage and the Southern Expedition of 1775-76, through the confusion over the campaign in 1777, to the handling of the resources in Europe and America to meet the Bourbon threat in 1778-79, the ministry appears to have made decisions without a thorough investigation of the situation by its experts.[36] Instructions were sent to America in the same manner as William Pitt had done in 1757, but the conditions were very different. The balance of resources was not what it was in 1759-63. Pitt epitomized the decisive man of action that was appreciated at the time and most admired by statesmen and scholars at the beginning of this century. They overlooked the dangers of Pitt's approach and blamed later failures on personalities. The defeat of 1775-83 occurred because Germain was no Pitt. In fact it took a long time and many more defeats to re-establish the culture of detailed analysis of information by expert military and naval officers relating to offensive operations. It was apparent in planning during 1799, but it still remains to be shown if the period 1793-99, in which so many plans were explored, adopted, adapted in London, contributed to what has been called "the apogee of sophistication during the age of sail" by 1801.[37] The evidence is too scanty and to date too little work has been done to establish the precise role that planning and intelligence analysis might have had on British amphibious operations between 1739 and 1783, but there do appear to have been differences over the period and it would be wrong to neglect them. Though William Pitt and the Seven Years War have been seen as a high point of British amphibious strategy, the legacy and particularly the admiration for Pitt's methods may have carried the seeds of humiliating defeat.

NOTES

[1] D. Syrett, "The Methodology of British Amphibious Operations during the Seven Years War and the American War," *Mariner's Mirror* 58 (1972), 269-280.

[2]J. S. Corbett, *England in the Seven Years War*, 2 vols., (London: Longmans Green, 1907), I, 375; B. Williams, *The Whig Supremacy* (Oxford: Oxford University Press, 1939), 336; P. Padfield, *Tides of Empire: Decisive Naval Campaigns in the Rise of the West*, 2 vols., (London: RKP, 1979 and 1982), 2:234; R. Mackay, *Admiral Hawke* (Oxford: Oxford University Press, 1965), 158.

[3]G. S. Kimball, (ed.), *The Correspondence of William Pitt*, 2 vols., (New York: Macmillan, 1902-3), i, xxix-xxxiii. This view is less pronounced in C. Buchett, "The Royal Navy in the Caribbean, 1689-1763," *Mariner's Mirror*, 80 (1994), 30-44.

[4]R. Middleton, *The Bells of Victory; The Pitt-Newcastle Ministry and the Conduct of the Seven Years War, 1757-1762* (Cambridge: Cambridge University Press, 1985), 164; J. Black, *Pitt the Elder* (Cambridge: Cambridge University Press, 1992), 164.

[5]H. W. Richmond, *The Navy in the War of 1739-1748*, 3 vols., (Cambridge: Cambridge University Press, 1920), 3:35.

[6]R. Harding, *Amphibious Warfare in the Eighteenth Century: The British Expedition to the West Indies, 1740-1742* (Woodbridge: Royal Historical Society, 1991), 31-2.

[7]The Newcastle Papers contain several examples of information sent to the Duke as secretary of State, which remained in his personal papers. See especially, British Library (B. L.), Additional Manuscripts 32694, ff. 1-165.

[8]Newcastle to Warren, 14 Mar. 1746 in J. Gwyn, (ed.), *The Warren Papers* (London: Navy Records Society, 1973), 221-2.

[9]Bedford to Newcastle, 24 Mar. 1746, PRO, CO42/13 (Miscellaneous Papers-Canada), unfoliated.

[10]Bedford, Wade and St Clair to Newcastle, 30 Mar. 1746, Bedford Estate Archive, Letter Book, 9:46-7.

[11]St Clair and Lestock to Newcastle, 21 Aug. 1746, PRO, SP42/98(Brittany Papers), f.128.

[12]PRO, PRO 30/8/74 (Chatham Deposit), f. 178.

[13]P. Le Fevre, "To Save Some Guesses: The Later Seventeenth-Century Navy, Information and Propaganda from Rupert to Rooke," in W. B. Cogar (ed.), *New Interpretations of Naval History: Selected Papers from the Twelfth Naval History Symposium* (Annapolis: U. S. Naval Institute Press, 1997), 79-92.

[14]J.C. Sainty, *Admiralty Officials, 1660-1870* (London: University of London, 1975), 7.

[15]For examples of Richard Wolters activities, see his correspondence relating to the situation after the defeat at Fontenoy and the Jacobite Rising in Wolters to Fawkener, 1 and 12 Aug 1745, in Royal Archives, Windsor, Cumberland Papers, Box 3, f. 311, and Box 4, f.35. For Wolters' views on the quality of information from France, see, Wolters to Stephens, 28 Feb. 1769, PRO, Adm/3972(Intelligence 1761-1778), unfoliated. On Margaret Wolters see, F. P. Renaut, *Le Secret Service de l'Amirauté Britannique au temps de la Guerre d'Amerique, 1776-1783* (Paris: Du Graouli, 1936), passim.

[16]Hardwicke to Newcastle, 11 Sept. 1746, B. L., Add. Ms. 32708 (Newcastle Papers), f. 263.

[17]Court Minutes (12 April 1738 - 11 April 1740), India Office Library, B/65, 269, 364.

[18]On the personal nature of financial planning, see L. Sutherland, "The City of London and the Pitt-Devonshire Administration, 1756-7" and "Samson Gideon and the Reduction of Interest, 1749-50," in L. Sutherland, *Politics and Finance in the Eighteenth Century*, (London: Hambledon Press, 1984), 67-114, 399-414. On the formalization of the role of the Secret Committee, see, C. H. Philips, *The East India Company, 1784-1834* (Manchester: Manchester University Press, 1940), 9-10.

[19]L.M. Penson, *The Colonial Agents of the British West Indies*, (London: 1924); I.K. Steele, *Politics of Colonial Policy: The Board of Trade in Colonial Admin-istration, 1696-1720* (Oxford: Oxford University Press, 1968), 167-170.

[20]J.A. Henretta, *Salutory Neglect: Colonial Administration under the Duke of Newcastle* (Princeton: Princeton University Press, 1972); T.R. Clayton, "The Duke of Newcastle, The Earl of Halifax, and the American Origins of the Seven Years War," *Historical Journal* 24 (1981), 571-603.

[21] R. Middleton, "A Reinforcement for North America, Summer 1757," *Bulletin of the Institute of Historical Research* (1968), 58-72.

[22] The Rochefort operation can be followed in detail in PRO, WO72/4 (Rochefort Papers).

[23] Newcastle Papers-Cabinet Memoranda, BL, Add. Ms 32998, f. 39.

[24] Marlborough to Pitt, 24 June 1758, Shelburne Papers, item 55, W. L. Clements Library.

[25] Lady Anson to Lord Anson, 11 July 1758, Staffordshire Record Office, Anson Papers, D615/P (S)1/2, item 9.

[26] Newcastle to Hardwicke, 4 Sept. 1758, and Hardwicke to Newcastle, 5 Sept. 1758, British Library Add. Ms 32883 (Newcastle Papers), f.273-5, f.298; Newcastle to Hardwicke, 17 Sept. 1758, Add. Ms 32884 (Newcastle Papers), f.27.

[27] Knowles Papers (private collection of Sir Charles Knowles bart), "A Sketch of the Services of Admiral Sir Charles Henry Knowles and those rendered by his father." Knowles' role in planning the Havana campaign is reasonably clear. His "Narrative of Intelligence before going to Havana," attached to a copy of Lieu-tenant Colonel Mackellar's journal, suggests that his advice was sought. See BL, Add. Ms 23678(Journal of the Siege of Havana). There is also a letter from the Duke of Cumberland to Albemarle noting Knowles continually "croaking" on about the operation (quoted in S. Keppel, *Three Brothers at Havana 1762* [Salisbury: Michael Russell, 1981], 15). In the Knowles archive there is also "An Original Journal of the Siege of Havana." It is anonymous, but most likely the Earl of Albemarle's personal account. This is kept together with a metal cylinder containing maps of Havana during the siege. His access to this material might suggest that Knowles was acting in an advisory capacity to Bute's ministry. I am indebted to the present Sir Charles Knowles for permission to consult these papers.

[28] Hopson to Pitt, 30 Jan. 1759, PRO, CO110/1(Guadeloupe Papers), f. 59.

[29] Rodney to Clevland, 19 Jan. 1762. PRO, CO166/2 (Martinique Papers), f.21.

[30] D. Syrett, *The Siege and Capture of Havana 1762* (London: Navy Records Society, 1970) xxi; S. Keppel, *Three Brothers at Havana 1762*, 15.

[31] B. Williams, The *Life of William Pitt, Earl of Chatham*, 1:301.

[32] Pitt to Amherst, 17 Dec. 1760 and 7 Jan. 1761, in G.S. Kimball, (ed.), *The Correspondence of William Pitt*, 1:370-73, 384-87.

[33] N. Tracy, *Manila Ransomed. The British Assault on Manila in the Seven Years War* (Exeter: Exeter University Press, 1995), 14.

[34] D.F. Marley, "Havana Surprised: Prelude to the British Invasion, 1762," *Mariner's Mirror* 78 (1992), 296-305.

[35] I am grateful to the staff of the W. L. Clements Library for their assistance with these papers.

[36] I. D. Gruber, *Howe Brothers and the American Revolution*, (New York: Atheneum, 1972), 12-30; E. Robson, "The Expedition to the Southern Colonies, 1775-1776," *English Historical Review*, 66 (1953), 535-560, especially 539-541; W. Willcox, "Too Many Cooks: British Planning Before Saratoga," *Journal of British Studies*, 2 (1962), 56-90; D. Syrett, "The Failure of the British Effort in America, 1777" in J. Black and P. Woodfine (eds.), *The British Navy and the Use of Naval Power in the Eighteenth Century* (Leicester, 1988), 171-190; G.S. Brown, "The Anglo-French Naval Crisis, 1778," *William and Mary Quarterly*, 13 (Jan. 1956), 1-25.

[37] University of Durham, Earl Grey Papers, 2252, 2253, 2256 (Examination of the Coast of France). Quotation from P.C. Krajeski, "The Foundations of British Amphibious Warfare Methodology During the Napoleonic Era, 1793-1815," in C. Crouch, K. O. Eidahl, and D. D. Howard, (eds.), *Consortium on Revolutionary Europe, 1750-1830*, (Florida, 1996), 198.

"Too Much Mixed in This Affair": The Impact of Ministerial Politics in the Eighteenth-Century Royal Navy

Daniel A. Baugh

> In addition to the external histories of navies (what navies *did*), naval historians also investigate the internal history of navies (what navies *were*). Here the concern of the historian focuses on how navies were organized, how they functioned, and especially their place within the social and political system that created them. The relationship between national politics and naval politics is a fertile one, and few scholars have tilled this field more satisfactorily than Daniel A. Baugh. In this essay, Professor Baugh focuses on the period between the War of 1739-48 and the American Revolution to investigate the extent to which Royal Navy policy in this era was influenced by ministerial politics.

Historians dealing with the eighteenth-century British ruling class have explored how the influence of the aristocracy penetrated almost every government, social, and cultural institution of the time. Only a few, however, have included a consideration of how this influence affected the Royal Navy and its officer corps. In 1986, J. V. Beckett in his survey of *The Aristocracy in England* confined his observations about the Royal Navy to the office of the First Lord, noting that nineteen of twenty-three eighteenth-century First Lords were either peers themselves or closely related to the peerage. For this information, Beckett cited John Cannon's brief and thoughtful survey, *Aristocratic Century*, published two years earlier. Cannon had addressed the matter more broadly and included the observation that "there were enough external connections to keep the navy securely within the aristocratic network."[1] His citation is the present author. However, the full passage (written in 1977) was: "What was unusual about naval appointments was that so much patronage was internal to the naval establishment. Still, there were enough external connections to keep the navy securely within the aristocratic network that

---

Daniel A. Baugh is Professor Emeritus at Cornell University.

controlled British government in the Georgian era."[2] The two elements of this passage that Cannon omitted are highly relevant to the theme of this paper: one, that naval patronage was largely naval; and the other, that the network that controlled British government was what mattered.

The first makes the point that aristocratic patronage did not dominate the Navy; its influence was clearly visible, but its impact on the profession was limited by the fact that naval connections were more important than aristocratic ones. The dominance of naval connections was partly a product of tradition, since the pride, cohesiveness, and professional attitudes and expectations of the officer corps were in no small degree created by the officers themselves.[3] This corporate sense was sustained by an important feature of the system of promotion—the power of flag officers abroad to make promotions by filling vacancies. For these as well as other reasons (which there is not space to explore here), aristocratic or politically-inspired requests for young men to be promoted were best addressed to admirals and commodores rather than to the Admiralty. Moreover, the navy's captains, in aggregate, had acquired by about 1730 almost total control over the entry of youngsters into the navy. Nicholas Rodger, who has read more private and public officer correspondence from the mid-eighteenth century than anyone else, rightly insists on the importance of *de facto* retention of naval patronage in the hands of naval officers themselves; there is plenty of evidence. Finally, any captain had to be wary of recommending incompetent people; in the long run they would do his reputation no good, nor be of use to him as followers and supporters in meeting the challenges of active service. A rather sad indication that the system was preponderantly naval is that some of the worst officers in the annals of the eighteenth century received promotion not because they were sons of peers but because they were sons of captains or admirals—promoted by their fathers or by a befriended admiral or commodore, men who usually set a higher standard for other sorts of young men.[4]

Instead of asking whether the naval profession was seriously affected by steady aristocratic intrusion, one should focus on the network that controlled British government. It is more interesting to ask whether the conduct of the king's ministers, parliamentary politics, or even popular politics had disturbing effects upon it.

There is surprisingly little to read on this subject. In the heyday of naval history, great historians from Sir John Laughton to Admiral Sir Herbert Richmond did not want to look at it. They regarded politics, whether professional or parliamentary, as bothersome background noise. They were well aware that political favor or timidity sometimes put or left the wrong men in charge and that political animosities sometimes influenced performance, but they were not motivated to venture into those thickets.

A particularly useful example is the botched battle of Toulon (February 1744) and the court martial (1746) that tried the two admirals, Thomas Mathews and Richard Lestock. Herbert Richmond's scholarly probing of this was exhaustive; he even consulted surviving log books, finding some of them to have been crudely altered or showing crucial pages to have been torn out. He came to the conclusion that in completely exonerating Lestock, the court had acted with "extraordinary partiality." The proceedings and the finding were, he commented, "such a travesty of administration of justice that one can hardly regard any of the other findings as honest and untinged by partisanship." At the end of his discussion he wrote:

> [I]t can hardly be wondered that people drew the conclusion that the decision had been made on party lines, and smacked rather of political affairs than of justice; and that the common report grew up that the Court was determined to acquit not Lestock the Admiral, but Lestock the Whig, and acted up to that determination.[5]

In short, Richmond employed the coy tactic of mentioning what people commonly thought—though the reader cannot doubt that this is what *he* thought, too. It was his way of announcing that unraveling the political pressures which accounted for the "extraordinary partiality" was not part of his historical mission.

Sir John Laughton, writing about Lestock a dozen years earlier for the *Dictionary of National Biography*, commented that the court's "finding has often been spoken of as a gross miscarriage of justice" but suggested that Lestock's conduct during the battle, if morally suspect, was probably technically correct. Laughton chiefly blamed the ministry and the Admiralty: Whitehall had no business leaving two admirals who openly disliked and mistrusted each other in a situation where they would have to cooperate. This was a valid criticism, but Laughton went no further.[6] His historical objectives were naval; any intrusion by politics would muddy up the lessons of naval history. Yet it may be protested that his entries for a general work of biographical reference should not have excluded politics to the extent that they did. Those who are currently working on the *New Dictionary of National Biography*—and it has to be said that a large platoon of scholars is required to redo the approximately 900 naval entries that he did single-handedly a century ago[7]—have commonly found that they must fill in the "political," as well as the strictly "naval" aspects of the topic.

It is best to state at the outset that if one considers the eighteenth century as a whole, the worst effects of an interaction of national political and professional politics were experienced during the American Revolutionary War when the earl of Sandwich was First Lord. At that time relations between the government and a considerable segment of the officer corps were unusually strained, probably to a degree even more injurious to the conduct of naval warfare than during a similarly intense bout of partisanship in the reign of Queen Anne. This statement is based on impressions rather than a detailed comparison, and may be controversial. But the evidence of strained relations during the period from 1775 to about 1780 is abundant. This is not to say that the chief cause of the naval failures of that war was factional strife in the officer corps. The basic source of trouble was inadequate and late mobilization, as well as the government's reluctance to build more ships of the types needed when it became fairly obvious that they would be needed. Regarding the latter, some new frigates should have been ordered immediately in 1775; this failure was followed by a dreadfully inadequate response to the looming threat posed by the naval programs of France and Spain.[8] Nevertheless, the mistrust of the

Admiralty that welled up in the officer corps after 1775 had strategic and operational consequences. The impact is impossible to ascertain precisely — things could have gone far better, or perhaps far worse; one is dealing with contingencies. Yet some important instances of strained relations are easy to detect. Even before the horrendous Keppel-Palliser court martial which resulted in a flat refusal to serve by a number of reliable, experienced admirals and captains, some men in these ranks were unusually wary when assigned to fleet commands — behaving like dogs who fear being beaten for no good reason. Richard, Lord Howe's extreme caution in all his dealings with Sandwich, and Augustus Keppel's anxious inquiries about his orders upon assuming the Channel command are two prominent examples.[9] The mistrust resulted ultimately from the First Lord's failure to shield the corps both from the whims and biases of his ministerial colleagues and a noisy public.

In December 1738 Admiral Sir Charles Wager, First Lord since 1733, wrote to the duke of Newcastle to tell him that Admiral Philip Cavendish, whom the government had in mind to command the squadron that was fitting out to make war on Spain in the West Indies, was physically too "infirm" for the appointment. Wager then added:

> I wish the King could be persuaded to let Vernon have this command. He is certainly much properer than any officer we have to send, being very well acquainted in all that part of the West Indies and is a very good sea officer, whatever he may be, or has been, in the House of Commons. Whether your Grace will move this matter again I don't know. But if Cavendish goes, in all probability he might die, and then the command would fall upon Brown, who your Grace don't like....[10]

In this deft, honest, and frank manner — typical of Wager — the First Lord managed to get the best man for the job appointed to a highly visible command against the wishes of the duke of Newcastle and King George II. Edward Vernon, who had earlier been passed over for promotion to admiral because of his bold opinions as an Opposition "Patriot" in the House of Commons, was plainly the man Wager wanted for the task.

There was an ironic political sequel. Vernon, having been given a chance to become a great hero, did so, most definitely, when he captured Porto Bello.[11] Wager sat in parliament as one of the two members for the popular borough of Westminster. For the general election of 1741, a local caucus nominated Vernon, and as the polling progressed it was so obvious that the opposition's naval hero would win that Lord Sundon (the other pro-government member) allowed, or directed perhaps, the high bailiff to force a premature closure of the poll. This high-handed, highly visible stroke prompted an explosion of popular outrage. (Wager was unfortunately not present to provide steadying advice because he was shepherding the king across to the Continent.) The election of Wager and Sundon was soon overturned on appeal, and all this led to a further diminishment of the Walpole administration's majority in the House of Commons; in due course the great minister was forced to resign. Wager was a popular admiral, but he was known to be a strong adherent and friend of Walpole's and left office at the same time.

Sir Charles Wager has lacked appropriate historical recognition. His retirement (at seventy-six) in February 1742 was inevitable—though at that moment he seemed as energetic and alert as ever—but the loss to the navy was considerable. Besides being extremely well informed on maritime and colonial matters, he was honest, likable, and trusted. He understood the necessities of politics, but kept them under limits. Everyone knew he cared deeply about the navy and its reputation, and he had practically no enemies, in or outside the service.[12] In sum, Sir Charles Wager was not only a naval expert but a respected, first-class leader.

The new First Lord (in March 1742) was the earl of Winchilsea, a man who had no expertise whatsoever in sea affairs nor, as it proved, any talent for leadership. Admiral Sir John Norris had been slated to be his number two board member, but Norris insisted on being First Lord and when this was refused he declined to sit on the board. As a result, the only well informed sea officer on Winchilsea's Board of Admiralty was Cavendish (long a friend of Wager's) and it appears that Cavendish felt he was rarely listened to. Sometimes, as he later told Vernon, his only recourse was to refuse to be a signer of orders that he considered unrealistic and ill-advised.[13] As it happened, the worst blunder of Winchilsea's board was an inaction—the failure to transfer Richard Lestock away from his second-in-command position in the Mediterranean. Given the known mutual dislike of Mathews and Lestock, there was a strong likelihood of trouble, and what Lestock eventually did was worse than even a cynical man might have imagined.

Before continuing, an observation is in order. There were, on the whole, fewer problems involving the officer corps when the First Lord of the Admiralty was a sea officer rather than a civilian. The next best situation was to have a civilian First Lord who was ready to listen regularly to the advice of a respected sea officer, with regard to both strategy and appointments—as the duke of Bedford quickly learned to do in 1745, the officer being George Anson. But whoever was in charge on high, the surest guarantee of officer morale was a strong inclination to recognize professional merit in any political quarter.[14]

The cluster of courts martial that came in the wake of the battle of Toulon made for a tremendous affair of naval and national politics. When Vice Admiral Lestock returned to England under suspension in 1744 he made formal accusations of misconduct against no less than seven captains as well as Admiral Mathews. The total number of appearances by witnesses was close to 300. Almost 200 different officers were involved, most as witnesses, some as members of the courts—and the witnesses included not just captains and lieutenants, but masters, boatswains and carpenters.[15] Approximately ninety witnesses were called home from the Mediterranean. Eventually four lieutenants, eleven captains, and two admirals were court-martialed in England. Only one captain, Richard Norris (a son of Sir John Norris, Admiral of the Fleet) was court-martialed in the Mediterranean and, although he was plainly guilty of cowardice, the flag officer in charge, Rear Admiral William Rowley, contrived to let him off. When news of this reached London, Rowley was soon called home and barred from further command.

British naval officers of the eighteenth century were frequently exposed to courts martial in one way or another, whether as sitting members, witnesses, or the accused. A surviving commander who lost his ship by shipwreck was routinely court-martialed. If he surrendered his ship in combat, he could expect to be on trial for his life. One of the many merits of C.S. Forester's *Flying Colors* is the way in which Captain Hornblower, during his hair-raising attempt to escape from France—he had surrendered and was made prisoner when no longer able to repel four powerful enemy ships—recurrently conjures up dark thoughts about the court martial that awaits him if he makes it home. Even the situation of a witness could be traumatic. Lieutenants normally dreaded having to testify against their superiors or their friends. It was an inevitable part of a career. Yet there was something special about the proceedings in the wake of the battle of Toulon. Naval events always attracted public attention in this era, but this was an extraordinarily dramatic occasion—an ongoing "media event," we might say—heated up in advance by a full-fledged pamphlet war and plenty of newspaper publicity. Among the lieutenants who testified at Admiral Lestock's trial in 1746 were some who would figure more or less prominently in the American Revolutionary war: Hugh Palliser, Edward Hughes, and Edward Affleck, to name just three. The number of participants in these trials was large, and they cannot have ever forgotten what happened on that stressful occasion.

So great was the political excitement generated by the search for blamability that even the dockyard workers at Chatham got actively involved, holding what we would refer to as a demonstration. A group stood at the gate during the captains' trials in autumn 1745 and demanded to know of each worker as he passed through whether he would be for Mathews or Lestock. Because the workers overwhelmingly declared for Mathews (who had been a popular commissioner there), the Admiralty Board decided to move the locale of the trials to Deptford.

Political intervention in a matter of naval justice made the occasion all the more memorable. There was a striking instance of overt intervention. Its underlying cause was the existing turmoil of parliamentary politics in the aftermath of the fall of Walpole. Some ambitious young Whigs latched on to Lestock's cause in order to further their own prospects. They used him and he used them. Unlike Mathews, Lestock had not hitherto shown much interest in parliamentary politics, but it was the only way he could save himself for he was tremendously unpopular "out of doors." He was very fortunate in the political timing of his career crisis, but the result was a nightmare for the navy.

Lestock's friends managed to get the House of Commons to conduct its own inquiry into the battle. From a list of those ordered by the navy for the coming courts martial eighty-nine were selected to report to the House, and during March–April 1745 a committee of the whole spent two full days each week for over a month examining them.[16] A debate followed in which Henry Fox and George Grenville, ambitious Whigs, spoke strongly against Mathews while feigning impartiality. After this debate the House voted to submit a petition to the king which recommended *by name* the captains and admirals who should be tried by court martial. In short, parliament had heard testimony from the naval professionals and was asking the king to give directions about naval justice to the Admiralty. Henry Pelham, the emerging leader of the House of Commons, deplored this proceeding, but the political temperature was so high that he could not stand in the way.

After the courts martial were over, Lord Anson protested to the duke of Newcastle that royal directions in the matter of naval justice were dangerous and contrary to tradition and law. It never happened again, nor did parliament ever again inquire into matters for which a naval court martial would be the proper instrument. Admiral Rowley's recall from the Mediterranean command was also prompted by a resolution of the House of Commons. It may be indicative of Anson's abhorrence of overt parliamentary intervention in naval discipline that he made sure of Rowley's continued promotion in the flag ranks. He appears to have considered Rowley a worthy officer: Rowley came onto the Admiralty Board when Anson became First Lord in June 1751.[17]

Formal parliamentary intervention prior to courts martial was understood to be a threat to the navy's institutional independence and was soon after squelched for good. There were, however, covert (and poisonous) actions by three civilian members of the Board of Admiralty who maneuvered to influence the outcomes of the trials of the admirals. George Grenville was one of the participants. Another was his political ally on the board, Henry Bilson Legge, the partiality of whom is clear from Legge's letters to the Duke of Bedford. The third was the young Lord Sandwich. His attitude is discernible from the hope he expressed privately to Bedford that the president of the court would "summon some other Captains" to sit as members of the court in order to counter some of those who had shown in the trials of the captains that they were prejudiced (he believed) in favor of Mathews. Such additions to the court may not have actually been made (further research is needed), but the verdicts indicate that the majority of the judges understood that higher authority wanted Lestock excused and the blame placed on Mathews.[18] The preponderance of testimony condemned Lestock's conduct, yet he was exonerated. The manuscript record of testimony survives in the Admiralty archives and, in view of the verdict, it is easy to see why the Admiralty decided against publishing it, as had been done after the trials of the captains.[19] Consequently, neither the public nor, more importantly, the officer corps as a whole realized that the majority of the professionals who were actually present at the battle had testified that Mathews, however clumsily he may have signaled his intentions and wishes, had essentially done what had to be done, and that Lestock's contention that a perfect line engagement could have been fought— van to van, center to center, rear to rear—was nonsense; an attempt to do that would have resulted in no battle at all.

The influence of the Admiralty Board's partiality on the court martial and the decision to seal up the evidence had two terrible effects on the naval service. One effect concerned battle tactics. The court's findings in the admirals' trials gave dramatic endorsement to an idealized, rigid interpretation of the line-of-battle that was ill-suited to the Royal Navy's actual circumstances and purposes after 1740. It has been noted by historians that Captain John Byng was a member of this court and that he had its findings in mind—there is direct evidence—when admiral in command at Minorca in 1756. But this was just the most prominent instance of many. In retrospect it is clear that an important opportunity was missed in 1746. The line-of-battle doctrine could have been usefully and wisely rendered less rigid, but the court's finding worked in precisely the opposite direction, and this occurred in circumstances which plainly implied official approval.

Standard line-of-battle tactics made sense when both opposing fleets were determined to stand and fight, as happened often in the seventeenth century but seldom in the eighteenth, when French battle squadrons generally had other plans and purposes.[20] As naval historians have commonly recognized, successful British fleet battles in the eighteenth century were fought by commanders who either issued special instructions and signals designed beforehand to deal with the inevitable problems or took a chance on success, knowing that a combat victory would vindicate them. Most of them understood, as Mathews had believed, that failure to bring about an engagement where feasible would be ruinous. Some historians have been aware of the role of the 1746 courts martial in perpetuating this awkward and operationally detrimental situation.[21] What has not been known is the particular nature of the politics that penetrated the naval judicial process. The attractiveness to members of parliament of Admiral Lestock's claims about the indispensability of "discipline" (a word which in that era meant fighting in good order, in this case, according to the Fighting Instructions) had combined with a factional politics which invaded the Board of Admiralty. Under these influences the accounts of tactical circumstances provided by professional eyewitnesses under oath were overridden and obscured.

The other damaging effect was the impact on morale in the naval profession. Every sea officer was aware that a court martial, like any trial, might have an unjust result, but when serving on a court martial most officers realized that an unjustified finding would call into question their professional judgment. The Mathews-Lestock court, by contrast, was influenced by a Board of Admiralty infected by political motives, and the constraints that normally would arise from thoughts about professional reputation were therefore eroded. Officers of the time did not need to know the precise facts in order to guess that something like this had happened to the Mathews–Lestock court.

This issue of officers fearing injustice through political influence will come up again in a moment. First, however, there is one last question about the findings of 1746 with which to contend. Historically, the most respected naval leader of the mid-eighteenth century has been Admiral George Anson—a fine officer and an alert, fair-minded man who cared deeply about the reputation and efficiency of the naval service. Anson was a member of the Board of Admiralty while all this was going on, and his influence with the duke of Bedford, First Lord, was substantial. Was he aware of what his civilian colleagues on the board were doing, and what did he think about it? Anson never wrote much down, never even said much except in very private circles, but he must have known of their partiality—in Admiralty circles there was no secret about the favoring of Lestock over Mathews. Commodore Peter Warren, at Louisbourg, assumed that Anson knew. He could only conclude that power had altered Anson, because "I always imagined the evenness of his temper his greatest virtue." Then he added (in a letter to a fellow officer): "This to ourselves: if he can look askew upon Mr. Mathews, as you observe, he may crush me to atoms."[22]

Everything we know about Anson suggests that he preferred to think about policy rather than politics and that he would be inclined toward favoring "discipline," so the question may come down to whether he had really taken the trouble to analyze the evidence of the circumstances of the battle carefully. What is known with certainty is that a year later when commanding a battle squadron at sea and approaching an enemy squadron, he halted for two hours to form a proper line before engaging (First Battle of Cape Finisterre) while his second-in-command, Warren, was itching to hurry down upon the enemy. Warren did so as soon as Anson's signal to attack was flown, without appearing to care about how ragged the line thus became.[23] So Anson does seem to have been inclined to stick to the "discipline" as expressed in the Fighting Instructions. It is not unreasonable to suppose, therefore, that he had been inclined to favor the sort of argument that Lestock had put forward the year before and did not inquire more fully. Whatever the reason, when he was older and wiser he may have regretted that he did not try to restrain his colleagues on the board from allowing their bias to influence the court.

That said, it must also be said that Anson rescued this particular Admiralty Board from what would have been not just unpopularity but probable removal from office. It was not a board that cared about popularity—quite the opposite, it acted as if virtue lay in eliminating popular admirals like Mathews and Vernon. (Its desire to get rid of the obstreperous Vernon in 1745 was understandable, but to strike him from the admirals list suddenly and summarily was unnecessary and excessive—and remembered by the public.) A more serious problem for this board was its lack of visible naval achievement during its first two years in office (1745-6). It was Anson who, in 1746, insisted upon maintaining a strong Western Squadron at sea despite the heavy sacrifices required and prolonged strategic disappointment. Eventually the strategy and sacrifices were handsomely rewarded, with Anson himself winning a decisive battle in May 1747 off Cape Finisterre. This was followed in October by Sir Edward Hawke's interception of a French fleet, which led to the Second Battle of Cape Finisterre.[24] These two great victories brought acclaim to the navy and the Board of Admiralty, and gave the public something else to discuss besides the battle of Toulon. They played an important role in bringing an end to the war the following year.

As is well known, Lord Anson was a reformer. When the war was over, with the Admiralty's reputation high, he undertook to get the navy's Articles of War codified and overhauled. This would require an Act of Parliament. Certain features of court-martial proceedings were to be revised, but the most controversial element was a new article, one which would subject a half-pay officer who refused an Admiralty assignment in wartime to discipline by court martial. Such refusals had been fairly frequent during the war just concluded.

Such a reform seems sensible on the surface, but two important objections soon come to mind. One was immediate and heartfelt at the time, though perhaps ephemeral; the other was fundamental. The first stems from the fact that this proposal came from a Board of Admiralty that was regarded by quite a few officers as being high-handed without being even-handed, and, given the outcomes in 1746, any officer might be inclined to wonder about the quality of justice handed down by a court martial convened under Admiralty influence.

The second objection—more fundamental than the first—is that such a proceeding had the potential of completely altering the manner in which the officer corps functioned. Nicholas Rodger has written that the "Admiralty controlled the Navy, not by formal bonds of discipline, and obedience, but by its control of patronage."[25] It is a good point—the essential truth. But courts martial, as emphasized above, were also part of the career picture, and would have become a much bigger factor if this article had been adopted. The Admiralty would have been able to rely on something besides patronage to exert its influence; the balance of the system could have changed. One almost certain result would have been to render the navy less insulated from ministerial politics. The implications were so revolutionary that one wonders whether, in actual practice, the navy would have wished to see the threat used. Nor was there a dire need for the measure since, in the most egregious cases of refusal, the Admiralty could, and did, strike the officer's name from the half-pay list. The regular use of this innovation might have meant greater efficiency in a managerial sense, but it was a form of efficiency that the eighteenth-century navy could not afford.

A very considerable body of officers, led by Captain Augustus Hervey—and joined, interestingly, by Sir Peter Warren, though Warren tried to soften the nature of Hervey's opposition—petitioned the Admiralty to drop this article and then lobbied against it in parliament. Actually, more officers signed a letter in support of the measure than signed the petition against it, but the number of officers who privately disapproved was undoubtedly greater. And it is significant that the letter from those who did support the Admiralty was very cautiously worded; it contained this sentence: "We . . . are convinced that what is intended as a reasonable expedient and necessary part of discipline is not made to serve the purposes of cruelty and oppression." In other words: We trust that you will restrain yourselves. When the bill came to be considered by the House of Commons the opponents of this article had a substantial advantage: members of parliament were habitually inclined to reject proposals which tended to increase the power of the executive. A majority of naval officers who sat as MPs spoke against it, among them Admiral Rowley, who had earlier signed the letter in support.[26] Here was an instance where thirty or so naval officers who held seats in parliament helped to keep parliamentary politics at a distance from professional politics.

At first glance one would think that the tremendous uproar in the nation over the loss of Minorca in 1756, the court martial of Admiral John Byng, and the subsequent, highly controversial carrying out of his execution on the quarterdeck of a man of war should have had a deeply disturbing effect on the officer corps. Yet this was a case where a botched naval mission which brought on a hugely publicized court martial in England had very little effect on naval politics, though it had an enormous impact on national politics — in fact, the government was forced out of office by it. Why did it have so little impact on the officer corps?

The main reason was that the actual carrying out of the sentence of death was the only truly controversial aspect of the case, and even that was carried out — though it could have been commuted — by the successor administration, which was of a very different political coloring and could not be supposed to be out for blood. It also mattered that in the end it was the king who decided against mercy. George II was furious at Byng's conduct. He had guessed from the tenor of the admiral's early letter from Gibraltar that the man would not fight and had said so loudly in the presence of others at court. Although, of course, Byng did fight a sea battle — leading his squadron against the French without showing any sign of cowardice — he did nothing else. Despite the various options available to him (most of which involved only moderate risk) for using his force to harass the French and encourage the garrison of Fort St. Philip to hold out, he saw nothing but obstacles and probable futility. In other words, though physically brave, Byng was destitute of determination, and in this important sense he did not fight.

George II's refusal of mercy had a lot of popular support in the nation. Nevertheless, many naval officers wished the sentence had not been carried out. The officers of the court who reached the verdict formally recorded their regret that they were required by the rules to sentence Byng to death and after doing so they recommended mercy. Yet if the actual carrying out of the sentence was controversial, practically everyone in the profession agreed that Byng had failed in his duty. Sea officers grasped very quickly that Byng's strategic "errors of judgment" were not only colossal but craven. From news reports they could readily discern that it was not really Byng's conduct of the battle that deserved censure; rather it was his failure to make any further efforts to help the garrison at Minorca hold out. Although his conduct of the sea battle was unimaginative, the evidence of the court martial, which was fully published, eventually confirmed this line of analysis. The legally disfiguring aspects of the case were therefore technical, arising from the circumstance that the Articles of War were not geared for non-combat failings (the court, not wanting to find Byng guiltless, stretched the law) and from the fact that the punishment of death, thanks to a change made in the Articles of War in 1749, was mandatory. Very few officers defended Byng; many were furious that a British force commander under such circumstances should have attempted so little. Thus, distressing though it all was, the officer corps did not divide over this episode. Captain Augustus Hervey, who was in Byng's squadron during the battle, was one of the few who tried to make a naval case on behalf of the admiral. The others who were sympathetic talked about mercy.

No one has analyzed with any degree of comprehensiveness the affiliations of the officer corps during the two decades after 1763. Much of what follows must be regarded as provisional. There were two root causes of trouble. Most fundamental was the transformative political effect of the accession of George III. A new set of politicians came to the fore and many of the older Whigs died off or became enfeebled by age or illness.

In the naval sphere the death of Lord Anson in 1762 at age sixty-five (while still in office as First Lord) was of great significance. For one thing, he had been remarkably even-handed in his dealings with the officer corps, especially during the Seven Years War, when he plainly favored men of ability from all points of the political compass. For example, Augustus Hervey could not bring himself personally to reconcile with Anson and Anson well knew it, but the First Lord recognized his professional skill and dedication, and made sure that he was promoted to flag rank and given important assignments.[27] Anson was the son-in-law of the earl of Hardwicke, the most astute among the former Whig leaders. Many of the best admirals and captains, promoted during Anson's long tenure at the Admiralty, had been aligned with those Whigs, and after the peace of 1763 they did not enjoy comfortable relationships with most of the governments that assumed power. Among these Whigs Admiral Augustus Keppel was a leading figure.

Under ordinary circumstances this situation would not have been professionally injurious, but the war to put down the American rebellion was not an ordinary war; it was unusual not only in terms of strategy and the nature of the challenge but also in terms of politics. It was a war in which the king himself felt he had a personal stake in the navy's success. The experience of Admiral Samuel Graves, naval commander at Boston when hostilities erupted in 1775, is a case in point. Having failed to provide Graves with promised reinforcements and also failing to state candidly to king or country how weak Graves's squadron was, Lord Sandwich, the First Lord, was consequently unable to explain why Graves had failed to act as vigorously as expected against the Americans. And so, without warning, Graves found himself recalled under a cloud, Sandwich lamely explaining to him that the "torrent" of criticism was "too strong for me to be able to withstand it." (It cannot be doubted that a good deal of the torrent was supplied by George III.) Upon arriving home Graves asked for a clear public statement from the Admiralty about the difficulties he had confronted with his inadequate squadron. This was not forthcoming, and Graves thereupon requested a court martial to "justify his conduct to the publick." The request was denied. He was never again offered active employment at sea.[28] This sort of thing—continual interference by the king, pressures from the ministry (especially from Germain), and weakness of the First Lord in the face of these—naturally created uneasiness in the corps.

To top it off, there was the mishandling of the notorious Keppel-Palliser affair of 1778-9. In this affair Lord Sandwich made three decisions which did colossal damage to the navy. The trouble began with his decision to appoint Vice Admiral Sir Hugh Palliser, his right-hand man on the Admiralty Board, to be a division commander of Keppel's Channel fleet. Although Palliser had known Keppel from early career circumstances and evidently got along well with him, a lot had happened since those years. The two men had hotly argued naval matters from opposite sides of the House of Commons, and Palliser was recognized as a naval man who was intensely supportive of the government. Upon Sandwich's recommendation he had been rewarded with a valuable sinecure which, in the eyes of many senior naval officers, his seniority and measure of professional distinction did not warrant. Everyone knew how close Palliser was to Sandwich.

The unsatisfactory action off Ushant on July 27, 1778, was a vibrant topic when parliament assembled in late November. Sandwich, speaking in the House of Lords, ably and wisely headed off a parliamentary enquiry, saying that it "would divide the officers and seamen into factions." He reminded his listeners of what he had personally witnessed thirty years ago: "Such precisely were the consequences of the miscarriage of Matthews [sic] and Lestock . . . ; the enquiry raised a kind of commotion in the nation; and at the conclusion no one good purpose was answered." The public and parliamentary expectation was that, instead, a court martial would be convened and the accused officer would be Palliser, who would welcome it as a means of defending his honor in response to insinuations of serious misconduct published in a newspaper which, as he averred publicly, made him furious. Yet it was Admiral Keppel who was court-martialed. Why this happened is unclear.

The usual explanation is that an angry Palliser precipitately filed charges at the Board of Admiralty against Admiral Keppel and, however much their Lordships might regret the fact, once these charges were received there was no room for discretion: the

Admiralty could not legally deny an officer his supposed right to clear off a slur on his reputation in this way. This interpretation was sharply disputed in the House of Commons. Opposition MPs denied that the Admiralty could not exercise discretion in such instances. In support of the Admiralty an amazing argument was made that this court martial had to go ahead because Keppel had refused to charge Palliser; since the public would absolutely demand some sort of court martial (true enough) it was necessary to try Keppel! A body of sea officers including the aged Lord Hawke submitted a memorial to the Privy Council giving reasons why the Admiralty must not let Keppel be court-martialed. In retrospect, it is clear that Sandwich should have denied Palliser's demand (a step that the First Lord's personal relationship with Palliser would surely have allowed) and suggested to him that, since his stated object had always been to clear his own name, he should request a court martial on himself. Lord Sandwich did not do this—a second dreadful decision.[29]

As every professional realized, given the nature of Palliser's charges of misconduct, Keppel was now to be put on trial for his life. The court assembled at Portsmouth in early 1779 in an atmosphere of enormous public excitement. Keppel was completely exonerated. Indeed, the court's finding pronounced the charges "malicious and ill-founded." The testimony quickly became public knowledge. At this point practically everyone realized that Palliser was thoroughly discredited—even the king, who felt sorry for him, observed that "his bringing a capital charge and yet not having proved the smallest appearance of ground" for it had shocked even "moderate men." Sandwich now persuaded Palliser to accept a court martial upon himself, a step that was politically unavoidable. Initially, Sandwich asked Keppel to bring charges of tactical misconduct against Palliser, but Keppel refused to do it. (Keppel, who had started out with an almost paranoid suspicion of Sandwich's Admiralty Board, was by this point steaming with fury and resentment, but continued to feign coolness and aloofness.) The trial went ahead anyway. To recover some of the Admiralty's moral authority in the officer corps, Sandwich needed to stand clear of the proceedings, but he evidently did the opposite. The rumors ran to the extent of supposing that certain captains were ordered to sea and others called home so that the composition of the court would be favorable to Palliser. At length, the court found Palliser's conduct to be no better or worse than Keppel had publicly said it was, which did him little good. That Sandwich continued to try to defend Palliser long after everyone else had abandoned him was a third damaging decision.[30]

Palliser lost everything. He had to resign his place at the Admiralty and his lucrative sinecures. But this retribution did not prevent a horrendous political divide from opening up in the officer corps; quite a few officers among those affiliated with the older Whig connection refused to serve. The worst consequence was a thinning of the ranks of able, experienced, and respected admirals still fit for sea service, since a number of these, following Keppel's lead, expressed strong doubts about serving while Lord Sandwich remained head of the Admiralty. In respect to younger officers the effects were considerably ameliorated within a few years, because so many ships were put in commission as the war continued that a new generation of officers could be brought forward. To be sure, the suspicions and resentments aroused in the Keppel-Palliser affair tempted men in all quarters to misbehave, but Lord Sandwich was the man in the responsible position. His decisions were the crucial ones.

These experiences of the American Revolutionary War call to mind two earlier topics and may thus serve the purposes of conclusion. First, given the divisive political atmosphere that accompanied this war from the beginning, the Admiralty very much needed to be headed by a respected sea officer who would do his utmost to keep national politics from seriously affecting the profession; if not the First Lord, then it needed to be one of the members of the board. Someone had to try to dampen the influence of combative politics on the corps — as Sir Charles Wager had done when necessary many years before — someone who was disposed to be more concerned with morale in the profession than accommodating the desires of the ministry. To say the least, neither Sandwich nor Palliser filled the bill. Sandwich and Palliser were indeed naval experts and hard-working men, but in this crucial respect they were the wrong men for the navy in this difficult passage of national politics.

Second, once again one sees the devastating effect that a court martial convened in response to accusations by a vice admiral against his superior after a disappointing battle could have on the officer corps. Similarities to the aftermath of the battle of Toulon were numerous and were often recalled on this occasion. Yet the differences between 1779 and 1746 were greater than the similarities. The most important difference was that the Admiralty was not in a position to influence the outcome of the court martial of Admiral Keppel, so that, unlike what happened in 1746, the nation believed that naval justice was done. The exoneration of Keppel was dictated by the evidence but—and this was another difference—it was also an indication of how many senior sea officers in 1779 were not disposed to sympathize with the Admiralty.

On this point King George III understood what needed to be done even while the Admiralty Board was reaching its fateful decision to let the court-martial of Keppel go forward. The king advised his prime minister in mid-December 1778 that Lord Sandwich should be removed from the Admiralty and made a Secretary of State, commenting: "Administration will somehow or other be too much mixed in this affair, unless a change is made in that department."[31] But Lord North felt that his government was too weak to survive so dramatic a move at this juncture, and the king did not persist. That it was not done is an important fact not only in the history of naval politics but in the larger political history of the American war. The theme of this paper has been chiefly the manner in which the importation of political history provides a better understanding of the navy and naval history, but here is an instance where an understanding of the navy helps to bring national political history into sharper focus.

NOTES

[1] J. V. Beckett, *The Aristocracy in England, 1660-1914* (Oxford, 1986), 410; John Cannon, *Aristocratic Century: The Peerage of Eighteenth-Century England* (Cambridge, 1984), 118.

[2] Daniel A. Baugh, ed., *Naval Administration, 1715-1750*, Navy Records Society (London, 1977), 5.

[3] J. D. Davies, *Gentlemen and Tarpaulins: The Officers and Men of the Restoration Navy* (Oxford, 1991) has insisted on the key role of the officers them-selves (with some assistance from Charles II and James, duke of York); Samuel Pepys helped but did not create the officer corps (see esp. pp. 228-32).

[4] N. A .M. Rodger, *The Wooden World: An Anatomy of the Georgian Navy* (London, 1986), passim.

[5] Herbert W. Richmond, *The Navy in the War of 1739-48* (Cambridge, 1920), 2:57, 268-71.

[6] *Dictionary of National Biography*, "Lestock," "Mathews." Understandably, Laughton was far less sure of the facts in this instance, writing before Richmond studied them.

[7] Andrew Lambert, *The Foundations of Naval History: Sir John Knox Laughton, the Royal Navy and the Historical Profession* (London, 1998), 91.

[8] Daniel A. Baugh, "Why Did Britain Lose Command of the Sea During the War for America?" in *The British Navy and the Use of Naval Power in the Eighteenth Century*, ed. Jeremy Black and Philip Woodfine (Leicester, 1988), 152-6. Daniel A. Baugh, "The Politics of British Naval Failure, 1775-1777," *The American Neptune* 52 (1992), 242-5.

[9] *Ibid.*, 235-8. *The Private Papers of John, Earl of Sandwich, First Lord of the Admiralty 1771-1782*, ed. G.R. Barnes and J.H. Owen, Navy Records Society (London, 1933), 2:54-105.

[10] Baugh, *Naval Administration, 1715-1750*, 15.

[11] For the pervasiveness and intensity of Vernon's popularity at this time see Kathleen Wilson, *The Sense of the People: Politics, Culture and Imperialism in England, 1715-1785* (Cambridge, 1995), 142-52.

[12] Wager's character and abilities will be exhibited in the entry I am writing for the *New Dictionary of National Biography* as well as in a forthcoming book with the proposed title "Precursors of Nelson," edited by Richard Harding and Peter Le Fevre. For the point that Wager was widely esteemed across political divides, see William Pulteney's letter to Vernon of June 16, 1741 in B. McL. Ranft, ed., *The Vernon Papers*, Navy Records Society (London, 1958), 240.

[13] Richmond, *Navy in the War of 1739-48*, 1:225.

[14] Rodger, *The Wooden World*, 302.

[15] These numbers are very rough estimates based on incomplete surviving records and printed accounts.

[16] P. A. Luff, "Mathews v. Lestock: Parliament, Politics and the Navy in Mid-Eighteenth-Century England," *Parliamentary History* 19 (1991), 51.

[17] *Cobbett's Parliamentary History*, 13:1250-1299; Sir John Barrow, *The Life of George Lord Anson* (London, 1839), 125; *Dictionary of National Biography*, "Rowley."

[18] Some of the evidence for these activities by Admiralty Board members will appear in my entries for "Thomas Mathews" and "Richard Lestock" in the *New Dictionary of National Biography* (forthcoming).

[19] Court martial records, PRO Adm. 1/5280-1.

[20] An insightful study of tactics is John Creswell, *British Admirals of the Eighteenth Century: Tactics in Battle* (London, 1972), but its working assumption that both battle fleets will stay to fight narrows its applicability.

[21] Often David Hannay's judgments ninety years ago were flawed by lack of

knowledge and particular prejudices, but he did emphasize, as many others writing on tactics have not, the great impact of the 1746 trials: "The consequence of their finding was to rivet the tyranny of a pedantic rule so firmly that it required forty years of war" to clear it away (*A Short History of the Royal Navy, 1217-1815* [London, 1909], 2:117).

[22]Julian Gwyn, ed., *The Royal Navy in North America: The Warren Papers, 1736-1752*, Navy Records Society (London, 1973), 249.

[23]Richmond, *Navy in the War of 1739-48*, 3:89-91.

[24]Ruddock F. Mackay, *Admiral Hawke* (Oxford, 1965), 63-5.

[25]Rodger, *Wooden World*, 303.

[26]David Erskine, ed., *Augustus Hervey's Journal* (London, 1953), 78-84; Baugh, *Naval Administration, 1715-1750*, 86-7.

[27]Erskine, *Augustus Hervey's Journal*, xxv-xxvi, 305-8.

[28]Baugh, "Politics of British Naval Failure," 226-9.

[29]The debate of December 11, 1778, concerning whether the Admiralty could exercise discretion is to be found in *The Parliamentary Register; or, History of the Proceedings and Debates of the House of Commons*, (London: J. Almon, 1779), 11: 131-52. The possibility cannot be completely ruled out that Sandwich and Palliser colluded and agreed that Palliser should preemptively file charges against Keppel; this was suspected by some members of the opposition though categorically denied by the two men. See in particular a letter printed in *Sandwich Papers* (2: 218).

[30]For a useful recent scholarly account see N. A. M. Rodger, *The Insatiable Earl: A Life of John Montague, Fourth Earl of Sandwich, 1718-1792* (London, 1993), 240-50, from which some quotations in this and the preceding paragraph are drawn. The interpretation differs from mine, particularly regarding whether Sandwich, as Dr. Rodger believes, had little choice in these decisions. For a view less sympathetic to Palliser and Sandwich see Laughton's entry for "Palliser" in the *Dictionary of National Biography*. The reader will readily surmise that the history of the whole sorry business is still by no means settled and that it is difficult to write about it without taking sides.

[31]Quoted in J. H. Bloomfield, "The Keppel-Palliser Affair, 1778-1779," *Mariner's Mirror* 47 (1961), 203.

In the Shadow of Marder: A New Perspective of British Naval Administration and the Naval Defense Act of 1889

Robert E. Mullins

> Arthur Marder was one of the most prolific and influential scholars of the Royal Navy in the Age of Steam and Steel. Writing in the 1930s and 1940s, Marder crafted an entire historiography based on detailed assessments of external threats and internal politics. In Marder's geopolitical world, external provocation, threat assessment, and the intervention of civilian politicians drove British naval policy in the years prior to the First World War. Recently, however, some naval scholars have begun to reexamine the underpinnings of that historiography. In this essay, Robert Mullins reexamines the Naval Defense Act of 1889 and suggests that it was less the product of external provocation and threat assessment than it was the result of a concerted effort by senior naval officers to impress upon their civilian counterparts the importance of continued British preeminence at sea: "the culmination of a struggle in civil-military relations."

It was a year of impressive naval revival in Britain, a period rendered significant by a series of strategic and force structure choices in 1889 that essentially predestined the course of modern naval history prior to the nuclear age. In that year, the Admiralty proposed the largest shipbuilding program ever formulated in peacetime during the nineteenth century. The Naval Defense Act, as it became known when formally approved by Parliament in May 1889, authorized the construction of ten battleships, forty-two cruisers and eighteen torpedo-gunboats at the cost of £21,500,000. The strategic rationale used to underwrite the five-year program was so persuasive in fact that Parliament also restored the two-power standard, in which the combined naval strength of France and Russia were to be used as a barometer for British shipbuilding requirements. What followed in the 1890s was a naval arms race, as both France, Russia and then Germany struggled to rival British naval power and the line of ancestors to the *Royal Sovereigns*, the first class of predreadnought battleships

---

Robert E. Mullins holds a Ph.D. in War Studies from Kings College, London.

that heralded a new era of capital ship design to maximize offensive naval power in future contests for control of the seas.

For over sixty years, the study of these events has been defined primarily by the research of the late Arthur Marder, whose special access to Admiralty archives in the 1930s led to findings later published in *The Anatomy of British Seapower* in 1940.[1] In what is undeniably the most widely cited reference on the subject, Professor Marder portrayed the Naval Defense Act as a reaction to widespread fears of a possible Franco–Russian naval combination. In his view, the strategic and force structure choices embodied in the Act were made at the behest of civilian authorities and not by the Admiralty. The Salisbury ministry was compelled to intervene when a reluctant Admiralty Board, unwilling to concede the disparity in naval strength *vis-à-vis* France and Russia, insisted that it possessed sufficient numbers of battleships and cruisers to fulfill the strategic missions of the Royal Navy in wartime.

The primary aim of this article is twofold. With the Marder account upheld in recent biographies of Lord Salisbury, it first becomes necessary to reassess it in light of underutilized archival materials and the supporting research of other naval historians.[2] In shaping this discussion precisely around external provocations, threat perceptions and civilian intervention, the reader will quickly acquire an appreciation for how British naval policy in the 1880s was motivated more by the budgetary concerns of politicians than the threats posed by France and Russia. For purposes of comparison, this will be followed by an organizational perspective of the Naval Defense Act, as seen through an analytic lens which describes the decisions of 1889 generally in terms of the culture, history and strategy of the Royal Navy. The last half of this article, in particular, concerns itself mainly with the origin and substance of the strategic ideas behind the Naval Defense Act. Their resurgence in the 1870s and 1880s is shown here to have occurred at the behest of John Knox Laughton, the pioneer naval educator and historian who encouraged naval officers to apply naval history to the solving of strategic problems in modern naval warfare. Whether he intended to or not, Laughton succeeded in inspiring a campaign for strategic awareness that culminated in 1889 with the formulation and passage of the Naval Defense Act.

In essence, the explanatory value of the Marder thesis rests upon whether or not the reader accepts three fundamental arguments presented in *The Anatomy of British Seapower*:

- British naval supremacy was in serious jeopardy in the 1880s, due mainly to the progress of naval modernization in France and Russia, and the prospect that these two countries would somehow form an effective naval combination and succeed in defeating the Royal Navy. According to Marder, the Franco-Russian threat to Britain at the time was more than credible, inferring that the latter was falling behind their potential adversaries in such crucial areas as materiel, armament, and rate of construction.[3]

- Not only was the prospect of a Franco-Russian naval combination a serious challenge to British naval supremacy, but the threat was perceived as such by those responsible for naval policy formulation in and outside of the Admiralty. This is critical to the Marder thesis, as threat perceptions from external provocations formed the basis of the British reaction that was eventually manifested in the Naval Defense Act. Marder referred to these threat perceptions and the reactions of British policymakers collectively as "the navy scare of 1888."[4]

- The strategic and force structure choices embodied in the Naval Defense Act were made at the behest of the Salisbury ministry and not from the Admiralty itself. According to Marder, Salisbury was compelled to intervene into the strategic calculus when a reluctant Admiralty Board, unwilling to concede the disparity in naval strength *vis-à-vis* France and Russia, remained adamant that it possessed sufficient numbers of battleships and cruisers to fulfill the roles and missions of the service in the event of war.[5]

With the vantage of hindsight, the threat posed from a Franco-Russian naval combination was a product more of anxiety than reality. Referring to the apprehension of British policymakers over such a likelihood, Theodore Ropp concluded that "[t]hese fears were largely illusory—even though France and Russia had signed an alliance in 1892, they did not enter into naval conversations until 1900, and the French naval command not only never considered the possibility of a union between the two fleets but was unanimously opposed to it."[6] Paul Kennedy also faulted the British for blowing the threat out of proportion, noting that "it seems in retrospect that they probably overestimated the danger from this direction, forgetting the weaknesses of their rivals and seeing only those in their own fleet."[7] What appears to be a clear and explicit departure from the Marder thesis, however, is in actuality a tacit admission that the threat posed from a Franco-Russian naval combination, or more precisely the *misperception* of the threat, was indeed the underlying factor behind the passage of the Naval Defense Act. In the end, Professor Kennedy would echo Marder and invoke a causal linkage between the threat the shipbuilding program endorsed by the Salisbury ministry: "The prospect of a Franco-Russian naval alliance, which would pincer the understrength Mediterranean Fleet and cut that vital line of communication in time of war, was too grim to be dismissed with soothing phrases and half-measures."[8]

Thus, whether the threat was real, imagined or exaggerated, the Marder thesis remains undisputed so long as the mere *perception* of a Franco-Russian naval threat existed within the Admiralty prior to 1889. Admiralty records pertaining to the years in question are readily available, and noticeably absent from these reports is any indication that the Admiralty—through the workings of the newly created intelligence department—was needlessly preoccupied with the prospect of a Franco-Russian naval combination. The sole exception is a report written by Captain William H. Hall, the first Director of Naval Intelligence, which was intended as an innovative force-planning analysis based on a worst-case scenario in the near future—so innovative, in fact, that the Hall report and the conclusions reached therein were suppressed by the First Lord and the First Naval Lord until July 1888, when the latter used it as the basis for the shipbuilding program that would become the Naval Defense Act.

Given the importance of the Eastern Mediterranean to British access to India and other colonial possessions, it was entirely understandable for the Admiralty to be well informed of naval developments in Russia, even though Russia had never posed a serious challenge to British naval supremacy at any time before, during or after the Crimean War.[9] Even though the Admiralty in the latter stages of the Eastern Crisis of 1876–78 sought to purchase four ironclads being built in British dockyards for the Ottoman Empire and Brazil, the supplement in naval strength was viewed mainly as a measure to ensure that the vessels were not transferred to hostile parties. "In none of the surviving correspondence regarding the 'war scare' purchases of 1878," observed John Beeler, "is there any indication that [the] Admiralty or cabinet was motivated by a sense of urgency, much less necessity."[10] During the 1870s, the Russian battlefleet was composed mainly of coastal-defense turret ships with inadequate armor protection and armament, a material weakness for a defensive force designed principally for coastal defense and not for offensive naval operations.[11] An American observer underscored this point in 1877, writing in his report that "Except for coast defense, the Russian fleet is rather numerous than powerful. The *Peter the Great* and the *Minin* [an armored cruiser] are the only two vessels on the list which approach the modern standard of fighting efficiency."[12]

Attempts by Russia to redress the profound disparity in naval strength during the 1880s was largely an incremental enterprise. This was not due to any shortage of funds. On the contrary, the Russian Government since 1878 demonstrated that it was willing to expend the resources necessary to subsidize an investment that was expected to yield a naval force roughly comparable to that possessed by Britain. Russian naval expenditures steadily increased throughout the decade, from £4,200,000 in 1880 to £5,828,571 in 1889—an increase of roughly 39% since 1880.[13] Admiralty estimates of Russian naval expenditures would seem to be more alarming; one intelligence report calculated that Russian naval spending increased by almost 54% during the same period.[14] The fact that this failed to stir pangs of anxiety within the Admiralty is a testimonial to the level of overwhelming confidence in the multi-faceted capabilities of the Royal Navy. It was also due to a realistic appraisal of relative capabilities *vis-à-vis* Russia. The British recognized that the Imperial Russian Navy had remained in a relative stage of infancy since the 1870s, while the Royal Navy was years ahead in terms of strategy, fleet composition, logistics and naval construction. It was more than obvious to Admiralty officials that the Russian battlefleet, such that it was, first had to learn to walk before it could run—and the Royal Navy was for decades accustomed to running at a pace heretofore unmatched by the principal maritime powers of the nineteenth century.

Captain Henry Kane observed the annual maneuvers of the Russian Baltic Fleet in 1884 and what he observed only reinforced Admiralty perceptions of the diminutive condition of the Baltic Fleet, which in effect constituted the bulk of the Imperial Russian Navy. Kane's report contained observations that bordered on condescension for a grossly inferior naval service, including a notation that "a great deal of practice was given to the [Russian] officers, if not in 'maneuvering' as we understand the word, at least in managing their ships."[15] His most pointed and particularly insightful criticism was reserved for the absence of what was commonly known as "steam tactics," consisting of tightly choreographed geometrical evolutions controlled by flag signals between warships. "Fleet Maneuvering or 'steam tactics,' which the Russians were famous for, in theory, in the days of Admiral Boutakoff," Kane observed, "seems to have been completely overlooked. They did not have a single day's drill of that sort. They never cruised in any formation but the single line ahead. They appear to have devoted themselves to torpedo warfare as not to be able to think of anything else."[16]

In effect, the Russian naval maneuvers of 1884 were merely a reflection of a naval strategy formulated along a defensive orientation, a fact that was later underscored by an article written by a senior Russian naval officer and translated by the Foreign Office. Forwarded to the intelligence department in April 1888, the officer reinforced the notion that the Baltic fleet was in reality a coastal defense force of secondary importance to the army: "It is difficult to admit the idea that Russia is striving for mastery over the Baltic. The attainment of this objective would not be worth the sanguinary struggle which it would involve, and moreover, the same result could be gained by Russian troops on the plains of Pomerania."[17] Captain Hall's written comments on the jacket of this report reveal the extent to which the Admiralty was well apprised of what the Russians could and could not do with respect to their navy: "Recent reports in Russian papers lead me to think it will be some time before steps are commenced to make a military harbor inside the Gulf of Finland."[18]

The impression fostered by Captain Hall and his staff about Russian naval capabilities was also grounded firmly in observations rendered by the naval attaché following his periodic inspections of Russian dockyards and other naval facilities. This was a most informative exercise, for the types and qualities of warships building in the dockyards were typically an indication of the expected roles and missions of the subject navy.[19] It was also an opportunity to assess Russian shipbuilding practices and activities, as well as the expected combat effectiveness of the future additions to the battlefleet. For most of the 1880s, Russian activities in these dockyards were limited mainly to the completion of a small number of ironclads and cruisers in various stages of construction, most of which were begun in the late 1870s.[20] As a result, the Russian battlefleet of the 1880s consisted only of two first-class ironclads, four second-class ironclads (late armored cruisers) and twenty-one coastal-defense ironclads.[21] Most of these vessels were unsuitable for extended operations abroad, particularly those in the latter category, a fact that spurred Russian shipbuilders to emulate British and French warship designs. On his visit to inspect the Baltic naval dockyards and facilities in early 1887, Captain Kane observed that "the Russians pay great attention to English and French shipbuilding, and every detail concerning our ships is well known and studied here. There is a reading-room at the 'New Admiralty' Dockyard, at which . . . English professional papers and magazines are more read than Russian."[22]

It was thus not surprising to the British when the Russians began construction of five new first-class ironclads between 1886 and 1888, most of which were roughly comparable to British first-class ironclads in terms of size and speed. Three of these ironclads—*Tchesma*, *Sinope* and *Ekaterina II*—were being built at Black Sea dockyards, while the remaining two ironclads—*Alexander I* and *Nicolas I*—were laid down in the Baltic.[23] A significant development in Russian naval modernization, the progress of these new vessels undoubtedly attracted the attention of the Admiralty back in London, but the new construction did not seem to arouse any sense of unwarranted anxiety. While recognized as an "important subject" by the Foreign Office, Admiralty records again reveal a well-informed yet muted approach to what could have been a contentious issue between the two countries, that being the implications stemming from the presence of three new Russian ironclads in the Black Sea.[24] In response to a request from the Foreign Office for more information about the new ironclads, Captain Hall provided a rather benign assessment of the new vessels, noting that their completion would be delayed until 1890 at the earliest. At the same time, Hall also referred to the deplorable state of the Russian Black Sea Fleet, noting that "such a force can hardly be capable of coping with the ironclads Turkey possesses though these are not modern vessels and it doubtful all are efficient."[25] In his estimate, the presence of the three ironclads would indeed alter the balance of naval power between Turkey and Russia in the Black Sea, but their presence was more of a Turkish concern than a British one. "But as there seems no disposition on the part of Turkey to acquire new ironclads," Hall observed, "it is evident that in 1890, Russia with three powerful ironclads will be relatively much stronger than at present."[26]

In sum, there is little evidence in Admiralty records to denote a sense of anxiety over Russian naval developments in the 1880s. Rather, the scores of intelligence reports and other correspondence to and from the Admiralty during this period reveal a much different image than that offered by Professor Marder in *The Anatomy of British Seapower*. The image presented above describes a confident and well-informed Admiralty, complete with an intelligence function perceptive not only of British naval capabilities, but how they also compare with the capabilities of the other principal maritime powers. Russia, as one of these maritime powers, lagged far behind the British standard for a modern seapower. What Russia considered to be a battlefleet, was more impressive on paper than in action, as amply demonstrated by its mediocre performance in the 1884 naval maneuvers. Between 1884 and 1888, Russia would embark on a shipbuilding program to remedy its reliance on numerous but ineffective and obsolete coastal-defense monitors, but the addition of five first-class ironclads was modest and simply not enough to bolster France in a credible challenge to British naval supremacy. For these reasons, it is quite understandable why the French considered any future cooperation with their incompatible Russian counterparts in the 1890s to be of minimal benefit. It is with France in mind that we now turn to British perceptions of the navy that would have been the senior partner in the phantom Franco–Russian naval combination.

A number of factors traditionally complicated the British strategic calculus when contemplating the prospect of naval warfare with France, much more so than those likely to be encountered in preparations for a one-sided contest with the Imperial Russian Navy. The first two can be reduced to geographical and meteorological circumstances. The obvious distances between the three countries aside, Russian naval operations were largely hindered by the lack of unfettered access to naval ports and sea lanes in the Gulf of Finland, a shoal-infested body of water that is ice-bound for much of the year. For this very reason, the intelligence department in the Admiralty never seriously considered the employment of offensive coastal operations for the reduction of Cronstadt, but instead planned for a blockade to be established at the entrance to the Gulf of Finland.[27] The proximity between Britain and France posed a much larger problem, as the second largest naval power possessed an extensive coastline with a number of excellent naval ports, which included Toulon, Cherbourg, Brest, Lorient and Rochefort. The idea of an invasion force crossing the English Channel from French ports certainly brought about a considerable feeling of anxiety from time to time among British politicians and military officers. "For the present the enemy is France," Lord Salisbury observed in 1887.[28] In the following year, he cautioned that "France is, and must always remain, England's greatest danger."[29]

The factor that mattered most in resolving this strategic dilemma was the naval balance between the two countries, as British naval officers were confident in the knowledge that French naval capabilities between 1860 and 1890 were largely substandard when compared to the warships, personnel and administration of the Royal Navy. This despite the occasional "invasion scare" which was exploited by British naval officers to justify increased naval expenditures to reluctant government ministers. In fact, France was no more a threat to British naval supremacy than Russia, especially in the aftermath of the Franco–German War of 1870–71. In the years following, the French were more preoccupied with overland threats from Germany than the prospect of yet another challenge to British naval supremacy. The French navy suffered as a result, as governmental expenditures were diverted to other priorities, chief among them was the rehabilitation of the army. "For the majority of the decade," observed John Beeler, "the French navy was deprived of the funding to maintain its existing navy, much less renew the challenge to Britain. The immediate need to rebuild and remodel the French military establishment, coupled with the futility of naval operations during the war and the necessity of paying a huge war indemnity, made naval construction a low-priority item during the years immediately following the humiliation."[30]

In the 1870s, the French navy thus consisted mainly of wooden-hulled ironclads built during the course of an ambitious shipbuilding program in the early 1860s.[31] These vessels were no match for British warships in the same category, the latter having been designed with durable iron hulls, watertight compartments and thicker armor.[32] By the end of the decade, the Admiralty estimated that the disparity in ironclads between the two countries was nine to five in favor of the British, who during the course of the decade completed the construction of thirteen ironclads and eight coastal defense vessels.[33] In contrast, French shipbuilders completed only seven such vessels, three of which were originally designed in 1865 or earlier. While the French managed to begin construction of nine first-class ironclads in the latter half of the 1870s, most of these vessels were completed between 1886 and 1889. This trend in French shipbuilding would be greatly exacerbated in the 1880s by pervasive dockyard inefficiency, the burden of additional naval construction, as well as the frequent design changes made at the insistence of the *Conseil des Travaux*, an advisory board that convened back in Paris and was responsible for the approval and modification of warship designs.[34]

The Admiralty back in London was well aware of the problems that beset French shipbuilders, having been kept informed of their progress and working conditions by Captain Kane and his periodic visits to French dockyards. After one such visit in early 1884, Kane referred to the *Conseil des Travaux* as "the final court of appeals on questions of naval construction" that was "in the vein of altering many things."[35] To underscore his point, he recounted the frustrations of a French naval officer, who lamented that "it is impossible to know what one of our ships will be like when completed, but it is very easy to see what she will not be; look at the design on which they begin her construction."[36] In this same report, Kane also provided Captain Hall and the intelligence department with some preliminary insight into the fractious atmosphere in the French Admiralty, contributed in part by the workings of the politically-motivated oversight board: "[T]he re-organization of the *Conseil des Travaux* amounted to quite a revolution at the French Ministry of Marine, and was directed against M. De Bussy, who . . . had made himself too autocratic, and had forced designs on the department which were generally condemned. . . ."[37]

In sum, this report and those that followed were read quite enthusiastically by the Admiralty, and their contents undoubtedly shaped the outlook of Admiral Sir Cooper Key, who served as First Naval Lord from 1880 to 1885. In a letter to Admiral Sir Geoffrey Phipps Hornby in December 1884, Key exuded the level of confidence that was commonplace in the Admiralty, especially over the reported disparity in naval strength between Britain and France:

> We now have twenty-seven ironclads in commission. The French have eleven. We could commission thirteen more in a month. I cannot find that the French have more than two ready and one of these has her boilers condemned (*Richelieu*). Many of our ships are of obsolete types—so are many of theirs. Moreover, being of wood theirs cannot last long. *I should have no fear whatever with France and Russia now, so far as our Navy is concerned* [emphasis added].[38]

The situation in the French Admiralty would only get worse in the second half of the decade, before improving somewhat between 1887 and 1890. This can be traced not only to dockyard inefficiency and the workings of *Conseil des Travaux*, but also to the high policy naval debates that further divided the Ministry of Marine over competing schools of naval thought. The result was incessant vacillation between naval strategies and capital ship design policies, as successive naval administrations selected their preference for one over the other. To complicate matters even further were the ascendance of Vice Admiral Theophile Aube and his fellow disciples of the *Jeune Ecole*. These reform-minded officers maintained since the 1870s that French naval strategy should be based on the *guerre de course*, complete with a fleet of fast cruisers and torpedo boats to destroy enemy commerce and the vulnerable ironclad forces that protected it. In January 1886, the views of the *Jeune Ecole* would receive a short-lived priority over all others with the appointment of its principal spokesman as Minister of Marine. Never reticent to express his views on the subject, Admiral Aube received Captain Kane in his office on 10 February for a general discussion of naval strategy. In his report subsequently filed to the Admiralty, the naval attaché recounted his meeting with the new Minister of Marine, including the latter's assertion that "no blockade will now prevent fast ships from putting to sea, and that it is therefore impossible for any nation to make herself Mistress of the Seas, in the way [the British] were after Trafalgar, however powerful she may be in ironclads."[39] This and other comments made by Aube, however, did not have the desired effect of invoking any sense of anxiety within the Admiralty. Upon reading the report, Captain Hall merely noted that "Admiral Aube's views on naval policy given by him to Captain Kane agree with those expressed by him in French periodicals before his accession to office."[40]

It was thus no surprise to the British that in the first few months of the Aube ministry, the construction of the ironclads in the dockyards were either delayed—as in the case of the ironclads of the *Magenta* class—or halted altogether in favor of new construction priorities.[41] The lack of progress in building these iron-clads, as evidenced first hand by the naval attaché, eventually prompted a staff officer in the intelligence department to claim that "the armorclad fleet is not only now, but will be, when all ships of both nations building are completed, inferior to that of England."[42] The French instead exhausted their materiel and financial resources in the procurement of fast cruisers and torpedo boats. In the case of the former, the Aube ministry solicited designs for a number of cruisers of various types, the first among them a third-class cruiser of moderate tonnage with a speed of nineteen knots and fair armament.[43] Three vessels of this description were eventually laid down in 1886, and the dockyards labored to complete these ships as quickly as possible.[44] Also laid down in 1886 were two large first-class cruisers—*Tage* and *Cecille*—that were specifically designed for commerce interdiction and destruction, for both vessels possessed the speed, coal capacity, and armament for such missions.[45] Finally, Admiral Aube sought funding for three more first-class cruisers, two second-class cruisers of an intermediate design, and six third-class cruisers, all of which were expected to be commenced in 1887.[46] All of these events, either in progress or expected, were known by the Admiralty in time to respond if necessary.

The Admiralty was also well-informed of the latest developments in French construction of torpedo boats and their experimental deployment in the annual naval maneuvers. By the end of 1886, the intelligence department calculated that the French navy possessed eighteen first-class and thirty-nine second-class torpedo boats, with fifty-one of the former in various stages of construction.⁴⁷ The department also documented the sizeable budgetary request from the French Government, where Aube requested funding for 100 additional torpedo boats to be built over four years.⁴⁸ Over the protests of Aube, the government failed to accede to the broad outlines of the request, but his failure to obtain the funds was the least of his worries at the moment. The experimental deployment of the torpedo boats in the 1886 annual maneuvers in the Mediterranean was inconclusive at best, a mediocre result that was known shortly thereafter by the Admiralty back in London. In the absence of the observations from the naval attaché, who for obvious reasons was not invited to attend the maneuvers, the intelligence department instead secured first-hand accounts published in French periodicals. The subsequent report, written by Captain Reginald Custance, referred to eyewitness accounts of French naval officers, who publicly expressed their doubts over the torpedo boat and its suitability for fleet operations.⁴⁹

The results of the 1887 annual maneuvers proved no better for the besieged vessel.⁵⁰ The performance of the torpedo boat was again left in doubt, especially when the remaining portion of the exercises were cancelled when Admiral Aube and the rest of the French cabinet fell from power in May 1887. While his tenure as Minister of Marine lasted less than fifteen months, the aftermath of the Aube ministry revealed the extent to which the *Jeune Ecole* experiment was a complete and utter disaster for French naval policy. This point was underscored by Theodore Ropp, who observes that the "*Jeune Ecole* split the French Navy wide open, and the next fifteen years (1885–1890) was a period of incredible confusion. . . . [W]ith an increasingly complicated ministry, an increasing confusion in strategic ideas, and an increasing number of civilian ministers, it is a wonder that France had any naval policy at all. At times it is certainly difficult to find it."⁵¹ Aube's immediate successor was Edouard Barbey, who served essentially as a caretaker until the appointment of Admiral Jules-Francois-Emile Krantz in January 1888.

Barbey and Krantz inherited a French navy in a state of grave disorder, stemming mainly from financial mismanagement, dockyard inefficiency, and the existence of divisive opinions over the future course of strategy and force planning.[52] Burdened by deficit spending and debt incurred from private borrowings, both ministers initiated measures to remedy the rather deplorable conditions found by the new British naval attaché in his visits to French dockyards. In a report filed in April 1888, Captain Sir W. Cecil Domville, who had succeeded Kane in 1887, noted that financial considerations were responsible for a reduction in the number of workmen at the Toulon dockyard from 5,000 to 4,400.[53] Following the necessary reforms advocated by Barbey and Krantz, the efforts of the remaining workmen were focused on the completion of contract vessels and the repairs of vessels already in commission. These efforts were given a boost somewhat by the prospect of war with Italy in the early months of 1888. "There is no doubt that a month or so ago the French armorclads were in a deplorable state of unreadiness for war," wrote Domville, "a fact of which apparently no notice was taken till recent political events brought war with Italy within a measurable distance."[54] But by then, the Admiralty had already realized that the French navy was in no condition to pose a viable threat to Britain for some time. Admiralty confidence in this respect was so high that even the First Lord, Lord George Hamilton, relished the disparity between the two navies, boasting in February 1888 that "many abuses and evils which we have eradicated here, flourish with exuberance in [French] dockyards, and the changes in policy and consequent waste of money in their building program during the past two years contrast unfavorably with the continuity and consistency of action of the English Admiralty during the same period."[55]

Perhaps the best example of this perception of the French navy was reflected in the muted reaction by the Admiralty to alleged French naval provocations in the Mediterranean. Despite newspaper reports in 1888 of unusual naval activity in Toulon, and dire warnings that "everything is being done to place a squadron of ironclads and all available cruisers in reading to sail," Admiralty reaction was decidedly benign.[56] Arthur Hood suggested that it would not be advisable to "create feelings of distrust or tension in the French government, by otherwise strengthening the [British] squadron in the Mediterranean."[57] Lord George Hamilton concurred, noting that French ambitions exceeded French capability, and that the French Navy was likely to find itself "in greater difficulties" trying to complete the program already approved.[58] Such reactions do not suggest men who were filled with anxiety about the threat of French naval power.

It is abundantly clear from the analysis above that both the professional and civilian elements within the Admiralty did not perceive Russian and French naval developments in the 1880s to be particularly alarming, anymore so than the hints at naval modernization from Germany and the United States in the 1890s. This is especially apparent in the tone of the numerous reports generated by the intelligence department during this period, which as a whole instilled an image of the Admiralty as both proactive and extremely confident of British naval capabilities, an image that inevitably conflicts with conventional wisdom and the conclusions reached by the late Professor Marder. Indeed, the Admiralty depicted in *The Anatomy of British Seapower* is a much different entity altogether, complete with a complacent and ineffective Admiralty Board that was slow to respond to the naval provocations of France and Russia, and did so only when prompted by the intervention of the Salisbury ministry. But upon further inquiry the Marder thesis can now be seriously questioned, as its favored combination of external provocations, threat perceptions and civilian intervention to explain the Naval Defense Act. The input of the first two elements has already been shown here to be peripheral to the decision to proceed with the largest peacetime shipbuilding program in the nineteenth century. This section will consider the last element, that being the impact of civilian intervention upon the strategic and force structure choices embodied in the Act, with a particular emphasis on the roles of Lord Salisbury and his civilian appointees in the formulation of British naval policy in the late 1880s.

While two biographies of Lord Salisbury have been published within the past year, little is said about Salibury's role in the formulation of the Naval Defense Act.[59] Yet according to Lady Gwendolyn Cecil in a multi-volume biography of her father, it was Salisbury who presided over the cabinet-level strategic review and intervened when the Admiralty Board proved reluctant to concede the dangers to Britain from the threat of a Franco-Russian naval combination. "The attitude of the Board of Admiralty on this occasion—its failure to appreciate deficiencies until their existence was driven home to it by Cabinet cross-examination—presents a curious inversion of the parts ordinarily played by Service officials and their political masters."[60] In a letter to George J. Goschen and reprinted in the biography,[61] Salisbury alluded to his repeated exasperation over Admiralty administration, and ultimately credited civilian intervention as the underlying motivation behind the measure. "As to the mere question of enlarging the fleet," wrote Salisbury, "we were able to do some good by making a sort of raid upon [the Admiralty] and carrying back the Naval Defense Act as the spoils of victory. But we cannot govern the Admiralty from day to day by raids of this kind."[62]

While Salisbury ultimately claims credit for the Naval Defense Act, the historical accuracy of his account is suspect for a number of reasons. At no time previously during his tenure as either prime minister or foreign secretary did Salisbury express an interest in British naval policy, other than that required to ensure that service expenditures were minimized for purposes of political expediency. He almost admitted as such in a rather acrimonious exchange with Viscount Wolseley in the House of Lords in May 1888, acknowledging that he could not remember ever having seen a plan of campaign before.[63] Like many of his immediate predecessors in office, Salisbury always presumed that British naval supremacy would be just that, and never thought it necessary to depart from the *ad hoc* treatment of strategy and other defense policy issues before the Cabinet.[64] He especially resented the published opinions of naval and military officers who criticized the Government for its failure to attend to the more important matters of national defense.

At the height of the public campaign over the naval defenses of the country, Salisbury protested strongly "against the tones of panic which prevail and the language which is used, as though the Government were [sic] passing by all these matters in utter apathy. . . ."[65] This served only to reinforce Salisbury's rather cynical and long-held view of the professional element in military affairs. "I think you listen too much to the soldiers," Salisbury once observed to Lord Lytton in 1871. "No lesson seems to be so deeply inculcated by the experience of life as that you never should trust experts. If you believe the doctors, nothing is wholesome; if you believe the theologians, nothing is innocent; if you believe the soldiers nothing is safe. They all require to have their strong wine diluted by a very large admixture of common sense."[66]

In spite of their vast differences on most political subjects, Salisbury was also no different from his political rival Gladstone when it came to the matters of naval policy, as both statesmen were acutely sensitive to public reactions to increased naval expenditures. Gladstone, in fact, believed strongly that the formula for his own political success, and that of the Liberal Party, rested in their ability to "frame a budget large enough and palpably beneficial enough, not only to do much good to the country, but to sensibly lift the party in the public view & estimation."[67] But to accomplish this required substantial reductions in naval and military expenditures. According to Gladstone: "If we can get from three-quarters of a million upwards towards a million off the naval & military estimates jointly, then as far as I can judge we have left the country no reason to complain, and may proceed cheerily with our work."[68] Upon his succession into office in 1868, Gladstone immediately instituted a policy of financial retrenchment and installed a reform-minded political supporter—Hugh Childers—as First Lord of the Admiralty. Accepting the view that the Royal Navy should be a *defensive* force and not an instrument of an interventionist foreign policy, Childers immediately sought to reduce naval obligations abroad and wasteful expenditures in the dockyards, while at the same time moderating current and existing shipbuilding programs to prescribed levels. The result was annual service estimates that were palatable to the fiscally conservative Gladstone. "The first of Childer's budgets was indicative of the Liberals' naval and fiscal policies over the next five years," observed John Beeler in his seminal study of British naval policy during the Gladstone and Disraeli ministries. "During the period [1868-74], naval spending topped £10 million only twice, in one instance from the addition of £600,000 allocated to the navy from the vote of credit occasioned by the outbreak of the Franco-German War."[69]

Gladstone would continue his struggle to limit naval expenditures throughout each of his four ministries, and when in opposition would repeatedly denounce the Disraeli and Salisbury ministries for their extravagant use of the Treasury. During his famous Midlothian campaign of 1879—which resulted in a Liberal victory at the polls and hence a second Gladstone ministry (1880-84)—Gladstone returned to a familiar theme that struck a chord within the public domain: "If all the millions bestowed upon giving effect to the warlike policy of the Government had, instead, of being so applied, been thrown down to the bottom of the sea, you would have been better off, with such a mode of disposing of the funds, than you are now."[70] The success of the rhetoric used by Gladstone in the Midlothian campaign was not lost upon Lord Salisbury. In his own biography of Salisbury, historian A. L. Kennedy observed that his subject "appreciated at its true value the tremendous impression which Gladstone's exploitation of Conservative mistakes, and even of Conservative achievements, had made and was making all over the country. The success of the famous Midlothian campaign, indeed, had a lasting effect on Lord Salisbury. . . ."[71] Until 1889, Salisbury was also willing to adhere to the Gladstonian approach to the annual naval estimates, using finance essentially as the final arbiter of naval policy. In this endeavor he was amply supported by his two civilian agents of naval reform at the Admiralty—Lord George Hamilton and Arthur Bower Forwood.

Salisbury's decision to appoint both Hamilton and Forwood to the Admiralty is of some significance when attempting to apportion credit or blame for the strategic, political and economic circumstances behind the Naval Defense Act. It is also indicative of the countenance of Lord Salisbury and his competing desires to undertake a passive personal interest in naval matters while leaving it to his appointees to limit naval expenditures through increased efficiency in administration. Ironically, his decision in 1885 to appoint Lord George Hamilton to the post of First Lord reflected more of a desire to placate a dependable political supporter in the

House of Commons than an intention to effect the level of reform necessary to restrain naval expenditures. Salisbury originally had every intention of appointing Hamilton to the War Office and returning W. H. Smith to the Admiralty as First Lord, an experienced naval and treasury minister who had held the same post from 1877 to 1880.[72] According to Beeler, Smith enjoyed a "high reputation as an administrator and, by carrying out a comprehensive reform of the Admiralty secretariat, he showed that he shared other qualities with [Hugh] Childers"—Gladstone's own appointee to the Admiralty in 1868. "But as a man of business," continued Beeler, "he fell squarely into the 'economical' camp along with Childers, and both men seem to have rated political considerations higher than the often alarmist pronouncements of their naval advisors."[73] Given his utter contempt for service experts, Salisbury undoubtedly viewed Smith to be an ideal choice for what he had in mind for the Admiralty. But at the suggestion of Hamilton, Salisbury reversed his decision and appointed Smith to the War Office and Hamilton to the Admiralty, the latter insisting that he could not deal effectively with the Duke of Cambridge.[74]

With limited ministerial experience at the India Office and Education, Hamilton was a virtual neophyte when it came to naval matters. Despite his shortcomings of experience in naval administration, his admirers later professed his tenure at the Admiralty to be a resounding success. His entry in the *Dictionary of National Biography* proclaimed that "Hamilton's administration was a period of extensive naval reform, during which the principles which were to govern organization of the fleet were formulated. Some great defects in departmental administration had been revealed, particularly in connexion [sic] with finance, repairs and ship-building."[75] These achievements if true are indeed worthy of such affirmation, but the process in which Hamilton labored to place the naval service within the "compass of finance"[76] was in actuality more harmful than beneficial, so much so that his words and actions eventually invoked the consternation of Queen Victoria and even caused Lord Salisbury to consider replacing him. In June 1888, the Queen wrote to Salisbury at the height of the public debate over British naval strength and expressed her displeasure with Hamilton and his naval administration. She thought Hamilton to be "not near strong enough" for the post of First Lord, and decried his propensity to "declare *all* is *right*, which we *know* is *not*."[77] Her concern for the course of British naval policy prompted a muted reply from Salisbury, in which he confessed that the discipline in the Admiralty was unsatisfactory and reassured the Sovereign that Hamilton was well aware of the "great deal to be done" in order to remedy the defects in his administration.[78] In the aftermath of the debate and passage of the Naval Defense Act, Salisbury visited Queen Victoria at Windsor and broached the idea of replacing Hamilton with his original nominee Smith, who in poor health was unable to continue as Leader in the House of Commons.[79]

Salisbury recognized that Hamilton was relatively inexperienced in naval affairs. For this reason he appointed Arthur Forwood as the Parliamentary and Financial Secretary of the Admiralty. Forwood was not only an outspoken supporter of the Salisbury ministry but also a former mayor of Liverpool with thirty-five years of experience in the commercial shipping sector. "Your commercial knowledge and experience would be of great value," wrote Salisbury in offering the post to Forwood in August 1886.[80] Forwood promptly accepted the invitation, and Hamilton welcomed his expertise to the Admiralty, despite the fact that his appointment was made explicitly at the behest of Salisbury. His presence at the Admiralty was undoubtedly viewed with suspicion by the four Naval Lords, who were especially resentful of his meddling into the technical aspects of naval policy. In explaining his *modus operandi* to Hamilton, Forwood admitted that "I quite appreciate that I may have departed from the course of my predecessors in dealing with some questions that have been before me in considerable detail."[81] The traditional role of the Parliamentary Secretary, however, did not preclude him from expanding his responsibilities in the Admiralty. "For a business life of thirty-five years I have been in the practical management of ships and steamers," continued Forwood in November 1886, "and with the knowledge thus acquired I cannot refrain from commenting on the papers that come before me. It may be that having this knowledge was a reason for placing me in my present position."[82]

Forwood amply returned the contempt of his naval colleagues with an equally critical view of the naval element of the Admiralty Board. He reserved his harshest criticism for their attitudes toward the annual naval estimates, the overall form and content of which was a responsibility shared by him and the First Lord. Forwood simply viewed the civil-military differences over the estimates as a contest of competing motivations. As for his naval colleagues, Forwood privately held that "[t]hey have at hand the old traditional policy that the Service exists for the Service, and support the naval as against the civil control which so excites service feeling when called into action. The question of civil control of expenditure is more or less at stake.[83] Lacking the subtlety and refinement for a minister in his position, his contempt for the Naval Lords eventually became a public spectacle, with statements to the press outlining his repeated frustration with them over such issues as the naval estimates, dockyard administration, and future shipbuilding requirements. His antagonism of the Naval Lords—both in public and private—was so scathing in fact that it inevitably resulted in the second resignation from the Admiralty Board in less than three months. The first had occurred in January 1888 when Captain Lord Charles Beresford resigned his position as Junior Naval Lord in protest over Hamilton's decision to reduce the funding and relative importance of the intelligence department. This time it was Vice Admiral William Graham who, as the Third Naval Lord and Controller of the Navy, chose to resign in April 1888 rather than continue to be subjected to the constant interference and criticism of the outspoken Parliamentary Secretary. For his part, Hamilton did what he could to restrain Forwood and preserve the appearance of harmony on the Admiralty Board, to the point where the latter felt that the First Lord was not providing his junior minister with the backing necessary to offset the demands of the Naval Lords.

If Forwood worried that Lord George Hamilton would capitulate to the demands of his naval colleagues, it was a needless sentiment. When it came to the formulation of naval policy in the Admiralty, the First Lord was supreme and as such exercised complete control over the nature and conduct of business performed by the Admiralty Board. The responsibilities of each member of the Board were assigned by the First Lord, and subject to review and amendment when deemed necessary. The Board itself convened on a weekly basis, with the agenda of each meeting having been approved and distributed to Board members beforehand. Any member wishing to forward an issue for discussion at the meeting had to receive the necessary sanction by Hamilton before it was raised before the Board as a whole. This arrangement was confirmed by Admiral Hood, the First Naval Lord who once conceded to a House select committee that "[c]onsultation takes place at the Board on any point which the First Lord thinks it is right and advisable that the Board should consider and adjudicate upon."[84] Since no votes were taken at these meetings, the role of the naval element of the Admiralty Board was limited to the provision of technical advice and additional consultation when requested by the First Lord. The only viable recourse to a dissenting Board member was to offer his opinion in a minute to be included in the official record. His opposition then muted, the Board had no choice but accept and abide by the decisions of the First Lord. Alternatively, he could resign, in which he would then forfeit his generous salary of at least £1,200 per annum as well as the house and other privileges afforded to a Board member.[85]

While Hamilton exercised the power afforded to his position sparingly and with considerable discretion, he was more than willing to allow the independently wealthy Beresford and Graham to resign in protest rather than undermine Forwood and their collective efforts to place the Admiralty within the "compass of finance."[86] In this endeavor the two civilian agents of naval reform were strongly supported by Lord Salisbury who, along with the First Lord and the Chancellor of the Exchequer, were ultimately responsible for determining just how much the Admiralty could expect to receive in appropriations from the Treasury. It was then left to the First Lord and the Admiralty Board to identify the needs of the service and frame a budget within the financial parameters established previously by the Cabinet. Salisbury would later note that before the Naval Defense Act, "Questions of Estimate which are not settled by personal conference between the Chancellor of the Exchequer and the War Office or Admiralty, as the case may be, are usually arranged in concert with the Prime Minister."[87] His participation in the budgetary process, moreover, was seen as instrumental to brokering a reasonable compromise between economy and service efficiency, particularly since "[t]he Chancellor of the Exchequer, little familiar with the defensive services, is rightly the spokesman of economy. The heads of the War Office and Admiralty, unacquainted with the precise position of the Exchequer, are the natural and proper advocates of efficiency."[88] Given his role as arbiter in the budgetary process, it is thus not surprising that Lord Salisbury would ultimately take issue with the pointed criticism of Hamilton and Forwood in 1888 over the inadequacies of the annual estimates and what the proposed budget actually meant to the wartime roles and missions of the service.

In the first six months of 1888, the Salisbury ministry witnessed a rather extraordinary public debate between naval officers and cabinet officials over the strategic and policy implications of the naval estimates. This was a most critical period for the supporters of naval estimates. This represented a critical period for the supporters of naval modernization, as their collective efforts in the public domain eventually compelled Lord Salisbury to react with a cabinet-level strategic review that essentially framed the strategic and force structure choices embodied in the Naval Defense Act. For purposes of this immediate discussion, it is important here to underscore the public indifference of Salisbury toward the policy questions brought up in the course of the public debate, preferring instead to allow the principal spokesmen of his naval policy—Hamilton and Forwood—to respond in kind to the numerous speeches and editorials written by the "service experts" that he despised so much.

His first definitive public statement on the subject was reserved for the second week of May 1888, when he found it necessary to respond to the more serious charges leveled by the critics of the Cabinet's naval administration. In making this statement, Salisbury appeared to be motivated more by a desire to rebuke the service experts than to reassure the public at large that the naval defenses of the country were exactly what they should be. He angrily protested that his silence was not due to negligence or absence of concern, but rather from his insistence that discussions of defense policy should held in private and not in a public forum. Salisbury then proceeded to defend the policies of his ministry, stating that "there is no ground whatever for the implied reproach of parsimony and that we are neglecting the defenses of the country."[89] When it came to the subject of naval preparedness, Salisbury referred to the upward trend in naval construction, and even commented that the terms "strength" and "weakness" were relative and thus inappropriate to describe British naval capabilities. But Salisbury ultimately returned to the overall theme of his message. "[B]efore I sit down I feel that I cannot avoid to enter a protest against another practice. That is, the practice of those who are, or ought to be, distinguished authorities upon military affairs making statements against the Government under whom they serve, and making them in a place where they cannot be answered."[90]

In stressing his conviction that these policy questions should be addressed in a private forum by the Cabinet, Salisbury committed himself to conducting an *ad hoc* strategic review of the armed forces. In approving the cabinet-level initiative the very next month, Salisbury essentially conceded that he was reacting to what others thought was a necessary investigation to determine the military and naval requirements of the country. Selected to participate in the review were Hamilton and his counterpart in the War Office. The scope of the review, however, was curiously limited to the traditional invasion threat posed by France. "The one subject with which I propose to deal with is the alleged inability of our military organization to protect us from the invasion of London," Salisbury wrote in a memorandum to the participants on 6 June.[91] "I presume the examination may be confined to the danger of the occupation of London by France, for an attempt by any other Power to conduct such an operation does not seem to be within the widest limits of probability."[92] Salisbury, moreover, seemed more interested in the plans of the War Office to repel a French invasion than with

Admiralty plans to prevent the invasion force from crossing the Channel in the first place. The Admiralty initially contributed very little to the strategic review, that is until Salisbury agreed to allow the Naval Lords to submit a proposal for a shipbuilding program on the basis of two hypothetical planning scenarios. In a subsequent memorandum, Hamilton confirmed the departure from the traditional budget-driven approach to force planning: "The Cabinet in July determined that Admiral Sir Arthur Hood should be requested to state the amount of force which he would require under certain eventualities. The questions . . . were drawn up after personal consultation with the Prime Minister."[93] Admiral Hood, in fact, offered to submit the proposed shipbuilding program within a half-an-hour of being told what scenarios to consider.[94] He was able to make such a bold offer because the strategic framework for the shipbuilding program had already been prepared in May 1888 by Captain Hall and the intelligence department. The opportunity merely presented itself to submit the ambitious proposal, which no doubt would have been rejected summarily had public attitudes toward naval modernization not changed to render it politically acceptable to the Salisbury ministry.

As to who should be ultimately credited for the Naval Defense Act, the events outlined above simply do not support the version offered by Lord Salisbury and subsequently reiterated in the Marder account. Contrary to the Cecil biography and even his own recollections of the events of 1888, Salisbury was clearly not the savior of the naval defenses of the country, nor was he remotely interested in naval affairs other than what was required of him during the annual budgetary process. Instead, Salisbury reacted rather reluctantly to the public movement that originated with the Beresford resignation in January 1888.

In the wake of widespread criticism of his cabinet's naval policies, the prime minister quickly consented to a cabinet-level strategic review which at first focused mostly on the army and little on the navy. The latter finally received the focus of attention at the conclusion of the review, when the political atmosphere and the consternation of Queen Victoria provided Salisbury with the incentive to consider the prospect of naval modernization for the first time. The Admiralty Board responded to this shift in priorities quite enthusiastically, having submitted within hours a proposal for an ambitious shipbuilding program that was based on hypothetical planning scenarios already considered by the Naval Intelligence Department. The Board was well aware for some time of the naval capabilities of its potential adversaries relative to that of the Royal Navy; what it lacked was a healthy appreciation of the implications posed by the absence of a clearly articulated strategic doctrine and how that void compromised the future capabilities of the service to perform its traditional roles and missions. But this was a strategic dilemma that Salisbury and his agents of naval reform had very little interest in resolving until faced essentially with a *fait accompli* by the Admiralty Board in July 1888. From that point forward, Admiralty force planning would be determined more by strategic considerations than the economic constraints imposed for purposes of political parsimony.

Then who or what should ultimately be credited for the Naval Defense Act? As shown above, the answer to this question lies not in the Marder thesis and its curious blend of external provocations, threat perceptions and civilian intervention. The motivation for strategic revitalization originated not from external factors, but from a renewed internal movement for strategic awareness at a time when the Admiralty Board was ineffective in tending to the more important matters germane to strategic and force planning. This movement was inspired instead by the strategic ideas of British naval officers, whose actions in support of them typifies how organizational cultures in navies can shape the decision-making process so that the outcomes match, as close as possible, the preferences of the senior officer corps and how it conceptualizes the wartime functions of the service.[95] Fearing that these ideas were being muddled by administrative complacency, technological determinism and a general failure to enunciate a coherent strategic doctrine from which to contemplate future shipbuilding requirements, a series of respected naval officers attempted in the late 1870s and 1880s to promote a new brand of strategic thinking and essentially rescue the Admiralty Board from itself. The first opportunity to do so occurred in late 1882, when the Board authorized to the creation of the Foreign Intelligence Committee, supervised by a talented officer whose well-conceived articulations of British naval strategy provided the foundation of a strategic framework for British naval operations. In time, Captain Hall would also establish an intellectual tradition that would be sustained by other strategic thinkers in residence within the Naval Intelligence Department, including among them his successors Cyprian Bridge, Prince Louis of Battenberg, Reginald Custance, Edmund Slade, Charles Ottley and even his own son, Reginald "Blinker" Hall.

The second important event of this kind occurred in 1886, when Captain Lord Charles Beresford was selected to serve as Junior Naval Lord on the Admiralty Board. Beresford was a reform-minded officer who also grasped the necessity for both the civilian and naval elements within the Admiralty to embrace the demands for increased strategic awareness in upper level policy debates. He quickly sought to expand and formalize the intelligence function from an *ad hoc* committee to a full-fledged department, and resigned in protest when he viewed salary cutbacks in the newly created department as a reduction of the overall value of the tasks performed by Hall and his small staff of officers. Fearing that the Admiralty would return to business as usual, Beresford sought to enlist the most prominent naval officers outside the confines of the Admiralty—Admiral Sir Geoffrey Phipps Hornby and Rear Admiral Philip Colomb in particular—to educate the public and government ministers of the dangers stemming from the defects in naval administration and the necessity for naval modernization.

What these officers achieved during the course of a six-month public campaign was a firm repudiation of the naval policies endorsed by the Salisbury ministry. Eventually, even the editor of the *Times*, George E. Buckle, who had originally sided with the ministry only months before on this issue, was persuaded by professional opinion. An admirer of Salisbury and his policies, Buckle warned the Government in May 1888 of the public support emerging in favor of naval modernization: "[T]he country will not now be satisfied until the Government is able to assure it that, whatever plan of defense may be ultimately adopted, the Navy is strong enough to carry it into effect."[96] The desired effect of these sentiments was achieved in July 1888, with the proposed shipbuilding program that ultimately became embodied in the Naval Defense Act.

When viewed in this way, the Act can thus be seen more as the culmination of a struggle in civil-military relations rather than a reaction to external provocations, threat perceptions and civilian intervention. On one side were civilian agents of naval reform who were strongly encouraged by Lord Salisbury to place the service within the "compass of finance" and minimize naval expenditures for purposes of domestic political consumption. Opposing this short-sighted approach to naval policy formulation was a self-selected group of prominent naval officers who conducted themselves as guardians of the strategic ideas that prevailed within the Royal Navy. These ideas were largely expressions of strategic predisposition firmly rooted in the wartime experiences of their predecessors—the naval element to what has been described as the "British way of warfare."[97] British naval officers were taught from the earliest stages of their careers that British naval supremacy was the only means to ensure the copious flow of commerce while protecting the home islands from invasion. From the words and actions of their predecessors they further viewed the exploitation of British naval supremacy as the logical outgrowth of a forward offensive naval strategy, itself founded on a commonly held belief within the service that the territorial boundaries of the British Empire extended beyond the demarcations of maps or charts. "The frontier of our Empire is the enemies coastline," Colomb remarked in May 1888. "At the beginning of this century, there was a certain defined way of looking at the situation of these islands surrounded by water, at the water surrounding them, and at the possible enemies' coasts which bounded the water. Our islands were strictly regarded as the capital of an empire, surrounded by a water territory, the frontier of which was the enemy's coast."[98]

The underlying essence of this linkage between culture and strategy in the Royal Navy during the nineteenth century is ultimately captured by the fact that, between 1650 and 1815, British naval officers gradually developed a highly effective strategic doctrine but never once felt it necessary to promulgate it in service manuals or sweeping doctrinal pronouncements. Instead, the senior officers corps of the service inculcated the next generation of British naval officers and ensured that their successors were intellectually prepared to fulfill the traditional roles and missions of the Royal Navy. This point is underscored by the research of Andrew Lambert, who referred to the simple fact that "[t]he Royal Navy did not create doctrine in the nineteenth century, in contrast to the French, Russian, American and German navies, because it was neither rebuilding after defeat nor creating a new service. It relied on its corporate memory, its history for guidance. The transmission of this knowledge was a major part of the intellectual development of career sea officers."[99] The currency of British strategic doctrine in the nineteenth century, and later in the twentieth century as well, was thus founded in the shared interpretations of historical precedent. Looking to the past reminded naval officers of the strategic benefits of the close blockade and other traditional applications of British naval policy. From 1815 through to about the mid–1850s, the principal expression of British naval strategy in peacetime remained the impressive power projection capabilities of a heavily-armed wooden battlefleet under sail, consisting of two and three-decked warships that were capable of conducting offensive missions such as the blockade and coastal bombardment.

Perhaps the best reflection of the strategic ideas preponderant in the Royal Navy occurred in the mid–1850s, in the years just prior to the confusion in the Admiralty over the unknown potential of steam propulsion and the implications to both naval strategy in general and the future determinants of capital ship design policy. In what became known as the "Cherbourg Strategy," the Admiralty planned for renewed naval operations to thwart a French invasion of the home islands following the completion of a well-fortified naval base and dockyard at Cherbourg, on the northwest coast of France.[100] The primary objective of this strategy was to ensure British naval supremacy in the Channel through the blockade and eventual destruction of the new naval base and dockyard. To accomplish the latter task, Admiralty planners decided to exploit the lessons learned during the last naval campaign against France. "The logic of war at sea after 1805 suggested that the Royal Navy would face its most difficult tasks ashore, or even inside the arsenals of its rivals," continues Lambert.[101] "In consequence of a new strand of naval thought, pioneered during the Napoleonic conflict, employed technology to enhance the capability of warships to act against the shore, both for amphibious power projection and for the direct assault of fortified harbors."[102] The strand that Lambert refers to here is an important corollary to the forward offensive naval strategy that prevailed within the Royal Navy during the eighteenth and nineteenth centuries. While blockading operations would ensure command of the sea for Britain, the employment of offensive coastal operations would ensure the destruction of the enemy battlefleet once command of the sea was no longer in doubt. This combination proved especially useful when the enemy was predisposed to safeguard its "fleet-in-being" rather than risk the loss of its naval assets at sea in a contest with the Royal Navy.

After the technological uncertainties of the 1860s and 1870s, the Royal Navy gradually began to regain its traditional strategic footing, due mainly to the widespread introduction of water-tube boilers and triple-expansion engines in British capital ship design. With faster and more efficient steam engines, the application of the close blockade was again feasible to thwart the egress of commerce-raiders from enemy ports. Meanwhile, offensive coastal operations continued to remain an essential mission of the service, as evidenced by the Egyptian campaign and the bombardment of Alexandria in 1882. It became abundantly clear at the outset of the decade, however, that the Admiralty had yet to emerge from the 1860s and 1870s with a clear sense of the roles and missions it was expected to perform, compounded further by the bewilderment over the optimal mixture of forces required to accomplish them. This point was underscored by John Beeler: "The British navy was expected (and did) perform a multitude of operations worldwide. This salient fact largely explains why the formulation of a coherent strategy, and, much more, the construction of a fleet with which to implement it, were so problematic during the mid-Victorian era."[103]

What was required in the Admiralty were civilian ministers and naval officers who shared an avid interest in strategic issues and could work together to devise a force structure that best reflected the roles and missions of the service in wartime. That these men were largely absent from the Admiralty in the 1880s was a function of individual personalities and the appointment of senior naval officers who were generally amenable to the political mandate of the First Lord.

It soon became evident that if the Admiralty was ever to embrace the demand for heightened strategic awareness, the impetus for such an overture would have to originate from within the senior officer corps, particularly from officers with the intellectual foundation and strategic vision to articulate the future requirements of the service. The officers who qualified for this distinction were undoubtedly encouraged by the writings and teachings of Sir John Knox Laughton, the influential naval educator and historian who advocated from as early as the 1870 that history was the servant of strategic naval thought and as such was the basis for the development of modern tactics, service doctrine and national strategy.[104] What appealed to these naval officers, was Laughton's revival of the strategic ideas that were obfuscated by the economic and technological determinism that defined British naval policy in the 1860s and 1870s. Laughton, a naval instructor who served in the Baltic campaigns of 1854 and 1855, first gained widespread notoriety in the service as a distinguished lecturer in naval history at the Naval War College, Greenwich. The audience that he wished to influence most during the course of these annual lectures courses were the junior officers in attendance at the college, among them future flag officers and framers of naval policy.

But his initiative and enthusiasm for the subject gradually expanded the audience to include most of the senior officer corps of the service. His most important convert was Admiral Sir Astley Cooper-Key, the first president of the college at Greenwich and First Naval Lord from 1879 to 1885.[105] Cooper-Key encouraged Laughton to continue his academic pursuits and introduce them to the mainstream of strategic naval thought. In his presence in 1874, Laughton read a seminal paper at the Royal United Services

Institution (RUSI), where he introduced the audience to what he termed "The Scientific Study of Naval History." In this paper he argued rather convincingly that naval history, if properly studied with accurate and exact knowledge, can yield insightful lessons that are just as relevant in the ironclad era as they once were in the age of sail. "I have argued against the idea that the study of naval history is useless—is a waste of time; I have argued that, on the contrary, it is a study of vital importance, and that the lessons it conveys are of very direct and practical meaning."[106] In the following year, Laughton reminded his listeners and readers that the study of naval history extended beyond mere tactical considerations. "A great deal has been said at different times about the study of tactics, but the scientific study of history is the study of tactics; it is a great deal more; it is the study of strategy, of organization, and of discipline, and it is the only sound basis of that study."[107]

Remaining at his teaching post at the Royal Naval College until 1885, Laughton received preferential access to the Admiralty archives and labored to refine the causal linkage between naval history and strategy development. In this endeavor he received considerable support from the intellectual elite of the senior officer corps, chief among them Admiral Sir Geoffrey Phipps Hornby and Rear Admiral Philip Colomb. Hornby was an ardent supporter of Laughton, so much so that the naval historian honored Hornby by dedicating his *Letters and Despatches of Horatio, Viscount Nelson* (1886) to him. Colomb also shared Laughton's enthusiasm for naval history, and was later appointed to succeed him as lecturer in naval history at the Naval War College in 1887.[108] Beside these two prominent naval officers, both of whom would later play critical roles in the public campaign for heightened strategic awareness in 1888, Laughton also interacted extensively with a number of current and future strategic thinkers in the newly formed intelligence department in the Admiralty. During the critical years of 1887 and 1888, for example, Laughton undoubtedly came into frequent contact with Captains (later Admirals) Reginald N. Custance and S. M. Eardley-Wilmot, both of whom were members of RUSI and even served on the executive council of the institution.

He was also well acquainted with Captain W. H. Hall, having previously served with the first Director of Naval Intelligence for three years while onboard the Gunnery Training Ship H.M.S. *Excellent*. In later years, the appointment of Captains (later Admirals) Cyprian A.G. Bridge—Laughton's oldest friend and intellectual companion—and Prince Louis of Battenberg to the intelligence department brought Laughton even closer to the formulation of strategic policy within the Admiralty. Thus, while Laughton never overtly sought to influence the framing of British naval policy during the 1880s, his imprint on the discourse that occurred among naval intellectuals and ultimately manifested itself in the Naval Defense Act is unmistakable and hence subject to reassessment.

While the writing of British naval history has improved in recent years, naval historians continue to struggle with their individual assessments of the contributions of the late Arthur Marder. Following Marder's lead, historians have heretofore explained the Naval Defense Act as an outgrowth of external provocations, threat perceptions and civilian intervention, when in fact the archival evidence available simply does not support the version made popular by Marder in *The Anatomy of British Seapower*. When replacing the conventional with the cultural lens to strategic revitalization in Britain, it becomes readily apparent that the decisions of 1889 can be attributed to a well-concerted effort to impress upon civilian authorities, as well as the general public at large, the necessity for heightened strategic awareness in naval policy formulation. The motivation for this effort came not from outside of the service, as commonly believed, but from within the senior officer corps and the prevailing organizational culture of the Royal Navy. The common bond shared between the naval officers who cultivated the trend toward heightened strategic awareness in the Admiralty—Hornby, Colomb, Beresford and Hall to name a few—was a set of strategic ideas that defined the culture of the service and was subsequently revived by the teachings of Sir John Knox Laughton after years of uncertainty and obfuscation. It was thus a combination of three critical elements—culture, history and strategy—that accounted for the promotion of a new British standard for a modern seapower, as codified in the Naval Defense Act and the force structure choices that shaped British naval policy in the pre-dreadnought era.

NOTES

[1] Arthur J. Marder, *The Anatomy of British Seapower: A History of British Naval Policy in the Pre-Dreadnought Era, 1880-1905* (New York: Alfred Knopf, 1940), 120-141.

[2] Andrew Roberts, *Salisbury: Victorian Titan* (London: Weidenfeld & Nicolson, 1999) and David Steele, *Lord Salisbury: A Political Biography* (London: UCL Press, 1999).

[3] Ibid., 120 and 131.

[4] Ibid., 131.

[5] Ibid., 132.

[6] Theodore Ropp, *The Development of a Modern Navy: French Naval Policy, 1871-1914*, Stephen Roberts (ed.) (Annapolis, Maryland: Naval Institute Press, 1987), 205.

[7] Paul Kennedy, *The Rise and Fall of British Naval Mastery*, Third Edition (London: HarperCollins Publishers, 1991), 210.

[8] Ibid. Kennedy in his citations refers to the Marder account as the "definitive treatment" on the "navy scares of 1884-94." See 440.

[9] For an overview of Anglo-Russian relations in the nineteenth century, see Andrew D. Lambert, "Great Britain and the Baltic, 1809-1890" in Goren Rystad, Klaus R. Bohme and Wilhelm M. Carlgren, eds., *In Quest of Trade and Security: The Baltic in Power Politics, 1500-1990* (Stockholm: Probus Forlag, 1994), 1:297-334.

[10] John F. Beeler, *British Naval Policy in the Gladstone-Disraeli Era, 1866-1880* (Stanford, California: Stanford University Press, 1997), 203.

[11] Roger Chesneau and Eugene Kolesnik, *Conway's All the World's Fighting Ships, 1860-1905* (London: Conway Maritime Press, 1979), 172; and ibid., 202-203.

[12] J. W. King, *European Ships of War and Their Armament, Naval Admini-stration, etc.* (Washington: U.S. Government Printing Office, 1877), 167. Cited in Beeler, 202-203.

[13] John F. Beeler, "A One Power Standard? Great Britain and the Balance of Naval Power, 1860-1880," *The Journal of Strategic Studies* (December 1992), 551.

[14] N.I.D. Report No. 119b, "Present and Prospective Shipbuilding Policy of the Principal Maritime Nations," March 1889, ADM 231/15.

[15] F[oreign] I[ntelligence] C[ommittee] Report No. 50, "Naval Maneuvers in the Baltic," October 1884, ADM 231/5. The Foreign Intelligence Committee preceded the establishment of the Naval Intelligence Department in 1886.

[16] Ibid.

[17] Foreign Office to Admiralty, "The Establishment of a Russian Military Harbor at Libau or Windau in the Baltic, or on the Arctic Ocean near the Norwegian Frontier," 18 April 1888, ADM 1/6933.

[18] Ibid.

[19] I am indebted to Professor Andrew Lambert for this point.

[20] Donald W. Mitchell, *A History of Russian and Soviet Sea Power* (New York: MacMillan and Co., 1974), 192-197; Fred T. Jane, *The Imperial Russian Navy* (London: Conway Maritime Press, 1983), 202-251.

[21] Beeler, *British Naval Policy*, 275.

[22] N.I.D. Report No. 118, "Russian Fleet and Dockyards (The Baltic)," January 1887, ADM 231/10.

23Chesneau and Kolesnik, 172 and 178; and Jane, 223-229.
24Foreign Office to Admiralty, "Russian Naval Armaments in the Black Sea," 11 June 1888, ADM 1/6934. The date of the response from Captain Hall was 22 June 1888.
25Ibid.
26Ibid.
27F.I.C. Report No. 64, "General Outline of Possible Naval Operations Against Russia," March 1885, ADM 231/6.
28Lady Gwendolen Cecil, *Life of Robert Marquis of Salisbury* (London: Hodder and Stoughton), 4:50.
29Ibid., 106.
30Beeler, *British Navy Policy*, 205.
31Chesneau and Kolesnik, 282 and Ropp, 41.
32Beeler, *British Naval Policy*, 204-205.
33Ibid., 208 and Chesneau and Kolesnik, 15-25.
34Ropp, 221 and 267-280.
35F.I.C. Report No. 35, "French Fleet and Dockyards (South Coast)," May 1884, ADM 231/4.
36Ibid.
37Ibid. Note that M. De Bussy was at the time the French Chief of Naval Construction.
38Cooper Key to Geoffrey Phipps Hornby, 2 December 1884. Printed in Oscar Parkes, *British Battleships, 1860-1890* (London: Seeley Service Co., 1957), 328.
39War Office to Admiralty, "Complaint of Want of Reciprocity in Affording Information to Foreign Governments," February 1886, ADM 1/6942.
40Ibid.
41F.I.C. Report No. 101, "French Fleet and Dockyards," April 1886, ADM 231/9.
42F.I.C. Report No. 119, "Present and Prospective Ship-Building Policy of Foreign Nations," November 1886, ADM 231/10.
43F.I.C. Report No. 112, "French Fleet and Dockyards (North and West Coasts)," September 1886, ADM 231/10.
44Chesneau and Kolesnik, 309.
45Ibid., 307.
46Ropp, 221 and 267-280.
47F.I.C. Report No. 8Ba, "Naval Dockyard Ports and LaRochelle," December 1886, ADM 231/10.
48Ropp, 172.
49F.I.C. Report No. 108, "Naval Maneuvers in the Mediterranean," August 1886, ADM 231/9.
50N.I.D. Report No. 130, "Naval Maneuvers in the Mediterranean," August 1887. ADM 231/11.
51Ropp, 178 and 180.
52Ibid., 181.
53N.I.D. Report No. 150, "French Fleet and Dockyards (Toulon and La Seyne)," April 1888, ADM 231/12.
54Ibid.
55*The Times*, 4 February 1888, 12.
56Hall to Admiralty, "Information Respecting Alleged Naval Activity at Toulon," 21 January 1888. ADM 1/6932.
57Foreign Office to Admiralty, "Mobilization of the French Fleet and Concentration in the Mediterranean; Desirability of Strengthening of the Mediterranean Squadron Suggested," 3 February 1888, ADM1/6392. Hood surmised correctly that Germany's warnings about France were an attempt to push Britain closer to Germany, while Italy was hoping for a defensive naval alliance with England for the sole purpose of deterring French aspirations in the Mediterranean. For a

general discussion of these events, see A.J.P. Taylor, *The Struggle for Mastery in Europe, 1848-1918* (London: Oxford University Press, 1954), 302-324.

[58] Foreign Office to Admiralty, "Copy of Dispatch from Sir E. Malet Relating to Alleged Increased Activity in Toulon Dockyard," 7 February 1888, ADM 1/6932.

[59] Andrew Roberts, *Salisbury* and David Steele, *Lord Salisbury*.

[60] See Lady Gwendolyn Cecil, *Life of Robert Marquis of Salisbury*. Marder cites the fourth volume in his own account of the Naval Defense Act, and even uses similar language to that employed by Cecil in her biography of her father. See Marder, *Anatomy of Sea Power*, 143 and Cecil, op. cit., 188.

[61] Ibid.

[62] Salisbury to Goschen, 10 February 1892. Cited in Cecil, *Life of Robert Marquis of Salisbury*, 188. Goschen served in the Salisbury Ministry as Chancellor of the Exchequer from 1886-1892. He later served in the third Salisbury ministry as First Lord of the Admiralty.

[63] *Hansard*, 3rd Series, 14 May 1888, Col. 105-106. ZHC 2/288. This point was also made in Richards, 496.

[64] Edgar Feuchtwanger and William J. Philpott, "Civil-Military Relations in a Period Without Major Wars, 1855-85," in Paul Smith, ed., *Government and the Armed Forces of Britain*, (London: The Hambledon Press, 1996), 7.

[65] *Hansard*, 3rd Series, 11 May 1888, col. 5. ZHC 2/288.

[66] Algernon Cecil, *Queen Victoria and Her Prime Ministers* (London: Eyre and Spottiswoode, 1953), 294.

[67] Gladstone to Granville, 8 January 1874. Printed in John Morley, *The Life of William Ewart Gladstone*, (New York: Macmillan and Co., 1910-20), 2:482.

[68] Ibid.

[69] Beeler, *British Naval Policy*, 59. See also 154-155.

[70] William Gladstone, *The Midlothian Speeches, 1879*, reprint (New York: Humanities Press, 1981), 130-157. Cited in Ibid., 169.

[71] A. L. Kennedy, *Salisbury, 1830-1903: Portrait of a Statesman* (London: John Murray, 1953), 135.

[72] Lord George Hamilton, *Parliamentary Reminiscences and Reflections, 1868-1885*, (London: John Murray, 1953), 135.

[73] Beeler, *British Naval Policy*, 244.

[74] Hamilton, 266-277 and Roberts, 330.

[75] *Dictionary of National Biography* (Onslow).

[76] Hamilton used this term in a speech in February 1888 to describe his primary objective during his tenure at the Admiralty. *The Times*, 4 February 1888, 12.

[77] Queen Victoria to Salisbury, 8 June 1888, in George Earle Buckle, ed., *The Letters of Queen Victoria* (London: John Murray, 1930), 413. Emphasis in the original.

[78] Salisbury to Queen Victoria, 12 June 1888, ibid., 414-415.

[79] Extracts from the Queen's Journal, 5 April 1889, ibid., 490.

[80] Salisbury to Forwood, 1 August 1886, in Paul Smith, "Ruling the Waves: Government, the Service and the Cost of Naval Supremacy, 1885-99," in Smith, ed., *Government and the Armed Forces in Britain*, 27.

[81] Forwood to Hamilton, 17 November 1886, ibid., 27.

[82] Ibid.

[83] Forwood to Hamilton, 24 November 1887, ibid., 32.

[84] *Parliamentary Papers*, Select Committee on Navy Estimates, Fourth Report.

[85] Ibid.

[86] Beresford at one point attested to the discretion used by Hamilton in his dealings with the Admiralty Board. *Hansard*, 3rd Series, 12 March 1888, col. 938-941. ZHC2/285.

[87] *Evidence, Written and Oral, taken by the Royal Commission appointed to Enquire into the Civil and Professional Administration of the Naval and Military Departments and the Relationship of those Departments to each other and to the Treasury* (known as the Hartington Commission). HO73/35/3.

[88]Ibid.
[89]*Hansard*, 3rd Series, 11 May 1888, col. 5-6.
[90]Ibid. Salisbury would repeat these sentiments in the House of Lords on 14 May 1888.
[91]Salisbury to Cabinet, "French Invasion (Most Confidential)," 6 June 1888, CAB 37/21/14.
[92]Ibid.
[93]Hamilton to Cabinet, "Navy Estimates," 10 November 1888, CAB 37/21/24.
[94]Smith, "Ruling the Waves," 36. Hood submitted the proposal on 1 July 1888. See Admiralty to Cabinet, "The Requirements of the British Navy," July 1888, CAB 37/22/36. See also *The Times*, 12 April 1889, for references made by Hood to the proposal.
[95]On the usage of organizational culture to explain strategic choices and instances of military innovation in peacetime, see Williamson Murray, "Does Military Culture Matter?" *Orbis* (Winter 1999), 27-42; and idem., "Innovation: Past and Future," in Williamson Murray and Alan R. Millett, *Military Innovation in the Interwar Period* (Cambridge: Cambridge University Press, 1996), 300-328.
[96]Ibid.
[97]For more on the naval element to the British way of warfare, see David French, *The British Way in Warfare 1688-2000* (London: Unwin Hyman, 1990); and Geoffrey Till, "Sir Julian Corbett and the British Way of Warfare: Problems of Effectiveness and Implementation," in Elizabeth J. Errington and Keith, Neilson, ed., *Navies and Global Defense: Theories and Strategy* (Westport, Connecticut: Praeger, 1996), 23-50.
[98]Cited in [John Knox Laughton], "Naval Supremacy and Naval Tactics," *Edinburgh Review* (January 1890), 148.
[99]Andrew D. Lambert, "The Royal Navy, 1856-1914: Deterrence and the Strategy of World Power," in Elizabeth J. Errington and Keith Neilson, ed., *Navies and Global Defense: Theories and Strategy* (Westport, Connecticut: Praeger, 1996), 81.
[100]For more on British reactions to the naval base at Cherbourg, see Andrew D. Lambert, *The Last Sailing Battlefleet: Maintaining Naval Mastery 1815-1850* (London: Conway Maritime Press, 1991), 11.
[101]Lambert, "The Royal Navy, 1856-1914," 78.
[102]Ibid.
[103]Ibid., 234.
[104]For the definitive historical treatment of Sir John Knox Laughton and the formal study of naval history, see Andrew Lambert, *The Foundations of Naval History: John Knox Laughton, the Royal Navy and the Historical Profession* (London: Chatham Publishing, 1998); and A.D. Lambert "History, Strategy and Doctrine: Sir John Knox Laughton and the Education of the Royal Navy," in William B. Cogar, ed., *New Interpretations in Naval History: Selected Papers from the Twelfth Naval History Symposium* (Annapolis, Maryland: Naval Institute Press, 1996), 173-187.
[105]Lambert, *Foundations*, 34, 46-49 and 74.
[106]J.K. Laughton, "The Scientific Study of Naval History," *RUSI Journal* (1874), 525.
[107]J.K. Laughton, "Scientific Instruction in the Royal Navy," *RUSI Journal* (1875), 233-34.
[108]Lambert, *Foundations*, 106.

Holding The Ring: The Royal Navy's Palestine Patrol, 1945-1948

Ninian L. Stewart

In the immediate aftermath of the Second World War, the Royal Navy undertook a variety of peacetime functions which, if less dramatic and glorious than its wartime operations, were often just as difficult and more frustrating. Among these was the maintenance of what came to be known as the Palestine Patrol: deterring the illegal immigration of European Jews into Palestine. This duty fell to the Royal Navy because Palestine was still technically under British control as a League of Nations mandate. The legal, political, and moral issues involved in this operation made it difficult enough; trying to play the role of honest broker between historic enemies made it dangerous as well. In this essay, a Royal Navy veteran offers a vivid and informed view of the difficulties and successes of the Palestine patrol, 1945-1948.

In 1945 a British administration governed Palestine under a mandate from the League of Nations whose activities were by then suspended. The extent to which immigration should be controlled had been under consideration when the outbreak of the Second World War ended the League's deliberations, and for the time being there was no international organization to take its place and decide the future of Palestine.[1] When peace returned to Europe, the monthly quota set by the British for Jewish immigrants became completely taken up by applicants, and in the late summer of 1945 small, primitive Mediterranean coastal trading craft started to make clandestine landings of Jewish immigrants from Central Europe on Palestine's beaches. The Arab inhabitants maintained their longstanding hostility to the growing size of the Jewish minority population, and they were supported strongly by the adjacent Arab nations. In October the Palestine Government requested military assistance for the Palestine marine police and the

---

Ninian Stewart served in and later worked for the Royal Navy from 1946-1997. His experience of patrol activities ranged from command of a patrol craft in Hong Kong 1955-1957 to Polaris SSBN operations in the 1970s.

British Government authorized the use of warships of the Mediterranean Fleet to intercept and search vessels suspected of carrying illegal immigrants.[2]

When issuing instructions for the conduct of the Palestine Patrol, as the operation became known, the Admiralty ruled that the warships did not enjoy belligerent rights on the high seas.[3] The damages awarded against the United States after an incident in international waters during the era of prohibition in the United States weighed heavily in this decision.[4] In addition, the Prime Minister did not want the Government's efforts to bring about a better ordered international community through the creation of the United Nations Organization undermined by doubts or questions concerning the legality of any aspect of the operation.[5] Thus the patrol was not empowered to divert, board or arrest any vessel suspected of being inbound with illegal immigrants embarked until after she had entered Palestine's territorial waters, extending three miles from land. Outside that distance, Commanding Officers could issue warnings but were not to back these up by the use of force.

The patrol started at comparatively short notice. At first it was controlled by a Flag Officer in a light cruiser stationed alongside a jetty in Haifa harbor. The cruiser provided the communication facilities which would otherwise have been lacking for the taxing task of linking the Admiral with army and air commanders, the Palestine central administration in Jerusalem, and ships allocated to the patrol. Later, when the duration of the task became long-term and the threat of sabotage in port became serious, the cruiser was replaced by a small Command, Control, and Communications shore station with a Commodore in charge and co-located with the local Army commander.[6]

The first warning of the approach of a vessel likely to be carrying illegal immigrants usually came from intelligence sources, prompting searches by Royal Air Force aircraft, which then homed a warship onto the vessel. A few illegal vessels penetrated without being detected from the air, and initially reconnaissance was hampered by lack of maritime patrol aircraft. After a visual check of a suspicious vessel, the intercepting warship would give a verbal warning of the likely consequences of any attempt at a landing. Once inside territorial waters orders to stop could be given and a boarding party was sent across by boat to inspect the cargo and, if necessary, make an arrest.[7] As time went by, the scale of the operation grew, with ships replacing the earlier illegal small craft and some starting their voyages outside the Straits of Gibraltar, the more sizeable being shadowed from the air and by warships the whole length of the Mediterranean.

Ships employed in the patrol needed speed, maneuverability and a strong and well trained boarding party. For those reasons, most of the interceptions were undertaken by destroyers, of which about four were kept available in or off Haifa. More lightly manned and less speedy sloops, frigates, and minesweepers also played important parts, the latter being particularly suitable if a tow became necessary.[8]

The warships were manned by regular sailors, reservists and wartime conscripts. At the start, most of these had not seen the British Isles since the war ended and were keen to return to their families, homes, and peacetime occupations. The Navy was under great pressure to release manpower to restore the United Kingdom's peacetime economy and rebuild bombed housing. As a result, morale was not a factor which could be taken for granted, and in addition the warships were often undermanned. Even when at anchor off Haifa, there was little rest since extensive precautions had to be taken against attack by underwater swimmers which included dropping explosive charges into the water at frequent intervals. Individual ships spent periods of up to four months in the Patrol and, although liable to be involved in the Mediterranean Fleet's other pressing postwar duties, were programmed in the intervals to enjoy visits to areas of the Mediterranean renowned for their attractions.[9] Families at home sometimes questioned the involvement of their menfolk with measures against refugees, but in those days the British press was more supportive of national activities, and murders committed by extremist elements on land played a significant part in limiting sympathy for illegal immigrants.[10]

Attempts at landings concentrated on the northern half of Palestine's coast, the sixty-mile stretch down to Tel Aviv. Further to the south, the population of the coastal area was almost solely Arab and the topography inland equally unwelcoming. In the first eight months that the patrol operated, all attempts at landings but one were intercepted, and in all cases but two everyone onboard was arrested and taken into Haifa.[11] This was the only port capable of berthing even small craft of the size being employed, but it had several disadvantages. The hillside above the harbor provided both an excellent grandstand from which events could be viewed by the large proportion of the community that supported the would-be immigrants, and it was also a good base for attempts to sabotage warships. Outside the port, winter weather made the approaches dangerous for craft without fully reliable means of propulsion, such was the case by accident or design with many immigrant vessels.

Vessels arrested and brought into Haifa were confiscated by the Palestine Government and attempts by owners to regain possession through the courts invariably proved unsuccessful. It was the other way round with their crews; after a number of prosecutions brought by the civil authorities had failed, they were deported if they could be identified, and so were free to try again in other vessels.[12] The arrested immigrants were not deported. Instead, their names were entered in the list of those applying for entry within the legal quota, and they were detained until reaching their turn for admission. This practice was viewed by others in and outside Palestine as permitting queue jumping at the expense of law abiding applicants for entry. Not surprisingly, Arabs protested that the Navy was easing the path of illegals by ensuring they were taken safely into harbor and not exposed to attempts to reach the shore from a grounded vessel through surf.[13]

Illegal vessels of over 1,000 tons displacement soon started to arrive. Their greater size facilitated identification by intelligence agencies when preparing for a voyage, and hence aided efforts through diplomatic channels to hinder their sailing. Once they were in transit, location by aircraft was easier and warships had less difficulty in picking them out amongst coastal traffic. But they were more difficult to stop, thus ending the Navy's hope that in time a better equipped Marine Division of the Palestine Police would be able to take over the Navy's task. Whatever their size, vessels carrying illegal immigrants—men, women and children—were always overcrowded, frequently dangerously so, and were generally in a thoroughly bad material state with terrible living conditions. After interception, and while outside territorial waters, those in charge onboard often sought to win time by prevarication or simulated breakdown. A favorite course of action was to attempt to obtain a tow from a warship, with the aim of claiming later that entry into territorial waters had not been voluntary.[14]

At the start of August 1946 six ships were arrested in one period of seventeen days. The numbers of illegal immigrants held in detention camps was by then considerable, and attempts by armed supporters to release them were difficult to repulse. The United Kingdom and Palestine Governments therefore arranged for fresh arrivals to be taken in British Government transports from Haifa to Cyprus, another British dependency, escorted by the Navy. Those concerned could still expect to return to Palestine when their names had gone through the quota waiting list.

The instant it became known to passengers for the first time that their period of waiting in detention would be spent away from Promised Land, the whole situation changed.[15] For a start, illegal vessels would no longer stop when told to do so.[16] Use of weapons to hold up a ship would have caused heavy casualties, and no other satisfactory mechanical means could be found. So the warships had to place themselves alongside their targets, which remained under way, and attempt to board. The illegal vessels maneuvered violently to shake them off, a process which threatened a serious collision, and which might have led to capsizing and sinking. Fortunately, the recent war had ensured that the Navy was provided with many experienced small ship officers, and the Commander-in-Chief, Mediterranean insisted that only officers with the necessary ability were appointed to commands in his fleet.[17] In fact, no crewmember or passenger was ever seriously injured during this phase of an arrest.

When attempting to board, and once onboard illegal vessels, members of boarding parties often met violent resistance, with the crews and immigrants throwing missiles and wielding iron bars, clubs, axes and other implements, hat pins being a particular menace. Boarders were sometimes overpowered and thrown overboard. All survived, although three boarders drowned when a frigate's boat capsized in surf during the later stages of an interception. With the exception of two occasions when Royal Marines took part, boarding parties were composed solely of sailors, crewmembers of intercepting warships, and although they disliked having to fight with immigrants, especially when women took part, and accusations of persecution, their determination was not affected.

Once violence of so extreme a nature began to be encountered, special training courses were started at a Royal Marine training establishment in Malta. These were particularly successful in developing willpower, confidence, teamwork and morale. But such arduous training made considerable physical demands, and care had to be taken to avoid injuries which reduced the availability of sailors since the ships had only a small reservoir of manpower.[18]

There was a tacit understanding on both sides that no firearms would be used; although boarders were armed, the training was intended to ensure success by other means, and boarders were permitted to open fire only as a last resort if in peril of their lives. Indeed, frequently the possession of a firearm turned into an embarrassment rather than a help. On one occasion shots were fired on the advice of a policeman in an attempt to bring down an illegal vessel's overhead wireless aerials. Not only was this unsuccessful, but the immigrants gained the wrong impression, believing themselves to be the target, and the fighting intensified.[19] In cases of civil disorder it is British practice to use tear gas (CS) to disperse crowds and quell opposition, and it was used by boarding parties and occasionally by their opponents.[20]

Once a boarding operation had been successfully completed, the engines and steering gear of the illegal vessel were sometimes found to be unusable due to mechanical failure or sabotage. The boarders had then to act as a salvage party, occasionally with little time to effect repairs or connect a tow before the vessel drifted into the breakers.[21] After control over the immigrants had been achieved, the affinity of seafarers faced by the perils of the sea had its effect and relationships often improved. Individual boarders invariably behaved with great humanity, on one occasion delivering a baby using medical procedures signalled to them by their parent warship.[22]

The Patrol undertook a rescue when at the end of 1946 a vessel in poor condition grounded on a remote and barren Greek isle and sank with the loss of eight of her 780 immigrant passengers. At the request of the Jewish Agency, two Royal Navy destroyers brought off all the survivors, despite continuing bad weather.[23] Three months later, a salvage party was sent to a seventy-year-old immigration vessel listing eighteen degrees and transmitting an SOS. The majority of the passengers transferred willingly to the two intercepting warships, 550 embarking in a destroyer, and 260 in a minesweeper, and their vessel was then towed to Haifa. There were other such incidents with aged, overloaded, and unseaworthy vessels.

Events showed that a three-mile limit allowed insufficient time to board and gain control of a vessel determined to reach the beach. But the British Government's chief law officer, the Lord Chancellor, remained adamantly opposed to arrests on the high seas. He also held that it would be unwise to rely on agreements that regimes whose flags were being misused by illegal immigrant vessels would not object. Just at this moment the United Kingdom was bringing a case against Albania for mining the Corfu Channel and damaging two British destroyers, making absolute adherence to the letter of international law all the more necessary. But the Lord Chancellor was realistic, and from January 1947 commanding officers were allowed to start arrests at such distance from the coast that, taking into account the uncertainties and imprecision of marine navigation, their action could not be seriously challenged.[24]

The best known incident during the patrol, the former Chesapeake steamer *President Warfield's* attempt to bring in 4,500 embarked in France, has been greatly embellished by folklore and fiction. By the time the *President Warfield*, bearing the name *Exodus*, approached Palestine, she was being shadowed by four destroyers and a frigate, supported by a cruiser. The boarding operation started at a distance from the Palestine coast which made the maximum possible use of the relaxation now permitted. The destroyers had a very difficult time getting alongside an elusive quarry in the dark and remaining there for sufficient time to put over sufficient boarders to effect an arrest. But careful preparations achieved a degree of surprise, and after two hours of fierce, but intermittent, fighting, morale onboard collapsed and the boarders secured control of the vessel.[25] Had she reached a beach there would have been a situation of great danger and disorder, with large numbers of passengers struggling to reach the shore and a reception party attempting to spirit them away from the clutches of the police, all in full sight of media representatives.

Numbers carried in the *President Warfield* were far in excess of anything met before, and by now camps in Cyprus contained well over 18,000 immigrants. On this occasion the U.K. government decided to implement *Refoulement,* a League of Nations' term for returning refugees whence they came. The Navy then had the task of escorting transports carrying the passengers first back to France, and finally to a port in the British occupied zone of Germany.

The likelihood of even larger illegal vessels being employed meant that arrests could not be completed without a possibility that both sides would suffer casualties too severe to be justified. In any case during the *President Warfield* operation, the destroyers had incurred considerable damage and one was out of action for over six months. So the Commander in Chief, concerned by the demands being placed on his fleet, sought and obtained approval for a vessel to be deemed "Unboardable." If an RN officer declared an illegal ship "unboardable" he could restrict naval operations to "marking" her and signaling her movements. Forces on land would then be placed so the passengers could be arrested as they landed.[26] But the firm action taken with the *President Warfield* and her passengers, timely agreement by the newly created United Nations Organization that Palestine should be partitioned, and steps taken by several governments to reduce the support available to illegal vessels, this all contributed to a less heated situation. In January 1948 a pair of well found 7,000 ton vessels carrying between them 15,000 immigrants were intercepted by a force of two cruisers with destroyers and frigates. Negotiations between the British and

Jewish authorities in Palestine and the show of force led them to agree to go peacefully to Cyprus.[27]

As the British mandate drew to its close, the patrol continued to make arrests. A lookout was also kept for gun running in preparation for settling scores between Jew and Arab and in defiance of a United Nations embargo.[28] The final stages of the operation were conducted amongst craft carrying Arab refugees fleeing from the Acre, Haifa and Jaffa areas. At the end of May 1948 partition came into effect and the British withdrew from Palestine, which was at that point being invaded by the armies of the surrounding Arab nations.

During the period when the future of Palestine was being decided, the Royal Navy intercepted and arrested some forty-nine illegal immigration vessels and detained some 66,000 illegal immigrants and crew. Only six small vessels, carrying between them about 2,200 immigrants, reached a beach without being arrested, and many of their passengers were rounded up ashore.[29] Despite dangerous maneuvers by often unstable and unseaworthy immigrant vessels attempting to avoid being boarded and violent resistance, there was no major mishap. Sadly, nine persons are known to have died as a result of injuries received when boarding parties were resisted.[30] But in the years which followed, hard feelings between those involved died away remarkably quickly, which would not have been the case had less restraint been exercised.[31]

Intelligence gathering, together with diplomatic and air force activities, all contributed to the end result—successful naval interceptions. The speedy provision of a local Command, Control and Communication organization ensured coordination with the other interested but widely dispersed authorities from the outset. Nevertheless it was the warships which had the most demanding tasks. Although the hull damage they suffered during interceptions became a cause for concern, this factor never led to the strength or efficiency of the patrol being reduced. It was a price worth paying. Had the *President Warfield* broken through, confidence in the patrol would have been lost and later attempts by large ships would have been more determined and perhaps more numerous. The success of the naval operation was ultimately due to good ship handling at close quarters and above all the courage and resolve of individual members of the well trained boarding parties, who performed their jobs with dedication and efficiency despite the unpleasant nature of their task.

Just as the patrol ended, the Supreme Court for Palestine rejected a ship owner's appeal for the return of a vessel arrested during one of the early voyages and then confiscated.[32] The court added that arrest outside territorial waters would have been legitimate on the grounds of Palestine's right of self-defense.[33] In other words, the voyage was viewed as an attempt at an invasion. But the British Government had adopted its more limited policy not only on legal grounds but with other objectives also in mind.

Events since the end of the Cold War, and the separate problem of very large cargoes of illegal drugs being shipped by sea, have brought boarding operations from warships back into prominence. An easier means of arrival is available now and sailors today rope down from helicopters as skillfully as their ancestors came down topmast backstays two hundred years ago. But prosecutions brought in the British courts following the arrest of suspected drug runners in international waters have met setbacks, while in the Kosovo operation, the legal issues were not resolved in time to allow suspicious vessels to be boarded. The legal regime affecting the use of warships to intercept commercial shipping thus remains very complicated and restrictive.

NOTES

[1]*Origins and Evolution of the Palestine Problem* (New York: United Nations, 1978); Annual *Register—A Review of Public Events at Home and Abroad*, various editors (Longmans, Green & Co., 1936–46).
[2]United Kingdom Public Records Office (PRO) Adm 1 series: 18584 & 19358; *Flag Officer Levant & Middle East,* hereafter cited as *(FOLEM), Reports of Proceedings* (October & December, 1945).
[3]Ibid.
[4]This refers to the pursuit and sinking of a Canadian Liquor Ship *I'm Alone* ten to fourteen miles from the U.S. coast, by a Revenue Cutter. See HBM Ambassador, Washington DC dispatch to Foreign Office, 22 April 1929.
[5]Adm1/20677 quotes a directive issued by Prime Minister Attlee requiring strict observance of international law by all arms of government.
[6]Adm1/19377 & 19401 *FOLEM Reports* (October & December, 1945); 19402 Captain (D) Third Destroyer Flotilla Report (November 1945); 19433 *Flag Officer,*

Fifteenth Cruiser Squadron Report (December 1945); *Commander-in-Chief (CinC) Mediterranean Report* (August & September, 1946).

[7]Accounts of events during arrests are summarized from reports of Senior and Commanding Officers held in Adm1 series. In addition, the author was present during the 1997 reunion of clandestine immigration crewmembers held in Haifa and Tel-Aviv where he was entertained most hospitably.

[8]Sloop: type of minor war vessel slightly less powerful than a destroyer, very suitable for independent operations at British dependencies and later recategorized as frigate. Location and employment of Flag Officers, Senior Officers and individual warships are taken from the weekly issues of Admiralty *Pink Lists*, 1945-1948.

[9]Adm1/18542: *CinC Mediterranean's Peacetime Policy for the Mediterranean Fleet*.

[10]London & Glasgow daily newspapers, 1945-1948.

[11]Admiralty *Pink Lists, 1945-48*. Other documents consulted include: synopsis by Lieutenant Commander (later Rear Adm.) D. A. Dunbar-Nasmith, DSC, RN, who commanded a patrol vessel; PRO records in the Colonial Office, CO537 series & Foreign Office 371/61802; record displayed at Haifa in Naval & Clandestine Immigration Museum; Mordechai Naor, *HAAPALA Clandestine Immigration 1931-1948* (State of Israel Ministry of Defense, 1987); Capt. Rudolph W. Patzert, *Running the Palestine Blockade, The Last Voyage of Paducah* (Annapolis, Md.: U.S. Naval Institute Press, 1994). I am also grateful to Fritz M. Liebreich for invaluable assistance. Mr. Liebreich landed from SS *Tiger Hill*, a clandestine immigration vessel, at Tel-Aviv on 3 September 1939, and has recently com-pleted a doctoral dissertation on illegal seaborne immigration into Palestine.

[12]Adm1/19615 *CinC Mediterranean Reports* (August-September, 1946).

[13]View forwarded to Admiralty by both the CinC & FOLEM in documents already listed.

[14]Adm1/9993 & 10202. This practice was encountered first during the summer of 1939 when, for some four months, the Royal Navy assisted the Palestine Marine Police intercept clandestine immigration vessels.

[15]Recollections of Captain P. S. Hicks-Beach, OBE, RN. As a Lieutenant, he was Boarding Officer onboard the arrested vessel Katriel *Yaffe* when after anchoring off Haifa the passengers became the first to learn that they would be detained in Cyprus and not the Promised Land. Considerable disorder ensued.

[16]In the first instance during interception of *Fede* II by HMS *Childers* (Lieutenant Commander E. A. S. Bailey, RN) on 2 September 1946. Bailey had been warned to expect trouble and the *Childers* was well prepared. After the arrest, recommendations made by Bailey led to additional training mentioned in the main text. (Adm1/19616) Later he was instrumental in devising a means for boarding the *President Warfield (Exodus)*.

[17]Recollections of Commander A. D. Casswell, RN, who served as Lieutenant Commander in command of one of the destroyers.

[18]Adm1/20621 *Mediterranean Fleet Reports* (August-December 1947). Recollections of Captain Hicks-Beach and also former Engineer Mechanic E.J.P. Barrett (HMS *Chaplet* boarding party). Both underwent the course, as did the author ten years later in preparation for another operation. Mr. Barrett spoke at the reunions already mentioned and the arduous nature of the training caused great surprise amongst his former adversaries.

[19]Adm1/20643 *Arrest of Guardian 13th April 1946*. There were three deaths due to small arms fire by the boarding party when fighting became particularly violent.

[20]Tear gas was not always very effective and on one occasion, the boarding of the *Ulua* (an 800 ton ex-US Coastguard Cutter) required an eighty-four strong boarding party to complete the arrest.

[21]The *Guardian's* engine and rudder were found immobilized by a boarding party. Weather conditions were very bad and after a warship had towed her to Haifa she was transferred to a harbor tug, whose tow parted. With an onshore gale

blowing, a minesweeper plucked *Guardian* from the surf in Acre Bay with only a few hundred feet to spare.

[22]Adm1/20630 & 20671 contain details of arrest of the *Merica*.

[23]The Jewish Agency represented Jewish religious and other interests in Palestine. Adm1/20595 *Athina Rescue* & Adm1/20777 *Sirina Island – Behavior of Survivors During Passage*. Also recollections of Lieutenant Commander (then Lieutenant) A. J. L. Tyler, RN, (published in *The Jewish Chronicle* February 1947 edition and also given in his talk at the reunions) and Mr. G. Morter, both of whom were serving in the destroyer commanded by the senior officer present. As a young sailor Mr. Morter had served ashore in Palestine during the 1936–1939 Arab revolt.

[24]Adm1/19615 *Mediterranean Fleet Reports*.

[25]Adm1/20685 *The President Warfield* & Adm1/20684 *Return of Illegal Immigrants to France*. Also recollections of Rear Admiral G. P. Gerard-Pearse, CB, and Lieutenant Commander E. Ravenscroft, RN, who, as Lieutenant and Engine Room Artificer respectively, boarded the *President Warfield*. Also, David C Holly, *Exodus 1947*, rev. ed. (Annapolis, Md.: U.S. Naval Institute Press, 1995); N. Degani, *Exodus Calling*, rev. ed. (New York: Herzl Press, 1997).

[26]Adm1/20677. CinC Mediterranean letter 47/001415/6/16 dated 30 August 1947.

[27]Boarding was by agreement and unopposed, being the second of two occasions when Royal Marines took part. Adm1/20789 *Palestine Illegal Immigration Policy Post the President Warfield*. Adm1/20793 *The Pan York & Pan Crescent*. Adm1/21087 *The Pan York & Pan Crescent* (December 1947–January 1948). Also talk by Mr. Y. Harel (overall commander onboard the *Pans* and the *Exodus*) at crew reunions already mentioned.

[28]In March HMS *St. Austell Bay* found the American vessel *Flying Anchor* at anchor off Tel-Aviv disembarking half tracked vehicles and she was escorted to Port Said.

[29]The authorities listed in Footnote 11 are in close agreement on the outcome of each voyage and do not differ widely on numbers onboard.

[30]Three died as result of fighting in the *President Warfield*, three in the *Guardian*, one each in *Ariella*, *Merica* and *Despite All*. Out of those nine, seven died as a result of small arms fire. Additionally two who jumped overboard from the *Fede II* drowned. There were many less serious casualties on both sides and the need for medical attention was one of the main reasons for resistance ceasing onboard *President Warfield*.

[31]After the formation of the Israeli Navy, contact with the Royal Navy was soon established. Several of the Palestine Patrol's adversaries came to do British training courses while Lieutenant Tyler went with his wife to Israel to qualify as an interpreter. Later the former Master of *Exodus* was the guest of (the now Captain) E.A.S. Bailey at his home.

[32]The Judicial Committee of the King's (or Queen's) Privy Council acts as the Supreme Court for British dependencies which do not have their own, as was the case with Palestine. Some former dependencies now independent continue to utilize this committee.

[33]Adm1/21106 *Maritime International Law: Detention and Diversion of Vessels on the High Seas*.

Part II

French Naval History and Historiography

Marines and Martial Races: The Recruitment of the *Tirailleurs Sénégalais* in French West Africa, 1857–1914

Bruce Vandervort

> In the late 19th and early 20th centuries, France ruled great portions of extra-national territory, particularly in north Africa. Like the British and other imperial powers of this era, the French relied on a combination of regulars and native troops to protect its territory overseas. The most famous element of this colonial force was the French Foreign legion, but in addition to these expatriates, the French also recruited native soldiers and in particular the *Tirailleurs Sénégalais* or Senegalese Light Infantry. In this essay, Bruce Vandervort discusses the extent to which French marine recruiters for this force were influenced by contemporary assumptions about race, geography, and character when recruiting native soldiers for French service.

The history of the various marine corps of the Western world is replete with accounts of their roles as colonial light infantry, elite assault troops, or shipboard sharpshooters. Much less attention has been paid to their equally remarkable historical role as recruiters, trainers, and leaders in combat of indigenous colonial troops. Readers will recall, for example, the part played by the U.S. Marine Corps in the formation of the *Garde d'Haiti* and the *Guardias Nacionales* of the Dominican Republic and Nicaragua.[1]

These forces, of course, were trained by the U.S. Marines for use in keeping internal order in their respective countries. Once they were up and running, the departing Marines pretty much left them to their own devices, like the clockmaker's god of the deists.

This was not the case, however, with what was destined to become the largest indigenous colonial force ever formed by marines, the *Tirailleurs Sénégalais* or Senegalese light infantry. Organized under the auspices of the French marine corps or *Troupes de la marine* in 1857, the role of the *Tirailleurs Sénégalais*

Bruce Vandervort is a Professor of History at the Virginia Military Institute and editor of *The Journal of Military History*.

was not confined to maintaining domestic order. From the beginning of its existence, this force was intended to serve as an instrument of conquest and an army of occupation in Africa and, if need be, as a reserve army for the defense of the Fatherland.[2]

This black colonial army was not an arm's-length creation, as were the New World formations sponsored by the U.S. Marines, but an integral part of the French *Troupes de la marine*. It was recruited, trained, and led by French marines and fought alongside them in battles ranging over a full century, from West Africa to Madagascar in the nineteenth century, and from Morocco to Gallipoli and the Western Front in World War I, to North Africa and Western Europe in World War II, and finally to Indochina and Algeria in the post–1945 era. Comprising a single battalion of 500 men in 1857, the force increased to just under 6,000 men in 1895, rose steadily in numbers during the early years of the twentieth century, and then mushroomed to over 170,000 men during the 1914–1918 war.[3] At that point and on into the interwar era, the *Tirailleurs Sénégalais* ranked as the largest indigenous colonial army in the world, after the British Indian Army.

This paper will address two related problems concerning the formation and growth of France's black marine force. First, it will review the reasons why France and her marine corps felt compelled to create such a force in the first place and why its growth became a matter of considerable national importance in the last decades of the nineteenth century. Second, it will explain how and why the French came to select certain groups in West African society for inclusion in the Senegalese light infantry, and why they decided to exclude others. One particularly interesting aspect of this second issue is the evidence that French recruiters sought especially to attract the so-called "martial races."

This is a topic of more than incidental importance. It helps to broaden discussion of the ethnic and cultural categories by which France's colonial governors and soldiers sought to understand and ultimately to rule the indigenous peoples of their West African empire. Of course, it also adds a vital dimension to our appreciation of the crucial role played the French marines in the foundation and defense of France's colonies in Africa.

Scholarly debate continues over the origins of the *Tirailleurs Sénégalais*. Some historians have argued that they were modeled on the *cipayes* or sepoys, native troops raised by the French in India in the eighteenth century.[4] Others trace their origins to the indigenous light infantry units formed in Algeria following the French invasion of 1830.[5] Still others view the *Tirailleurs Sénégalais* as the fruit of efforts to recruit indigenous fighting forces in Senegal going all the way back to the 1600s.[6]

The best evidence seems to indicate that the *Tirailleurs Sénégalais* were brought into existence largely in response to concerns that were specific to Senegal and should be viewed as the latest and most successful of a number of attempts to create such a force in the West African colony. It is nonetheless true, however, that the structure and mission of the force owed much to France's experience with colonial troops in Algeria. The link was General Louis César Faidherbe, army engineer, veteran of colonial warfare in Algeria, and governor of Senegal in the 1850s and 60s. Faidherbe has rightly been accorded the title of "founding father" of the *Tirailleurs Sénégalais*.

Whatever impetus may have brought them to life, the *Tirailleurs Sénégalais* are probably best seen as one example among many of indigenous colonial forces raised by France over the centuries: in Canada, the West Indies, India, West Africa, and Indochina. The French were perhaps more active in this field than other colonial powers, with the possible exception of the Portuguese. This need not be taken to mean, however, that France had a special gift for organizing and leading colonial troops, as Marine Colonel Charles Mangin insisted in 1910. Mangin was a veteran colonial officer and the primary exponent of the *Force Noire*, a large African army for service in defense of France.

> The aptitude of our race for managing indigenous troops is very old [he wrote]. Already in the 18th century, it served us well in India and Canada, even against a European enemy. This aptitude comes from our greater politeness, our habit of speaking to others as we would want others to speak to us, and

from the natural cordiality of our people, which, alas, sometimes degenerates into familiarity. Also, we don't feel a need for the kind of external distinctions that show contempt for subordinates, but which other civilized peoples seem to need to set themselves apart from their subjects.[7]

The *Tirailleurs Sénégalais* were founded in 1857 to supplement the French marine infantry in Senegal, which had borne the main burden of colonial defense and internal expansion up to that point. The decree authorizing the creation of the force was a result of pressure put on the government of Louis Napoleon by the governor of Senegal, General Faidherbe, who had begun to despair of losses of European troops to tropical diseases and heatstroke. Faidherbe not only believed that African troops were better suited to warfare in the tropics, but being an amateur ethnographer of some renown, he contended that with proper training, carefully-chosen African soldiers could be effectively employed as line infantry—provided they were officered by French marines and "stiffened" by French marine units held in reserve behind them.

Clearly the threat of European losses due to tropical diseases was a major stimulus to the creation of a large indigenous fighting force in West Africa. Although advances in tropical medicine, such as the use of quinine to combat malaria, had managed to reduce the incidence of deaths due to disease among European troops in Africa by the 1850s, the effect was much more pronounced among troops in barracks than among troops in the field. French medical records of the time show that whereas deaths due to disease among European soldiers in barracks in Senegal had dropped from an annual average of 200 men per 1,000 in the 1830s to a yearly average of seventy-two per 1,000 in the 1857–1872 period, there was almost no impact on deaths among European troops in the field.[8] Indeed, as the following figures illustrate, deaths due to disease among European troops in the field actually rose over the years of imperial conquest in West Africa.[9]

Years	Deaths per 1,000 Troops
1857–1872	200
1885–1886	201
1886–1887	222
1891–1892	300

But malaria, yellow fever, and typhoid epidemics notwithstanding, until the 1880s it was still considered the better part of wisdom to field more European than African troops from the marines' advance base in Kayes (in present-day Mali) to do battle during the West African dry season. Marine officers still questioned the battle worthiness of their African charges and feared desertion of Muslim soldiers to the largely Muslim enemy.

All of this began to change in 1886 when the great marine officer and future savior of France at the First Battle of the Marne, then-colonel Joseph-Simon Galliéni, set forth from Kayes with a force composed largely of *Tirailleurs Sénégalais*. Ultimate pragmatist that he was, Galliéni had refused to be burdened with troops that could not withstand the pestilence and heat of tropical warfare. "It would be a good idea," he wrote, "to get rid of most of the European troops in the Sudan, who only encumber our ambulances and die like flies, and replace them with indigenous elements."[10] By mounting the few European troops in his column on mules, Galliéni served notice that henceforth the *Tirailleurs Sénégalais* would play the primary role in the French conquest of West Africa. "The Senegalese light infantry are the real soldiers of the Sudan." "By turns engineers, gunners, couriers, porters, always ready, always loyal, it is because of them that we hold the vast territory [from the Senegal River] to the Niger River."[11]

The *Tirailleurs Sénégalais* officially acceded to their role as the dominant force in the French conquest of West Africa in 1891 when the marine commander in the Sudan, Colonel Louis Archinard, took a column composed entirely of African troops into battle against the jihad army of Sultan Ahmadu.[12] By the eve of the First World War, Europeans were almost entirely absent from the French marine forces in West Africa. Wrote Colonel Charles Mangin, the veteran colonial soldier quoted above:

> Today [1910] a force of 12,500 [*Tirailleurs Sénégalais*] guards the whole of our possessions in West Africa and the Congo-Chad region, for, in all of this area, larger than Europe, there is now only a single European unit, a battalion of three companies (450 men) of colonial infantry, stationed at Dakar to defend the main [South Atlantic] base of our fleet.[13]

All of the European imperial powers, France included, had large populations from which to draw their indigenous soldiers, but in almost no cases did they simply recruit as they would have done in Europe, that is, from the population at large. Almost always, they fastened their attention on certain selected parts of the population, from which they proceeded to draw the bulk of their indigenous troops. Thus, the British army in India recruited heavily among Punjabis, but tried to avoid taking in Bengalis or Madrassis. Likewise, Britain's West African Frontier Force in Nigeria eagerly sought out recruits among the Hausas of the North but shunned the Ibos of the South. The French, in the process of carving out an extensive empire in West and Equatorial Africa in the last half of the nineteenth century, were no exception to this general rule. They, too, created a large indigenous army and recruited its rank-and-file not from the population at large, a reservoir of some five million people, but from carefully-chosen segments of the populace.

But on what basis were these recruits chosen? On what basis were others rejected? It has become notorious that nineteenth century British army recruiters picked their indigenous troops on the basis of a presumed membership of what were believed to be "martial races." This approach, while best known in connection with the recruiting practices of the British Indian Army from around 1880 down to the Second World War, also operated to some extent with regard to Britain's indigenous armed forces in Africa—for example, the West African Frontier Force and the King's African Rifles in East Africa. But, while the "martial races" concept probably achieved its most elaborate formulation in the recruiting handbooks of the British Indian Army, "martial races" criteria seem to have been employed extensively by the recruiters of other European colonial powers as well. Whereas "martial races" criteria probably were not decisive in determining who served in France's indigenous West African forces, they did play a more important role than has been recognized.

The "martial races" doctrine derived in part from observation and partly from supposition. Some colonial peoples—ethnic groups or tribes—were observed by European authorities to have a penchant for warfare. Others were classified as "martial races" because they seemed to possess what Europeans liked to think were "martial" characteristics. This more speculative, less pragmatic, side of the "martial races" doctrine was reinforced in the second half of the nineteenth century by the biological determinism that stemmed in the Anglo-Saxon world from the thought of Charles Darwin or, among the French, from the writings of Jean-Baptiste Lamarck.

Certain physical characteristics were taken as signs of martial potential. These usually included light skin. British officials in late nineteenth century India tended to believe that "the dawn of Indian history discloses two races struggling for the soil." The winner in this struggle, and thus the subcontinent's premier "martial race," was "a fair-complexioned Sanskrit-speaking people of Aryan lineage" (the Punjabis of northwestern India), while the loser, and thus the segment of the Indian population to be shunned by army recruiters, was "a dark-skinned race of lower type" (the Madrassis of southern India).[14]

By contrast, French marine recruiters in West Africa, however willing they might have been to make a connection between fairness of skin and martial propensities, found less scope for its application than did the British in India. For example, the fair-skinned Berber and Tuareg warriors of the Sahel region were much admired by French officers, but, unfortunately, were nomads and thus had to be written off as completely averse to military discipline.[15] Racial distinctions did, however, come into play in the matter of the French hankering after the Tukolor warriors of the Futa Toro in the middle Senegal River region and the Western Sudan. The Tukolors were *métis*, a mélange of the dark-skinned

Wolofs of Senegal and the fair-skinned Fulani pastoral nomads of the Central Sudan. French soldiers, beginning with Faidherbe in the 1850s, considered them the most warlike of the West African peoples and, as empire builders in their own right, the most gifted leaders. A widely held view was that if ever there were to be native officers in the *Tirailleurs Sénégalais*, they ought to be Tukolors.[16]

There was, however, a major obstacle to recruiting Tukolors for the French service. "Their religious fanaticism and the memory of their former power [broken by France in thirty years of warfare]," wrote Marine Colonel Albert Ditte in 1905, "have given them an immense sense of pride and an instinctive hatred for our authority."[17] Thus, although a fair number of Tukolors were eventually recruited for service in the *Tirailleurs Sénégalais* in the years following their defeat by the French, they were never sufficiently trusted to be given the posts of responsibility their reputation as a "martial race" supposedly had earned them.

Geography was also believed to be a determining factor in the evolution of "martial" characteristics. People from temperate climates, such as mountainous regions, were expected to be more "martial" than denizens of tropical areas. Lord Elphinstone, the commander of the ill-fated British "retreat from Kabul" in 1842, believed that in India "The inhabitants of the dry country to the North are comparatively manly and active, while the Bengalis with their moist climate and their double crops of rice, . . . are more effeminate than any other people in India."[18] French marine officers in West Africa also believed that "martial" aptitude deteriorated with proximity to the equator. Colonel Mangin, writing in 1911, argued that the Sudanic peoples, the inhabitants of the dry plains just to the south of the Sahara, were the only suitable candidates for service in the *Tirailleurs Sénégalais*. The tribes of the forest zone, in the Côte d'Ivoire and French Equatorial Africa, for example, lacked the discipline and stamina to be good soldiers, he contended.[19]

But "martial races" doctrine also contained a good-sized dose of the noble savage fixations of the eighteenth century. Thus, some officers held that the more primitive a people were, the less they had been influenced by Western civilization, the more desirable they were as colonial soldiers. Unlike city folks, rustics, so the story went, were not only healthy and strong but unspoiled and uncomplicated. Military men, unfortunately, tended to interpret primitive characteristics somewhat more cynically. Bumpkins were welcomed to the colors because they tended to be unschooled, often even illiterate, and hence didn't ask questions. Country lads also respected hierarchies and were amenable to discipline.

By way of contrast, it may be interesting to point out that some U.S. cavalry officers in the West preferred to recruit their Indian allies from among the tribes they considered the most "civilized," like the Delawares, who had lived alongside whites for the better part of two centuries before migrating to the plains from the eastern woodlands.[20] This notion, as has already been suggested, was anathema to most European military men in Africa. General Sir Garnet Wolseley, Gilbert & Sullivan's "very model of a modern major general," spurned assistance from the African inhabitants of the Gold Coast towns when he set out to wage war against the Ashantis in 1873. He found the westernized "town negro an objectionable animal [whose] vanity, pretensions . . . and vulgar swagger made one feel how much more useful he would be if we had never emancipated him."[21] French marine captain Hippolyte-Victor Marceau felt the same way about the town-dwelling Wolof people of western Senegal, who had been granted French citizenship following the Revolution of 1848. The Wolof, he wrote, "is a 'Rights of Man' negro; a citizen without civilization; an elector who disdains our uniforms; he is no longer fit to be a *tirailleur*."[22]

Almost from the very beginning, the Africans who were deemed most "fit to be a *tirailleur*" by French marine recruiters were the Bambara people of the region between the Senegal and Niger rivers. As Colonel Ditte of the marines made clear in a lecture to the *Ecole Supérieure de Guerre* in 1905, the Bambara possessed the salient characteristics of a "martial race." "Of average height, sometimes quite tall," Ditte said, "the Bambara is stocky, powerfully-muscled, and exhibits a remarkable vigor. What most distinguishes the Bambara *tirailleur*, however, is his limitless confidence in his European superiors and a devotion that knows no bounds. All of his other characteristics, his endurance, his quiet and stubborn courage, flow from that one essential quality."[23]

Other marine officers took a more negative view of the alleged virtues of these peasant warriors of the Sudan. Captain Marceau, for example, described the typical Bambara soldier as "an uncouth fellow who possessed all the martial virtues, but who, unfortunately, did not exhibit a great deal of intelligence." Not that this was necessarily a bad thing, the captain hastened to add. Much better a slow-witted Bambara than a Wolof barrack-room lawyer from Dakar.[24] What all of this seems to underscore is that, yes, French marine recruiters valued "martial" virtues such as strength, endurance, and courage in the Africans they enrolled in the *Tirailleurs Sénégalais*, but that they prized the qualities of obedience, docility, and devotion even more. Winston Churchill's remarkable tribute to the Sudanese soldiers who fought with Kitchener's British army at Omdurman in 1898 would not be out of place here. "To the faithful loyalty of a dog," the young Winston wrote, "he added the heart of a lion. He loved his officer, and feared nothing in the world."[25]

Religion was an important ingredient in the make-up of the "martial races," according to British recruiting officers. In both India and Africa, they tended to view Islam as a martial creed and thus made a concerted effort to recruit Muslims for their colonial armies.[26]

French recruiters were much more ambivalent about Muslim soldiers. Faidherbe, in the 1850s and 60s, had looked upon Islam as a boon for Black Africa, as a progressive faith that would help Africa to make the transition to the modern world.[27] This view was not shared, however, by many of his successors. Galliéni, for example, was harshly critical of Islam's impact on Africa and demonstrated a marked preference for the animist religion followed by most of the Bambaras.[28] French officers in Africa continued to be haunted by the specter of Muslim mutinies throughout the colonial period. This fear of Islam, and the assumed receptiveness of the Bambaras to Christian missionaries, made Bambara recruits all the more desirable in the eyes of the French marines.

While there can be no doubt that French marine officers in Africa subscribed to the terminology of a "martial races" doctrine, and probably even believed much of it to be valid, it would be a mistake to see this as the exclusive foundation on which the *Tirailleurs Sénégalais* regiments were built. It is extremely likely that the *Tirailleurs Sénégalais* would have been recruited largely from the Bambara people, even if the "martial races" doctrine had never been heard of. There are two good reasons for suggesting this.

The Bambara, one could easily argue, became the backbone of the *Tirailleurs Sénégalais* largely by a process of elimination. The Wolof, who had supplied the troops for France's early conquests in Senegal, opted out of military service after the 1850s, not because they disdained the uniform, as Captain Marceau preferred to believe, but because more promising careers beckoned in the booming commerce and burgeoning bureaucracy of urban Senegal.[29] The Tukolors, every marine's first choice as the premier fighting men of the Sudan, unfortunately could be recruited only in small numbers due to their reputation as fanatical Muslims and unreconstructed enemies of French expansion. The Mandingo peoples of Guinea, meanwhile, were at war with France under their great leader Samori Touré during the last three decades of the nineteenth century. This pretty much left the Bambaras.

But the Bambaras were the logical target of marine recruiters for another, equally important reason. Beginning in the 1850s and continuing into the 1890s, they were engaged in a bitter struggle to preserve their political independence and animist faith against Tukolor expansionism. The Tukolors were at the same time the main bulwark against French conquest of the Sudan. A tired cliché it may be, but the old adage, "My enemy's enemy is my friend," seems entirely apropos in this case. War and politics threw the Bambaras and the French into each other's arms and virtually assured that the bulk of the *Tirailleurs Sénégalais* would be recruited from out of their ranks.

In conclusion, the "martial races" doctrine, while it clearly affected some French military officers in West Africa during the colonial period, served as a kind of intellectual patina for policies that were dictated by necessity. France needed an indigenous colonial army to supplement and ultimately replace her marines, a force that was expensive to maintain, vulnerable to tropical diseases, and much in demand elsewhere. She needed an army of hardy, obedient and loyal native infantrymen who could defend her colonies against Muslim jihads and move their frontiers forward into Chad, Dahomey, Madagascar, and the Congo. France found them where they were most available, among the stolid Bambaras of the Western Sudan.

NOTES

[1] For a one-volume popular account of U.S. interventions in Latin America in this century, including those of the U.S. Marine Corps during the interwar years, see Ivan Musicant, *The Banana Wars: A History of United States Military Inter-vention in Latin America, from the Spanish-American War to the Invasion of Panama* (New York: Macmillan, 1990).

[2] There is great need for an up-to-date, comprehensive history of the *Tirailleurs Sénégalais* in French. The early period is covered adequately by Pierre Gentil's dense *Les Troupes du Sénégal de 1816 a 1890*, vol. I, *Soldats au Sénégal du Colonel Schmaltz au Général Faidherbe (1816-1865)* (Dakar-Abidjan: Les Nouvelles Editions Africaines, 1978). General Albert Duboc's *Les Sénégalais au service de la France* (Paris: Edgar Malfère, 1939), continues the story. There is a remarkable output of scholarly writing in English on the *Tirailleurs Sénégalais*. The two most useful works are Charles Balesi's *From Adversaries to Comrades-in-arms: West Africans and the French military, 1885-1918* (Waltham, Mass.: Crossroads Books, 1979), and Myron Echenburg's *Colonial Conscripts: the Tirailleurs Sénégalais in French West Africa, 1857-1960* (Portsmouth, N.H.: Heinemann, 1991).

[3] Echenburg, *Colonial Conscripts*, 7, Table 2.1.

[4] P. Cogniet, ed., *Histoire et épopée des Troupes coloniales* (Paris: Presse Moderne, 1955), 82.

[5] For this viewpoint, see especially R. Pasquier, "L'influence de l'expérience algérienne sur la politique de la France au Sénégal (1842-1869)," in *Perspectives nouvelles sur le passé de l'Afrique noire et de Madagascar. Mélanges offerts à Hubert Deschamps*, ed. C. A. Julien (Paris: Publications de la Sorbonne, 1974), 263-284.

[6] The first four chapters of Gentil, *Les Troupes du Sénégal*, give an extremely detailed account of the early attempts to create an indigenous army in the colony.

[7] Mangin, *La Force Noire* (Paris: Hachette, 1910), 297-298.

[8] Borius, Alfred, "Topographie médicale du Sénégal," *Archives de Médicine navale* 37 (1882), 401; Jean-Pierre F. Thévènot, *Traité des maladies des Européens en pays chaud, et spécialement au Sénégal, ou essai statistique, médicale et hygiénique sur le sol, le climat et les maladies de cette partie de l'Afrique* (Paris, 1840), 195. Cited in Philip D. Curtin, *Disease and empire: the health of European troops in the conquest of Africa* (Cambridge: Cambridge University Press, 1998), 26.

[9] Borius, ibid.; Dr. Laffont, "Rapport médical sur la campagne de 1887-1888 dans le Soudan français," *Archives de Médicine navale* 51 (1880), 292, 348-53; Primet, "Rapport sur l'épidemie de fièvre jaune au Soudan," *Archives de Médicine navale* 59 (1893), 376. Cited in Curtin, ibid., 78, 85.

[10] Galliéni, *Deux campagnes au Soudan français, 1886-1888* (Paris: Hachette, 1891), 626.

[11] Quoted in Marc Michel, *Galliéni* (Paris: Fayard, 1989), 119.

[12] Georges Pasquier, *L'Organisation des troupes indigenes en Afrique Occidentale Française* (Paris: Larose, 1912), 34.

[13] Mangin, *La Force noire*, 175-176.

[14] David Omissi, *The Sepoy and the Raj: the Indian Army, 1860-1940* (London: Macmillan, 1994), 32.

[15] Lt. Colonel Albert Ditte, *Observations sur la guerre dans les colonies: organisation – execution. Conferences faites à l'Ecole Supérieure de Guerre* (Paris: Henri Charles-Lavauzelle, 1905), 53-54. Ditte was an officer in the *Infanterie coloniale*, i.e. the former *Troupes de la Marine*. His collected lectures at the Ecole Supérieure de Guerre constitute a French primer on "small wars" or what we would today call "low-intensity warfare." Ditte's book is in some respects superior to the most famous study of this subject in the English language, Colonel Charles Callwell's *Small wars: their principles and practice*, first published by the British government in 1896 and currently in its sixth edition (Lincoln: University of Nebraska Press, 1996).

[16] See, for example, Capt. Hippolye-Victor Marceau, *Le Tirailleur soudanais* (Paris: Berger-Levrault, 1911), 2-3.

[17] Ditte, *Observations sur la guerre dans les colonies*, 53.

[18] Omissi, *The Sepoy and the Raj*, 29.

[19] Mangin, *La mission des troupes noires, compte-rendu fait devant le Comité de l'Afrique française* (Paris: Comité de l'Afrique française, 1911), 29.

[20] Thomas W. Dunlay, *Wolves for the Blue Soldiers: Indian scouts and auxiliaries with the United States Army, 1860-90* (Lincoln: University of Nebraska Press, 1982), 18.

[21] Wolseley, *The Story of a Soldier's Life*, Vol. II (New York: Charles Scribner's Sons, 1903), 288.

[22] Marceau, *Le Tirailleur soudanais*, 2-3.

[23] Ditte, *La guerre dans les colonies*, 52-53.

[24] Marceau, *Le Tirailleur soudanais*, 2.

[25] Quoted in I.H. Zulfo, *Karari: the Sudanese account of the battle of Omdurman* (London: Zed Press, 1980), 97.

[26] Omissi, *The Sepoy and the Raj*, 24; Sam C. Ukpabi, *The Origins of the Nigerian Army: a history of the West African Frontier Force (1897-1914)* (Zaria, Nigeria: Gaskiya Corporation, Ltd., 1987), 97.

[27] Georges Hardy, *Faidherbe* (Paris: Editions de l'Encyclopédie de l'Empire Français, 1947), 82.

[28] Michel, *Galliéni*, 109-110.

[29] Pasquier, *L'Organisation des troupes indigènes*, 64-65.

Officers in Charge of the French Navy Department during the Third Republic, 1870–1940

Jean Martinant de Préneuf

> In the early years of the Third Republic, the French Minister of Marine was almost always a senior serving officer, generally an admiral. As time passed, however, this tradition began to erode as civilians held the post with greater frequency, until by the mid-twentieth century the Minister of Marine was nearly always a civilian official. In this essay, Jean de Préneuf explains how and why this transformation took place, and what it suggests about the whole issue of civil-naval relations in a modern democracy.

From 1870 to 1917, half of the Ministers of Marine in France were naval officers. The appointment of military ministers became less frequent as the republic became more established. The appointment of an officer to oversee the Navy was a deliberate political strategy which evolved with the regime.

Until 1898, naval officers were appointed because they were supposed to be more competent. Politicians wanted to gain the political impartiality of a corps considered as hostile to the Republic and to keep the *Arche sainte* apart from political struggles. A study of service records shows that some military and even political skills were required to be an effective minister. But the powerlessness of the Navy during the Fachoda crisis, as well as the Navy's annoyance with the Radical's policy of secularization and republicanization ended this system. From 1898 to 1909, cabinets were composed exclusively of civilians because the Radicals were convinced that only a politician could successfully effect compliance with policies from naval officers.

The declining presence of professional officers raises the question of their influence on and within the government. The

---

Jean Martinant de Préneuf, agrégé in History, is deputy chief historian of the Research Department of the Naval Historical Service (*Service Historique de la Marine*) at Vincennes. He would like to thank R. Chalmers Hood for proofreading this essay.

parliamentary system, governmental instability and the administrative organization of the Navy Department were factors that served to limit officers' influence. That influence depended on contacts officers established during their careers with politicians, as well as the officer's experience with law making. Consequently, the concept of apolitical ministers is a myth. They were, in fact, involved in political struggles despite their presumed neutrality.

At least three times during the Third Republic, officers in charge of the War Department put the government in danger. In 1877 General de Rochebouët considered an attack against the Parliament.[1] In 1889, General Boulanger came close to crossing the Rubicon by following supporters who advised him to march on the presidential palace.[2] General André was personally implicated in the "Fiches" scandal at the beginning of the century when, as war minister of the radical anticlerical Combes cabinet, he initiated a registration system of religious and political opinions of officers in order to get rid of conservative elements in the army.[3] Despite those painful but rare episodes,[4] the Republic did not hesitate to entrust the management of the Navy and the Army to military officers.[5] The fifty-six officers appointed as ministers represent the second most common group in those cabinets, just behind lawyers.[6] From Admiral Fourichon in September 1870 to Admiral Darlan in June 1940, no fewer than nineteen different officers were in charge of the Navy. It is also possible to add the textile businessman Barbey, and the state attorney (*conseiller d'Etat*) Gougeard, both of whom were former naval officers.

This presence of officers was not consistent over time. As the Republic became stronger, officers were less frequently appointed as ministers, as the following tables show.

Naval Officers in Charge of the Navy Department 1870-1940

1. 1871-1883 Naval Officer Monopoly

1870-1871	Fourichon I
1871-1873	Pothuau I-II
1873-1874	Dompierre d'Hornoy I-II
1874-1876	De Montaignac de Chauvance I-II
1876	Fourichon II
1876-1877	Roussin I
1877	Gicquel des Touches
1877	Roussin II
1877-1879	Pothuau III
1879-1880	Jauréguiberry I-II
1880-1881	Cloué
1881-1882	Gougeard
1882-1883	Jauréguiberry III-IV

2. 1883-1898 Alternation Between Civilians and Officers

1884-1885	Peyron
1885-1886	Galiber
1886-1887	Aube
1888-1889	Krantz I
1889	Jaurès
1889	Krantz II
1893	Rieunier
1893-1894	Lefèvre
1895	Besnard I
1896-1898	Besnard II

3. 1898-1940 Civilians Predominate

1909-1911	Boué de Lapeyrère
1915-1917	Lacaze I
1917	Lacaze II
1940	Darlan

From 1870 to 1881 (1883 if we consider Gougeard an officer), the Navy department remained the exclusive territory of admiral-ministers. From 1883 to 1898, an almost regular alternation between civilians and officers was evident. Finally, from 1898 to

1940, the appointment of an officer to *rue Royale* became exceptional with only three officer ministers in forty-two years (Boué de Lapeyrère, Lacaze, and Darlan).[7] These last two were appointed during wars, in circumstances where normal political rules were not applied.

This strong but declining presence of officers originated from the complex relationship between the Republic and the Navy, in particular with the officer corps.[8] The appointment of an officer or a civilian to lead the *Royale* was dictated by a deliberate political strategy which evolved with the regime. What was the political influence of those military ministers? This question begs three more: Why were officers appointed to run the Navy? What was their professional political profile? What was the institutional context for their leadership?[9]

The use of officers to run military departments had its roots in a long political tradition which originated at the beginning of the century. The Third Republic followed the example of monarchies. The republican monarch assumed the *Imperium*. According to this concept, it was not necessary to appoint a politician to lead military departments.[10]

This tradition fit in well with the reason commonly invoked to justify the use of soldiers: the presumed competence attributed to naval officers.[11] According to this view, only specialists were in a position to run technical departments. Jules Simon, prime minister from December 1876 to May 1877, explained this view to the deputies a *propos* the appointment of Admiral Fourichon: "It is necessary to have been a good sailor to be a good minister of the Navy, to have been a good soldier to be a good minister of War, to have been a good engineer to be a good minister of Public Works."[12]

However, this way of thinking did not last very long. If everyone agreed on the technical competence of the minister-admirals during the first years following the defeat of 1870, as early as 1879, the sponsor of the Navy budget, Eugène Lamy, criticized the poor standard of the *Royale* and the choice of the naval officers who had run the department for the previous nine years.[13] The Fachoda crisis revealed the weakness of the French Navy and destroyed the already weakened trust of the politicians in the professional competence of naval officers.[14]

But competence was never the only criteria in the choice of an officer. The use of military officers in the Cabinet was also determined by political motivations. Politicians had always been eager to make sure of the political loyalty and neutrality of their Minister of Marine. French politicians remembered the Bonapartist *coup d'Etat* in 1851, and after 1889 they wanted to avoid a second one with a new General Boulanger.[15]

In the early years of the Third Republic, naval officers were part of the conservative cabinets which ruled the country until 1877. Politicians like Thiers and de Broglie trusted those men who more or less shared their political ideas. (Fourichon and Pothuau ,who were former Orleanists joined the *centre gauche* when they were elected senator. Dompierre d'Hornoy was a convinced legitimist and Montaignac de Chauvance was royalist too.)[16] "The Navy has to sacrifice itself on the sacred altar of *la Patrie!*" said admiral Pothuau when he addressed the House to present his budget for 1872. He got tremendous applause from the deputies elected in February 1871 by a population that aspired above all to peace after a bloody defeat.[17]

Conversely, moderate republicans called *Opportunistes* who led later cabinets included few political supporters among senior officers.[18] Those pragmatic politicians wanted to strengthen the republican regime safely. Appointing an officer rather than a civilian was first of all a political message sent to other officers. Essentially it was saying: "We respect your independence, so respect the independence of civil power." Among the eleven naval officers appointed to the government from 1879 to 1898, no fewer than eight served in the Government of National Defense armies during the war of 1870-71.[19] Some of them were certainly not fervent supporters of the opportunists. But that experience was regarded by the moderate republicans as a proof of their impartiality.

This decision was sound. In a country still deeply injured by the terrible defeat of 1870,[20] calling an officer to the government also sent a political message to the citizens. Navy officers who had fought with the army during the Franco-Prussian War were popular, and five of the ministers—Montaignac de Chauvance, Jauréguiberry, Pothuau, Dompierre d'Hornoy, and Fourichon—had been elected as Deputies in February, 1871.[21] Their appointment was expected to show the French people the cabinet's commitment to keep the *Arche sainte* apart from the political struggle.[22] For instance, Admiral Jauréguiberry's appointment was a sound idea for three reasons: he was appreciated for his military skills by the officer corps, he was popular throughout the country, and his political loyalty had already been tested.[23]

The selection of officers as ministers was based on the candidate's name and his ideas. The first President, Marshall de Mac-Mahon chose men who were regarded as the sailors' representative; after 1879, prime ministers needed men who shared their political ideas. Generally, men were not chosen for their seniority, though all of them were rear admirals or vice admirals except captain Gougeard.[24]

Their personal files usually reveal complete and brilliant service records. This is not really a surprise for men who reached the top of the hierarchy. The files show that there was no single prerequisite skill for becoming a minister. Admiral Gicquel des Touches, in charge of the Navy Department in the monarchist cabinet of the Duke de Broglie in 1877, is a good example. He had a competent record but not an outstanding one. He had always showed his loathing for parliament, even in public. He was appointed because of direct and decisive intervention by the president of the Republic, Marshall de Mac-Mahon along with de Broglie. Mac-Mahon had appreciated this monarchist and clerical sailor in Algeria in 1868-1869, then in Lorient in 1873 when Gicquel des Touches received him very warmly as port commander.[25]

Despite this example, certain military duties seem to have been especially helpful for ministerial candidates. Jobs such as aide-de-camp or principal private secretary of the minister, chief of staff or governor of a colony were good launching pads to ministerial responsibilities. Succeeding at diplomatic missions sometimes entrusted to naval officers was also a good way to draw attention of a future president of the council.[26]

Finally, officers choosen to join a cabinet were those who had become accustomed to working with politicians during their careers in the Navy. But, one often needed more to become a minister. To circulate for a long time in political circles within parliament or the salons was often decisive.[27] As long as the officers were authorized to be elected to parliament, most of the secretaries of state for the Navy, essentially Vice Ministers of Marine were former deputies or senators. They were appreciated by politicians because their political ideas were well-known and they were used to the law making process. Captain Gougeard, Admirals Jaurès, Aube, and Jauréguiberry were all regular visitors of the Juliette Adam's Salon, a circle very popular among Republican leaders like Gambetta or Ferry.[28]

Admiral Jauréguiberry had all the necessary qualifications. A former governor of Senegal, he was supported by the colonial lobby; as member of the French Protestant church council, he was an influential personality among high Protestant society; and last but not least, he was elected deputy in 1871 and senator for life in 1879.[29]

Things changed with the Dreyfus Affair and the nationalist unrest at the turn of the century. Radical-socialist governments mistrusted the officer corps which they judged hostile to their policy of secularization and republicanization. Indeed, during the radical leadership from 1898 to 1909, no naval officers were appointed to *rue Royale*. The leftist politicians believed that only a civilian could impose these objectives on the Navy.[30] Lockroy, De Lanessan and Delcassé's actions strongly contrast with their military predecessor's inability to reform the Navy during the 1890s. This difference had its roots in the political evolution of the republican regime and the institutional context. Naval officers were at a disadvantage compared to politicians.

Naval officers who were called upon to head the navy might have seemed powerful. In fact however, the in-fighting at both *la Royale* and in the Parliament significantly limited their power. Until the beginning of the twentieth century, control of promotions, authority to make technical and strategic decisions, and the control of spending largely bypassed the minister.[31] Until 1902, this organization of the central administration led to a "substantial weakening of the Secretary of State's power."[32] Flanked by a powerful chief of staff, admiral ministers had also to take into account advices given by committees of the Navy.[33] In the eyes of their former comrades, military ministers still remained members of their corps, a sort of fleeting *primar inter pares*. It was difficult for them to not follow their colleagues' decisions because they needed to keep the support of the top ranking officers. The only room for maneuver was to capitalize on the deep divisions which existed between admirals over naval topics. But it was a dangerous game for men in this position because some of them returned to the fleet.

In 1894, the Minister of Marine lost control of civil administration in the colonies when the parliament established the colonial ministry ruled by civilians. This loss of influence was almost certainly related to the rise of colonial lobbies led by politicians and businessmen. Some of them, such as Félix Faure and de Lanessan, were Ministers of Marine. A time of military conquest was giving way to an era of civil administration.[34]

Having lost their administrative control of the colonies, the Ministers of Marine were also unable to retain their authority over *troupes de marine* who served there. However, officers who were still looking for new bases where French ships could call played a leading role in renewing colonial conquest.[35] But times had changed. Colonization expanded into the interior and there were not enough Marines to defend this huge colonial empire. The Minister of Marine asked for troops from the War Department and gradually had to hand over colonial leadership. In Madagascar, for instance, where the conquest had begun in 1885 by sailors, the Army took control ten years later.[36] Moreover, several bills proposed by members of Parliament close to the colonial lobby aimed to separate *troupes de marine* from the Navy in order to create a Colonial Army. At the end of a long process, by the law of 7 July 1900, the navy handed over its colonial troops to the War Department.[37] Only with many difficulties, did the Minister of Marine manage to retain control of the harbor and navy yards defenses throughout the empire. Thus, at the beginning of the century, the traditional colonial power of the navy disappeared at the very moment France achieved the conquest of the second largest empire in the world. Thereafter, the political influence of the Minister of Marine was diminished.

Restricted to administrative issues, a Minister's powers remained more theoretical than real for military questions except in the cases of Admirals Lacaze and Darlan during the World Wars. At the beginning of the Republic, the Minister was considered Commander in Chief of the fleet, but because of the lack of modern communications, the squadron commanders were actually largely independent. As the minister was busy with the civil administration of his department, he was not able to prepare efficiently for war. So, in 1902, de Lanessan, a Radical Party civilian serving as Minister of Marine, limited the authority of Navy Chief of Staff just to war planning. This reform, which took administrative oversight of the Department away from the Chief of Staff, actually strengthened the Minister's powers by relieving him of strictly military matters. Henceforth, the Minister of Marine became an administrator rather than a military leader. Increasingly, the Navy needed experts able to defend projects before the Parliament. In this political system, executive power was weak and parliamentary committees waxed more powerful until 1917. Ministers had to compromise with the Navy and Budget committees which refused to vote credits for multi-year naval programs for the same reasons as in the United States and Britain.[38]

Under such conditions, the influence of these admiral-ministers was limited because of governmental instability.[39] Nevertheless, the subject remained tied up in political quarrels. In the long term, the conflicting decisions which demonstrate that these men were associated with government policy, proves that the political neutrality of these admiral-ministers is a myth. Two examples will suffice. Admirals Pothuau and Galiber generally tried to stop colonial expansion in order to increase spending on coastal defenses in European France. By contrast, Admirals Jauréguiberry, Montaignac de Chauvance, and Rieunier wanted to make the Navy an instrument of colonization. As for ship construction, Admirals Gougeard and Besnard were fervent supporters of the *Jeune Ecole*, while Admirals Lacaze, Darlan, and Boué de Lapeyrère preferred to give priority to battleships.⁴⁰ Each of them had a fairly profound political influence. Success depended on their ability to win parliamentary votes, forcing each of them into an uncomfortable position, sandwiched between Deputies in Parliament and the admirals in the fleet. The debate was unequal because experienced and savvy politicians such as Gambetta, Ferry, and Clemenceau faced naval officers who were mere amateurs at the political game. The officer's arguments for or against the small ship theories of the *Jeune Ecole* were ignored by the politicians.⁴¹ Moreover, the officer's attempts to keep the colonies under the Ministry of Marine were in vain, losing out to the Parliamentary Committee members who were lobbying for an independent colonial administration and colonial army. On the other side, the admiral-ministers were not effective as administrative reformers of the Navy because of their proximity to, indeed membership in, the career officer corps.

The experience of Admiral Boué de Lapeyrère is typical. He was in charge of the navy from July 1909 to November 1910. As a follower of Mahan and one of the fathers of French rearmament before World War I, he was convinced of the need to build dreadnoughts. One month before he became Minister of Marine, he supported an unrealistic naval construction project for forty-five battleships. Then, awkwardly and tactlessly, he asked Parliament for more than 30 billion francs. Despite this attempt to woo the Deputies, who remained reluctant to vote multi-year credits, he was defeated and Prime Minister Aristide Briand, the pragmatic politician who understood parliamentary power, refused to support him. Two years later, Delcassé, a centrist politician and former Minister of Foreign Affairs, who likewise understood law-making and political alliances, managed to get the votes for a program of twenty-eight battleships. Poincaré, the next Prime Minister, supported this influential deputy.⁴²

In the complex French parliamentary system, military officers were gradually excluded from ministerial positions except during wartime. In the history of the Third Republic, civilians such as de Lanessan, Delcassé, and Leygues contributed more to the Navy's modernization than the military ministers could have achieved. To effectively oversee this vast department, a politician well aware of naval matters and capable of defending his projects within Parliament was more useful an officer. The Third Republic, now more widely accepted by the public than at the time of its inception, no longer needed to appoint admirals from *rue Royale* as proof of professional skill or as a guarantee of naval officers' political support. As said Georges Clemenceau, who led France to victory in 1918: "War has became a too serious business to be handed over to military officers."[43]

NOTES

[1]Fresnette Pisani-Ferry, *Le coup d'Etat manqué du 16 mai 1877*, 1965 and Benoît Yvert (ed.), *Dictionnaire des ministres (1789–1989)*, (Paris: Perrin, 1990), 598.

[2]Philippe Levillain, *Boulanger, fossoyeur de la Monarchie*, (Paris: Flammarion, 1982).

[3]François Vinde, *L'Affaire des Fiches 1900–1904, chronique d'un scandale*, (Paris: Editions universitaires, 1989).

[4]In the long term, the pronunciamento temptation does not appear among the traditions of either the French Navy or the French Army. There is no doubt on that point for French and foreign scholarship alike. The most recent synthesis about French historiography on the issue is, "L'histoire politique des armées et des militaires dans la France Républicaine (1871–1996): essai d'historiographie," by Olivier Forcade, in *Jean Jaurès. Cahiers trimestriels*, 142 (1996), 7-24. For Anglo-Saxon interpretations, look at G. Chapman, "France: The French Army and Politics," in *Soldiers and Governments. Nine Studies in Civil-Military Relations*, M. Howard (ed.), (Bloomington: Indiana University Press, 1957), 51–72; David B. Ralston, *The Army of the Republic. The Place of the Military in the Political Evolution of France, 1871–1914*, (Cambridge, Mass.: MIT Press, 1967); A. Horne, *The French Army in Politics, 1870–1970*, (London: Macmillan Press, 1984), Klaus-Jûrgen Müller (ed.), *The Military in Politics and Society in France and Germany in the Twentieth Century*, (Oxford-Washington DC: Berg Publishers Ltd., 1995).

[5]From 1870 to 1940, fifty-five of the 635 ministers were generals or admirals. Mattei Dogan, "Les officiers dans la carrière politique (du maréchal de Mac-Mahon au général de Gaulle)," *Revue française de sociologie*, II (1961), 2:89.

[6]Jean Estebe, "Prosoprographie des militaires ministres sous la Troisième République," in *Militaires en République 1871–1962; Les officiers, la pouvoir et la vie publique en France*, Olivier Forcade, Eric Duhamel and Philippe Vial (eds.), (Paris: Publications de la Sorbonne, 1999), 199. For more details, have a look at his Ph.D.dissertation, entitled *Les ministres de la République 1871–1914*, (University of Toulouse le Mirail, 1978), 3 vols.

[7]Estebe, "Prosoprographie des militaires," 202.

[8]This issue is still little studied unlike the relationship with Army officers with a few exceptions, such as the pioneering work of R. Chalmers Hood, published as *Royal Republicans. The French Naval Dynasties Between the World Wars*, (Baton Rouge-London: Louisiana State University Press, 1985).

[9]Roland Drago, "Le chef des armées de la Troisième à la Cinquième République," *Militaires en République 1870–1962*, 45-51.

[10]Serge Berstein, "Les militaires ministres de la guerre," *Militaires en République 1870–1962*, 211.

[11]Journal officiel. Débats. Assemblée nationale. 10.11.1875. Quoted by Roland d'Ornano, *Gouvernement et haut-commandement en régime parlementaire français 1814–1914*, (Aix-en-Provence: La Pensée universitaire, 1958), 107.
[12]Quoted by Philippe Masson, *Histoire de la Marine*, vol. II *De la vapeur à l'atome*, (Paris-Limoges, Lavauzelle, 1983), 151–152.
[13]Renée Masson, *La Marine française lors de la crise de Fachoda 1898–1899*, (M.A. dissertation, University of Panthéon-Sorbonne, 1955); Edouard Lockroy, Minister of Marine, *La défense navale*, (Paris, 1900); Thierry Billard, *Félix Faure* (Paris: Julliard, 1995), 888; Jean-Charles Jauffret, "The Army and the Appel au soldat," *Nationhood and Nationalism in France from Boulangism to the Great War*, Robert Tombs (ed.), (London: Harper-Collins, 1991).
[14]Jean-Charles Jauffret, "The Army and the Appel au soldat," *Nationhood and Nationalism in France from Boulangism to the Great War*, Robert Tombs (ed.), (London, Harper&Collins, 1991).
[15]Alain Corbin et Jean-Marie Mayeur, *Les immortels du Sénat 1875–1918. Les cent seize inamovibles de la Troisième République*, (Paris: Publications de la Sorbonne, 1995).
[16]Alfred Barbou, *L'amiral Pothuau*, (Paris: Jouvet, 1882).
[17]François Bédarida, "L'armée et la République: les opinion politiques des officiers français en 1876–1877," *Revue historique*, 232 (1964): 119–164.
[18]Jérôme Grévy, *La République des oppportunistes 1870–1885*, (Paris: Perrin, 1998), 29–48; Jauréguiberry, Gougeard, Aube, Krantz, Jaurès, Rieunier, Lefèvre and Besnard. Jean-Paul Bertaud and William Serman, *Nouvelle histoire militaire de la France 1879–1919*, (Paris: Fayard, 1998), 610.
[19]For example, admiral Rieunier was Minister of Marine from January to November 1893. He was elected deputy of Charente-Inférieure in 1898 and sat in Parliament with the liberal nationalists and strongly criticized the republican government. Etienne Taillemite, *Dictionnaire des marins français*, (Paris: Editions Maritimes et d'Outre-Mer, 1982), 289–290; Estebe,"Militaires ministres," 209.
[20]Stéphane Audouin-Rouzeau et Jean-Jacques Becker, *la France, la nation, la guerre: 1850–1920*, (Paris: Sedes, 1995), 387.
[21]Taillemite, *Dictionnaire des marins*. Twenty-nine officers in activity were elected as deputy in 1871. Jean-Paul Charnay, *Société militaire et suffrage politique en France depuis 1789*, (Paris: SEVPEN, 1964), 107.
[22]Raoul Girardet, *La société militaire dans la France contemporaine (1815–1939)*, (Paris: Plon, 1952). Reed, *La société militaire de 1815 à nos jours* (Paris: Perrin, 1998), 121–144.
[23]Noël Kerbourc'h, *Marine et opérations terrestres. L'exemple de la guerre franco-allemande de 1870–1871. Quand l'armée de mer devient armée de terre* (Ph.D. diss., Université de Paris IV, 1995); Jérôme Grévy, *République des Opportunistes*, 124; Vincent Sciama, *L'action politique de Charles de Freycinet "Scientifique de la politique" (1848–1886,*(Master's thesis, University of Paris I Panthéon-Sorbonne, 1998); Henri Wesseling, *Le partage de l'Afrique 1880–1914*, (Paris, Denoël, 1996), 25 and 243–244.
[24]François Roth, "Mac-Mahon, le maréchal-président 24 mai 1873–30 janvier 1879," *Militaires en République 1870–1962*, 115.
[25]Admiral Gicquel des Touches, *Journal, vol.X : Le cabinet du 16 mai 1877*, Family archives, 9; Gisquel des Touches, *Journal*, 4.
[26]One of the best examples is given by Admiral Jaurès, Minister of Marine from February to March 1889. This officer had all skills needed to be a minister: he fought brilliantly in the Gambetta's armies in 1870–1871, he had been elected deputy of the Tarn in July 1871 and reelected in 1875 as conservative republican. Jean Jaurès' uncle, he was a regular visitor of republican circles like Juliette Adam's salon. He sat within the Left when he was elected senator for life in December 1875. Commander in chief of the training squadron, he was known for his diplomatic flair during a mission in Eastern Mediterranean in 1876. He had been appointed ambassador in Madrid (1878) then in Saint-Petersburg (1882). Boudon, *Immortels du Sénat*, 356–358. Taillemite, *Dictionnaire des marins français*, 170–171.
[27]Estèbe, "Prosoprographie des militaires," 208.

28After the July 1872 law which prohibited active duty military men from voting, the October 1875 law determined eligibility for Deputies. But, some officers remained in the *Sénat* because, between 1875 and 1884, twenty-eight military men were allowed to be elected senator for life. Nine of them were naval officers, retired or on active duty (Jaurès, Jauréguiberry, Pothuau, Fourichon, Montaignac de Chauvance, Frébaut, Peyron, Galiber). Their election was often a political reward after governmental responsibilities, sometimes a step toward the Secretary of State for Navy. Jacques-Olivier Boudon, "L'Armée au Sénat," *Immortels du Sénat*, 99-111. The traditional use of military ministers ends at the turn of the century—it is certainly not unrelated to the progressive extinction of parliamentary officers. Boudon, *Immortels du Sénat*, 111; Grévy, *République des oppportunistes*. Saad Marcos, *Juliette Adam*, (Cairo: Dar al Maaref, 1961).

29Jacques-Olivier Boudon, "Jauréguiberry Bernard 1815-1887," *Immortels du Sénat*, 353-356.

30Camille Pelletan, Minister of Marine from 1902 to 1905, represents a sort of caricature of this attitude. Paul Baquiat, *Une dynastie de la bourgeoisie républicaine. Les Pelletan*, (Ph.D. diss., University of Paris IV-Sorbonne, 1995).

31Jean-Paul Redon, *l'évolution de l'organisation centrale du ministre de la marine de Malouet à Lanessan (1814-1902), à travers les textes règlementaires (odonnances, décrets, arrêtés ministériels, etc)*, (Master's thesis, University of Paris I Panthéon-Sorbonne, 1989), 1:84-254.

32Jean-Louis de Lanessan, "Rapport au président de la République," *Bulletin officiel de la marine*, I (1902): 198.

33Service historique de la Marine, *Historique des fonctions de Chef d'Etat-major de la Marine*, (Vincennes: SHM, 1992), 1-9; Serman, *Nouvelle histoire militaire*, 613.

34François Bergé, *Le Sous-secrétariat et les sous-secrétaires d'Etat aux colonies: Histoire de l'émancipation de l'administration coloniale*, (Paris: Société française d'histoire d'Outre-Mer, 1962); Charles-Robert Ageron, *France coloniale ou parti colonial?*, (Paris: PUF, 1978); For Jean Louis de lanessan, former governor of Indochina and future Minister of Marine from 1900 to 1902, "Il ne faut surtout jamais confier à l'autorité militaire la direction des affaires d'aucune colonie," *principes de colonisation*, (Paris: Alcan, 1897), 151.

35 Jacques Thobie, "La France coloniale de 1870 à 1914," in Gibert Meynier and Jacques Thobie (ed.), *Histoire coloniale de la France*, vol. II *L'apogée 1871-1931*, (Paris: Armand Colin, 1991), 19-30.

36Bruno Buchet, *L'expédition française à Madagascar en 1895*, (Master's thesis, University Paris IV-Sorbonne, 1986), 20-21.

37Jeauffret, *Parlement, gouvernement, commandement: l'armée de métier sous la Toirisème République 1871-1914*, (Ph.D. diss., University of Paris I Panthéon-Sorbonne, 1987), Vincennes: SHAT, 1987, 651-931.

38Bertraand Gérard, *L'organisation de l'administration centrale de la marine au vingtième siècle*, (Vincennes: SHM, 1991), 29; Jauffret, *Parlement, gouvernement, commandment*, 14; Bock, *Un parlementarisme de guerre. Recherches sur le fonctionnement de la Troisième République pendant la Grande Guere*, (Ph.D. diss., Institute for Policy Studies of Paris, 1998); Hood, *Royal Republicans*, 128-147; Masson, *Histoire de la Marine*, 166-167.

39No fewer than fifty-four cabinets succeeded from February 1871 to August 1914. Jacques Ollé-Laprune, *La stabilité des ministères sous la Troisième République 1870-1940*, (Paris, LGDJ, 1962).

40Théodore Ropp, *The Development of a Modern Navy: French Naval Policy 1871-1914*, (Annapolis: Naval Institute Press, 1987); Stephen S. Roberts (ed.), 155-201 and 254-280.

41Masson, *Histoire de la Marine*, 166, 180-182.

42Masson, *Histoire de la Marine*, 215.

43Jean-Baptiste Duroselle, *Clemenceau*, (Paris: Fayard, 1988).

Colbert's Legacy: The French Navy and Her Inheritors in the Early 20th Century

R. Chalmers Hood
with Phillippe Vial

> The following commentary was presented at the Fourteenth Naval History Symposium in response to the foregoing papers by Bruce Vandervort and Jean Martinet de Préneuf. In these remarks, R. Chalmers Hood offers a brief introduction to some of the broader issues they raise, and attempts to show how their work is likely to contribute to a new consideration of French naval history.

In the battles for power and influence at Versailles, Louis XIV, the *roi de soliel*, divided up France between two great families of the new nobility of the robe. To Louvois he gave control of the army, which had been engaged for years in expanding France's frontier to the Rhine and into the Low Countries. To Louvois's rival, Colbert, the king gave authority over everything from the high water mark on the French coast out beyond the seas to encompass the French speaking world. The French still call this "*La France d'outre-mer,*" or France overseas. This meant that in addition to serving as Minister of the Navy, Colbert was responsible for the colonies, the colonial army, the merchant navy, the fishing fleet, and even the consulates which were traditionally staffed by admirals rather than diplomats. For Americans, shadows of Colbert's legacy can be seen in the French military cemetery at Yorktown and at the crest of the Appalachian Mountains where, near a place called Fort Necessity, a force of French Marines helped defeat the British General Braddock and his colonial ally George Washington, during the French and Indian War. On a mountain peak three quarters of a mile above sea level, a huge obelisk now marks the spot where French Marines killed Braddock, a very high water

Chalmers Hood is an independent research scholar who lives in Woodbridge, Virginia. Phillippe Vial is Chief Historian at the *Service Historique de la Marine*.

mark for the French Navy and the empire which Colbert helped to create.

France continued on her unique path at sea and *d'outre mer* well into the twentieth century. Though arriving at the same point as her friends and opponents, it is this other way taken by the Navy sometimes called *La Royale* which is the subject of the research being conducted by both Bruce Vandervort and Jean Martinant de Préneuf. Both have chosen to study military organizations by examining what those organizations do during the ninety-nine percent of the time that they are not engaged in combat operations. While naval history has most often focused either on battles (such as, for example, Mahan) or on the study of technology these two authors instead focus on the behavior of naval leaders in peacetime, thereby implying (at least) that to know the mind of the sailor is to know how he will behave in battle.

Vandervort's study builds upon the work concerning French colonial policy first broached some years ago by Henri Brunschwig in his *French Colonialism, 1871-1914: Myths and Realities* (New York: Praeger, 1964) and Raymond F. Betts in *Assimilation and Association in French Colonial Theory, 1890-1914* (New York: AMS Press, 1960) by exploring the unique patterns developed by the French colonial army for recruiting men into native infantry regiments. Until the passage of a 1902 reorganization law, the responsibility of the colonial army remained as envisioned by Colbert: that is, as subordinate to the Ministry of Marine. While the core of this overseas French army was made up of Europeans who had settled in the colonies, wartime expansion was possible only by tapping native manpower reserves. As with other European colonial powers, habits which evolved over time guided recruiters toward certain tribes or nationalities that seemed to adapt more easily to the military life. In the case of France, the colonial army included Vietnamese, Pacific islanders, Caribbean "Indians," Moroccans, Tunisians, and most significantly, large numbers of Saharan natives who were collectively identified as "Senegalese."

Vandervort takes the Betts-Brunschwig argument about how well France did in its relations with her colonial subjects, and applies it to the huge effort of recruiting upwards of 200,000 men who fought in the European trenches during the First World War. Which tribes should be approached, and why? What he discovered was that French colonial army generals and recruiters had very specific preferences, finding some groups far better suited (in their view at least) for the military than others. In his study he uncovers a mix of feelings about these preferences varying from the very practical Generals Mangin and Gallieni whose opinions were formed during small colonial campaigns, to the more theoretical arguments of other recruiters who reflected the popular Social Darwinism of the day.

In his paper, Jean Martinant de Préneuf undertakes the kind of work that Gordon Craig pursued in his popular and influential *Politics of the Prussian Army, 1640-1945* (Oxford: Clarendon Press, 1955). De Préneuf explains the evolution of civilian control of the French Navy, which by comparison with other western democracies came fairly late. He suggests that under the Third Republic (which was established only because there was less opposition to a republic than to a monarchy), it was important for the civilian politicians to include career military officers in the cabinet in order to ensure the support of the army and navy. The pattern of selecting an admiral as Minister of Marine, along with the other jobs inherited from Colbert, dates from the early nineteenth century and continued until 1940. It was only in the early twentieth century that French governments turned more often to civilians to fill this cabinet position—Admirals Lacaze and Darlan during the two world wars being the last two (and very notable) exceptions to this rule.

De Préneuf has dug into private papers and memoirs to find the reasons behind the earlier preference for appointing admirals to these political jobs and to determine why change came so slowly. Throughout the nineteenth century, a number of cabinet positions were regarded as "technical" ministries, best left to management by experts. These included the national highway department (or *Pont Chausees*), the Army, and the Navy. At the close of the nineteenth century, however, several unforeseen political incidents tested this theory and proved it wrong. The Navy's poor showing at the time of the Fashoda crisis, and the decade of repercussions that followed the painful Dreyfus Affair, made it clear that the two military ministries needed skilled politicians more than technical experts at the helm. For an American to understand the impact of Dreyfus on the French military, one needs to consider the emotional responses to Truman's order to integrate the armed forces or Clinton's efforts concerning gays in the military. There were even a few incidents during America's war in Vietnam, notably that of army doctor Howard Levy, that seemed to echo the antisemitic and secret evidence issues of the Dreyfus case, though none of them generated the kind of outcry that the Dreyfus case did in France.

Obviously, change had to be made carefully to avoid a rupture between the military caste and the French public. The term "caste" seems particularly suitable in this case. Again, since the days of Colbert, specific regions of the country had been set aside as exclusive recruiting territories for the Navy. Well into the twentieth century, the enlisted ranks were filled by men who came from these coastal zones, dividing their lives between the Navy and the merchant or fishing fleets. The same was true of the naval office corps which for centuries came predominately from six small regions in France, each the size on an American county. Slowly, during the first half of the twentieth century, this concentration was diminished, but significant change came only after 1945. As with other French institutions to which certain families attached themselves, the Navy was very much a world unto itself, quite isolated from the others because most of their lives were spent abroad or at sea rather than at home. It was only after World War II when, in an effort to integrate the military elite back into French society, that career military personnel received the right to vote.

Foreign friends and foes alike became concerned about the chance of another military coup in the tradition of General Boulanger and about the reliability of the French Navy, following the exposure of the secret Corvignole group within the army officer corps in 1934. During the 1930s when French civil-military relations reached a new low point, there were officers who looked at Franco and Mussolini as good role models, and while observers did not predict a coup in France, they did worry about what might happen in some future crisis. Some would argue that these dark fears came alive at Vichy, and indeed, the division within the officer corps between those who remained with Darlan at Vichy, and those who followed De Gaulle took years to repair and was not achieved until the 1980s with the retirement of the wartime generation of officers.

In the film *The Longest Day*, there is a scene that takes place on the eve of the Normandy landings in which the French Admiral Jaujard addresses his cruiser squadron over a loudspeaker. He explains how the rounds that they are about to fire represent the French Navy's return to the fight. In a metaphoric sense, the presence here of both Jean de Préneuf and his colleague Philippe Vial does much the same thing. They are part of a new generation of French historians who are interested in military and naval matters and who are anxious to join the international discussion of these issues. With the inclusion of their voices, along with those of others like Claude d'Abzac at the French military historical officers at Vincennes, and American scholars like Bruce Vandervort, the long-term benefit will be an international shift to a new emphasis on France's contribution to the art of war. This new work is likely to be less burdened by the baggage of old arguments and just as likely to be inter-disciplinary, combining social, political and diplomatic themes. It will be exciting and stimulating to explore this new chapter in French naval history.

Part III

The 19th Century U.S. Navy

"To Strike a Blow in the World that Shall Resound through the Universe": American Naval Operations and Options at the Start of the War of 1812

Jeff Seiken

> Particularly in terms of national acceptance, the War of 1812 marked a kind of coming out party for the United States Navy. In the first six months of that war, American warships won a number of signal victories over their British counterparts that boosted morale at home and led eventually to a dramatic naval expansion in the immediate post-war years. But in this essay, Jeff Seiken argues that despite these much-ballyhooed successes, American naval strategy in these first six months of war was flawed, and that the U.S. Navy missed "a brief but golden opportunity" to have a dramatic and disproportionate impact on the course of the war. In the process, he has a great deal to say about the historiography of the naval war as well, and alert readers should not overlook his thoughtful endnotes as well as the text.

Much of the recent scholarship on the War of 1812 has claimed to illuminate overlooked or forgotten aspects of the conflict. The opening phase of the war at sea, however, is one subject that has definitely not suffered from a lack of scholarly attention. Since the days of A. T. Mahan, naval historians have debated and dissected in detail the relative merits of the strategy adopted by American commodore John Rodgers at the outset of the conflict. Nonetheless, this subject deserves another look for two reasons: first to reassess Rodgers's motives for the actions he took at the start of the war; and second, to examine some of the other strategic options the U.S. Navy might have pursued early on in the conflict. Historians have generally viewed the first six months of the war as the high-water mark of the American naval effort on the high seas. Compared to what followed in 1813

Jeff Seiken is a Ph.D. candidate in military history at Ohio State University working on American naval policy and planning in the War of 1812. His research has been supported by a Rear Adm. John D. Hayes pre-doctoral fellowship from the Naval Historical Center.

and 1814, this is certainly true. But the U.S. Navy missed a brief but golden opportunity in the summer of 1812—an opportunity not only to inflict serious harm on the British but perhaps also in some small but still meaningful way to alter the course of the war.

Posterity has not been kind to Paul Hamilton, the congenial rice planter from South Carolina who served as the navy's civilian chief in 1812. His fondness for alcohol has long been a matter of the historical record.[1] More recently, his shortcomings as an administrator have been meticulously documented by Christopher McKee in his magisterial study of early navy's officer corps.[2] Yet, historians have said comparatively little about his most serious weakness—his inept performance as a strategist. He must bear at least part of the blame for the administration's failure to establish a naval force on the Great Lakes prior to the war. Hamilton and his counterpart in the War Department flirted briefly with the idea in April 1812 before dismissing it as impractical, a decision that would have disastrous consequences for the American invasion of Upper Canada.[3] Hamilton acted with scarcely more decisiveness, however, when it came to preparing for the onset of hostilities on the high seas. Although war had been in the offing for months, Hamilton as of May 1812 had yet to formulate even a preliminary plan of operations for the five frigates and seven smaller ships that constituted the whole of his bluewater fleet.[4] Given the great disparity in size between the contending navies, the most logical strategy for the Americans to follow was the *guerre de course*, the traditional recourse of the weaker fleet. But that still left the question of how the handful of ships at Hamilton's disposal should be deployed to best effect against British shipping. And that was the question that Hamilton seemed at a loss to answer as the administration's self-imposed deadline for war drew nearer.[5]

Towards the end of May, Hamilton finally roused himself from his strategic stupor and took the long overdue step of seeking the advice of his two senior officers afloat, John Rodgers and Stephen Decatur.[6] Each replied with detailed if somewhat different proposals for raiding British shipping in various quarters of the Atlantic.[7] Their recommendations, however, failed to produce any sort of conclusive determination on Hamilton's part. His only response was to direct Decatur's squadron to link up with Rodgers's division at New York.[8] The declaration of war on June 18 brought Hamilton no closer to a resolution on strategy. He granted Rodgers and Decatur limited permission to strike at any British cruisers near New York, provided they returned promptly to port. Otherwise, both were told to wait for more "extensive" instructions to come.[9] The promised orders eventually did materialize, but only after Treasury Secretary Albert Gallatin prodded Hamilton into action. At Gallatin's urging, Hamilton ordered the two commodores to take up station along the coast, where they were to cruise with their respective squadrons to protect returning American merchant vessels.[10] Hamilton issued these instructions on June 22, four full days after the official start of the conflict. But by then it was too late. Rodgers and Decatur had already sailed in company from New York with the frigates *President*, *United States*, and *Congress*, the brig *Argus*, and the sloop *Hornet*. And Hamilton's directive of the 18th notwithstanding, they would not be heard from again for more than two months.

Rodgers's and Decatur's decision to lead the bulk of the navy's active force on a lengthy cruise without authorization from the secretary was certainly a bold one. But more than that, it was a blatant act of insubordination and a potentially court-martialable offense. So why did they do it? To answer that question, it is necessary to back up and consider the general mindset of the officer corps on the eve of the war.

The five years preceding the War of 1812 were a trying time for the navy's senior officers. The *Chesapeake* affair in 1807 had left the service disgraced and humiliated, and, afterwards, the captains faced the additional ignominy of seeing most of the oceangoing warships consigned to ordinary while the government spent almost a million dollars on building more gunboats. Equally demoralizing was Congress's repeated refusal to authorize any new construction after 1808 despite the steady deterioration of relations with Great Britain. But the disappointment that cut deepest of all was the treatment the officers received at the hands of Congress on another matter, one that touched their personal lives as much as their professional identities. The issue in question was officer pay and benefits.

A number of years earlier, Navy Secretary Robert Smith had approached the legislature on his officers' behalf, seeking an increase in the salaries of midshipmen, lieutenants, and captains not on active service.[11] That effort failed, but during the winter of 1807–08, the group of officers assembled to sit on the court-martial of the *Chesapeake*'s commander decided to petition Congress again. This time, however, they requested much more extensive changes in the laws regulating their compensation. Among other provisions, their memorial asked for improvements in the supplemental pay of all officers as well as the awarding of pensions to the families of navy officers killed in battle.[12]

Ten officers signed the memorial, but it was John Rodgers who supplied most of the initiative behind the drafting of the document. As he explained to his wife in January 1808, he had long contemplated such a project and had merely been waiting for a favorable moment to make an overture to Congress.[13] His sense of timing, however, turned out to be less than astute. The navy's political stock in the wake of the *Chesapeake* affair could hardly have been lower, while the question of what to do about the latest assaults on the nation's neutral rights consumed most of the legislators' attention. In the end, a House committee reported a bill embodying the officers' requests, but it was tabled due to the press of other business. Worse was yet to come. Rodgers and the other officers renewed their petition over the winter of 1809–10, this time buttressed by the signatures of another forty or so members of the officer corps.[14] More delays followed, though, and the House did not get around to discussing the bill until February 1811. In the ensuing debate, every section was struck out, after which the House decided to postpone the bill indefinitely, effectively killing it.[15]

The rejection of their memorial was a bitter blow for the officers, but what rankled the most was the callous way Congress had dismissed their concerns about the welfare of their families.[16] Rodgers, whose wife had given birth to their second child in 1809, felt particularly betrayed by the outcome.[17] He had chosen to devote the whole of his adult life to the navy, he wrote to his wife in

1810, despite the financial hardship and numerous absences from home such service entailed. Yet, he now believed the navy "will never compensate me for such a personal sacrifice for its good." His own country, he maintained, was "a stranger to those feelings of gratitude which individual sacrifices have a claim to."[18] After the bill met its final death on the floor of the House, Rodgers's friend and fellow captain William Bainbridge took an equally bleak view of their situation. Since Congress appears unwilling to give us subsistence, Bainbridge wrote Rodgers, then we must either starve or attain it by our extra exertions. He was referring to the practice of officers going on furlough for the purpose of participating in private trading voyages overseas.[19] Bainbridge knew from personal experience that such commercial ventures could be profitable, and he was about to embark on another expedition himself.[20] But his words would assume an altogether different meaning once the war began.

The evidence is spotty, but from the scattered personal correspondence that survives it appears that the officer corps welcomed the onset of war with Great Britain. Armed conflict with Britain meant the opportunity to erase the stain of the *Chesapeake* incident and redeem the nation's tarnished honor. At the same time, war held out the sparkling prospects of winning fame, promotion and prize money—in other words, the realization of the officers' most cherished professional aspirations. The letters of Samuel R. Trevett, a surgeon in Decatur's squadron, vividly capture the mood of giddy excitement that gripped the navy as the war became imminent. "We are calculating to make our fortunes in a few weeks after war is declared and let the world know that I intend to make a sort of triumphant entry into Boston in a car more splendid than that which glitters over Neptune's *gate*," he predicted to one friend. A few days later, he informed another that "The fever of war and ambition burn here [in Virginia] with a force superior to a Norfolk sun and *yellow* fever." Everyone in the squadron was on tiptoe, ready to "strike a blow in the world that shall resound through the universe."[21] The only question was where.

As John Rodgers prepared to go to sea on June 20, he was not certain himself. A day earlier, he had suggested to Navy Secretary

Hamilton that his squadron in conjunction with Decatur's might surprise some of the enemy warships cruising offshore before the British learned of the declaration of war and could collect their scattered fleet.[22] But by the time Rodgers joined Decatur off Sandy Hook, the commodore had a different target in mind. He had received word of a large, lightly defended Jamaican convoy that was making its way homeward along the edge of the Gulf Stream to the southeast.[23] Here, indeed, was a chance to strike a blow that, if it did not resound through the universe, would at least reverberate through the corridors of Parliament and London's leading commercial houses. Equally important, here was an opportunity to snatch up perhaps dozens of heavily laden merchantmen and earn a small fortune in prize money. For Rodgers, whose wife was now expecting their third child, such a windfall would set up his growing family for good, pension or no pension. He confided his hopes in a last minute letter to his wife, written just as he and Decatur were getting underway on the 21st. "Between you and I my object at present is to make your circumstances such as I could wish them to be and this I hope to affect without any risk." He signed off with an injunction to be thankful that heaven "has not only afforded me an opportunity of breathing pure air but at the same time the prospect of making all those who are most dear to me comfortable for life."[24]

Rodgers could hardly have made his motives any clearer, and the considerations outlined above—his anger at Congress and his apprehensions about the financial future of his family—hold the key to understanding his behavior at the outset of the war. These two factors help explain not only his original determination to go after the Jamaican fleet, but also his far more questionable decision to defy his orders and leave the American station in pursuit of the convoy. Alas, the documentary record is silent on Decatur's side, but it seems safe to assume that he was a willing accomplice.[25] That the two commodores shared some of the same personal concerns can be seen in the unusual agreement they signed before sailing. They pledged to split all prize money for the duration of the war and to continue such payments to their widows in the case one or the other fell in battle.[26]

Rodgers and Decatur never did catch up to the convoy. Their combined squadron returned to Boston on August 31 riddled with scurvy and with only seven prizes to show for their ten weeks at sea. Rodgers acknowledged the disappointing outcome of the cruise. But he justified his conduct to the secretary by claiming that he had still accomplished an important strategic objective: "[O]ur being at Sea obliged the Enemy to concentrate a considerable portion of his most active force and thereby prevented his capturing an incalculable amount of American property that would otherwise have fallen a sacrifice."[27] Hamilton readily accepted this explanation and congratulated Rodgers on the success of his stratagem. President James Madison likewise commended Rodgers in his annual address to Congress in November 1812.[28] Most historians, taking their cue from Mahan's favorable verdict, have also been inclined to credit Rodgers with creating an effective diversion.[29]

But was this really part of Rodgers' plan? A careful review of his correspondence casts doubt on this interpretation. To be fair, in their earlier letters counseling Hamilton on strategy, both Rodgers and Decatur had mentioned that a policy of distant cruising would force the British to deploy a large number of naval vessels in the defense of their own trade. Yet, if Rodgers calculated that his pursuit of the convoy would "distract the enemy," as he later avowed, two things seem rather puzzling.[30] First, in his final communication to the secretary before leaving Sandy Hook on June 21, Rodgers briefly outlined his cruising plans but said nothing about trying to draw the British away from the coast.[31] Second, the initial dispatch he filed upon reaching Boston on August 31 was also silent on the subject.[32] Only in his follow-up report, written on September 1, did Rodgers make the assertion quoted above about his cruise being of great benefit to American commerce. By this time, though, he would have had ample opportunity to take stock of the public reaction to his lengthy absence. Throughout July and August, the whereabouts and fortunes of his squadron had been the subject of much speculation and rumor in the nation's newspapers.[33] But as the summer wore on and reports of American merchant losses mounted, this general discussion took a critical turn.³⁴ Writers in anti-administration papers lambasted the government for leaving the American seaboard and merchant fleet bereft of defense against marauding enemy warships. Ironically, most of the hostile commentators were careful to absolve Rodgers of any wrongdoing, explaining that he was no doubt simply following the administration's orders.³⁵ Towards the end of the summer, however, some critics began to aim their barbs in Rodgers's direction. The very day of his arrival in port, he was greeted by a pointed editorial in the Boston *Gazette* censuring him for foolishly exposing his force to destruction in a distant sea instead of cruising close to home where he might have done the most good.³⁶ Seen in this context, Rodgers's after-the-fact defense of his conduct looks more like an attempt at damage control than an honest accounting of his intentions.³⁷ That Hamilton and later Madison warmly praised him for his actions should also come as no surprise, for the administration would have been every bit as anxious to deflect criticism and put a positive spin on events.

Of course, it can still be argued that his cruise provided a great assist to returning American vessels regardless of what he actually intended. There is a fair amount of truth to this statement. The knowledge that Rodgers was at large and sailing in squadron strength did disrupt the plans of the commander of the Halifax station, Vice Adm. Herbert Sawyer, and his subordinate, Capt. Philip B. V. Broke. In early July, Sawyer sent Broke to sea with the sixty-four-gun ship-of-the-line *Africa* and three frigates, with orders to sweep the coast of American commerce and find Rodgers.³⁸ By the middle of the month, Broke had arrived off Sandy Hook, which he judged "a most advantageous position for the destruction of the Enemy's trade and for intercepting his Ships of War." But news that Rodgers had gone to the Grand Banks compelled Broke to abandon this cruising ground and speed northward. He ended up escorting a Jamaican convoy of about sixty sail to the edge of the Banks, a detour that led him far afield from the main American shipping lanes.³⁹ Broke expressed some of his frustration in a letter to the Admiralty on July 30. Since leaving the coast, he informed his superiors, he had seen few vessels and destroyed only two, "being studious whilst seeking Commodore Rogers [sic] to avoid separation in chase after single merchant ships."[40]

Broke's complaint offers compelling evidence that Rodgers did indeed render an essential service to the American merchant fleet. But it is important to note that the benefits were of limited duration.[41] In early August, Broke learned that his opponent had long since vacated the western Atlantic and so he felt free to disperse his own ships. By August 19, the frigates *Shannon* and *Aeolus* were returning to their former station off New York, while the *Belvidera* was also cruising in search of prizes.[42] Furthermore, even while Broke was busy scouring the seas in search of Rodgers, other British warships enjoyed basically free run of the American coast and racked up impressive numbers of captures. For instance, in the space of a single week in July, the brig *Emulous* grabbed eight merchant ships bound for New York or New England. Overall, the Royal Navy seized and sent into Halifax forty prizes in July and another forty-five in August, which represented the two highest totals for any single month of the war.[43] These figures should be used with caution, as a fair proportion of the vessels taken were either recaptures or privateers. Nonetheless, they demonstrate that the British were far from paralyzed by their efforts to track Rodgers down.

If the effects of Rodgers's cruise were less than they appeared to be, could the administration have made more efficient use of its naval assets by adopting a different strategy? Some students of the navy think so, and they have argued that the strategic dividends would have been much greater if Hamilton had dispatched ships individually, on distant commerce-raiding missions.[44] Advocates of independent cruising have often pointed to the spectacular victories registered by the *Constitution* and her sister frigate *United States* as proof of the superiority of such a strategy. This argument has merit, but it also overlooks several important considerations. First, had Hamilton scattered the navy to the winds in this fashion, returning American merchant ships would have been deprived of any protection whatsoever, leading to losses that might have totaled in the millions of dollars. Second, for solitary cruisers, the risks of being run down and captured by a superior force were not insubstantial. The brig *Nautilus* fell victim to Broke's squadron in the summer of 1812 and only skilful seamanship preserved the *Constitution* from a similar fate. Finally, while the early American victories at sea were indeed dramatic, one point needs to be remembered: from a strategic standpoint, these triumphs were largely barren of result. In fact, they were counterproductive, for even after a successful action, the victorious vessel had to cut short its cruise and return to port for a lengthy refit.[45]

If independent cruising was unlikely to produce the results its latter day advocates have claimed for it, perhaps Rodgers's original strategic instincts deserve a second look.

Rodgers's decision to sail in squadron strength in hopes of intercepting the Jamaican convoy was, in fact, a sound one. The destruction of a significant part of the convoy would have embarrassed the British government, created a panic among the London merchants, and probably stirred up immediate opposition to the war.[46] Where Rodgers erred was in choosing to continue pursuit of the convoy across the Atlantic. By doing so, he removed the most powerful elements of the American navy from the one theater where they could have done the most harm to the British. The Maritime Provinces of Canada were a critical hub in the commercial network linking North America, the Caribbean, and Great Britain. Between March and September of every year, large convoys from Britain and the West Indies sailed for Canada at the rate of one or two per month. The traffic in the opposite direction was equally heavy, with convoys departing from Halifax, Quebec, and New Brunswick at regular intervals beginning in early summer.[47] Finally, as Rodgers himself discovered, even those convoys bound from Jamaica directly to Britain looped close to the North American coast on the first leg of their journey before turning eastward.

Had Rodgers confined his cruising grounds to the stretch of water between the Grand Banks to the north and the Bay of Fundy to the south, he would have placed himself in an excellent position to intercept one or more of these convoys. None were heavily guarded, and some during the summer of 1812 were not even aware that a state of war existed between the United States and

Great Britain. This area also offered many other tempting targets such as captured American merchant vessels on their way to Halifax and small British cruisers on privateer patrol. Rodgers would have also stood a good chance of ambushing some of the heavier British warships as they straggled in ones and twos into Halifax from their winter rendezvous at Bermuda. Finally, Rodgers might have fallen in with one of the most valuable prizes of all: the troop and supply convoys that the British were sending to Quebec for the defense of Canada. David Porter in the frigate *Essex* managed to intercept one of these convoys carrying a battalion of Royal Scots from the West Indies. He captured a single transport loaded with 200 soldiers, but was obliged to let the rest pass unmolested. He afterwards lamented that he could have taken the entire convoy if there had been another American warship on hand to assist him.[48] Instead, the rest of the transports arrived safely at Quebec in mid-August, enabling British Lt. Gen. Sir George Prevost to rush desperately needed reinforcements to Upper Canada.[49]

Admittedly, such a strategy entailed some significant dangers. Not the least were the navigational hazards associated with the treacherous winds, currents, and coastline of the Maritimes.[50] Then there was always the chance that Rodgers's three frigates and two lesser rates might have met up with the 64-gun *Africa* and four frigates that formed Broke's command. The possibility of such an engagement must go down as one of the more intriguing what-ifs of the war. Yet, it is worth noting that the British squadron was by no means as powerful as it looked on paper. The *Africa* was a decrepit old war-horse of more than 30-years service and judged to be in such poor shape that she was sent back to England in the fall of 1812. Even if unable to avoid an encounter with Broke, Rodgers by crowding on more sail could have forced the British to give chase, thereby leaving the slow-sailing *Africa* far behind and improving the odds considerably in the event a battle did occur.[51]

Whatever the risks might have been, they were outweighed by the potential gains. At the very least, by taking up station in the sea-lanes around Canada, Rodgers would have seized the initiative at sea, forcing the British entirely onto the defensive. Rodgers's presence off the coast would have inhibited British efforts to protect their own shipping against American privateers while also denying the Royal Navy much of any opportunity to interdict American commerce. Destruction of one of the military convoys would have seriously compromised the defense of Canada, while loss of one of the merchant convoys might have turned British public opinion against the war at the outset. That none of these greater or lesser possibilities was realized can be attributed to the lack of strategic vision at the top. Neither Navy Secretary Paul Hamilton nor anyone else in the administration showed much appreciation for the range of options open to the navy at the beginning of the war. John Rodgers, too, must shoulder some of the blame. There was no more conscientious, professional, or dedicated officer than Rodgers in the entire service. Yet, his normally sound judgement failed him at a critical moment, costing him and the United States Navy the chance to strike a truly damaging and memorable blow.

NOTES

[1] See, for instance, Irving Brant, *James Madison: Commander in Chief, 1812–1836* (Indianapolis: Bobbs-Merrill, 1961), 125–26; John K. Mahon, *The War of 1812* (Gainsville, Fla.: University of Florida Press, 1972), 5; Frank L. Owsley, Jr., "Paul Hamilton," in *American Secretaries of the Navy*, Paolo Coletta, ed. (Annapolis: Naval Institute Press, 1980), I:93, 97.

[2] Christopher McKee, *A Gentlemanly and Honorable Profession: The Creation of the U.S. Naval Officer Corps, 1794–1815* (Annapolis: Naval Institute Press, 1991), 9–11. McKee believes that accounts of his alcoholism may have been exaggerated and that the real reason for his eventual removal from the cabinet was his slipshod management of the Navy Department. McKee is correct that Hamilton was guilty of many administrative lapses, but the true extent of the department's disorganization did not become apparent until *after* his departure. Furthermore, the specific complaints leveled against Hamilton as an administrator were hardly so serious as to account for the vehemence with which his critics in Congress demanded his resignation—or the vindictiveness they afterwards showed in rejecting his nomination to a minor government post in South Carolina. For details about some of the questionable contracts he awarded during his tenure as navy secretary, see the correspondence in SEN 13B-A1, A3, Record Group 46, (NA).

[3] For background on the American policy of disinterest regarding naval control of the Great Lakes before the War of 1812, see Jeff Seiken, "To Obtain Command of the Lakes: The United States and the Contest for Lakes Erie and Ontario, 1812-15," in *60 Year's War for the Great Lakes, 1754–1814*, David C. Skaggs and Larry L. Nelson, eds. (Lansing, Mich.: Michigan State University Press, forthcoming).

[4] According to the Navy Department's official list, the number of vessels in active service along the coast actually amounted to fourteen. However, at the time of the declaration of war, the ship *John Adams* was undergoing an extensive refit, while the sloop *Wasp* was absent in Europe on a diplomatic mission. See Paul Hamilton to the House of Representatives, December 3, 1811, *American State Papers, Class VI, Naval Affairs* (Washington: Gales and Seaton, 1834), I:83. (Hereafter

American Naval Operations at the Start of the War of 1812   143

referred to as *ASP:NA*.) Even the figure of five frigates being fit for service is misleading, as neither the *Constitution* nor the *Essex* was ready to sail at the war's outbreak.

[5] Peter Kastor maintains that the administration initially had no plans to deploy the navy in the event of war. Only after Congress declared a temporary embargo on foreign trade in early April 1812 did Madison experience a change-of-heart and decide to send the navy to sea. See Peter Kastor, "Toward 'The Maritime War Only': The Question of Naval Mobilization, 1811-1812," *The Journal of Military History*, 61 (July 1997): 455-480, especially 477-78. Kastor's argument however, is flatly contradicted by the documentary record. He obviously failed to consult either *Secretary of the Navy Letters to Officers, Ships of War*, Microfilm Series M-149, or *Captains Letters to the Secretary of the Navy*, Microfilm Series M-125.

[6] Hamilton to Rodgers, May 21, 1812, to Decatur, May 21, 1812, *Secretary of the Navy Letters to Officers, Ships of War*, Microfilm Series M-149, Record Group 45 (RG45), National Archives (NA). Both captains were currently patrolling the coast with the squadrons under their command. Because he waited until such an advanced date to write them, Hamilton was certain to have at most a handful of days to digest their advice before the war commenced. In fact, Decatur's letter reached the Secretary exactly one week prior to the declaration of war. See Hamilton to Decatur, June 11, 1812, ibid.

[7] Rodgers to Hamilton, June 3, 1812, Decatur to Hamilton, June 8, 1812, *Captains Letters to the Secretary of the Navy*, Microfilm Series M-125, RG45, NA. Much has been written about the contrasting nature of Rodgers's and Decatur's advice, but the differences were by no means as great as some historians have maintained. Decatur favored sending out American warships individually or in pairs, leaving it to the captains to choose their cruising grounds. In the body of his letter, though, he laid particular stress on the benefits of cruising in tandem. Rodgers's plan was more prescriptive. He suggested dispatching a squadron of two or three swift-sailing frigates plus a sloop to cruise off the British Isles. The remaining frigates, he thought, acting either independently or as a squadron, should be deployed to intercept shipping bound to and from British North America while the lighter vessels preyed on the enemy's West Indies commerce. Occasionally, the entire fleet might unite if a particularly valuable target presented itself, like an East Indies convoy.

[8] As of early June, Rodgers's squadron consisted of the frigates *President* and *Essex* and the sloop *Hornet*. Decatur's squadron was composed of the frigates *United States* and *Congress* and the brig *Argus*, although the latter had been temporarily detached. For the secretary's orders to rendezvous at New York, see Hamilton to Rodgers, June 5, 1812, to Decatur, June 5, 11, 1812, Letters Sent to Officers, RG45, NA.

[9] Hamilton to Rodgers, June 18, 1812, to Decatur, June 18, 1812, ibid. Hamilton was dilatory even in issuing these brief orders. As a result, his dispatch to Rodgers reached New York on the 21st, one day after the express from the War Department arrived in the city. It was from the latter source that Rodgers learned of the declaration of war. See Rodgers to Hamilton, June 21, 1812, Captains Letters, RG45, NA. Hamilton's tardiness in alerting his officers to the war news provoked an angry outburst about the secretary's incompetence from Lt. James Biddle. See James Biddle to H., June 27, 1812 [but misdated by archivist as 1813], James Biddle Papers, Historical Society of Pennsylvania (HSP). Biddle also vented his disgust to his father, who relayed his complaints to Pennsylvania Congressman Jonathan Roberts. See Charles Biddle to Roberts, June 27, 1812, Jonathan Roberts Papers, HSP. Roberts was part of the Congressional delegation that pressed for Hamilton's removal in December 1812. See Roberts to Charles J. Ingersoll, January 19, 1813, Charles J. Ingersoll Papers, HSP.

[10] See Gallatin to James Madison, [June 20, 1812], Madison Papers, Library of Congress (microfilm edition); Hamilton to Rodgers, June 22, 1812, to Decatur, June

22, 1812, Letters Sent to Officers, RG45, NA. These orders were a recipe for disaster. As Alfred T. Mahan has argued, splitting up the meager American naval force in such a manner risked exposing each division to defeat at the hands of a superior British squadron. See *Sea Power in its Relations to the War of 1812* (Boston: Little, Brown, and Co., 1905), I:320-21. Hamilton's vague instructions for the two commanders to cooperate as circumstances dictated also created the potential for trouble due to the service's rudimentary command structure. The navy had no rank higher than captain, but officers in charge of squadrons received the courtesy title of commodore and were permitted to fly a broad penant from their masthead. In theory, when two squadrons met, overall command fell to the commodore with seniority—in this case, Rodgers. But this point of protocol was not clearly established in practice, at least so far as Decatur was concerned. Rodgers and Decatur had already clashed over the question of seniority just a few weeks before the start of the war during a meeting off the Delaware Capes. Decatur apparently refused to concede that he was subordinate to Rodgers and subject to the latter's orders. The encounter ended with Decatur summarily departing with his squadron. Rodgers tried to be diplomatic about the incident and proposed discussing their differences in person with Paul Hamilton on the next available occasion. See Rodgers to Decatur, May 28, 1812, Rodger's Family Papers (RFP), Box 64, Library of Congress (LC). Rodgers also wrote Hamilton directly, suggesting a solution of sorts to the problem that arose with Decatur. He recommended the creation of three different classes of penants which could be used as needed to indicate the relative rank of commodores sailing in company with one another. Hamilton liked the idea and ordered Rodgers to implement it immediately. See Rodgers to Hamilton, June 3, 1812, Captains Letters; Hamilton to Rodgers, June 10, 1812, Letters Sent to Officers, RG45, NA.

[11]Smith to William Eustis, December 24, 26, 1803, Letters to Congress, RG45, NA. Smith did not seek to change the base pay given to officers who were not on active service. Rather, he asked that such men also be allowed to draw rations—essentially a food allowance that could be converted into cash at the rate of $0.20 per ration beyond the first—that were normally given to officers on active duty. For a general discussion of the system of naval pay and benefits, see McKee, *A Gentlemanly Profession*, 331-337.

[12]Four copies of the petition—two handwritten and two printed—can be found in folder HR 11A-F6.1, Record Group 233, NA.

[13]Rodgers to Minerva Rodgers, January 25, 1808, RFP, Box 13, LC.

[14]The officers also tried their luck with the upper house of Congress in 1809. See copy of William Bainbridge's letter to Paul Hamilton, May 23, 1809, Letters to Congress, RG45, LC. Hamilton submitted the copy as Paper D in his report to the Senate, June 6, 1809. The report and accompanying enclosures—except for Bainbridge's letter—are printed in *ASP:NA*, 1:194-97. The Senate, however, does not appear to have taken any subsequent action on the petition.

[15]*The Debates and Proceedings of the Congress of the United States*, 11th Congress, 3rd Session (Washington: Gales and Seaton, 1853), 860-862.

[16]Three years later, the memory of the debate still infuriated Isaac Hull. "[O]ur memorial presented to Congress a few years since was treated with so much indelicacy (I may say indecency) that every officer has determined never to ask again for anything," he wrote David Daggett, a senator from Connecticut, in 1814. "They even went so far as to say that the daughters of officers killed fighting for their country, could when *fifteen* get a living for themselves, meaning, I suppose, that they could take in washing or something still worse." Quoted in Linda M. Maloney, *The Captain from Connecticut: The Life and Naval Times of Isaac Hull* (Boston: Northeastern University Press, 1986), 259-60.

[17]Only the second child, Robert, survived. The first died after thirteen months. See Charles O. Paullin, *Commodore John Rodgers* (Annapolis: Naval Institute Press, 1967; originally published 1909), 191, 279.

[18]Rodgers to Minerva Rodgers, April 26, 1810, RFP, Box 13, LC.
[19]Bainbridge to Rodgers, April 1, 1811, RFP, Box 49, LC. Apparently, Rodgers was giving serious consideration to undertaking such a voyage himself. See Rodgers to Burwell Bassett, February 2, 1811, RFP, Box 64, LC; Thomas Tingey to Rodgers, March 15, 1811, RFP, Box 49, LC.
[20]David F. Long, *Ready to Hazard: A Biography of Commodore William Bainbridge, 1774-1833* (Hanover, N.H.: University Press of New England, 1981), 106-08, 119-29.
[21]Trevett to Charles Morris, June 11, 1812, to Jacob Gates, June 13, 1812, Miscellaneous Manuscripts, LC. Emphasis in the original. Trevett enclosed this last phrase in quotes in his letter.
[22]Rodgers to Hamilton, June 19, 21 (written at 6 AM), 21 (written later in the day outside of Sandy Hook) 1812, Captains Letters, RG45, NA. See also Rodgers to Stephen Decatur, June 20, 1812, RFP, Box 64, LC.
[23]Rodgers to Hamilton, June 21 (written after the first two letters of that date, off Sandy Hook), September 1, 1812, Captains Letters, RG45, NA.
[24]Rodgers to Minerva Rodgers, [no date but written while at sea off Sandy Hook in company with Decatur's vessels], RFP, Box 13, LC.
[25]In fact, just before his departure from Norfolk on June 13, Decatur suggested to Hamilton the possibility of trying to intercept a British convoy known to have sailed from the Leeward Islands the previous month. Decatur to Hamilton, June 13, 1813, Captains Letters, RG45, NA.
[26]Memorandum, dated June 21, 1812 and witnessed by Jacob Morton and John Bullus, typescript copy, Area Files, reel 75, Microfilm Series M-625, RG45, NA. The original is in the library of the United States Naval Academy.
[27]Rodgers to Hamilton, September 1, 1812, Captains Letters, RG45, NA.
[28]Hamilton to Rodgers, September 8, 1812, Letters Sent to Officers, RG45, NA; James Madison, 4th Annual Message, November 4, 1812, *The Writings of James Madison*, Galliard Hunt, ed. (New York: G.P. Putnam's & Sons, 1900-1910), 8:221-31.
[29]Mahan, *Sea Power*, I:325-27. For other favorable views of Rodgers' cruise, see Brant, *James Madison*, 40-42; Leonard F. Guttridge and Jay D. Smith, *The Commodores* (New York: Harper & Row, 1969), 199; K. Jack Bauer, "John Rodgers: The Stalwart Conservative," *Command Under Sail: Makers of the American Naval Tradition, 1775-1850*, James C. Bradford, ed. (Annapolis: Naval Institute Press, 1985), 228; Donald R. Hickey, *The War of 1812: A Forgotten Conflict* (Urbana, Ill.: University of Illinois Press, 1989), 92-93.
[30]This passage is from Rodgers to Hamilton, September 14, 1812, Captains Letters, RG45. NA.
[31]See note 24 above. The same holds true for the private letter he sent to his wife.
[32]Rodgers to Hamilton, August 31, 1812, ibid.
[33]See, for instance, the New York *Columbian*, August 21, 1812; New York *Commercial-Advertiser*, July 17, 1812; Boston *Columbian-Centinel*, July 29, 1812; Charleston *Courier*, July 11, 1812.
[34]Many newspapers during the summer began publishing a running tally of American merchant ships captured or burnt by the British.
[35]See, for instance, the Boston *Columbian-Centinel*, August 1, 1812.
[36]Boston *Gazette*, August 31, 1812.
[37]Linda Maloney also casts a skeptical eye on Rodgers' attempts to play up the outcome of his cruise, although she attributes his attitude to a case of "sour grapes" arising from his jealousy over the *Constitution*'s defeat of the *Guerriere*. See "The War of 1812: What Role for Sea Power?" In *Peace and War: Interpretations of American Naval History, 1775-1984*, 2nd edition, Kenneth J. Hagan, ed. (Westport, Conn.: Greenwood Press, 1984), 49.

[38] Herbert Sawyer to John W. Croker, July 5, 1812, Admiralty Records (Adm.) 1/502; Sawyer to Broke, July 4, 1812, Adm. 1/1553, Public Records Office (PRO). A fourth frigate, the *Guerriere*, joined the squadron a few days after its departure from Halifax.

[39] This convoy should not be confused with the one Rodgers sought to intercept. The Jamaican fleet Broke was shepherding had sailed from the Caribbean around the 1st of July under convoy of the frigate *Thetis*. The convoy Rodgers hoped to find had left the islands in late May under the escort of the frigate *Thalia*. It reached England safely on July 23rd. News of its arrival was carried in the London *Times*, July 25, 1812.

[40] Broke to John W. Croker, July 30, 1812, Adm. 1/1553, PRO.

[41] An astute point made by Linda Maloney in "The War of 1812," 49. Yet, she is wrong to say that the British were not drawn away from the American coast.

[42] Sawyer to Croker, August 25, 1812, Adm. 1/502.

[43] Faye Margaret Kert, *Prize and Prejudice: Privateering and Naval Prize in Atlantic Canada in the War of 1812* (St. John's, Newfoundland: International Maritime Economic History Association, 1997), 131, 159-165. Vessels destroyed at sea, ransomed, or subsequently recaptured by the Americans were not included in these tallies. In addition to these captures, another 26 American merchantmen fell prey to British warships on the Newfoundland station during the same time period. See List of American Prizes at St. John's, Newfoundland, September 1, 1812, Naval History Manuscript Collection, Franklin D. Roosevelt Library.

[44] Three of the most vociferous advocates of this approach are Maloney, "The War of 1812," 47-49; Stephen Howarth, *To Shining Sea: A History of the United States Navy, 1775-1991* (New York: Random House, 1991), 98; Kenneth J. Hagan, *This People's Navy: The Making of American Sea Power* (New York: The Free Press, 1991), 80.

[45] This is not to say that such victories were meaningless, for they did have a tremendous impact on American morale. These triumphs also had an immense effect on naval politics. In fact, the navy had won such popular acclaim by the winter of 1812-13 that its future growth and vitality as a national institution were all but assured.

[46] The mere rumor that several West Indiamen had been captured by the Americans was enough to cause stock prices to fall on London's Royal Exchange. See the London *Times*, August 19, 1812.

[47] For details about the convoy schedule for 1812, see Adm. 1/4359, PRO. For a general discussion of the organization of British trade during this time period, see the essays in *The Trade Winds: A Study of British Overseas Trade during the French Wars 1793-1815*, C. Northcote Parkinson, ed. (London: George Allen and Unwin, 1948).

[48] Porter to Hamilton, September 7, 1812, Captains Letters, RG45, NA.

[49] J. Mackay Hitsman, *The Incredible War of 1812: A Military History* (Toronto: University of Toronto Press, 1965), 83-84.

[50] In the first six months of the war, the Royal Navy lost three vessels to shipwreck. See Barry J. Lohnes, "British Naval Problems at Halifax during the War of 1812," *The Mariner's Mirror*, 59 (August 1973): 322.

[51] For details about *Africa*'s condition, see Joseph A. Goldenberg, "The Royal Navy's Blockade in New England Waters, 1812-1815," *The International History Review*, 6 (August 1984), 425, 427. For a reference to *Africa*'s poor sailing qualities, see Broke to Croker, July 30, 1812, Adm. 1/1553, PRO.

"Concessions Where Concessions Could Be Made": The Naval Efficiency Boards of 1855–1857

Kenneth J. Blume

> In the mid-1850s, the United States Navy faced a problem not uncommon to navies struggling through periods of prolonged public indifference: it had more senior officers on the rolls than it had ships for them to command. Indeed, many senior (and elderly) naval officers treated their commissions as sinecures, languishing on shore and clogging up the promotion ladder for young and ambitious middle-grade officers. In 1855, Congress authorized an "Efficiency Board" to review the records of all U.S. Navy officers and recommend some for retirement. That "some" turned out to be 201 individuals! The resulting outcry from the victims and their political advocates created a political crisis. In this essay, Kenneth Blume assesses the motives and consequences of this incident and concludes that, "more damage was done to the navy's officer corps than at any other time in the nineteenth century."

In 1844, a minor mutiny broke out aboard the Frigate *Potomac*. In the course of quelling that mutiny, Passed Midshipman Julius S. Bohrer fractured his skull. This was just the beginning of the serious toll that professional duties took on his physical well-being. Serving aboard *Plymouth* in 1848, he contracted opthamalia, and two years later, serving off the coast of Africa, he suffered from such serious exposure to the tropical climate that he contracted "Chronic Rheumatism."[1]

Was Julius Bohrer fit to serve in the navy of the United States? By the 1850s it was a question that Congressmen were asking about many naval officers. In 1853, Secretary of the Navy James C. Dobbin had commented that "The great evil in our present system is, that neither merit, nor service, nor gallantry, nor capacity, *but*

Kenneth J. Blume is Associate Professor of History and Chair of the Department of Humanities and Social Sciences at the Albany College of Pharmacy in Albany, New York.

mere seniority of commission, regulates promotion and pay."[2] As a result, in 1855 Congress appointed a board to determine "the efficiency of the officers of the line."[3] Working in secret, and keeping no official records, the board examined the records of 712 officers. Of those, forty-nine officers were dropped as incompetent or unworthy, seventy-one were placed on the "reserved" (retired) list at leave-of-absence pay, and eighty-one were placed on the "reserved" (retired) list at furlough pay (½ of leave-of-absence pay). In all, 201 officers were affected—including Bohrer, who was dropped from the list on the grounds of physical unfitness for the service.

Bohrer himself was relatively unknown, but some of those affected were prominent, and many filed appeals with Congress—which, in turn, established yet another board to reexamine the cases. Julius S. Bohrer was one of those who appealed.

Three courts of inquiry met in 1857, reviewing appeals from 108 officers. The picture of Bohrer's physical condition was not encouraging. Vision in his right eye was limited, his right leg was contracted at the knee, and the mobility of his joint was impaired. Further, his hip joint was affected by "masting" and a lack of "pliancy" in the muscles and ligaments. He suffered from sciaticus and an enlargement of the spleen. The court of inquiry described him as "totally disabled from active duty." "It is quite apparent," the court reported, "that his condition . . . is permanent." Bohrer had established his "mental moral and professional fitness" for naval service, but he was "physically unfit for the active list." In the end, the court restored Boher to the naval lists, but placed him on the reserve list on leave of absence pay.

The case of Julius S. Bohrer was one of many. Like Bohrer, many naval officers were reinstated. But the episode scarred a generation of officers for the rest of the century.

In re-evaluating the cases of those sailors who appealed, the 1857 Boards of Inquiry considered four criteria: "physical, mental, professional, and moral fitness . . . for the naval service."[4] The application of these criteria illuminates not only personnel issues of the Antebellum navy, but also the functioning of naval bureaucracy, and the intersection of political forces with professional needs. In brief, the records provide a rich portrait of the United States Navy on the eve of the Civil War.

For example, Lt. J. B. Walbach had been dropped because of what we today would call a "drinking problem." By the time of his appeal, he was suffering from chronic disease of the prostate gland. Even though he had stopped drinking—which might have settled the issue of "moral fitness"—his health had declined and he was found not physically fit for service. The decision in this case was *not* to restore the officer to the naval ranks.[5]

Questions about "physical" fitness for naval service could be fairly objectively determined, but other criteria were more complex to assess. For example, Passed Midshipman Allen Byrens was found to be suffering from consumption and other maladies, but even more significantly, to have incurred a debt to a boardinghouse woman by not paying his rent.[6] The court would likely have lightened the original action (as it did in other instances) had not Byrens' ill-health been compounded by behavior that cast doubt on his "moral" qualifications for naval service.

Byrens' actions were doubly dishonorable because they involved inappropriate treatment of a woman. In this mid-century era, it is not surprising that the navy would have had strong views on the honor and appropriate treatment due "American Womanhood." Lt. Samuel Chase Barney, dropped from the naval lists by the original board, discovered that the navy was disinclined to ignore his treatment of his wife—despite his claim that the matter was a private affair of no concern to the United States Navy. The court of inquiry concurred that Barney should remain dropped from the list, not only because of his defective vision and hearing and his "flagrant contempt for authority" but also because he was a wife beater.[7]

Barney's attorney had argued "that the Court has no right to enquire into a party's 'domestic conduct or relations....'" But the appeals court disagreed, asserting that "Cruel and Scandalous treatment of a woman by a man, is no part of his 'domestic relations,' even though that woman be his wife .... No one will contend for a moment, that if an officer were cruelly to beat and misuse a woman who was *not* his wife, in some place other than his home, so as to bring him into notorious disrepute, that he would be utterly unworthy to hold a commission in the Navy—And will any one with a particle of sensibility contend that the offence is less scandalous, less outrageous, less morally disqualifying, because the woman maltreated was his wife, and the scene of the outrage was his own home?"[8]

Here we see no attempt at isolating the relevance of private behavior in the conduct of an individual's public responsibilities. "Suppose," the court asked, "an officer were to murder his wife, is it possible that a court constituted as this is, would be precluded from investigating the fact, upon the ground that it had no right to enquire [sic] with 'domestic relations'? . . . The . . . question . . . is, What effect has such conduct produced upon the fitness of the applicant for the Naval Service?"[9] The court's answer spoke directly to the connection between private behavior and fitness for a public position. "It is not enough that an officer should know his profession, to make him useful and efficient," the court advised. "An essential element for command, is a character and deportment that will inspire subordinates with respect, and any conduct which tends to impair or destroy this, and bring scandal and disrepute upon the Service, is a legitimate subject of inquiry . . . ."[10]

The case of Lt. William E. Hunt, reserved on furlough pay, provides further insight into the Navy's priorities for the behavior of its officers. The court explored reports of Hunt's intemperance. But that intemperance was not habitual—and could not be conclusively corroborated. However, the determining factor was that Hunt was a veteran of the Mexican War, where he had distinguished himself in battle. In consequence, Hunt was restored to the active naval list.[11] Here, the Court gave a veteran the benefit of the doubt, even as it acknowledged that "occasional" intemperance was a tolerable occupational hazard if the individual otherwise fulfilled his responsibilities.

Of course, an officer had to be able to do his job. Lt. William B. Whiting had been placed on furlough because of both professional *and* physical unfitness. While serving aboard *Vandalia*, 1853–1855, he had been unable to "perform his duty with energy and efficiency," and had "required a chair or camp stool on deck to sit down on during his watches at night."[12] Compounding his physical shortcomings were his mental limitations. One officer testified that "Whiting [never] had the mind to acquire a knowledge, from experience, of the common principles of his profession." The court of inquiry concluded, therefore, that Whiting lacked the "aptitude for and adaptation to the nautical and military branches of his profession" and "labor[ed] under an impediment of speech. These defects . . . are insuperable obstacles to his ever becoming an efficient and useful officer on active service afloat." In short, Whiting was no asset to the Navy and could perform no useful function. But the court took mercy on a hopeless case—because, again, of the "character issue." In this instance, "character" worked to the officer's advantage, because the court, "in view of his unimpeachable moral character, his general good conduct, and his efficiency in Hydrographic surveys and Chartography," recommended that Whiting be placed on "leave-of-absence pay" instead of the lower "furlough" pay.[13] By appealing, therefore, Whiting had managed to get his retirement pay doubled.

The seriousness with which the court of inquiry considered the criteria for moral, mental, physical, and professional fitness can be seen in the case of Comdr. Robert Ritchie, who had been moved to the "reserve" list on leave-of-absence pay.[14] Ritchie's reputation had originally been sullied by charges that he had committed perjury and was therefore morally unfit to serve. Here the court had to make a judgment about the nature of perjury. Ultimately, according to the court, "it matters not whether the alleged false swearing does, or does not constitute the technical offence of perjury. This Court, having no criminal jurisdiction, has only to inquire whether it was *false*, and whether it was *intentionally* so. If it was both, the court can not fail to perceive its bearing upon the question of his *moral fitness* for the rank of a commander in the American Navy, a proper regard for the interest and character of which would never permit the court to recommend to it one upon whom rested such a stain."[15] In this instance, having found no evidence of Ritchie's guilt, the court overturned the original decision and restored him to the active list.

Over the years, the navy had occasionally demonstrated intolerance of new ideas, of individualists, of people who were "different." The actions of the original "plucking board" reflected such narrow-mindedness, but the 1857 courts of inquiry demonstrated a broader appreciation of leadership in a modernizing navy. Cadwalader Ringgold, for example, one of the great navigator-scientists of the nineteenth century U.S. Navy, had been placed on leave-of-absence pay by the original board. Ringgold was viewed as an eccentric by more conventional officers. In addition, he had been ill during much of one of his famous cruises—and that illness had been taken by some as mental instability.[16] But a testament to the fundamental fairness of the 1857 hearing is the fact that it understood the situation and restored Ringgold to the active list.[17] It righted a wrong perpetrated out of vindictiveness by the original Efficiency Board.

The outcome was similar for Matthew F. Maury, known as the "Pathfinder of the Seas" and famous for the *Sailing Directions* that he had compiled. Maury had been retired from the service despite his accomplishments ostensibly because of a physical handicap. The inquiry revealed that Maury, despite a handicap resulting from an 1839 leg injury, could still function perfectly well as a naval officer. As a result of the inquiry, Maury was restored to the navy's active list.[18] Once again, "justice" had—eventually—prevailed, but at a considerable psychic and professional cost.

The 1857 court of inquiry, therefore, overturned a number of unjust dismissals or demotions. None had been more unjust than the dropping of Capt. Uriah P. Levy. Levy had at least three strikes against him as a naval officer. He was unorthodox; he was a reformer; and he was a Jew. He had worked to end flogging within the navy and to create the naval apprentice system—this in the years before the creation of the Naval Academy.[19] His resume caught up with him when the original Efficiency Board ordered him dropped from the naval list—one of only three captains so treated.

Levy based his appeal on the claim that he had been dropped because he was Jewish, and that throughout his naval career he had been persecuted because of his religious faith. Here, the Court of

Inquiry had to walk a fine line. Could it publicly acknowledge that such prejudice existed and had motivated the Efficiency Board? Could it, on the other hand, deny the existence of such prejudice, and therefore deny the basis of Levy's appeal? In the end, the court found a way to do justice for Levy and at the same time protect the image of the service. While acknowledging that *if* "such a prejudice does exist against him . . . and has pursued him at every step through a long life, he is indeed a most unfortunate man," the court announced that the testimony amounted to "vague and unsatisfactory inferences & suppositions" that did not prove "the existence of such a prejudice, and one capable of producing such tremendous results upon the prospects of almost an entire lifetime."[20] It was possible that such bigotry could exist in isolated instances, the court speculated, but not on such a wide scale. It was also possible that a "general prejudice" existed against Levy for reasons *other* than religion. "Does not the credit, good order, and efficiency of the service demand that even a *general prejudice* of so inveterate a character as that alleged, growing out of either of the causes last named," be taken seriously, the judge advocate asked?[21] Having considered Levy's charges, the court responded to them in a serious manner and could now proceed to do what was right—which was to order Levy restored to the active list of the navy.[22]

Other actions of the 1857 courts of inquiry reveal what kinds of behavior were considered important, and which were considered unacceptable. Lt. William Noland, for example, was one of those who had been dropped from the naval list. The court rejected his appeal because testimony revealed that he was intemperate and insubordinate and had disregarded orders in a way that the court described as "disgraceful."[23] Similarly, the court refused to dismiss *verifiable* cases of *habitual* drunkenness. Lt. Dominick Lynch had been furloughed for such problems. Because testimony revealed numerous serious incidents of intemperance, the court upheld the original decision.[24] In another case, the court upheld the original action placing Comdr. Thomas R. Gedney on furlough pay. Gedney claimed that exposure had harmed his health and that he should at very least be moved to the higher "leave-of-absence" pay. The hearing, on the other hand, produced considerable evidence of

Gedney's drunkenness.[25] So too, in the case of Lt. Junius Boyle, who also had been furloughed. The hearing produced evidence of his intemperance, and evidence that he was a "better seaman than officer." Therefore, the decision in this case, too, was to keep him on furlough pay.[26]

Where a sailor's problems were beyond his own control, the court was more sympathetic. Passed Midshipman Nathaniel West had been dropped because he was demonstrably insane. But the appeals inquiry revealed that West had been a good seaman *up until* his insanity, and so the court restored him to the reserve list with leave-of-absence pay.[27] In essence, this was a humanitarian gesture. The court was similarly humane in the case of Thomas Brownell, who had also been dropped from the lists. Brownell petitioned to be switched to leave-of-absence pay. His was an odd case. A distinguished veteran of the War of 1812—which worked to his advantage—he suffered from an "incurable" and disabling hernia. The case was complicated by the disappearance of his service records after the War of 1812, and by his temporary departure from the naval service after the war. The court went halfway toward granting his request and restored him to the reserve list on furlough, rather than leave-of-absence, pay.[28]

And so it went, throughout much of 1857. The hearings dragged on, as the three courts of inquiry gave every officer an opportunity to state his case in as much detail as he chose. Ultimately, the court itself wrote its own assessment. "The court is aware that, throughout this long and tedious investigation, the course pursued on [the] part of the government has been one of concession, in every instance where concessions could be made without involving a disregard of duty to the service and the country."[29]

Of the original Efficiency Board, certainly, there has been mixed assessment. Comdr. Samuel F. DuPont, a member of that board, wrote a friend: "I am free to say that the duty has been ably & fearlessly performed. . . . All motives of expediency were thrown aside—no connexions social or political, no friendships however strong, were permitted to weigh a feather, if the individual came under the law."[30] And, to be sure, over the years historians' assessments of this whole episode in American naval history have tended to be sober but positive—arguing that in the *long run* the success of the Board can be seen in the quality of the officer corps at the time of the Civil War.[31] On the other hand, some historians have dwelt on the negative aspects of this episode in American naval history. These historians, often the biographers of officers who suffered at the hands of the original Efficiency Board, not surprisingly argue that although the aims of naval reform were laudable, the methods of the Board were flawed and destructive.[32]

To be sure, many of the wrongs were righted—in John Newland Maffitt's case, and in Matthew F. Maury's, and Uriah P. Levy's, and Cadwalader Ringgold's, and others—but was it necessary to have those wrongs perpetrated in the first place? Certainly, Geoffrey Smith is correct when he says that "Scraping barnacles from a rotting hull would have proved easier than the attempt to cull the ranks of the aged and incompetent."[33] The heart of the service is its personnel, and lack of opportunities for promotion and significant command contributed considerably to low morale—or low "job satisfaction"—throughout the navy.[34] The promotion bottleneck— brought about by the absence of a standing bureaucratic mechanism for retiring old, infirm, or incompetent officers *without* a special act of Congress—was a cancer eating at the vitals of the antebellum navy. The Efficiency Board, in order to cut out the cancer, was willing to kill the patient. Harold Langley, using the Maury case as an example, admits that "the board's actions left deep wounds on many," but argues that "the coming of the Civil War helped to blot out the memory of this attempt at naval reform."[35]

But psychological trauma is not so easily erased—even by an admittedly greater trauma (the Civil War). The 1857 courts of inquiry righted many wrongs and demonstrated that the service could be scrupulously judicious and fair. But those same 1857 proceedings proved how injudicious and unfair the original Efficiency Board had been in too many cases. John Newland Maffitt was restored to the active naval ranks. But four years later, he abandoned his northern brothers and "went South"—perhaps with the hope that the naval service of the Confederacy would more appreciate his talents. Matthew F. Maury, too, was restored—but also "went South." We will never know how many of the sixty-two officers who won their appeals in 1857 completed their naval careers with an unhealed scar, a deep grudge, a persistent cause for dissatisfaction.

In at least one case, however, we can get a glimpse of the residue of the battle for reinstatement. Richard Worsam Meade II (brother of Gettysburg's George Gordon Meade) had entered the Navy in 1826 and after eleven years had finally achieved the rank of lieutenant. When the Efficiency Board made its recommendations in 1855, Meade was among the nineteen lieutenants dropped entirely from the active list of the service. He appealed to Congress and regained his commission with rank of commander. But for Meade the action of the Board was particularly humiliating since the category in which he had been placed implied that he was incompetent by his own fault. Furthermore, from the perspective of the Meade family, the two year period of struggle, tension, and humiliation—occurring while Meade's son was concluding his training at the Naval Academy and taking his first two cruises as a passed midshipman—offered a lesson that members of the family harbored with them for the rest of the century: great injustice was possible at the hands of both the Federal Government and the Navy Department. Henry Meigs—Meade's father-in-law—had sarcastically described Washington, D.C., as "that *Eternal Residence of all the Virtues*"[36]—and that attitude became the prevailing attitude in the Meade family. Meade's son rose to be a rear admiral—and the third-ranking officer in the navy—by the 1890s, but he held a grudge against the government and the navy that, in part, had its roots in the Plucking Board of 1855. He probably was not the only American naval officer carrying that psychological baggage.

It would be problematic to argue that the service should *not* have tried to weed out officers who were incompetent or too old to perform their duties, or to argue that there did *not* need to be an institutionalized structure for timely advancement within the ranks. But the 1855 Efficiency Board's most grievous sin was to punish the original thinkers. By doing so, the Antebellum Navy demonstrated in 1855 that it had no room for individuals, for thinkers, for leaders with "different" opinions. And as Capt. Philip A. Burdette, USMC, wrote recently, the service must have room for such officers because "mavericks" are the "lifeblood" of the service.[37]

Ultimately, the functioning and results of the 1857 courts of inquiry demonstrated that "the system worked." Those hearings were everything that the 1855 Efficiency Board deliberations were not: open, evidence-based, deliberate, and fair. Under incredible political and public pressure, the Navy demonstrated that it could clean house the right way and could make restitution for past errors. Had the 1855 Efficiency Board functioned according to the principles guiding the 1857 courts of inquiry, the results would have been altogether productive: the dead wood might have been pruned out while the qualified, responsible, and indeed in some cases imaginative officers who *wanted* to serve their country might have remained on the lists with realistic expectations of career advancement. But that did not happen. The judgments of the Naval Efficiency Board of 1855 were all too often wrong, arrived at in the wrong way. As a result, more damage was done to the navy's officer corps than at any other time in the nineteenth century.

NOTES

[1]United States. Navy Department. Office Of The Judge Advocate General. Records Relating to Personnel. *Records Of Proceedings Of Courts Of Inquiry Convened Under The Act Of January 16, 1875 [sic], Feb. 1857 - Feb. 1859.* RG 125, National Archives, Washington, D.C. [Hereafter cited as *1857 Inquiry Pro-ceedings*], Vol. 17.

[2]Quoted in Harold D. Langley, "James Cochrane Dobbin," *American Secretaries of the Navy*, ed. Paolo E. Coletta (Annapolis: Naval Institute Press, 1980), Vol. I, 290.

[3]Historians of the U.S. Navy have almost universally described the Antbellum navy as a service in desperate need of reform — and therefore the Efficiency Board as a necessary attempt at solving a vexing problem. See, for example, Harold D. Langley, *Social Reform in the United States Navy, 1798-1862*. (Chicago: University of Illinois, 1967), 34-35; and Charles Oscar Paullin, *Paullin's History of Naval Administration, 1775-1911*. (Annapolis: Naval Institute Press, 1968), 239-243; or Geoffrey S. Smith, "An Uncertain Passage: The Bureaus Run the Navy, 1842-1861," in Kenneth J. Hagan, Ed., *In Peace and War. Interpretations of American Naval History, 1775-1978.* (Westport, CT: Greenwood Press, 1978), 89.

[4]Isaac Toucey to E.A. Lavalette (for example), *1857 Inquiry Proceedings*, Vol. 17.

[5]*1857 Inquiry Proceedings*, Vol. 16. The Walbach case illustrates another feature of this story: the role of the president in the affairs of the military. Both the original 1855 Efficiency Board and the 1857 Courts of Inquiry were to make recommendations to the secretary of the navy, who, in turn, was to make recommendations to the president, who, in turn, would make the final personnel decision. So the process went. President Franklin Pierce, in 1855, approved the recommendations

transmitted to him by Secretary of the Navy John Dobbin. In 1857, the Courts of Inquiry reviewed the appeals of 108 officers, reversed sixty-two, and upheld forty-six. Secretary of the Navy Isaac Toucey, in turn, transmitted those findings to the new president, James Buchanan. The following year, Buchanan weighed in on the matter by restoring a number of the officers whom the Court of Inquiry had failed to restore. "The case of Lieutenant Walbach I consider clear," Buchanan commented. "He ought to be restored to the active list." Buchanan's action on Walbach's behalf was not an isolated example, and one of the goals of this study will be to assess the nature and implications of these presidential actions, on the eve of the Civil War, by a chief executive who has sometimes been accused of pro-Southern bias—a charge also leveled, of course, at his secretary of the navy. See, for example, Paolo E. Coletta, who says that "Isaac Toucey of Connecticut, was a southern sympathizer like the president he served, James Buchanan. *The American Naval Heritage in Brief* (Washington: University Press of America, 1978), 111.

[6] *1857 Inquiry Proceedings*, Vol. 19.
[7] In 1849 he had avoided an order to join *Falmouth* in Boston. Ibid.
[8] Ibid.
[9] Ibid.
[10] Ibid.
[11] Ibid.
[12] *1857 Inquiry Proceedings*, Vol. 17.
[13] Ibid.
[14] Ibid.
[15] Ibid.
[16] Commodore Matthew C. Perry "apparently used the Board to continue a vendetta" against Ringgold. See James E. Valle, *Rocks and Shoals. Order and Discipline in the Old Navy, 1800-1861* (Annapolis: Naval Institute Press, 1980), 68. For more on Ringgold, see Harrington, Gordon K, "The Ringgold Incident: A Matter of Judgement," in Clayton R. Barrow, ed. *America Spreads Her Sails.* (Annapolis, Md.: United States Naval Institute Press, 1973), 100–111; and Robert Erwin Johnson, *Rear Admiral John Rodgers, 1812-1882* (Annapolis: United States Naval Institute, 1967), 141. Unfortunately, Samuel Eliot Morison's classic biography of Perry (*"Old Bruin": Commodore Matthew C. Perry, 1794-1858* (Boston: Little, Brown, 1967) says virtually nothing about Perry's service on the Naval Efficiency Board.
[17] *1857 Inquiry Proceedings*, Vol. 18.
[18] *1857 Inquiry Proceedings*, Vol. 21. See also, Frances Leigh Williams, *Matthew Fontaine Maury. Scientist of the Sea* (New Brunswick: Rutgers University Press, 1963), 269-308. Not surprisingly, Williams takes Maury's side in the controversy.
[19] He was also a shrewd investor who became wealthy enough to purchase Monticello and restore it as a monument to his idol, Thomas Jefferson.
[20] *1857 Inquiry Proceedings*, Vol. 20.
[21] *1857 Inquiry Proceedings*, Vol. 20.
[22] The only full biography of Levy currently available is Donovan Fitzpatrick and Saul Saphire, *Navy Maverick: Uriah Phillips Levy* (Garden City: Doubleday, 1963).
[23] *1857 Inquiry Proceedings*, Vol. 19.
[24] *1857 Inquiry Proceedings*, Vol. 21.
[25] Ibid.
[26] Ibid.
[27] *1857 Inquiry Proceedings*, Vol. 19.
[28] *1857 Inquiry Proceedings*, Vol. 21.
[29] *1857 Inquiry Proceedings*, Vol. 20.
[30] Quoted in James M. Merrill, *Du Pont, The Making of an Admiral: A Biography of Samuel Francis Du Pont* (New York: Dodd, Mead, 1986), 220.

[31] For example, Charles Torodich says that the original act establishing the Efficiency Board "encouraged diligence among the midshipmen 'who could now look forward to promotion to the grade of Lieutenant before losing their useful vigor and inclination for the service.' The axe had fallen and had rooted out the navy's dead wood. Annapolites would soon have their day in the sun." (*The Spirited Years. A History of the Antebellum Naval Academy* [Annapolis: Naval Institute Press, 1984], 131, quoting Thomas G. Ford's 1887 unpublished manuscript, *History of the Naval Academy*.) Similarly, other historians have chosen to overlook the damage done by the Efficiency Board in favor of what they judge to be the longer-term benefits. Most recently, for example, Howard C. Westwood argues that, the period of turmoil aside, the "enhanced opportunity" that many officers experienced considerably strengthened the federal navy for its responsibilities in the Civil War. ("Reform in the United States Navy: The 'Plucking' of Officers in the Latter 1850s," *The American Neptune* L, 2 [Spring 1990], 118. See also Smith, "An Uncertain Passage," 89-90.) Ultimately, historians who view the work of the Efficiency Board as a success see that work through the prism of the Civil War. Harold Langley, who argues that the work of the board "established the principle of retirement and . . . did some good" ("Isaac Toucey," *American Secretaries of the Navy*, ed. Paolo E. Coletta [Annapolis: Naval Institute Press, 1980], Vol. I, 308), ultimately concludes: "When the [Civil] war began the wisdom of most of the board's actions was borne out in the cases of the older officers who could not serve."(*Social Reform*, 35).

[32] Frances Williams, Matthew Maury's biographer, for example, concludes that "the basic aim [of reforming the Navy] had been right and was eventually achieved, but the methods of the 1855 naval Board had deserved the condemnation they received." (*Matthew Fontaine Maury*, 308). Similarly, John Newland Maffitt's biographer, Royce Shingleton, describes the decision of the 1855 Efficiency Board to put Maffitt on the indefinite furlough list as "arbitrary." "His name should not have been on the list," Shingleton declares, "and the wrong was rectified." (*High Seas Confederate. The Life and Times of John Newland Maffitt* [Columbia, S.C.: University of South Carolina Press, 1994], 24. See also Emma Martin Maffitt, *The Life and Services of John Newland Maffitt* [New York and Washington: The Neale Publishing Co., 1906], pp. 136-198).

[33] Smith, "An Uncertain Passage," 89.

[34] On this issue during a later era see Kenneth J. Blume, "Career Frustration in the Late Nineteenth-Century Navy: The Case of Rear Admiral Richard Worsam Meade." Paper, Twelfth Naval History Symposium, U.S. Naval Academy, Annapolis, MD, Oct. 27, 1995.

[35] Langley, *Social Reform*, 35.

[36] Henry Meigs to Clara Forsythe Meigs Meade, September 1, 1839, Meade Family Papers, privately held.

[37] Philip A. Burdette, "Sheep, Mavericks, and Institutional Behavior." *United States Naval Institute Proceedings*, August 1999, 50-51. This essay was the "second cohonorable mention in the annual Vincent Astor Memorial Leadership Essay Contest.

"The Sudden Destruction of Bright Hopes": Union Shipbuilding Management, 1862-1865

William H. Roberts

> One important element of Union victory in the American Civil War was the possession of overwhelming naval superiority. That superiority was achieved and maintained not merely by the circumstance of superior resources but also by the successful mobilization and management of those resources. In this essay, William H. Roberts uses the monitor construction program as a model to show how the Union Navy developed a system of centralized design and a procurement organization that worked with civilian industry to establish an efficient system of industrial mobilization.

The Union victory in the American Civil War was due in great part to the North's overwhelming industrial preponderance over the South. Few would seriously dispute that statement, and some historians go even further and invoke a kind of industrial determinism to explain the outcome of the war.[1] In 1861, though, the Union's material superiority existed mostly in prospect. The process by which the Union mobilized—how it converted industrial potential into tangible materials of war—sheds considerable light upon the war years themselves. Beyond that, it illuminates the ways in which high technology development can be managed, the role of specialty producers in an industrializing economy, and the question of how the Civil War affected American industrialization.

One of the few authors to address the subject of Civil War mobilization is Paul Koistinen, who argues that the Civil War period was characterized by resources that were abundant compared to the war's requirements—at least on the northern side. Because of this, the North could obtain its war materials by offering money to contractors. It did not need to turn to the more-or-less government-directed sort of "command economy" that characterized the South during the Civil War and the United States

---

William H. Roberts holds a Ph.D. from the Ohio State University.

during 18th and 20th Century wars.² While this broad-brush analysis seems valid for most sectors of the northern economy, a closer look shows that in critical areas, the Union was indeed resource limited. For this reason, successful mobilization required more than financial incentive—it required some government action beyond throwing money at the problem.

One major area in which "mobilization by financial incentive" proved to be inadequate was the U.S. Navy's procurement of armored vessels. The Union Navy commissioned its first ocean-going ironclad ship in March 1862. By war's end three years later, it had nearly sixty such vessels built and building, most of which were monitors—low-lying armored ships with their guns mounted in revolving turrets. Because the navy built more than fifty monitors and only four ocean-going ironclads of other designs, this paper focuses on monitors.

The Civil War naval mobilization was unprecedented in the nation's history—far larger and more complex than any previous one, and undertaken by a government that was not used to large projects or to fast action.³ The navy's backlog of orders for steam engines and the army's shortage of small arms show that merely getting manufacturers to build more copies of proven designs was difficult enough. In the ironclad program, technological uncertainty complicated the issue. Ironclads were high tech—the "wonder weapons" of their day. Besides that, the navy had to develop the new ironclad technology under conditions of great urgency. The existing ship acquisition system simply could not meet those twin challenges of urgency and uncertainty.

The acquisition system with which the U.S. Navy began the Civil War was itself created in response to challenges. Until the coming of steam, the navy built its ships almost exclusively in navy yards. Because yard managers were naval officers or civilian navy employees, the Navy Department and its bureaus had complete control of the process. The vessels were usually built by ones and twos, to designs prepared or approved by the Bureau of Construction, Equipment and Repairs. Different yards might receive the same plans and specifications, but no one expected that every ship of a class would be identical—the vagaries of wood ensured uniqueness even without the natural human tendency to "improve" a design.[4]

Steam disrupted this time-tested system. Navy yards had no facilities to build boilers and engines, so despite the expertise of naval engineers, the navy of the 1850s had to turn to private contractors for its steam propulsion machinery.[5] In doing so, it lost control of a vital element of ship design and construction. New technology led to a new acquisition system designed to reassert the navy's control over its shipbuilding.[6]

To regain that control, the navy evolved a system to maximize the impact of the only element that contractors understood: money. This "carrot and stick" approach involved two major elements. First, to encourage timely completion and relieve contractors of financial burdens, the navy would make progress payments at certain construction milestones. Second, each contract included a performance guarantee for the finished product. The navy would "reserve"—that is, withhold—final payment until the contractor's machinery performed successfully at sea. A case study of the USS *Merrimack* shows that this apparatus proved itself in the "Young America" frigate program of the 1850s.[7]

By the end of that decade, the navy had developed a framework within which to manage high-tech acquisition. Technologically, it had created an in-house cadre of experts—its naval engineers and naval constructors. Organizationally, it had grouped these experts within the Bureau of Construction, Equipment and Repairs—ship design and machinery design under the same bureaucratic roof—and established the precedent for having government inspectors present in contractors' establishments. Contractually, it had developed language that reduced risk for government and contractors alike—provisions that protected the navy from charlatans and incompetents, while providing incentives to competent contractors for timeliness, reliability and performance.

When war came in 1861, President Abraham Lincoln's proclamation of a blockade left Secretary of the Navy Gideon Welles scrambling for ships. Besides purchasing and arming merchant ships, Welles immediately began to let contracts for wooden blockading vessels and to build others in navy yards using commercial- or navy-built engines. Although these efforts proceeded with relatively few technical or contractual problems, the success was deceptive—steam propulsion, of itself, was no longer high technology.

Armored ships, however, *were* high technology. Ironclads were still experimental, and shipbuilders had reached no consensus on their design and construction.[8] The Union Navy quickly recognized this technological uncertainty. To help resolve it, the navy undertook in autumn 1861 what we would now call a "parallel development" program, contracting with civilian shipyards to build three very different ships —*New Ironsides, Galena,* and *Monitor.*[9]

If one were to characterize the Union ironclad program in a single word, that word would be "urgency." Secretary Welles urgently needed ironclads, first to contain Confederate ironclads and then to take the offensive against the Confederacy.[10] Urgency pervaded the Union ironclad program, and urgency contributed significantly to the breakdown of the acquisition system. Urgency kept the navy from meeting the rigid testing schedules mandated by its 1850s-style contracts. Urgency prevented the navy from taking time to resolve technical ambiguities in advance. Urgency drove the navy to make production decisions in a partial vacuum, committing itself to produce several similar classes of ironclads in parallel before "lessons learned" from the first ships were available. Urgency rendered the navy highly vulnerable to pressure in making its acquisition decisions. Under such pressure, the deficiencies of the 1850s acquisition system quickly began to surface.

Secretary Welles responded to the sense of urgency by placing Assistant Secretary Gustavus Vasa Fox in charge of ironclad procurement. Fox, a former naval officer with good political connections, was an enthusiast and a driver.[11] In addition, after witnessing the Battle of Hampton Roads in March 1862, he became a "monitor man" through and through. Fox's "conversion" and the political machinations of John Ericsson's partners in the *Monitor* project derailed the navy's plans for parallel evolutionary development of ironclads. When the navy was finally able to contract for more ironclads in March and April 1862, Union efforts concentrated on Ericsson's design—after March 1862, monitors were where the action was.[12] Less than a week after the *Monitor's* March 9, 1862, battle with the *Virginia* at Hampton Roads (and ten days before the bidding for additional ironclads was to close), Ericsson received a verbal order for six improved monitors of the *Passaic* class.[13]

Fox quickly became impatient with the navy's ship acquisition organization. The established Bureaus of Construction and Repair and of Steam Engineering supported ironclads, but they were not nearly as committed to the monitor design as was Fox.[14] The chiefs of those bureaus, Chief Constructor John Lenthall and Engineer in Chief Benjamin Franklin Isherwood, also had broad responsibilities.[15] They could not drop all their other projects to concentrate on ironclads, and thus to Fox they appeared dilatory. The results-oriented Assistant Secretary decided that ironclad procurement required reform.

Fortunately, a model for reform already existed. Soon after the war began, Welles and Fox realized that the highly centralized system they inherited was adequate when ships were built in navy yards in ones and twos, but faltered when dozens of ships were being built and converted by contractors. Their solution was decentralization, and in July 1861, Capt. Francis Hoyt Gregory was recalled from retirement and appointed to supervise gunboat construction in New York.[16] Gregory had little to do with ironclads at first, since all three first-generation ships were supervised by Rear Adm. Joseph Smith of the Bureau of Yards and Docks. One may presume, however, that Gregory knew of the progress of the *Monitor*. One may also presume that Gregory knew of the navy's representative on the *Monitor* project: Chief Engineer Alban Crocker Stimers, with whom Gregory had served in the 1850s.

Stimers, a rising star in the engineer corps, was assigned in November 1861 to supervise construction of the *Monitor*.[17] Working closely with John Ericsson gave him great confidence in the Swedish inventor and an intimate knowledge of "Ericsson's battery." Accompanying *Monitor* to Hampton Roads in March 1862, Stimers almost single-handedly saved the ship from foundering. During the Battle of Hampton Roads, Stimers operated *Monitor's* turret, then took command of the gunnery division. During the last part of the battle, he was the only officer in the turret, occupying an operational command position quite extraordinary for a non-line officer. Fox praised him highly in both personal and official letters—heady stuff for a staff officer described by a line messmate as "smart but coarse—and like all of his kind [engineers] overbearing and disagreeable."[18]

Stimers stayed with the *Monitor* for weeks, using the time to develop improvements to the *Monitor* design, but as it became clear that the *Virginia* would not come out, he found the prospect of glory in battle to be less enticing than the chance to design and build monitors. He returned to New York in mid- to late-April 1862.[19] Once there, Stimers found "Ericsson's new plans so superior to anything I had expected" that he shelved those he had made.[20] He reported upon his arrival to Admiral Gregory, who on May 7, 1862, was designated General Superintendent of Ironclads and given responsibility for all the ironclads building under contract along the East Coast.[21]

Soon after, Stimers was assigned to be General Inspector of Ironclads. Gregory told Stimers of his appointment on May 23, 1862, laying down his duties in very broad terms.[22] Gregory, however, knew that Stimers had the ear of Assistant Secretary Fox; as he described it, "there came an order stating, very laconically, that Mr. Stimers would have charge of those vessels building on the Ericsson plan, and he took the charge." Stimers characterized their roles: Gregory "governing largely the personnel . . . I as general inspector governing wholly the construction itself."[23] Stimers' appointment began the process by which the General Superintendent's organization evolved into the "monitor bureau."

Stimers' initial task was to supervise the construction of the new monitors that Ericsson had designed, not to design monitors himself. Prewar practice included assigning inspectors to contractors' establishments, but urgency and cutting edge technology required expansion of the existing model. Stimers suddenly had to provide continuous in-depth inspection of many technically advanced vessels, which in turn required him to create overnight a large corps of inspectors. The General Inspector built his organization from two sources: naval engineers detailed to the Inspectorate and civilian engineers hired to serve in the same capacity.[24] These resident inspectors visited the ships they supervised at least daily to make sure that the contractors followed the specifications and used only good materials and workmanship. Besides forwarding the contractors' bills for progress payments and making regular progress reports to Stimers, the inspectors provided technical guidance to the contractors when required. Each vessel also had an assistant inspector of machinery, who reported to Stimers through one of his direct subordinates.[25] Stimers made frequent inspection trips up and down the seaboard, keeping an eye on both the contractors and the local inspectors.

This corps of local inspectors was more important than it at first seems, because each inspector had the authority to reject a contractor's workmanship or materials.[26] Rejection meant delay and increased expense; for example, the stern post forging for the monitor *Tippecanoe* cost the contractor two weeks work when the inspector condemned it as scant (too thin).[27] Because rejection could hinge on an inspector's interpretation, Stimers' authority to direct the local inspectors markedly increased his influence over ironclad contractors.[28]

Besides this explosive growth in personnel, the "monitor bureau" grew in scope as Stimers centralized technical authority for the monitor program. Ericsson had begun to think about his "second generation" design for the *Passaic* class well before *Monitor* was finished. He worked closely with Fox and Stimers, however, and the ships' characteristics remained under discussion into early April 1862.[29] Once the design was settled, several contractors built the *Passaics* from Ericsson's plans, a change from previous practice in which contractors developed their own detail drawings from general plans and specifications.[30]

Contractor inexperience with the new technology was a factor in this move to centralized design, but it was not the only impulse behind the navy's decision to enforce strict configuration control. Ericsson, who originated the designs, had a very high reputation, and Fox wanted to ensure that his wishes were followed.[31] The navy had begun to recognize that in the application of high technology, apparently insignificant details could have broad impact. In addition, the move would give the navy the benefits of production runs of identical units—increased output and decreased delivery time. For the "follow" yards, of course, there was an element of uneasiness in being forced to use someone else's plans; they had nothing beyond Ericsson's assurance that each part would fit "in the others like hand to glove." If the parts did not fit, the follow yard would have to pay for the wastage and rework.[32]

Centralized design made perfect sense—in theory. In practice, however, it massively increased the workload on the centralized designer, and by mid-1862, Ericsson was trying to supervise six monitors himself while producing the detail drawings for the entire *Passaic* class. The inventor's workload grew again in June 1863 when the navy awarded him contracts for two ocean-going monitors. These ships were Ericsson's pets and he lavished effort upon them; even with his remarkable capacity for work, he was nearing his limit. Yet the navy wanted at least two more classes of monitor, a "fast" monitor for "harbor and river" service (later called the *Tippecanoe* class) and a "light draft" monitor (later called the *Casco* class) for the Confederacy's shallow rivers. Someone had to design these ships.

Stimers accordingly established an office in which he placed a junior engineer and some draftsmen, who were to take Ericsson's general plans and fill in the details for Ericsson's approval. For the *Tippecanoe* class, Ericsson "drew up a general plan and submitted a general description," and Stimers consulted with Ericsson and Fox to develop the specifications, including "changes upon which we all agreed."[33] Over the autumn of 1862 and winter of 1863, Ericsson gradually withdrew from this arrangement and Stimers took over the design work, adding more engineers and more draftsmen.[34]

Ericsson's withdrawal from designing monitors left the General Inspector in sole possession of that field. As Stimers absorbed the design function into his organization, he had several skirmishes with Lenthall and Isherwood. By going directly to Fox, Stimers resolved these issues to his satisfaction and established monitor design as his own bureaucratic "turf." No longer would urgently-needed designs be delayed by the need to have them approved by the Bureaus; with regard to monitors, Lenthall and Isherwood had been reduced to rubber stamps.[35] Although in hindsight this may have seemed premature or too optimistic, in 1862 it was justifiable. There was so little "established practice" in the largely unexplored field of ironclad design that Stimers' credentials were as good as anyone else's—he was an experienced seagoing engineer, he had helped to build the *Monitor*, and he worked closely with John Ericsson. His experience in Hampton Roads enhanced his credibility—of the potential ironclad designers, only Stimers had actually engaged in ironclad combat. Fox felt that Ericsson's review of monitor drawings would be sufficient to ensure that the monitor program stayed firmly on the Ericsson track.

By mid- to late 1862, then, many elements of a revamped acquisition system were in place. Technologically, monitor design had been centralized in Ericsson and Stimers, and the innovation of providing Ericsson's drawings to each contractor promised significant benefits. Organizationally, almost all ironclad production on the East Coast came under the General Inspector's specialized establishment, and a corps of inspectors had been formed to ensure that Ericsson's drawings would be followed. In contracting, however, the navy lagged behind.

The lack of contractual progress was primarily due to overlap among contracts—the *Passaic* class contracts were let in the spring of 1862, before any of the first generation ironclad contracts were settled, and the follow-on *Tippecanoe* class contracts were let in autumn 1862 before any of the *Passaics* were even completed. Based on the machinery agreements of the 1850s, the contracts lacked two vital elements: a workable mechanism for incorporating technical changes, and a mechanism to account for the economic effects of war upon supplies of capital, materials, and skilled labor.

By late 1862, changes were becoming a major problem. Construction changes result from the natural desire to make each vessel the best she can be. Yet each change involves a tradeoff, since each disrupts the efficient construction of the ship. Eventually the design must be "frozen"—changes must stop—if the ship is to be finished. With vessels as novel as the monitors, designed and built in such haste, omissions were bound to occur and improvements were certain to suggest themselves. The navy's rudimentary mechanism for dealing with construction changes broke down under the stress.

The contracts for the *Passaic* class did include provision for changes, but they used unsophisticated language similar to that applied to the first-generation ironclads. Improvements "suggested by either party, and agreed upon, shall be adopted as the work progresses. All the modifications recommended and adopted" by the contractors would be warranted "to prove successful improvements, with any other improvements the parties to this contract may agree upon." A later clause reiterated that improvements "suggested and employed" by the contractor would be guaranteed "to work successfully."[36] While this language seemed to protect the government's interests, it failed to address important issues.

The most obvious was the question of who would pay for modifications "agreed upon" by the government and the contractor. The *New Ironsides* settlement, in which the contractors received additional money "by bill of extras allowed by agreement," shows what was apparently intended, but that contract was not finally settled until November 1862, long after the contracts for the *Passaic* class were made.[37] For the seagoing monitors, Ericsson merely received a promise from Fox that he would be compensated for his extra work, and Welles assured the inventor of the Navy Department's "interest and disposition to act in a liberal spirit towards you" with regard to changes on the *Passaics*.[38]

A more vexing question was that of pricing the modifications. The least sophisticated pricing model would cover the labor and material cost of doing new or revised work. This conformed to the practice in the closely related machine tool industry.[39] A more comprehensive model would include the labor cost of ripping out the old work and the labor and material involved in removing and replacing items that were in the way (interferences). The most complex model would include indirect costs: the increased cost of the original work due to delay and disruption incident to the additional work. This model would also involve extension of the end date of the contract so that the contractor would not be penalized for late delivery. At least at first, the government paid only for the new work and did not formally extend the end date.

Related in turn to this was the question of changes on which the government and the contractor did *not* agree. How would the system react to what in modern terms is a "unilateral" change? It was apparently understood that the government could compel the contractor to make such a change. The extent to which the government would then be liable for incidental claims (beyond the direct cost of the change itself) was unclear.

The looseness of the change provisions certainly affected the cost of the ships, but the financial aspects could have been worked out—in post-completion litigation, if necessary—without serious injury to the construction program.[40] More damaging, the lack of a contractual requirement to agree on design changes helped to camouflage their true cost in time and money and encouraged the navy to make them while the ships were still under construction. The "continuous improvement" philosophy that resulted led to gross delays, massive expenditure and technical failure.

The navy did at least examine the issue before deciding to incorporate the lessons of combat experience in later classes. Stimers observed that in a discussion at the Navy Department, "it was well shown that it would cost a great deal of money to make the changes, and would make great delay...." The goal, however, was combat effectiveness. The policy was established at least at the level of Assistant Secretary Fox, who "said he supposed if we went on in this way and made changes, every time a monitor was in a fight it would cost a million of dollars; but notwithstanding that, he supposed it was the best plan to pursue."[41]

Fox supposed that making changes during construction was the best plan, but the factors that influenced his conclusion are not recorded.[42] It is clear, however, that the navy explicitly weighed the potential for great expense and great delay before deciding to modify the ships under construction. Fox's supposition was a defensible policy decision, explicitly taken. Unfortunately, in implementing that policy Stimers piled change upon change and delay upon delay. A more sophisticated process, requiring the contractors and the navy to estimate the impact of each change before it was ordered, could have been extremely valuable in keeping the monitor program on track.[43]

An example of the "ripple effect" of technological change involves the ordnance of the *Passaic* class. The original *Monitor* carried two 11-inch guns, but these proved indecisive in her fight with the *Virginia*. Fox decided that larger guns were needed and ordered Capt. John A. Dahlgren, the navy's premier ordnance expert, to develop a 15-inch gun. Dahlgren took the job reluctantly.[44] Technical problems bedeviled the 15-inch program and production started very slowly. By the end of September 1862, when Ericsson was to have completed six monitors carrying twelve 15-inch guns, the first gun had not even arrived at the Washington Navy Yard for testing.[45]

Worse, Ericsson had designed the *Passaics*' turrets for 11-inch Dahlgren smoothbores. Although Dahlgren sent him the plans for the 15-inch guns, Ericsson failed to redesign the turrets accordingly.[46] When the 15-inch guns finally arrived, their muzzles would not fit through the monitors' gun ports. Widening the ports would have weakened the turrets, so an expensive and time-consuming crash program was needed to correct the problem. Enlargements of similar scale had been made to other ships, but Ericsson's very "tight" design had no margin for changes.[47]

Another example of the bad effects of "better" instead of "good enough" is the marked growth between the original specifications for the *Tippecanoe* class, shown to bidders in August 1862, and the specifications the navy sent to contractors in October.[48] Besides delaying the drawings, the aggregated changes made the ships too heavy and adversely affected their trim. To remedy the problems, the contractors had to disassemble the partially completed ships, at great cost in time and money.

By late 1862, then, the navy had made real progress in its organization and management of high-technology acquisition. Recognizing that only contractors could build the ships it needed, the navy adapted its procurement organization to work closely with civilian industry and to provide a single organization that could focus on the new technology. Yet despite the improvements, hidden difficulties remained. The program begun with such high hopes began to bog down, and successful and timely production of the new monitors would be a major task.

A major "hidden difficulty" was financial. The ironclad contracts of 1861 and 1862 were modeled on 1850s machinery contracts, in which the contractor agreed to produce a specified article for a stated price. Such contracts, now called "fixed price" contracts, assumed that the article could be specified—that the contract would be clear and unambiguous and that the specifications would not change before the contract was completed. They further assumed that economic conditions would remain stable—that the price and supply of labor and materials would not change dramatically—and they were laden with financial incentives and penalties.

Applied to the experimental technology of armored vessels, the first generation ironclad contracts did not protect the government from the contractors' technical failures.[49] Beyond that, the contracts contained no practical method for dealing with changes. In the 1850s system, the contractor built only the machinery, which was unlikely to change much between contract and delivery. No mechanism for processing major contract changes had evolved because none had been needed.

Yet changes were inevitable, especially when dealing with new technologies. Major changes during the building of the *New Ironsides* substituted 11-inch guns for 8-inch; more than doubled the crew; and added armored bulkheads, gun port shutters, and a pilothouse. The contractual result was a compromise: the contractor absorbed the "omissions" (such as the port shutters and pilothouse), and the navy paid for the items it considered to be changes.[50] Design changes and their technical, financial and schedule implications would become tremendously important as the ironclad program grew during 1862 and 1863.

Changing economic conditions also undercut the 1850s contracting system. Fixed price contracts worked in times of unchanging prices, but by 1862 the Union's economy was less stable. Wages and prices had begun to rise, inflation had begun to show itself, and the Treasury Department could not pay the navy's warrants promptly. It was, as Ericsson's biographer pointed out, "hazardous business to estimate upon government work."[51] The unstable environment made fixed price contracts unsuitable even for such simple and well-defined items such as clothing.[52] The emphasis on financial incentives and penalties built into the 1850s style contracts compounded the effect on shipbuilders.

compounded the effect on shipbuilders.

The navy stressed the fiscal side of its contracts because it wanted to get the government's money's worth and withholding funds was practically the only leverage it had. Early wartime experience with the first generation ironclads (as well as with other shipbuilding and conversion efforts) reinforced this mindset. The navy gave some credence to the constant complaints from ship and engine builders that their contracts were less profitable than anticipated, but mounting delays and increasing friction gave navy officials the impression that most contractors were more interested in money than in fulfilling their contracts.[53] Feeling that many contractors were no more scrupulous than they were forced to be, the navy adopted a wary, almost suspicious attitude, increased its inspection force, and mandated strict enforcement of contract provisions.[54]

Over time, the effect was to reinforce the lesson that withholding funds was the government's chief weapon and to inculcate the idea that the contractors' protests were only meant to increase their profits. Unfortunately, the navy's perception of shipbuilder profiteering was wrong. Most contractors were in fact hurting as they faced delays from their suppliers and poured more of their generally inadequate capital into their projects. The navy's reaction to contractor slowness was to withhold progress payments; the inflationary economic climate made withholding payments counterproductive.

Union industrial capacity formed a second major "hidden difficulty" for the monitor program. Although industrial mobilization is beyond the scope of this paper, by mid-1862, the navy's orders for the ten improved monitors of the *Passaic* class had backlogged the established shipyards of the East Coast. The *Tippecanoe* class of "fast monitors" was begun in early autumn 1862; of the nine ships, four were built in Cincinnati, Ohio, and Pittsburgh, Pennsylvania. By autumn 1862 and winter 1863, as the navy prepared for yet another class of monitors, navy officials were explicitly assessing the industrial capacity of the nation's shipbuilders to construct specific types of ships. Stimers' and Fox's very ambitious monitor program overtaxed the nation's resources and manpower and contributed to the sharp escalation of shipbuilding labor and materials prices.[55]

The third "hidden difficulty" for the monitor program, the monitor bureau itself did not become evident until late 1863 and 1864. During its first year, the monitor program enjoyed a string of technical and industrial successes, in large part traceable to the General Inspector's "project office." These advantages, all of which derived from the focused nature of the General Inspector's organization, offered the potential to develop better designs, better construction management, better alteration management, better logistics support, and better opportunities to integrate all facets of the ironclad program.

First and fundamentally, Stimers' organization had a single focus: monitors. Unlike the Bureaus of Construction and Repair and of Steam Engineering, responsible for everything from contract-built river gunboats to navy yard-built wooden cruisers, the General Inspector had a limited area of concern. The "project office" could concentrate its efforts, as it concentrated initially on providing ironclads quickly and in quantity. The *Passaic* class represented a very aggressive program of concurrent development and deployment, and the project office successfully integrated all the details required to produce serviceable ironclads in minimum time. As a single-focus organization, the "project office" could also be highly responsive to the concerns of the navy's leadership. This is evident not only in Stimers' ongoing relationship with Fox but in the considerable energy and inventiveness displayed in preparing Adm. Samuel F. Du Pont's ironclads for his April 1863 attack on Charleston and in modifying them afterwards.

Second, the "monitor project office" controlled the design details of its ships. Normally, a ship built by one bureau would be engined by another and armed by a third. If each bureau optimized its own systems with little regard for how they fit together, or if the three coordinated their efforts imperfectly, it would lessen the effectiveness of the ship. With a single agency responsible for all parts of the vessel, everything could be integrated to optimize the overall design.

Third, the "monitor project office" was uniquely well placed to provide integrated logistics support for its ships. Its centralized technical management gave it much more control over the ships' configuration than was common at the time, which meant that the ships could reasonably be expected to match the drawings on file at the project office. This, in turn, allowed the development of alteration "kits," like pilot house reinforcement sleeves or turret base rings, that reduced the time and effort needed to perform alterations in the field. Similarly, common designs and readily available drawings eased the problem of providing repair parts to deployed monitors. Involvement in every stage of design and construction allowed project office personnel to become "monitor specialists" and enabled the General Inspector to provide forces afloat with experts to alter and repair the ships on station.[56] Well-trained personnel, intimate knowledge of requirements, and close relations with contractors allowed such highly successful fleet support operations as the groups of workmen that made up the Port Royal Working Parties, their Hampton Roads Working Party counterpart, and the team that repaired the monitor *Weehawken's* engine in Port Royal.[57]

Fourth, the "monitor project office" was the central point for collection of feedback and "lessons learned" about the monitors. All of the complaints and difficulties attributed to the ships funneled back to the project office, either directly or through Fox. This provided an excellent opportunity to learn; as Fox wrote, "I like to hear their faults, because it teaches a lesson—Praise never does."[58] Despite the division between builders (engineers) and operators (line officers) and despite Ericsson's prickly attitude toward critics, the feedback from the fleet could be seen in alterations such as those that strengthened the pilot houses and turrets, reduced leakage under the turret bases, and increased the ships' capacity to remove flooding water.

The "monitor project office" organization suffered, however, from latent drawbacks, including the volume of work the office took on and the lack of independent technical review of its engineering decisions. The drawbacks stemmed from a combination of Stimers' personality and the ambiguous position of the project office in the navy's organization.

The volume of work assigned to or claimed by the project office grew dramatically in 1862 and 1863. Originally conceived as a production-oriented organization, the project office expanded to fill all the niches that opened in the monitor program. When Ericsson became too busy to perform the detail design of the harbor and river monitors, the project office first assumed the duty of turning the master's general plans into detailed drawings, and then began to develop its own monitor designs. When the deployed monitors required alterations and repairs, the project office assumed the organization and management of the work and the workers. When the design of the light draft monitors seemed stalled, the project office took it over. Stimers even made designs for a "fast sloop-of-war," to be called the *Mercury*, and a twin-turreted monitor.[59] Coupled with several temporary duty assignments to Port Royal and the demands of defending himself before a Court of Inquiry, the project officer's workload was a killing one. Stimers could not do it all and still do it correctly.

Yet flaws in the General Inspector's character kept him from seeking assistance. Jealous of his "turf" and ambitious for advancement, he would not turn to the established bureaus for assistance and in fact rebuffed them whenever he could. Neither would he ask Ericsson for help, at first because of Ericsson's egocentric resistance to "any other than himself" designing monitors and then because of a quarrel over the *Tippecanoe* class gun mountings.[60] Stimers became trapped in the cycle of overwork and cutting corners that may be characterized as "never time to do it right but always time to do it over."

Aggravating the problem of Stimers' rejection of bureau assistance was the attitude of the bureau chiefs themselves. Stimers had gained practical independence from the Bureaus of Construction and Repair and of Steam Engineering, and the bureau chiefs, in turn, washed their hands of Stimers' designs. While the independence and hand washing gratified the egos of those concerned, they removed an essential portion of an effective "project office" system: the second look. On the policy level, no one in a position of responsibility proposed alternatives to the monitors after Hampton Roads. On the technical level, no one in the navy double-checked Stimers' designs, while Stimers' growing coolness toward Ericsson and Ericsson's preoccupation with his "big pets" removed the informal "second look" upon which Fox depended. To be effective, a project office must have authority to make decisions on its project, but basing those decisions upon a single source of technical information and opinions is not sound management. Stimers succeeded so well in his autonomy campaign that he gave up the "safety net" that a second technical opinion would have provided.

Stimers' autonomy campaign illuminates the most serious deficiency in the navy's ironclad acquisition structure: excessive imbalance between the service's formal and informal organizations. Formally, Stimers' job was to ensure that the monitors being built met the specifications that others had prepared—a responsible assignment, but not one calculated to make an ambitious man stand out from his contemporaries. Informally, Stimers owned the entire monitor program in fee simple, from design through construction to in-service repairs.

Stimers thus exercised influence far out of proportion to his station, influence that he owed purely to his relationship with Fox. Yet with influence came insecurity. Fox had caused Secretary Welles to create Stimers' position and to order Stimers to the job; he could as readily remove Stimers and assign someone else as General Inspector. Stimers also knew that the General Superintendent's office was a wartime expedient; when the war ended, it would surely evaporate. Stimers' touchiness and hunger for autonomy were in part a response to the insecurity of his too-highly-exalted position.

Stimers' insecurity was aggravated by the relative position of the bureau chiefs, whom he saw as rivals. Unlike the General Superintendent's organization, the bureaus were permanent and established by law. Unlike the General Inspector, the bureau chiefs had been confirmed in their positions by Congress and could not be dismissed lightly. Isherwood and Lenthall thus had a much more secure institutional base than Stimers—and when the war ended, they would retain their high status, while he would return to relative obscurity. Although the bureau chiefs had little practical authority over the ironclad program, Stimers perceived their latent formal authority as a constant threat.

In February 1864, Stimers proposed to Fox that the Navy Department ask Congress to create a Bureau of Iron Clad Steamers. The new bureau would be headed by "a practical and scientific engineer" with a staff of thirteen.[61] Stimers' proposal would, in effect, institutionalize the monitor project office and make it permanent. By correcting the most insidious and corrosive flaw of the General Inspector of Ironclads organization—Stimers' total dependence upon Fox—it would have significantly improved the acquisition system. A permanent, formally established project office might have prevented or ameliorated the delay and disruption caused by the "continuous improvement" philosophy.

The legislation that Stimers proposed was quite general, perhaps deliberately so. It did not clearly define the administrative boundaries between the new bureau and the existing ship acquisition bureaus. Bureaucratic "turf" considerations, professional and personal animosity toward Stimers, and line officer reluctance to see a second bureau run by an engineer militated against it, but the proposal's demise was hardly foreordained. In its 1862 reorganization, the navy had acknowledged the need to institutionalize new technology, and the Bureau of Steam Engineering was the result. A similar move to institutionalize another new technology seemed distinctly possible.

Given the chance, the Bureau of Iron Clad Steamers could have corrected many problems. By reintegrating the ironclads into the navy's bureau system, it would have enforced cooperation among the navy's technical bureaus, or at the least ensured that controversies between them would reach the Secretary of the Navy for explicit resolution. By aligning the navy's formal and informal organizations and formalizing the General Inspector's informal control of the ironclad program, it would have removed much of the insecurity that drove Stimers' quest for autonomy.

Unfortunately, by the time Stimers made his proposal, he had already ensured its death. The mortal blow was the failure of the light draft monitors of the *Casco* class. Without examining the light draft effort in detail, the failure stemmed from Stimers' eagerness to elaborate on Ericsson's simple sketch design—to use the most elegant leading edge technology and get the maximum possible performance from the ships. As in many ambitious high-tech projects, leading edge became "bleeding edge." Great delay and massive cost overruns were the results. Worse was to come. When equipped for combat, the light draft monitors would not float.[62]

Fox took the news badly. Although the reasons for the delays and cost overruns might be clear to Stimers, Fox wrote, "to us it comes like the sudden destruction of bright hopes." The construction delays were fatal—"fatal to the ironclads, to the monitors, to the establishment of any proposition [the Bureau of Iron Clad Steamers] such as you have presented. . . ." The light drafts would not be done for the summer campaign of 1864, "though six of them would have given us the vitals of the South. What is the reason?—additions, alterations and improvements." Fox blamed himself for the everlasting alterations, because he "could and ought to have prevented it."[63]

The fiasco toppled Stimers, mortified Fox, embarrassed Welles, and set the navy's acquisition system back in a way that required decades to recoup. Stimers' need to please Fox and his urge to create the best technically possible ship led him to overcomplicate and overload the vessels. His autonomy campaign and his estrangement from Ericsson meant that no one outside his organization scrutinized his plans or restrained his urge to elaborate. Within his own organization, overwork kept Stimers from checking the calculations his subordinates made. The General Inspector's personality was clearly a factor, but the shortcomings of the monitor program's *ad hoc* organization prevented administrative structure from compensating for personal deficiencies. The very public failure of a multi-million dollar program discredited the idea of an independent project office.

It has been said about the armed forces of democracies that they hit their stride just about the time the war ends. This was certainly the case in the Civil War navy's ship acquisition programs. By late 1864, Fox had been weaned from the continuous improvement philosophy and the negotiation method of making changes was gaining momentum. The excesses of the monitor project office had been curbed and corrective action was being taken on the worst excess, the light draft monitors.⁶⁴ The acquisition bureaucracy had realized that withholding money from financially strained contractors was counterproductive, and Admiral Gregory's efforts to clear up the backlog of contractors' claims were bearing fruit. The expansion shipyards of the Ohio River valley were building quality ships as fast as the available labor supply would allow. The war had been a harsh teacher, but the navy appeared to have learned its lessons.

By the time the "new navy" of the 1880s began to appear, however, few traces remained of the massive industrial mobilization of the war years, and the lessons the war taught had been largely forgotten. Contracting had regressed, the wartime shipyards of Pittsburgh and Cincinnati had vanished, and the project office form of organization had evaporated. Some contend that after the Civil War, the navy returned to its prewar routine so completely that a visitor "returning in 1870 after ten years' absence might never have guessed that the Navy had passed through any war at all."⁶⁵

Administratively, the project office form of management was the major innovation of the war. It had many advantages, and Stimers' proposal to institutionalize it by creating a Bureau of Iron Clad Steamers would have been a step forward for the navy. The delays and expenses of western shipbuilding played their part in the reaction against the project office form of acquisition management, but it was primarily the light draft fiasco that killed Stimers' 1864 proposal and derailed the idea of making the "project office" permanent.⁶⁶ Similarly, a postwar reaction reversed the trend toward flexibility in naval acquisition. The result was a renewed exaltation of competitive bidding for government contracting and a proliferation of marginally successful rules to prevent fraud. Ship acquisition swung back toward an 1850s model; for a dozen years after the war, the navy built most of its ships in its own yards.

Despite some early successes, the monitor program could provide a case study in what one author calls "The Law of the Rathole: Know when to quit."⁶⁷ Fox had "married" Ericsson's technology by very publicly and whole-heartedly committing the navy to the monitor. Fox then failed to create a "rival rathole"—by eliminating technical competition and oversight, he eliminated the need for

Stimers to defend his decisions on technical grounds. By the time Stimers' technical failures became manifest, it was too late to save the program. The Assistant Secretary also failed to manage expectations. "Big projects draw lots of attention," and Fox fanned the public relations fire at every opportunity. Every news story meant that a bit more of the navy's prestige had been invested in the monitors, and the more prestige invested, the more difficult it was to change course. Finally, both Fox and Stimers failed to monitor their subordinates: just as Stimers accepted his assistant Theodore Allen's assurances that all was well with the light draft program, so did Fox accept Stimers' assurances.

Welles, too, bears his share of fault. Depending too heavily on Fox, he did not closely examine the program until the launch of the first light-draft monitor gave unmistakable evidence of failure.[68] He assumed that Lenthall and Isherwood were as involved in the monitors as they were in other programs and that no news was good news.[69] Welles never "pulled the string" far enough to find the knots and snarls; his neglect gave ammunition to the Lincoln Administration's political enemies and helped to discredit the project office system both inside and outside the navy.

After the original *Monitor* and the *Passaic* class, the navy ordered thirty-nine coastal and seagoing monitors. Of the nine *Tippecanoe* class ships, only five were completed while the Civil War lasted. Only five of the twenty light draft *Cascos* were finished by war's end. Of eight navy yard built monitors of the *Miantonomoh* and *Kalamazoo* classes, only *Monadnock* saw Civil War service, and of Ericsson's two "big pets," only *Dictator* was ever completed. When the war ended, twenty-seven of the thirty-nine monitors ordered after mid-1862 were still under construction. The resources wasted and the operational opportunities missed for lack of ships were staggering.

Civil War experience showed that the "continuous improvement" method applied to contract-built vessels would produce ships for the next war, not the current one. The institutional memory was short, however, and many lessons were lost. From the end of the Civil War through the 1870s, the navy commenced twenty-two ships, of which only three had iron hulls. Five were built by contractors, the others in navy yards.[70] After 1873, the navy did not again build iron or steel-hulled vessels until the "ABCD" ships (cruisers *Atlanta, Boston,* and *Chicago* and dispatch boat *Dolphin*) of 1883.

A recent study of navy-business relationships demonstrates how navy contracts of the 1870s and early 1880s evolved from those of the war years. By 1871, the navy had moved to ease the contractors' capital shortages by making permanent the reduced reservation percentage instituted in 1864 and by giving contractors more frequent progress payments. The contracts for the ABCD ships similarly incorporated some clauses and refined others from earlier contracts, mostly in ways that increased the navy's control of the shipbuilding process or protected the government's interests.[71]

Despite this contractual progress, the "ABCD" effort clearly showed that the navy had not internalized key lessons of the monitor program. First, the navy offered the ships for bid before the plans were completed. Next, rigid pro-competition laws forced the navy to award all four of the ABCD contracts to the low bidder, John Roach of Chester, Pennsylvania. During construction, Roach suffered from careless or late preparation of drawings by the navy and a constant stream of "additions, alterations and improvements." Thanks to delays and the growing amount of rework required, Roach's capital ran short and he had difficulty paying his workforce, slowing the work and further delaying progress payments.

In 1885, newly appointed (Democratic) Secretary of the Navy William C. Whitney withheld payments due to (Republican) contractor Roach, and Roach was forced into bankruptcy on July 18, 1885.[72] Thanks to even more design changes, the navy required twenty-two more months to finish the nearly completed ships after it took over Roach's shipyard. It was *"déja vu* all over again." The institutional consequences of the Civil War mobilization were as ephemeral as the physical ones. After its initial successes, the "monitor project office," lacking formal structure to compensate for its informal deficiencies, had failed. The reaction against its failure stunted the navy's ship acquisition system for decades.

NOTES

¹For example, Raimondo Luraghi sees Southern defeat as "inescapable." "No agricultural, underdeveloped country could ever defeat an industrial one," Luraghi writes, "and the South was no exception." The Confederacy's "few men endowed with genius" were doomed to failure "even before a single cannon shot had been fired." Raimondo Luraghi, *A History of the Confederate Navy* (Annapolis: Naval Institute Press, 1996), 347.

²Paul A. C. Koistinen, *Beating Plowshares into Swords: The Political Economy of American Warfare, 1606-1865* (Lawrence, KS: University Press of Kansas, 1996).

³The lack of attention paid to this issue is epitomized by one author's blithe assertion that the northern industrial base "merely" required an increase in tooling and production. Ervan G. Garrison, "Three Ironclad Warships—The Archaeology of Industrial Process and Historical Myth," *Historical Archaeology* 29 (1995), no. 4: 34.

⁴Howard I. Chapelle, *The History of the American Sailing Navy: The Ships and Their Development* (New York: Bonanza Books, 1949 (reprint)), 371-425.

⁵Barbara B. Tomblin, "From Sail to Steam: The Development of Steam Technology in the United States Navy, 1838-1865" (Ph.D. diss., Rutgers The State University of New Jersey-New Brunswick, 1988).

⁶Kurt Henry Hackemer, "From Peace to War: U.S. Naval Procurement, Private Enterprise, and the Integration of New Technology, 1850-1865" (Ph.D. diss., Texas A&M University, 1994).

⁷Ibid., 5-10.

⁸For a discussion of how engineers advance knowledge in the absence of sound theory, see Walter G. Vincenti's description of the process he calls "variation-selection." Walter G. Vincenti, *What Engineers Know and How They Know It: Analytical Studies from Aeronautical History* (Baltimore: Johns Hopkins University Press, 1990), 48-49, 241-50.

⁹The three vessels' design and construction may be found in, respectively, William H. Roberts, *USS New Ironsides in the Civil War* (Annapolis: Naval Institute Press, 1999); Hackemer, "From Peace to War"; and Stephen C. Thompson, "The Design and Construction of USS *Monitor*," *Warship International* 27, no. 3 (1990): 222-42.

¹⁰Welles to John P. Hale, February 7, 1862, National Archives, Record Group 45, Office of Naval Records and Library, Entry 5, Letters to Congress, vol. 11, labeled on spine "No. 13 Jan. 3, 1855 to May 12, 1862."

¹¹For more on Fox, see John D. Hayes, "Captain Fox—He is the Navy Department," *United States Naval Institute Proceedings* 91, no. 9 (September 1965), 65-67; and William J. Sullivan, "Gustavus Vasa Fox and Naval Administration" (Ph.D. diss., Catholic University of America, 1977).

¹²See William H. Roberts, "The Name of Ericsson: Political Engineering in the Union Ironclad Program 1861-1863," *Journal of Military History* 63 (October 1999), 823-44, and chapters 10 and 11 of Roberts, *USS New Ironsides*.

¹³Irene D. Neu, *Erastus Corning Merchant and Financier 1794-1872* (Ithaca, NY: Cornell University Press, 1960), 55. (The price increased from $325,000 in December 1861 to $400,000 after Hampton Roads.) For the verbal contract see William Conant Church, *The Life of John Ericsson* (New York: Charles Scribner's Sons, 1891), 2:5-6.

¹⁴James Phinney Baxter, III, *The Introduction of the Ironclad Warship* (Cambridge, MA: Harvard University Press, 1933; reprinted Hamden, CT: Archon Books, 1968), 284.

¹⁵The Bureau of Construction, Equipment and Repairs did not split into the Bureaus of Construction and Repair and of Steam Engineering until July 1862, but Isherwood was for practical purposes a bureau chief by mid-1861. For continuity's sake, I refer to him as such. Edward William Sloan III, *Benjamin Franklin Isherwood*

Naval Engineer: The Years as Engineer in Chief, 1861–1869 (Annapolis: Naval Institute Press, 1965), 28–29.

[16]Kenneth W. Munden and Henry Putney Beers, *The Union: A Guide to Federal Archives Relating to the Civil War* (Washington: National Archives and Records Administration, 1962), 484. Gregory was promoted to Rear Admiral on July 16, 1862. Similar decentralization took place in the West; when the navy expanded its riverine role, Welles sent Capt. Joseph B. Hull to St. Louis, Missouri, to take charge of navy shipbuilding on western waters. *Official Records of the Union and Confederate Navies in the War of the Rebellion* (Washington: Government Printing Office, 1894–1922), ser. 1, 23: 141. (Hereafter *ORN*.) Hull, also called back from retirement, was promoted to Commodore on July 16, 1862.

[17]Dana M. Wegner, "Alban C. Stimers and the Office of the General Inspector of Ironclads, 1862–1864" (Master's thesis, State University of New York College at Oneonta, 1979), 3–5. Smith to Stimers, November 5, 1861, in Julia Stimers Durbrow, *The Monitor and Alban C. Stimers* (Orlando, FL: Ferris Printing, 1936), 1–2.

[18]For Stimers' account, Alban C. Stimers, John D. Milligan, ed., "An Engineer Aboard the Monitor," *Civil War Times Illustrated* 9, no. 1 (April 1970), 28–35. Samuel D. Greene, "In the 'Monitor' Turret," in *The Opening Battles*, vol. 1 of *Battles and Leaders of the Civil War*, eds. Robert Underwood Johnson and Clarence C. Buel (New York: Appleton-Century-Crofts, 1956; reprint), 719–29. Fox to Welles, March 8, 1862, *ORN* 7:6 and Fox to Ericsson, March 9, 1862, ibid., 7; Fox to Stimers, March 10, 1862, in Durbrow, *The Monitor and Alban C. Stimers*, 10. John Barnes, quoted in Wegner, *Alban C. Stimers*, 4.

[19]In February Stimers told Fox he "would like to assist at getting up the specifications" of follow-on vessels. Stimers to Fox, February 3, 1862, Private, Gustavus V. Fox Papers, New York Historical Society (hereafter "Fox Papers"), Box 4. He wrote in mid-April, "I have my specifications completed now and the enemy has retreated to Norfolk." Stimers to Fox, April 14, 1862, ibid.

[20]Stimers to Fox, April 24, Fox Papers, Box 4. Ericsson had seen Stimers' plans, probably without Stimers' knowledge. He called them "utterly defective," with "not a redeeming feature in the whole production," and asked Fox not to require a formal report that would hurt Stimers. To prevent "serious injury to my excellent friend," Ericsson wanted Fox to smooth over the issue by ordering Stimers to "devote his whole time to the superintendence of the 6 vessels we are now building." Ericsson to Fox, April 23, 1862, Private, typescript, ibid., Box 3.

[21]Gregory to Welles, May 10, 1862, National Archives, Record Group 19, Records of the Bureau of Ships, Entry 1235, Correspondence of the General Superintendent of Ironclads, 18:41.

[22]Gregory to Stimers, May 23, 1862, NARG 19, Entry 1235, 18:42. Stimers told Fox that he highly approved of centralizing superintendency in Gregory because it would leave him with more time to attend to details than if he himself had been made General Superintendent. Stimers to Fox, May 10, 1862, Fox Papers, Box 4. Fox probably did not seriously consider Stimers for the higher post. The General Superintendent needed "clout" to deal with high-ranking officers; as a line admiral, even on the retired list, Gregory had far more clout than Stimers, a staff officer whose relative rank equaled that of a commander.

[23]Gregory testimony, in United States Congress, *Report of the Joint Committee on the Conduct of the War at the Second Session, Thirty-Eighth Congress* (Washington: Government Printing Office, 1865), "Light Draught Monitors"(hereafter "Light Draught Monitors"), 74. Deposition of Alban C. Stimers, August 11, 18, and 19, 1873, National Archives, Record Group 123, Records of the Court of Claims, Entry 1, General Jurisdiction Case Files, Case 6326/6327, Swift v. US. Case 6326 is "Alexander Swift et al. v. US,"dealing with light draft monitors *Klamath* and *Yuma*; Case 6327 is "Alexander Swift and the Niles Works v. US,"dealing with harbor and river monitors *Catawba* and *Oneota*. Principles, arguments and evidence were commingled. For brevity, they will be cited as "Case 6326/6327, Swift v. US."

[24]Isherwood testimony, "Light Draught Monitors,"116. For civilians, e.g.,

Welles to Thomas M. Griffith, January 2, 1863, and Welles to Thomas J. Griffin, April 18, 1863. NARG 45, Microfilm entry M209, Miscellaneous Letters Sent by the Secretary of the Navy, 68:57, 208.

[25]Reports from local inspectors are in NARG 19, Entry 64, and NARG 19, Entry 68, Reports Received from Superintendents Outside of Navy Yards and NARG 19, Entry 974 and 975, Reports of Inspectors of Machinery for Ironclad Steamers.

[26]I am indebted to Dr. Kurt H. Hackemer for this insight.

[27]Chief Engineer Charles H. Loring to Stimers, November 25, 1862, NARG 19, Entry 64, Box 1 (Jan 1862 – June 1863), 2:45.

[28]In 1863, Gregory revoked Stimers' authority to correspond directly with the contractors. Fox refused to intervene, so Stimers decided to evade Gregory's order. Although he could not instruct the contractors directly without going through Gregory, he reasoned, he *could* direct the government inspectors at each shipyard and have the inspectors direct the contractors. When this dodge came to Gregory's attention, the Admiral delivered a stinging rebuke. Gregory to Stimers, October 28, 1863, NARG 19, Entry 1235, 13:25.

[29]The navy and Ericsson tried to incorporate the lessons of Hampton Roads in follow-on ships, but the indecisive action taught few lessons. Baxter, *Ironclad Warship*, 359–60; Fox to J. Hayden, April 3, 1862, Robert Means Thompson and Richard Wainwright, eds., *Confidential Correspondence of Gustavus Vasa Fox Assistant Secretary of the Navy 1861–1865* (Freeport, NY: Books for Libraries Press, reprint of 1918–19 ed.), 2:285. Contracts with Ericsson for six vessels were signed March 31, 1862; NARG 19, Entry 235, Contracts for Construction of Naval Vessels 1861–1865, s.v. *Passaic*. Percival Drayton wrote that the experience gained from the Monitor "is so small that it is almost like beginning *de novo*." Drayton to Du Pont, November 24, 1862, in John D. Hayes, ed., *Samuel Francis Du Pont: A Selection from his Civil War Letters* (Ithaca, NY: Cornell University Press for The Eleutherian Mills Historical Library, 1969), *The Blockade: 1861–1862*, 2:293.

[30]Fox to Harrison Loring, April 14, 1862, NARG 45, Microfilm Entry M209, 68:63. Ericsson received $4,000 per vessel for the plans, which he furnished directly to other builders without going through any government agency. Nelson Curtis to Welles, May 11, 1862, NARG 45, Microfilm Entry M124, Miscellaneous Letters Received by the Secretary of the Navy, roll 407, 8; Deposition of Alban C. Stimers, August 25, 1873, NARG 123, Entry 1, Case #7157, Miles Greenwood vs. the United States.

[31]Deviation from Ericsson's drawings in the monitors *Passaic*, *Montauk* and *Kaatskill* resulted in severe leakage and expensive repairs aboard those three ships. Ericsson to Fox, January 10, 1863, NARG 45, Microfilm entry M124, roll 430, 168. The experience reinforced the navy's determination to enforce compliance with centrally issued drawings.

[32]Church, *Life of John Ericsson*, 2:5. Interchangeable parts were uncommon at this time, and interchangeability was generally achieved using a complicated and expensive system of inspection gauges. David A. Hounshell, *From the American System to Mass Production 1800–1932: The Development of Manufacturing Technology in the United States* (Baltimore: Johns Hopkins University Press, 1984), 27, 41–46. Ericsson's vast self-confidence and intolerance of criticism would not have diminished other shipbuilders' concerns.

[33]Stimers testimony, "Light Draught Monitors," 92, 95; Deposition of Alban C. Stimers, August 25, 1873, NARG 123, Entry 1, Case 7157, Greenwood v. US. Stimers stated that he "volunteered" to establish the office. Deposition of Alban C. Stimers, August 11, 18, 19, 1873, ibid., Case 6326/6327, Swift v. US.

[34]As Stimers observed, "these vessels were all of novel construction . . .," so the navy decided that the contractors would be required to work to the plans the navy furnished. One contractor noted, "we were not allowed to proceed with a single bolt without the drawings," and another recalled that his firm was "strictly forbidden" from proceeding without plans. Deposition of Alban C. Stimers, August 11, 18, 19, 1873, NARG 123, Entry 1, Case 6326/6327, Swift v. US; deposi-

tion of Nathaniel G. Thom, May 28, 1875, ibid.; Deposition of Joseph S. Kirk, May 30, 1876, ibid.

[35] From the *Passaic* class on, changes and characteristics came from the Fox-Stimers-Ericsson triumvirate, usually as the result of face-to-face interaction between Ericsson and Stimers and of exchanges of letters between Fox and Stimers and Fox and Ericsson. In its purest form: "Enclosed I send you the letter of recommendation which Mr. Lenthall can convert into an order and which covers the ground agreed upon at Capt. Ericsson's last night." Stimers to Fox, May 20, 1863, Fox Papers, Box 7.

[36] Blank form contract for *Passaic* class, NARG 45, Entry 464, Subject File, US Navy 1775-1910 (hereafter "NARG 45, Subject File"), AC—Construction, Box 22.

[37] National Archives, Record Group 71, Records of the Bureau of Yards and Docks, Entry 48, Contract Ledger for Iron Clads 1861-62, 1:11-12; Roberts, *USS New Ironsides*, 39.

[38] Church, *Life of John Ericsson*, 2:10; Welles to Ericsson, April 22, 1862, NARG 45, Microfilm entry M209, 68:108.

[39] Philip Scranton, *Endless Novelty: Specialty Production and American Industrialization, 1865-1925*, (Princeton: Princeton University Press, 1997), 45-46. Cost accounting may have advanced further than Scranton thinks; see Deposition of Cornelius H. Delamater, July 30, 1877, in Court of Claims 6327, Alexander Swift et al v. US, NARG 19, Entry 186, Papers Relating to Claims in Connection with the Construction of Civil War Vessels, 1862-1865, s.v. *Catawba*.

[40] The monitor contracts were not fully resolved until 1919, when the last Court of Claims cases were dismissed. James F. Secor and Anna A. Secor, Executors of the Will of James F. Secor, deceased, survivor of Zeno Secor and Charles A. Secor, v. The United States, 54 Court of Claims 92-107, December Term 1918-19.

[41] Deposition of Alban C. Stimers, August 11, 18, 19, 1873, NARG 123, Entry 1, Case 6326/6327, Swift v. US. Stimers' testimony in another case is in House Report 766, 51st Congress, 1st Session, March 10, 1890. He noted the desire to "make improvements as we went along, although we fully appreciated that it would delay [the ships'] completion and add to their cost." Ibid., 1.

[42] The alternative would have been to complete the ships, then make the changes. Later successful acquisition programs generally chose that "build it now, change it later" plan or incorporated modifications gradually in series production. Examples include the US B-29 bomber and submarine programs during World War II. Kenneth P. Werrell, *Blankets of Fire: U.S. Bombers over Japan during World War II* (Washington, DC: Smithsonian Institution Press, 1996), 82, 72, 75, 80; John D. Alden, *The Fleet Submarine in the U.S. Navy: A Design and Construction History* (Annapolis: Naval Institute Press, 1979), 78-79.

[43] The navy did try to institute a system of negotiating price and schedule before ordering its changes, but Stimers admitted, "that system applied to so small an amount as compared with the whole amount, that it didn't amount to much." Deposition of Alban C. Stimers, August 11, 18, and 19, 1873, NARG 123, Entry 1, Case 6326/6327, Swift v. US.

[44] Robert J. Schneller, *A Quest for Glory: A Biography of Rear Admiral John A. Dahlgren* (Annapolis: Naval Institute Press, 1996), 202-209, 218-23; telegram, Fox to Dahlgren, March 11, 1862, Library of Congress, Papers of John A. Dahlgren, Box 5, Folder "General Correspondence 1862."

[45] Fox to Ericsson, September 27, 1862, Reel 4, John Ericsson Papers, American Swedish Historical Foundation Microfilm Edition (Philadelphia, PA: Rhistoric Publications, 1970) (hereafter "Ericsson Papers"). The slow production of 15-inch guns forced builders to fit each *Passaic*-class ship (except *Camanche*) with one 15-inch and one smaller gun.

[46] Spencer C. Tucker, *Arming the Fleet: U.S. Navy Ordnance in the Muzzle-Loading Era* (Annapolis: Naval Institute Press, 1989), 220-21; Schneller, *Quest for Glory*, 208, 218-23.

[47] During construction, New Ironsides' guns were enlarged from 8 inch to 11

inch, multiplying the weight of the battery by a factor of about 2.6; increasing the *Passaics'* guns from 11 inch to 15 inch multiplied battery weight by a factor of about 2.5. The *Passaic* episode also displays a disadvantage of centralized design and concurrent production: if something is wrong with one unit, it will be wrong with the rest. Gun weights from U.S. Navy, Bureau of Ordnance, *Ordnance Instructions for the United States Navy* (Washington: Government Printing Office, 1866).

[48]Deposition of Alban C. Stimers, August 25, 1873, NARG 123, Entry 1, Case 7157, Greenwood v. US; deposition of Nathaniel G. Thom, December 29–30, 1876, January 2, 1877, July 9–10, 1877, ibid.

[49]Hackemer, "From Peace to War," 229; Kurt Hackemer, "Building the Military-Industrial Relationship: The U.S. Navy and American Business, 1854–1883," *Naval War College Review* 52, no. 2 (Spring 1999), 93–96.

[50]Roberts, *USS New Ironsides*, 14, 16, 21–23, 25; NARG 71, Entry 48, 1:11–12.

[51]Church, *Life of John Ericsson*, 1:270. Cost-plus contracts were used during the American Revolution to counter the inflation of that period, but post-Revolutionary reaction against fraud and perceived "excessive" profits led Congress gradually to idealize competitive bidding and fixed price contracting. James F. Nagle, *A History of Government Contracting* (Washington, DC: George Washington University, 1992), 7, 300.

[52]Consumer prices rose from an index value of 100 in 1860 to 121 in 1862, 151 in 1863, 189 in 1864, and 196 in 1865. John J. McCusker, *How Much Is That in Real Money? A Historical Price Index for Use as a Deflator of Money Values in the Economy of the United States* (Worcester, MA: American Antiquarian Society, 1992), 328. In 1863, the Chief of the Bureau of Provisions and Clothing wrote that inflation had caused most clothing contractors to default. *Annual Report of the Secretary of the Navy 1862–63* (Washington: Government Printing Office, 1863), 1033.

[53]Contractors, Stimers asserted, "really have no patriotism." He called them "people who remain at home and grow rich in time of war." Stimers to Fox, February 1, 1863, Fox Papers, Box 7. Rear Adm. Smith wrote, "I see you ready to propose sundry modifications to your contract, all of which lessen the expense to you. . . ." Smith to William H. Webb, August 8, 1862, NARG 45, Subject File AD—Ironclads, Box 51, typescript marked NWR (Naval War Records), 2634:367.

[54]A letter of January 1864 to machinery inspectors noted, "By the specifications you are entitled to demand the best materials that art can furnish, and a degree of workmanship which may be called perfect. It is impossible for the contractor to do more than comply. . . ." NARG 19, Entry 61, Letters Received by the Chief of the Bureau of Construction and Repair from the Secretary of the Navy, Box 2.

[55]See William H. Roberts, "'Irresistible Machines': Industrial Mobilization for the Union Navy 1861–1865" (Ph.D. diss., The Ohio State University, 1999).

[56]For example, Inspector Thomas J. Griffin, newly arrived in Port Royal, was able to repair *Passaic* on station when others thought she would have to be sent north to be fixed. Typescript copy of LCDR E. Simpson to Dahlgren, November 8, 1863, Naval Historical Center Operational Archives, ZB file, s.v. Griffin, Thomas Jefferson (Box 95).

[57]Dana M. Wegner, "The Port Royal Working Parties," *Civil War Times Illustrated* 15, no. 8 (December 1976): 22–31, and Roberts, "Irresistible Machines," chapter 7.

[58]Fox to Ericsson, December 30, 1862, Unofficial, typescript, Fox Papers, Box 3.

[59]Stimers to Fox, July 17, 1863, Fox Papers, Box 7; Stimers to Fox, July 24, 1863, ibid.

[60]Stimers testimony, "Light-Draught Monitors," 92; Stimers to Fox, February 29, 1864, Private, Fox Papers, Box 9.

[61]Stimers to Fox, February 18, 1864, Fox Papers, Box 9.

[62]The light drafts were designed to have 15 inches of freeboard. Fully loaded, *Chimo's* deck edges would have been submerged, and only the arched part of the

deck along the ship's fore-and-aft centerline would have been out of the water. Naval Constructor W. L. Hanscom called it, "Rather a small margin for a man to go to sea with." Fox to Benjamin F. Wade, December 15, 1864, in "Light Draught Monitors," 3-5; Aquila Adams testimony, ibid., 12-13; Hanscom testimony, ibid., 5-6.

[63] Fox to Stimers, February 25, 1864, Private, Fox Papers, Box 8.

[64] Stimers was relieved as General Inspector of Ironclads in June 1864. He correctly assessed the situation when he wrote that if he lost Fox's support, he would "drop out of sight immediately." Stimers to Fox, June 16, 1864, Fox Papers, Box 9. Stimers' replacement, Chief Engineer William W. Wood, wielded far less influence.

[65] Harold Sprout and Margaret Sprout, *The Rise of American Naval Power* (Princeton: Princeton University Press, 1946), 165.

[66] The General Superintendent's office was officially closed on November 1, 1866. Welles to Commodore Cadwalader Ringgold, October 26, 1866, quoted in *Charges Against the Navy Department*, House Miscellaneous Document 201, 42d Congress, 2d Session.

[67] G. Pascal Zachary, "The Law of the Rathole," *Technology Review* (May/June 1999), 33.

[68] Welles wrote, "Stimers and Fox have had [the light draft monitors] in charge, and each has assured me that my apprehensions were groundless. . . . I am not satisfied with Stimers's management, yet Fox has in this matter urged what has been done." Gideon Welles, *Diary of Gideon Welles Secretary of the Navy Under Lincoln and Johnson*, Howard K. Beale, ed. (New York: W. W. Norton, 1960), entry for June 10, 1864, 2:52-53.

[69] "Of course, I could not attempt to justify my own neglect. I had been too confiding . . . ." Welles, *Diary*, entry for February 21, 1865, 2:241-42. "When my attention was called to the question, Lenthall and Isherwood for the first time informed me that they had been excluded. . . ." Ibid., entry for August 2, 1865, 2:349-51.

[70] Robert Gardiner, ed., *Conway's All the World's Fighting Ships 1860-1905* (Annapolis: Naval Institute Press, 1979), 126-29. Donald L. Canney, *The Old Steam Navy*, vol. 1, *Frigates, Sloops and Gunboats, 1815-1885* (Annapolis: Naval Institute Press, 1990), 145-66, 172. The navy also "rebuilt" older ships to evade Congressional aversion to new construction. I have counted ships commenced as new construction or as rebuilds (*) between 1865 and 1880 as "new" ships. They comprise four new *Algoma* class ships (1867); *Tennessee**; six 1871 rebuilds called the *Galena* class (*Vandalia**, *Marion**, *Mohican**, *Galena**, *Quinnebaug** and *Swatara**); five *Enterprise* class in 1873 (four new and the rebuilt *Nipsic**); three new iron-hulled *Alert* class (1873); the new (1873) *Trenton*; the 1874 rebuild *Tallapoosa**; and the 1876 rebuild *Lancaster**.

[71] Hackemer, "Building the Military-Industrial Relationship," 100-107.

[72] Leonard Alexander Swann, Jr., *John Roach Maritime Entrepreneur: The Years as Naval Contractor, 1862-1886* (Annapolis: Naval Institute Press, 1965). Chapters 7-10 deal with the "new navy" ABCD ships. Benjamin Franklin Cooling, *Gray Steel and Blue Water Navy: The Formative Years of America's Military-Industrial Complex 1881-1917* (Hamden, CT: Archon Books, 1979), 36-39, 50-51, 57-58; Hackemer, "Building the Military-Industrial Relationship," 105-107.

Mahan *versus* the Pacifists

Suzanne Geissler

> Few naval thinkers have come in for more after-the-fact scrutiny than Alfred Thayer Mahan. He is lionized by his supporters as a prophet of naval power, and he is dismissed by his critics as a naval propagandist and an evangelist of Anglo–Saxon world supremacy—a racist vision not uncommon to his day. Less often scholars have attempted to deconstruct Mahan's personal views about man, God, and religion to determine the extent to which his religious convictions informed his geopolitical views. In this essay, Suzanne Geissler tackles that subject and concludes that Mahan's "Christian world view" was an important element of his Sea Power theories.

Though naval scholars are aware that Alfred Thayer Mahan was a devout Christian and active layman in the Episcopal Church, with few exceptions, they have not known what to make of this. They either ignore it as irrelevant to his naval thought or misinterpret it as a peculiar or in some cases even a pernicious, eccentricity.[1] But religion was not a hobby to Mahan nor was it irrelevant to his thinking. His Christian faith was the very core of his life and it influenced his naval and historical thought considerably. Nor was Mahan an amateur dabbler in this field. Though not a clergyman he was nonetheless a keen student of the Bible and theology. He certainly had the intellectual wherewithal to take on any clergyman in debate, which he often did in the letters to the editor columns of religious journals.

This paper looks at Mahan's views of warfare from a Christian perspective, and elaborates on some of the criticism he received in the press for his stand on war in general and the arbitration controversy in particular. This will illustrate some of the tensions present in Protestant Christianity in the early 1900s, as well as show how Mahan dealt with these thorny issues.

Suzanne Geissler is Assistant Professor of History at William Paterson University in Wayne, New Jersey.

Mahan is difficult to categorize religiously. We know he was a Christian, a Protestant, and an Episcopalian. But this only illustrates the danger of assigning labels glibly, for Mahan did not fit neatly into conventional classifications of Episcopalians. Mahan was something of a hybrid: a High Church Evangelical. He was High Church in his preference for a more formal ceremonial type of liturgy, the importance he accorded the sacraments and other rites of the church and in his view of the episcopate as being in "apostolic succession." However, he was also Evangelical in that he was a born-again Christian. He had had a clearly identifiable conversion experience at the age of thirty and he considered this experience, not his baptism as an infant, as the point in his life at which he truly became a Christian.[2] He felt that the essence of the Christian life was not church attendance, participation in the sacraments, or doing good to one's neighbor, but, as he put it, "a personal relationship with Christ crucified."[3] Indeed, he wrote an entire book on this theme, *The Harvest Within: Thoughts on the Life of a Christian,* published in 1909.[4] Mahan was also more Evangelical than High Church in his taking the Bible as the highest authority for Christians, as opposed to the High Church party which generally located authority in the three-fold formula of Scripture, tradition, and reason.[5]

Mahan was also "conservative" as opposed to "liberal" in his view of how Scripture should be interpreted. He accepted the Bible as the inerrant revealed Word of God and disdained the "higher criticism" method of Scriptural interpretation which posited the Bible as a culturally conditioned document which had many scientific and historical errors in it.[6] Mahan also leveled serious criticism at the Social Gospel (what might be called the religious wing of the Progressive Movement) which was then in its heyday, attempting to make Christianity more relevant to social and economic problems.[7] Briefly stated, Mahan's objection was that the Social Gospel movement reversed the priority of the two Great Commandments; it elevated love of neighbor over love of God. Put another way, it focused the Christian's attention on "external benevolent activities" rather than on building a personal relationship with Jesus Christ. He considered this a "capital mistake." Not that Mahan was against benevolent activities—he wasn't (though he strongly disapproved of the Social Gospellers' infatuation with socialism)—but he thought that they were the "fruit" of Christian life, not the essence of that life itself.[8]

Mahan's views on war are most clearly laid out in two pieces, "The Peace Conference and the Moral Aspect of War," an article which appeared in *North American Review* in 1899, and "War from the Christian Standpoint," a paper he gave at a church conference in 1900. Both later appeared as chapters in his book *Some Neglected Aspects of War* (1907). The starting point, though, for understanding Mahan's view of war is not the nature of war itself, but rather the nature of humanity. Mahan believed in Original Sin, the doctrine which states that because of Adam and Eve's disobedience in the Garden of Eden the entire human race (with the sole exception of Jesus) has an inborn predisposition to sin. All sin, and all are in need of a savior.[9] And because humans are sinful they do bad things. Violence, and eventually war, are the result. It is important to grasp that because of his theological views, Mahan did *not* view human nature as constantly improving—an idea that was a staple of Progressive thought. Therefore, he thought war never could or would be eliminated. This is the nub of his argument with the pacifists, as we shall see.

The fact that all humans are sinful, so evident to Mahan from his study of Scripture and history, did not in his view negate the existence of good in the world, or that there might be relative levels of good and evil. Nor did it negate the necessity or utility of societal controls, i.e., government, to keep the damage that evil could do to a minimum. This inevitably entails government-sanctioned use of force.

Though Mahan does not cite Augustine of Hippo (354–430) in his writings, it is nonetheless clear that Mahan's views on war stem, at least indirectly, from Augustine's just-war theory. This should not be surprising since Augustine's ideas could have come to him from any number of sources. Most just-war theories, whether they spring directly from Augustine or not, are similar because they are all based on the same premise, namely the reality of Original Sin. The thrust of Augustine's argument is that while war is *an* evil, it is not *the worst* evil. In fact, war is sometimes necessary to prevent a worse evil. This does not mean that all wars are just. Augustine distinguishes among such factors as: the reasons for the war, attempts made to avoid it, the means used to fight it, and the authority by which it is ordered. Basically, Augustine says that war is permitted if it is authorized by a legitimate authority, is fought for a just reason (defense against direct aggression or to protect a weaker party), is used only as a last resort, and is fought by means proportional to attaining victory without spilling over into needless slaughter.[10]

Mahan, who had clearly given the matter a lot of thought, was in the same camp. Because mankind had "a condition . . . obviously far removed from Christian perfection," wars were sometimes necessary. Mahan went on to say "that in the present imperfect and frequently wicked state of mankind, evil easily may, and often does, reach a point where it must be controlled, perhaps even destroyed, by physical force."[11] Contrary to what some of his detractors over the years have claimed, Mahan in no way glorified war; he admitted it was an evil, but believed that it was "justified" as "a remedy for greater evils."[12]

It is all very well to talk about a just-war theory, but how did Mahan reconcile this view with Christian teaching? After all, he claimed that he had arrived at his position solely from studying the Bible, not reading other authors. His argument rested on three points: First, Jesus used force to expel the money-changers from the Temple; moreover, he did so as Mahan points out, not "on his own behalf," but for the benefit of those who were being exploited. Second, no Christian soldier mentioned in the New Testament is ever told his faith requires him to abandon the profession of arms. And third, God has given authority (the "power of the sword,") to the state "to defend the right."[13]

Mahan's views on war began to receive publicity around the period 1899–1900 largely because of his participation in the First Hague Conference, which was held from May to July 1899. A detailed discussion of the Hague Conference and Mahan's role in it is beyond the scope of this paper, but certain issues arising out of that conference are germane because they brought Mahan criticism in the Christian press and Social Gospel circles. Briefly, the Hague Conference was a manifestation of a movement called Universal Arbitration, (or just "arbitration" for short), which was much in vogue at the time. The idea was that if international disputes could be arbitrated, war could be avoided. The advocates of this view wished to carry it one step further and make arbitration mandatory (which would, of course, entail setting up some sort of international tribunal to hear cases). Thus, if *all* international disputes could be subject to *mandatory* arbitration, war could be ended *forever*—or so it was thought. Many in the Progressive movement in general, and the Social Gospel movement in particular, latched onto this notion with great enthusiasm. It fit in nicely with their belief that mankind was progressing morally as well as materially and that war would become obsolete—a relic of the barbarian past.

Undoubtedly not all of the ninety-six delegates (representing twenty-six nations) attending had such lofty goals. Many were experienced diplomats who were there simply to get the best deal they could for their country in terms of arms limitation treaties. But a surprising number seemed to buy into the notion that even if war itself could not be outlawed, many of its nastier aspects could. Five out of six of the U.S. delegates held to this view. The lone naysayer, not surprisingly, was Mahan.

When President McKinley had appointed Mahan to the U.S. delegation, the other members were not altogether pleased because Mahan, alone among them, "had very little, if any, sympathy with the main purposes of the conference."[14] Those words were written by Andrew Dickson White, diplomat and former president of Cornell University, a member of the American delegation. White kept a diary during the proceedings and it provides an illuminating view of both Mahan's role at the conference and White's constant frustration with Mahan's raining on the arbitration parade. White considered Mahan wedded to old-fashioned militaristic ideas and admitted to his diary that he was "embarrassed" by Mahan's retrograde views, although he considered Mahan "a man of the highest character and of great ability."[15]

Two issues in particular caused friction between Mahan and the more idealistic delegates. One was the attempt by the conference to ban the use of "asphyxiating bombs." Mahan's position briefly stated was that such weapons had not been fully tested and developed, so that any discussion of their use or the damage they could cause was purely hypothetical. He also argued that the U.S. should never prohibit itself from using a weapon out of misplaced idealism because a less scrupulous enemy was unlikely to be bound by such prohibitions. And finally he noted that other weapons currently used, e.g., the torpedo, also brought its victims a horrible death, but that no one was proposing to ban them.[16]

The second issue had to do with a proposal to allow neutral hospital ships to pick up survivors of naval engagements and thereby confer the privileges of neutrality on those survivors. Mahan thought this was an unfair use of neutrality. In fact, he thought that a neutral ship voluntarily entering a war zone was not neutral at all. He believed it would avoid legal problems with neutral nations if hospital ships flew the flag of the country to which they had offered their services.[17] This question became tied up with technical issues revolving around the legal definition of neutrality, which were not easily explained to the general public. Nonetheless Mahan came off looking hardhearted—as though he was opposed to rescuing drowning sailors.

Mahan had an Olympian reputation in naval circles and to some extent in the general public as well—at least that portion of it that kept up with world events. He was also well known in religious circles. He was a frequent contributor to religious journals, mostly Episcopal. He wrote articles and book reviews and was an indefatigable writer of letters to the editor. He also wrote on religious topics for the secular press, mainly in the form of letters to the editors of publications such as the *New York Times* and the *New York Evening Post*. His comments on religious matters, e.g., in speeches to church groups, were also reported in the press.

Not surprisingly, his views on warfare, indeed his very status as a military commentator, generated some unfavorable comments in Social Gospel circles, especially the growing pacifist movement. Not all these critics were *absolute* pacifists, that is, against all war at any time for any reason. Most, in fact, were not. Nevertheless, they were what could be termed *functional* pacifists. They did not oppose all wars that had been fought in the past; some they could identify as having been fought for a moral purpose. The most obvious example was the Civil War, which they could see as good because it resulted in the freeing of the slaves. This should not be surprising when one considers that many of these Social Gospel pacifists considered themselves spiritual heirs of the abolitionists. What was turning them into functional pacifists at the beginning of the twentieth century was their belief that while war may once have had a moral purpose, that was no longer the case because humanity had morally evolved. War had become a relic of the barbarian past. It is immediately evident why they found Mahan's views so objectionable.

In 1900 Wallace Rice took on Mahan in the pages of a Progressive magazine, *The Dial*. The occasion was the publication of Mahan's book, *Lessons of the War with Spain*, which contained a reprint of "The Peace Conference and the Moral Aspect of War."[18] Rice considered Mahan a warmonger, and a hypocrite besides, for clothing his views in the garb of Christianity. Mahan, Rice said, "fails to show any higher notion of right than is held in the word might." This was not surprising, according to Rice, since Mahan's profession "is the art of killing his fellows." Just in case the reader did not get it the first time Rice repeated this charge at the end of the article.[19] He was particularly incensed that Mahan saw war as having a moral justification and that Mahan even invoked the name of God. Rice did not agree with Mahan's view that a nation's acting in its own self-interest is compatible with the larger purposes of Providence. "Captain Mahan forgets the appeal to the national conscience and the God he has been invoking and says baldly: 'it [American expansion] is our interest.'" He concludes his review by reiterating that Mahan's "profession is the art of killing his fellows, and that he is far too eager professionally to discern any of the possibilities of peace."[20]

A more extensive attack on Mahan was launched by Lucia Ames Mead, an anti-imperialist and peace activist, in *The Arena*, another Progressive–Social Gospel magazine, in 1908. It is not clear that her article is a book review, but it seems to have been written as a response to the publication of *Some Neglected Aspects of War*, which contained several of Mahan's articles on war and Christianity.

Mead, who considered herself an "abolitionist of war" and a member of "the new peace party," denied that she was an absolute pacifist, but she stated her belief that "human nature doubtless is improving." She expressed confidence that war would end "within a century," but worried that influential people such as Mahan could derail the process with their retrograde views. That Mahan was a professed Christian was even more dismaying to her. "When, therefore, a distinguished naval expert and exemplary Christian gentleman discourses on this theme and tells us that war is inevitable, the layman is overawed and dumb."[21] While less personally insulting than Rice, she offered a fuller critique. Her belief in human progress was unbounded, and she assailed Mahan for doubting it. Mahan believed that permanent peace, if such a thing even existed, would be a slow process that took centuries. Mead claimed that Mahan "ignores the fact that, in this age of endless forms of organization, rapid communication and widespread education, the progress of past centuries is now being equaled in decades, not merely in material achievements, but in mental and spiritual advance."[22] She also, not surprisingly, supported the arbitration movement and condemned Mahan for his rejection of it. She claimed that Mahan was unconcerned with justice and had an ulterior motive for his view of warfare—namely the continued existence and expansion of the navy. She admitted no protective or defensive function of a navy. "A navy exists simply that it may fight another navy." War is evil "because it never aims at justice" and in any case is uncivilized and outmoded. Her belief in peace rested on her belief in progress and "constructive, courageous statesmanship that forestalls enmity and turns it into bonded friendship."[23]

These were not the only critiques Mahan received from the "peace party." One which he reported himself in the preface to *Some Neglected Aspects of War*, was an anonymous letter he had received signed "A Lover of My Fellow Creatures." The writer said that upon reading one of Mahan's articles on the Hague Conference,

> I . . . deeply regret to find that you have used the great talent God gave you for the welfare of mankind to uphold and encourage instead War which is literally Hell upon earth, and the curse of mankind, at this exceedingly critical period when your opinion might have proved a feather weight in the scale in favour of International Arbitration. May God forgive you, and lead you to an altered and better mind.[24]

There is no evidence that Mahan responded directly to the public attacks of either Rice or Mead, but he did take on the anonymous correspondent. Mahan was willing to accept disagreement and he was a good enough historian to know that there were many and conflicting interpretations of a given issue. But he did not care for the implication of some of his critics that his views were unchristian or that he stood in need of God's forgiveness for holding them.

> To ask thus solemnly that God may forgive a man is to pronounce his guilt before God. Why? Because of the antecedent assumption, that all War is so certainly and entirely wicked, that a man cannot without sin present before the audience of his kind such considerations as those contained in the article, herein republished, "The Practical Aspect of War." That the author thereof may be conscientiously assured of the rightness of his contention counts for nothing; no opposite side of the case is admitted, as to War.[25]

Mahan goes on to say that the writer,

> takes the seat of the Almighty, and unhesitatingly declares the wickedness of his fellow. Judgment is

passed by one neither commissioned nor competent to it; a procedure as unchristian in spirit, and in manifestation, as War can be.[26]

Mahan continued to speak and write on the subject of war and its relation to Christianity. In 1912 he published *Armaments and Arbitration*, a full-length critique of the utopianism of the arbitration movement. In one of the articles in that book, "The Place of Force in International Relations," Mahan returned to the theme of viewing war through a Christian lens. He distinguished, as did Augustine, among the church, the state, and the private individual. God, he declared, gave the state the "power of the sword" to punish evildoers and protect the innocent. This meant that force must regrettably but necessarily be used. The horror of war can be redeemed by "the entrance of the human will into the Divine accomplishment." In other words, despite human sin God can use war to accomplish his divine purposes and humankind can participate in that. To Mahan this was noble, not evil.[27]

Mahan loved a good battle, in print as well as on the sea, and he was never reticent about stating his views as a Christian. His knowledge of the Bible, theology, and history made him an important figure in the religious circles of his day and gave his writings a profundity that many of the more sentimental and utopian critiques of war lacked. Mahan was above all a realist about human nature, and the roots of that realism lay in his Christian worldview.

NOTES

[1]Two books which, in this author's opinion, deal inadequately with Mahan's religious views are Peter Karsten, *The Naval Aristocracy: The Golden Age of Annapolis and the Emergence of Modern American Navalism* (New York, 1972) and Robert Seager, II, *Alfred Thayer Mahan: The Man and His Letters* (Annapolis, Md., 1977). Two studies that show a more sophisticated understanding of Mahan's theology are Reo N. Leslie, Jr., "Christianity and the Evangelist for Sea Power: The Religion of Alfred Thayer Mahan," in John B. Hattendorf, ed., *The Influence of History on Mahan* (Newport, R.I., 1991) and Jon Tetsuro Sumida, *Inventing Grand Strategy and Teaching Command: The Classic Works of Alfred Thayer Mahan Reconsidered* (Baltimore, 1997).

[2]Mahan discussed his conversion in a rarely noted but significant article, "The Apparent Decadence of the Church's Influence," *The Churchman* (25 April 1903), 546–47. See also, "Address Delivered at Holy Trinity Episcopal Church, Brooklyn,

N.Y.," March 1899, in Robert Seager, II, and Doris D. Maguire, eds., *Letters and Papers of Alfred Thayer Mahan* (Annapolis, Md., 1975), 3:599–600 [hereafter cited as *Letters*]; and "'The Practical in Christianity' An Address Delivered in the Church of the Holy Trinity, Middletown, Ct., 22 March 1899", in Alfred Thayer Mahan, *The Harvest Within: Thoughts on the Life of a Christian* (Boston, 1909), 267.
   ³Mahan, "Apparent Decadence," 547.
   ⁴See footnote 2 above.
   ⁵Alfred Thayer Mahan, "War from the Christian Standpoint," in *Some Neglected Aspects of War* (Boston, 1907), 97.
   ⁶*Ibid.*, 97; "Apparent Decadence," 545. I agree with Jon Sumida that this does not make Mahan a "fundamentalist" or a "literalist." See Jon Tetsuro Sumida, "The Problem of Learning in the Absence of Recent Experience: Alfred Thayer Mahan and the Uses of Naval History," paper delivered at the annual meeting of the American Historical Association, 3 January 1997; see also his *Inventing Grand Strategy*, 76–79.
   ⁷A good example of this is Mahan's scathing review of the 1913 Social Gospel novel *The Inside of the Cup* by Winston Churchill [the novelist, not the more famous British statesman] in *The Churchman* (30 August 1913), 277, 289–90.
   ⁸"Apparent Decadence," 545, 547.
   ⁹See, e.g., Mahan to Hugh R. Munro, 20 May 1910, *Letters*, 3:335–36.
   ¹⁰Augustine, *Political Writings*, ed. by Henry Paolucci (Chicago, 1962), 162–83. For a good analysis of Augustine's just-war theory see George Weigel, *Tranquillitas Ordinis: The Present Failure and Future Promise of American Catholic Thought on War and Peace* (New York, 1987), 28–32.
   ¹¹"War from the Christian Standpoint," 99–100.
   ¹²*Ibid.*, 98–99.
   ¹³*Ibid.*, 104–08.
   ¹⁴Andrew D. White, *Autobiography of Andrew Dickson White* (New York, 1905), 2:347.
   ¹⁵*Ibid.*, 347.
   ¹⁶*Ibid.*, 319–20; Mahan's report to U.S. delegation, *Letters*, 2:650–52.
   ¹⁷White, *Autobiography*, II, 343; Mahan's report to U.S. delegation, *Letters*, 2: 646–49.
   ¹⁸Mahan, *Lessons of the War with Spain, and Other Articles* (Boston, 1899).
   ¹⁹Wallace Rice, "Some Current Fallacies of Captain Mahan," *The Dial* (16 March 1900), 198, 200.
   ²⁰*Ibid.*, 199–200.
   ²¹Lucia Ames Mead, "Some Fallacies of Captain Mahan," *The Arena*, 40 (1908), 163–65. Mead was an officer of the Anti-Imperialist League, the Women's Peace Party, and the Women's International League for Peace and Freedom. See John M. Craig, *Lucia Ames Mead and the American Peace Movement* (Lewiston, N.Y., 1990).
   ²²*Ibid.*, 166.
   ²³*Ibid.*, 167–70.
   ²⁴*Some Neglected Aspects of War*, xiii.
   ²⁵*Ibid.*, xiii.
   ²⁶*Ibid.*, xiv.
   ²⁷Mahan, *Armaments and Arbitration, or the Place of Force in the International Relations of States* (New York, 1912), 116–20.

Part IV

Naval Forces in World War II

Breaking out of Prison: Italian Naval Policy and Operational Planning 1935–1938

Robert Mallett

>Even before the outbreak of World War II, naval planners in virtually all of the major powers were crafting plans to deal with possible contingencies. In Italy, this planning was complicated by the ambitions of a dictator whose appetite was larger than his realism, and by a shifting diplomatic situation that compelled naval planners like Admiral Domenico Cavagnari to plan in turn for naval wars against Ethiopia, Germany, and finally, Britain. In this essay, Robert Mallett illuminates the treacherous and ultimately disastrous path trod by Italian naval planners in the years between Mussolini's Ethiopian adventure and the Munich crisis.

In October 1926 Italian dictator Benito Mussolini enlightened a gathering at the Italian Army War College as to his geopolitical vision of Italy's future. "A nation," he noted in a much quoted speech, "which does not have free access to the sea cannot be considered a free nation; a nation which does not have free access to the oceans cannot be considered a Great Power; Italy must become a Great Power."[1] Fourteen years later, following a program of sustained Italian naval rearmament, and after Mussolini had aligned Fascist Italy with Europe's other major dictatorship, Nazi Germany, *Il Duce* declared war on Great Britain and France in order to resolve the question of Rome's "imprisonment" within its *mare nostrum*, the Mediterranean. On 31 March 1940, following his meeting with Adolf Hitler at the Brenner Pass a week earlier, Mussolini stressed to his chiefs-of-staff that Italy could not remain out of the conflict currently in progress. Only a war "parallel" to that of Germany could resolve Italy's geopolitical difficulties, and enable it to break out of its Mediterranean and Red Sea prison. The Italian Royal Navy, the *Regia Marina*, should therefore wage an offensive both within the Mediterranean, and outside, in order to drive Italy's foes out.[2]

Robert Mallett is the Leverhulme research Fellow at the University of Leeds in the United Kingdom. The author wishes to thank the British Academy and the School of History, University of Leeds, whose financial assistance allowed him to attend the Symposium. He is also grateful to the Ufficio Storico della Marina Militare, Rome.

The risk of conflict with the western European democracies had been a feature of Italian foreign and naval policy for some time before Mussolini's disastrous declaration of war on 10 June 1940. Throughout the late 1930s, the Italian naval staff, already planning, and having accordingly laid down construction programs, for the future confrontation with the British and French fleets that Italy's dictator regarded as "inevitable," had been compelled, as a consequence of Mussolini's aggressive, expansionist and pro-German policies, to contemplate a Mediterranean war with Italy's principal maritime competitors; and at a point when its long-term building programs—destined for completion no sooner than 1943—were far from complete.

The first flashpoint came during 1935–1936, when Fascist plans to attack and conquer the Ethiopian empire brought the Mussolini regime close to open hostility with Paris and London. After Mussolini issued his directive of 30 December 1934, ordering Italy's service chiefs to destroy the Ethiopian armed forces and conquer the entire territory, the under-secretary of state and chief-of-staff of the Italian navy, Admiral Domenico Cavagnari, expressed his outward approval of the dictator's plans for territorial expansion.[3] Given Anglo–French fears of a resurgent German Reich, Cavagnari noted in a memorandum for Mussolini in mid–January 1935, the international political configuration favored the execution of such a policy. In fact, he added, "as regards our expansion in Abyssinia, we may conclude as follows: now or never." However, the Cavagnari memorandum also contained more than a hint of caution. He warned that Mussolini's recent agreement with French foreign minister Pierre Laval did not guarantee that the British would stand aside in the face of an Italian assault on Ethiopia's territorial integrity. Given that Britain had substantial imperial interests in the eastern Mediterranean and Red Sea, and given that it effectively controlled access to the Suez Canal, Cavagnari urged that Mussolini also conclude a similar deal with London, thereby avoiding the risk of an Anglo–Italian confrontation.[4]

However, the subsequent efforts of Mussolini, via his ambassador in London, Count Dino Grandi, to persuade senior British officials to accept an alteration to the East African status quo in Italy's favor, met with a negative response. Both Sir Robert Vansittart, permanent under-secretary at the foreign office, and Sir John Simon, the foreign secretary, expressed clear reservations toward what Grandi had described as Italy's intention to reach a "peaceful" settlement to its territorial claims against Ethiopia. Clearly both had realized that Mussolini planned an outright annexation, and an annexation that might in itself eventually threaten Britain's own position in the region.[5]

When, in early March, the British government duly dispatched a note to Rome expressing concern about Italy's military build up in Eritrea and Italian Somaliland, its existing East African colonial territories, and following a report from the Italian naval attaché in London, Ferrante Capponi, that spoke of Admiralty determination to strengthen the Royal Navy's eastern Mediterranean presence, Cavagnari's predictions appeared to have been proved correct.[6] Later, in mid–April, back room negotiations between British and Italian diplomats at the Stresa Conference, only served further to demonstrate to Mussolini that "Italy could expect no cooperation from the United Kingdom in any attack on Ethiopia."[7] When Simon attempted to raise the Ethiopian question at the League of Nations Assembly in Geneva, the dictator angrily informed London that he would never accept League arbitration in the matter.[8]

Prior to the Stresa Conference, Cavagnari, clearly aware that Anglo–Italian tension over the Ethiopian question was mounting, had again warned Mussolini of the risks of antagonizing Britain unduly. Should the British government indeed place the Italo–Ethiopian dispute before the Geneva Assembly, he noted on 4 March, then there was every likelihood of a League application of collective sanctions under the terms of Article 16. In the event of this, the Italian navy could do nothing to counter Britain's control of the Suez Canal—an artery vital to the supplying of Italy's East African armies. Moreover, the British bases at both Gibraltar and Alexandria in Egypt remained out of the *Marina*'s operational range. Italian forces could mount an attack on Malta, but that island was hardly "Britain's Achilles heel in the Mediterranean." Therefore, the admiral noted, Mussolini should place political pressure on the British by threatening to abandon Italy's ties with Britain and France, at a point when Nazi revisionism had become an ominous feature of European politics. Such pressure might, Cavagnari added, induce Paris and London into giving Italy a mandate or protectorate over Ethiopia.[9]

The firm British stance at Stresa, however, coming as it did in the wake of Grandi's failed attempt to secure British agreement to an Italian annexation of Ethiopia, had greatly angered the temperamental Italian dictator. In fact, while still at the Conference, and while discussing issues of European peace with British and French statesmen, he ordered Cavagnari to prepare operational plans for offensive operations against the Royal Navy, and its bases in the Mediterranean and Red Sea.[10]

Such an order was inconsistent with Italian naval construction policy. Geared toward a future war against France and Yugoslavia, that policy had resulted in the laying down of a new type of capital ship, the *Littorio* class, in 1934, and the remodernization of Italy's four existing pre–World War One battleships, the *Cavour* and *Doria* classes. Mussolini's order therefore perplexed Cavagnari and the naval staff. The agreements reached with the French in January 1935 had already compelled the Italian navy to consider possible operations against Germany, in the event of an attempted Nazi takeover in Austria, which, at that point at least, Mussolini was determined to prevent. Now, the *Duce* had changed the focus of operational policy yet again, this time ordering the naval staff to consider Britain as a probable future enemy.

Cavagnari lost no time in voicing his concern. In an internal directive of 14 April, he advised the navy's planners that naval war planning now needed to take into account the possibility of a future Anglo–Italian clash in the waters of the Mediterranean. While a conflict with Germany still formed the basis of the recent political agreements with Paris, Cavagnari noted, the Italian fleet might well find itself at war with Britain, with France as Italy's principal ally.[11] Ten days later the admiral articulated his thoughts in greater detail. He ordered the navy's planners to prepare fresh operational directives in the event that Berlin attempted to occupy Austria, following the abortive Nazi *putsch* of mid–1934. Operations would take place within the framework of the new Italo–French alliance, and should include attacks on German merchant and naval traffic in the Mediterranean and Red Sea and in the Indian and Atlantic Oceans, as well as countering German fleet operations against metropolitan France and Italy. At the same time, however, naval planning should also prepare for a war with Britain. Principally, Cavagnari concluded, plans should focus on developing combined sea and air operations in the event that the British fleet abandoned its base on Malta and attempted to make for Gibraltar. The admiral noted, however, that he found the prospect of such a confrontation "alarming."[12]

Accordingly, by mid-May, the navy's war plans office had produced initial contingency plans in the event of an Anglo–Italian conflict. Codenamed *Operation B* the plan highlighted the clear disadvantages facing the Italian fleet in any sea war against the Royal Navy. Effectively, the planners had argued, in such a clash the Italian navy would need to conduct operations in two principal theatres: i) Malta and the central Mediterranean and ii) the Red Sea. The fleet's chief objective would be that of destroying all enemy naval units in the central Mediterranean, an objective that Italian forces would secure in two separate phases. During phase one, Italy's aeronaval forces would launch an offensive against Malta, and thus attempt to destroy all British bases on the island and force its abandonment. Prior to this initial phase of operations mines should be laid in the Sicilian Channel. Subsequently, *Operation B*'s second phase involved Italian air and naval units attacking the Mediterranean Fleet as it abandoned Malta and headed for either Gibraltar or Alexandria. Based on Sicily, the Italian battle squadrons along with submarine and air units would attack the enemy at the most strategically advantageous moment. However, if the Royal Navy successfully redeployed to Gibraltar, the Italian fleet could not conduct an offensive so far from its bases. On the other hand, should the British deploy their fleet at Alexandria, then the air force should mount attacks on it, and eventually be supported by further naval actions. In addition, the plan noted, there remained a strong possibility that Britain would reinforce its Mediterranean Fleet with units from home waters. The planners also echoed Cavagnari's earlier warning to Mussolini that Britain might close the Suez Canal—an action that would create considerable difficulties for the Italian expeditionary armies in East Africa. Finally, in the Red Sea theater Italian air units should attack the British bases at Aden and on the island of Perim, while submarine units concentrated on locating, and destroying, British naval forces operating in the region.[13]

Despite the fact that *Operation B* was, at least theoretically, to have taken place within the context of the Italo–French alliance, it is striking that the plan itself contained no specific reference as to how the alignment with France was to function in operational terms. This clearly demonstrated that, for the navy's planners, any future joint operations with the French navy—until recently the Italian naval staff's principal Mediterranean foe—remained highly unlikely. Moreover, Cavagnari himself had noted, in his March memorandum to Mussolini, that the French would never back any Italian war against Britain, given their obvious need of British support against Germany. Therefore, the Italian fleet faced the risk of a clash with the Royal Navy alone.

Undoubtedly any Anglo–Italian sea war in the Mediterranean and Red Sea in mid–1935 would have seen the *Regia Marina* swiftly defeated at the hands of the Royal Navy. By this stage the regime's capital ship building and remodernization programs had scarcely begun, and the Italian fleet possessed only two aging battleships to pit against British sea power, the *Doria* and the *Caio Duilio*, both laid down prior to World War One. The Italian navy had no effective independent air support for fleet operations—a capability essential to the success of *Operation B*—and had not, at this point, seriously considered the importance of anti-submarine or mine warfare.[14] The focus of the planners on the central Mediterranean again echoed the views of Cavagnari and demonstrated the impossibility of Italy countering any British blockade of the Mediterranean at Gibraltar and Suez. In other words, should the League of Nations choose to halt Mussolini's expansionist program, the Italian navy, indeed the Italian armed forces collectively, could do little to prevent it. Italian operations against British positions at Aden and Perim, in the southern Red Sea, could not in themselves resolve the problem of keeping open lines of communication between Italy and East Africa. Nor did cooperation between the air and naval staffs, a key element should *Operation B* be executed successfully, prove especially productive in the months that followed.15

Not surprisingly, throughout the rest of that summer Cavagnari and the naval high command continued to voice their anxiety about the real possibility of an Italian war with Britain, which Mussolini's uncompromising stance over the Ethiopian question seemed likely to provoke. Despite the fact that a tentative *rapprochement* between Rome and Berlin over Austria had taken place, and, duly, significantly reduced the likelihood of a war with Germany, Cavagnari continued to dread the prospect of a war against the Royal Navy.16

On 19 June, amid the news that London and Berlin had concluded a naval agreement limiting German capital ship building to 35% of Britain's, Cavagnari again warned Mussolini against war with the British. A few days earlier, the admiral had already notified the dictator of his view that the French might well increase their own naval building in the wake of the Anglo–German Agreement.17 Naturally, any Italian losses incurred in a bilateral war with the Royal Navy would clearly have an effect on Italy's long term naval policy in the Mediterranean. Cavagnari informed Mussolini that he had prepared the Italian fleet for conflict with Britain as best he could. Nevertheless, Italy would still find itself facing a more powerful enemy, armed with greatly superior means. Against such an adversary, the Italian navy would deploy its incomplete battle squadrons, and without any semblance of air support. Italy's navy might secure some initial successes in the early stages of such a war, Cavagnari concluded, but thereafter the fleet could only "attempt to resist enemy pressure that would gradually grow heavier by the day." The only means whereby Italy could take the offensive to the British would be if Mussolini authorized further naval building; such a program would subsequently permit the naval staff to create an effective guerrilla warfare arm. Otherwise, Italy's naval strategy would remain defensive, and concentrate on protecting lines of communication between Africa and the metropolitan sphere.[18]

But, in the months prior to Italy's war of conquest against Ethiopia, launched by the Italian army in early October, political relations between Rome and London worsened steadily, thereby greatly increasing the chances of an Anglo–Italian war. By early August, the temperature had reached boiling point, when Britain demonstrated increasing resistance toward Mussolini's imperial designs on the African continent. On 9 August, and on Mussolini's orders, Marshal Pietro Badoglio, technically head of Italy's chiefs-of-staff, convened a meeting of the Fascist military leadership to discuss the imminent prospect of a conflict with Britain. Their conclusions, and especially those of the naval high command, were overwhelmingly pessimistic. Cavagnari and his deputy chief-of-staff, Admiral Wladimiro Pini, argued that the Italian navy would find itself at a massive disadvantage if Mussolini ordered it to war against Britain. The Royal Navy overwhelmingly outnumbered it in almost every class of vessel, he noted, while Italian air power offered only a limited strike capability against enemy naval units. The fleet could not defend the Italian Dodecanese islands, could not adequately defend Italy's key naval base at Tobruk in Libya, could wage no offensive in the Red Sea and could not guarantee that communications with East Africa would remain open in wartime. Britain's huge naval superiority was matched by its dominance of important strategic positions within the Mediterranean. Even if Italy attacked and captured Malta, it remained unlikely that it could hold the island. Britain, Cavagnari concluded, could launch air and sea offensives against Italy with comparative ease. Only a genuine Italian threat to Britain's imperial defense mechanism might convince the British to avoid an all-out clash with Italy.[19]

Little more than a week later, the Italian naval high command learned that the Admiralty planned to reinforce its Mediterranean Station with units from the Home Fleet, as the planners had correctly predicted in May. Consequently, in a fresh version of *Operation B*, the plans office set out new operational directives for war with Britain. Given the risk of an Italian air and sea offensive against Malta, the Royal Navy was most unlikely to deploy to the island in any significant strength. Rather, the British fleet would remain based at the Mediterranean exits, with the Home Fleet at Gibraltar and the remainder at bases in the eastern basin. In order to prevent the British attacking mainland Italian naval bases or penetrating the Dodecanese and destroying Italian convoys bound for Africa, only limited options were open to the *Marina*. Cruisers, destroyers and torpedo boats could operate in the western and central Mediterranean theaters, while a similar force would deploy to the lower Ionian Sea. Such Italian forces would invariably face a British navy armed with powerful battleships, and with an aeronaval capability. Not surprisingly, by mid–September, the naval high command reached the conclusion that while Italy enjoyed an excellent strategic position within the Mediterranean, it currently lacked the means to exploit it. Neither did the fleet possess sufficient fuel stocks for a protracted sea war; the navy's bunkers contained enough fuel for only two and a half months of war. The conclusion was inescapable: the Italian navy would lose any war with Britain.[20]

It was, therefore, fortunate for Mussolini and his Fascist regime that the Stanley Baldwin administration did not wish to risk confrontation with Italy at a time of great international uncertainty. Faced with concomitant threats from Hitler's *Reich* and Imperial Japan, the British government notified Rome that it did not plan to close the Suez Canal and, ultimately, did not want an Anglo–Italian war over Ethiopia. Encouraged by British assurances, Mussolini ordered Italy's war of conquest to begin on 3 October.[21]

Aside from the political tensions that arose between Rome and London over the question of Italian intervention in the Spanish Civil War, that erupted in July 1936, the second major moment of Anglo–Italian conflict came in the autumn of 1938, when Hitler's claims against the Sudetan regions of Czechoslovakia brought Europe to the brink of war. By this point Mussolini had moved Fascist Italy ever closer toward a political and military alignment with Hitler's regime. His declaration of the Rome–Berlin Axis in November 1936, his visit to Germany in September 1937 and Hitler's return journey to Italy in 1938, did not simply mark a symbolic forging of links between the two dictator states. On the contrary, as bilateral relations steadily improved, and those between Italy and Britain and France duly worsened in the aftermath of the Ethiopian Crisis, so did Fascist strategic policy become increasingly focused on a Mediterranean expansionist war, and with Germany as Rome's chief ally.

As early as January 1936, Italian naval staff policy began to focus on driving the British and French from the Mediterranean and Red Sea in a war fought alongside the *Kriegsmarine*.[22] However, the vast expansion in Italian naval power demanded by the naval ministry in order to undertake such a war—ten new battleships, four aircraft carriers, thirty-six cruisers and up to seventy-five submarines—clearly lay well beyond national economic and industrial capacity. Existing building had already suffered delays of around two years owing to serious material shortages, primarily of iron and steel. This rendered a close alignment between Rome and Berlin indispensable if the Fascist regime was to achieve its wider imperial objective of conquering Egypt and the Sudan, and carving out a vast Italian empire in North Africa and the Middle East. Cavagnari later anticipated that Italy's alliance with Germany would lead to enough enemy forces being drawn off to other waters to enable Italy to fight, and win, its sea war in the Mediterranean.[23] But Italy received little material assistance from Germany prior to the outbreak of war in 1939. Berlin could only supply significant quantities of coal, and even these fell afoul of an inefficient rail link between Italy and Germany. Moreover, during the Italo–German naval conversations at Friedrichshafen in June 1939, though both sides agreed on the need to attack the British and French fleets in the Atlantic, they disagreed on future Italian strategy in the Mediterranean. Erich Raeder, commander-in-chief of the *Kriegsmarine*, pressed Cavagnari to abandon his focus on defense of the central Mediterranean in favor of a more offensive strategy in the western basin. Cavagnari refused, and no further talks were held prior to Italy's entry into the conflict in June 1940.[24]

By September 1937, in the wake of Mussolini's visit to Germany, the naval staff had determined that Italy's naval policy should in future be governed by a political formula whereby combined Axis quantitative fleet strength should eventually reach 50% of the Anglo–French.[25] As a result, over the course of the next year the

Fascist government financed further *Littorio* programs, and the naval planners began to develop operational contingencies for the future Axis war.[26]

However, while new Italian naval programs laid down in early 1938 were destined for completion no sooner than 1943 (the date later fixed for an Italo–German war against the western European democracies under the terms of the Pact of Steel), Hitler's revisionism brought the risk of war much sooner than that date. Following the Austro–German *Anschluss* of March 1938, Mussolini, who had by now grudgingly regarded it as an "inevitability," resisted German pressure to formalize the Italo–German relationship by concluding a full-blown military pact.[27] Nevertheless, he informed his foreign minister, Count Galeazzo Ciano, that eventually he would sign such a treaty with Germany, "because there were a thousand and one reasons why he did not trust the western democracies."[28] Germany and Italy were now "neighbors," the dictator declared. Rome and Berlin would form a "bloc" that would combine to fight the British and French.[29]

The opportunity for Mussolini to wage such a war was not long in coming. Over the summer of 1938, the Italian dictator appeared increasingly eager to discern Hitler's intended policy over the Czechoslovakian issue. Any war that might involve Germany, he argued, could not but involve Italy as well.[30] By early September, with Berlin still having given no concrete indication as to how Hitler intended to proceed, the Italian naval high command was suddenly issued, presumably by Mussolini, with a directive to prepare for an imminent, and undeclared, initiation of hostilities against Britain and France.

As had been the case during the Mediterranean Crisis three years earlier, Cavagnari and the naval leadership viewed the prospect of such a war with alarm. The Italian fleet faced the combined might of Britain and France in the Mediterranean, and, Cavagnari warned Ciano in late September, American intervention in the war remained a possibility.[31] Again, the naval staff's own perceptions of Italian strategic limitations were evident in the navy's operational planning. Plan *DG 1 Op. AG*, completed in early September, had as its primary objective an undeclared naval offensive aimed at capturing the Suez Canal and occupying Tunisia. Almost exclusively, the planners foresaw the use of "guerrilla" weapons, light surface vessels and submarines in a series of surprise operations against Anglo–French naval units, and their bases at Marseilles, Bizerte, Toulon and Malta. If the British Mediterranean Fleet could successfully be blockaded within its Maltese base, then the main Italian battle formations stood a reasonable chance against the Home Fleet, which the Admiralty would invariably re-deploy to the Mediterranean as it had done in 1935. If, however, the British elected *not* to deploy to Malta, but to Gibraltar or Alexandria, then the Italian fleet, with only two battleships—the remodernized *Cesare* and *Cavour*—faced the combined might of the Anglo–French navies alone, and, again, without any semblance of air cover.[32]

Had the Italian fleet been ordered to initiate hostilities, there can be little doubt that it would have fared poorly against its British and French adversaries. With its construction programs still far from complete, without air cover and with its "guerrilla" warfare capability still undeveloped, it would have faced crushingly superior enemies. Furthermore, Italian Naval Intelligence, the *Servizio Informazioni Segreti*, reported that the British had not based a substantial part of their fleet on Malta, but at Alexandria and Gibraltar, against which the naval planners had not anticipated operations.[33] Nor had there been any indication that the navy had cooperated closely with either the army or air staff—cooperation essential were Italy to take Suez. Finally, the alignment with the Germans remained in an embryonic stage, and clearly the Axis was neither politically nor militarily mature enough for a major war.[34] Only the following year did Rome and Berlin take the first tentative steps toward military cooperation.

Both the Mediterranean and Czech crises revealed Fascist Italy's unmistakably aggressive and expansionist tendencies. Mussolini's imperialist pronouncements were clearly not designed merely for internal propaganda consumption, but were, on the contrary, statements of intent. Yet, both crises also highlighted the all too evident limitations facing the Italian armed forces. The Italian dictator, eager to use each moment of international tension as a springboard for a successful Italian war of expansion in Africa and the Middle East, of which the conquest of Ethiopia marked simply the first stage, was, on each occasion, prevented from doing so by Italian strategic weakness and by the reluctance of the military leadership. The Fascist regime's major naval programs, initiated in the early 1930s as the principal means of driving Italy's foes out of its *mare nostrum*, were not destined for completion before the mid–1940s. Thus, while Mussolini hoped to challenge Anglo–French Mediterranean hegemony long before that time, he simply lacked the capability to do so. Such national debility only served to generate impetus for an Italo–German alignment that remained wholly unpopular within much of Italy and, ultimately, did not resolve the dictator's geopolitical "dilemma." By 1943 Mussolini's alliance with Germany, and subsequent war against Britain, saw Italy not liberated from Mediterranean incarceration, but invaded by vastly superior Allied forces. Italy's fleet had already been defeated two years before.

NOTES

[1] Cited in B.R. Sullivan, "A Fleet in Being: The Rise and Fall of Italian Sea Power, 1861–1943," *International History Review* 10 (1988): 115.

[2] R. Mallett, *The Italian Navy and Fascist Expansionism, 1935–1940* (London, 1998), 178.

[3] Memorandum by Mussolini, 30/12/1935, *I documenti diplomatici italiani* (*DDI*), settima serie, (Rome, 1990), 1922–1935, volume XVI, no. 358.

[4] "La questione italo–abissina," Cavagnari to Mussolini, 15/1/1935, Archivio Centrale dello Stato (ACS), Rome, Ministero della Marina: Gabinetto, busta: 199.

[5] Mallett, *The Italian Navy*, 13–14; a British naval intelligence report of January 1935 noted that ". . . in the event of Ethiopia becoming Italianised, Italy would be in a position to exert herself against British interests along practically the whole extent of British boundaries. She would also obtain control of the head waters of the Blue Nile." Confidential Admiralty Monthly Intelligence Report, (M.I.R.), No. 188, January 1935, Naval Historical Branch, (London).

[6] British embassy to Italian foreign ministry, 28/2/1935, *DDI*, 7, XVI, no. 677, (appendix); Capponi to naval staff, 3/3/1935, Archivio Storico del Ministero degli Affari Esteri (ASMAE), Rome, Ambasciata di Londra, busta: 891, fascicolo: 2.

[7] Conversation between Thompson, Guarnaschelli and Vitetti at Stresa, 12/4/1935, *Documents on British Foreign Policy* (*DBFP*), series 2, (London, 1949–57), volume XIV, no. 230 and no. 232.

[8] Mussolini to Grandi, 20/4/1935, *DDI*, ottava serie, 1935–1939, (Rome, 1952–92), volume I, no. 60.

[9] Cavagnari to Mussolini, 4/3/1935, *DDI*, 7, XVI, no. 694.

[10] "Operazione 'B,'" Cavagnari to army staff, 23/5/1935, Ufficio Storico della Marina Militare (USMM), Rome, Direttive Generali (DG), busta: O–L.

[11] "Piani di guerra," Cavagnari to naval staff, 14/4/1935, USMM, DG, busta: 1-D.

[12]"Piani di guerra," Cavagnari to naval staff, 24/4/1935, USMM, DG, busta: 1-D.

[13]"Documento di guerra L.G. 10-Piano B," naval war plans office, 16/5/1935, USMM, DG, busta: 1-D.

[14]Mallett, *The Italian Navy*, 23.

[15]Ibid., 25–27.

[16]Ibid., 27–29.

[17]"Conversazioni navali anglo–tedesche," Cavagnari to Mussolini, 15/6/1935, ASMAE, Affari Politici: Italia, busta: 27, fascicolo: 2.

[18]Cavagnari to Mussolini, 19/6/1935, USMM, DG, busta: 8-G.

[19]"Meeting of the Supreme High Command held at the *Palazzo Viminale*, Rome, 13 August 1935," in Mallett, *The Italian Navy*, appendix 2, 205–17.

[20]"Piano B - dislocazione iniziale ed impiego del naviglio di superfice," naval war plans office, 20/8/1935, USMM, DG, busta: 0-E; "Riunione Stato Maggiore," 19/9/1935 and 7/10/1935, USMM, DG, busta: 1-E.

[21]Mallett, *The Italian Navy*, 36.

[22]"Studio sul programma navale," naval war plans office, 13/1/1936, ACS, Min. Mar. Gab., busta: 195.

[23]Mallett, *The Italian Navy*, 58 and 94–96; "Progetti operativi," Cavagnari to Badoglio, 19/11/1937, USMM, DG, busta: 1–B,

[24]Mallett, *The Italian Navy*, 96; Cavagnari to Ciano, 20–1/6/1939, *DDI*, 8, XIII, appendix IV.

[25]"Studio circa la preparazione. Argomento I - Le forze navali," naval war plans office to Mussolini, 9/1937, USMM, DG, busta: 0-A1.

[26]Mallett, *The Italian Navy*, chapter 3.

[27]Ibid., 114.

[28]G. Ciano, *Diario: 1937–43*, ed. R. De Felice, (Milan, 1994), 5/5/1938.

[29]"Political Report," Mackensen to foreign ministry, 17/5/1938, *Documents on German Foreign Policy*, (*DGFP*), series D, (London, Washington and Paris, 1949–56), volume I, no. 764.

[30]"Memorandum by the foreign minister," 23/8/1938 and 27/8/1938, *DGFP*, D, II, no. 384, and no. 401.

[31]Ciano, *Diario*, 26/9/1938.

[32]"DG 1 Op. AG. Studio preliminare per operazioni contro Francia–Inghilterra," naval war plans office, 2/9/1938, USMM, DG, busta: 1-A.

[33]"Situazione delle forze," naval staff, 22/9/1938, USMM, DG, busta: 1-A.

[34]W. Murray, "Munich 1938: The Military Confrontation," *Journal of Strategic Studies* 2 (1979), 295.

Doyle's Dauntless Dory: USS *Nassau* and the Evolution of Carrier-Based Close Air Support

Hill Goodspeed

> Planning for war occupied American naval planners in the 1930s as well. Nevertheless, the war that came to America in 1941 brought with it tactical problems that the planners had not foreseen. A case in point was the need for carrier-based close air support, a need which led to the creation and development of the escort carrier as the U.S. Navy's primary platform for this mission. In this essay, Hill Goodspeed examines the history of U.S.S. *Nassau* from her commissioning to her participation in the operations in the Aleutians, where she became the first carrier whose primary mission was to support an amphibious assault in the Pacific. In the process, he traces the development of a tactical doctrine for the employment of this new type of warship.

In the years before World War II, whether on the war game table at Newport or at sea, naval officers evaluated the potential impact of the aircraft carrier in naval warfare. In a Navy that followed Alfred Thayer Mahan's dictum of the "decisive sea battle," proponents of naval aviation naturally advanced the carrier as a decisive element of the Navy of the future. In 1922 hearings before the House Naval Affairs Committee, Chief of the Bureau of Aeronautics Rear Adm. William A. Moffett testified that without aircraft carriers "our Navy can never be anything but a second-best Navy, which . . . has about the same value as a second-best poker hand."[1] Comdr. John H. Towers, the Navy's third aviator and overall commander of the successful transatlantic flight attempt of 1919, stated the case more boldly in 1925 testimony before the President's Aircraft Board, more commonly known as the Morrow Board. "Aviation is not only the eyes of the Navy but also its good right arm. It does not require a great deal of vision to see the day

---

Hill Goodspeed is the Historian at the National Museum of Naval Aviation in Pensacola, Florida. He is the author of one book, *The Spirit of Naval Aviation*, and his articles and book reviews have appeared in the *Journal of Military History*, *Naval History*, *Naval Aviation News*, *Foundation*, and the British publication, *Wings of Fame*.

when it may be both arms."[2] In advancing their case for the aircraft carrier, these officers naturally focused on the weapon's role in a ship vs. ship engagement, viewing that as its most important application. Wrote Lt. Logan C. Ramsey in the August 1930 issue of the *United States Naval Institute Proceedings*, ". . . the fleet required to assume the offensive must be prepared to contend . . . with aircraft carried by the opposing fleet."[3] Operations against land targets generally fell into the category of attacking major installations ashore, particularly naval bases.[4] Whether against ship or shore, proponents of naval aviation were unanimous in their opinion that aircraft, and as an extension the carriers from which they operated, were offensive weapons. As Comdr. Patrick N. L. Bellinger told an audience at the Naval War College in August 1924, "An aircraft is primarily an offensive weapon and if it fails to take advantage of any and every opportunity to do all the damage within its power, against the enemy . . . it will have failed in its maximum accomplishment."[5]

The United States Navy War Instructions issued in the years before World War II also turned a blind eye towards the carrier's role in landing operations, mainly emphasizing its role in a fleet action. The 1924 instructions assigned the support of landing operations to a "Control Force" consisting of cruiser divisions, destroyer squadrons, submarine squadrons, the supply train, and mine squadrons. No mention was made of carriers and aircraft squadrons fell into the category of "as may be assigned."[6] Though the Navy could be excused at this particular juncture given the fact that USS *Langley* (CV-1), the service's first carrier, had yet to formally join the fleet, such was not the case in future doctrine. In 1934 the War Instructions specifically outlined the role of aircraft carriers, concentrating mainly upon a fleet action in which they were to attack enemy vessels and aircraft, defend vessels and aircraft against attack, lay smoke, and scout tactically. Secondary missions outside a fleet action were to attack enemy forces or objectives *"at a distance"* and to act as cruisers when their aircraft were exhausted.[7] Clearly, operating in close proximity to an enemy-held shore was not viewed as an ideal tactical use of a carrier.

Hesitancy to engage flat-tops in direct support of landings against a hostile beachhead is also evident in War Plan Orange, the strategy against Japan that dated to the period before World War I. In his landmark study of the plan, Edward S. Miller highlights the fact that war planners could never come to grips with the problem of air cover for landings on a hostile shore. Debate in 1935 about an invasion of the Marshall Islands was a revealing example of this fact. U.S. planners believed that Japanese defensive strategy during the American offensive would be the entrapment of the Blue (U.S.) Fleet by tying it to the support of the invasion beaches, a vulnerable position in that the ships were relatively immobile and subject to air attack. Marine Corps officers on the war planning staff demanded that the invasion force receive carrier-based close air support for as long as they deemed necessary. However, members of the Navy's War Plans Division (OP-12) balked at this concept, which in their minds would take away the carrier's advantage of mobility. It was better for the available carriers to roam free throughout the entire theater, striking Japanese airfields from which the enemy could send air strikes against the invasion beaches.[8]

At sea, once the large-deck carriers *Lexington* (CV-2) and *Saratoga* (CV-3) joined the fleet in 1927, the annual Fleet Problems conducted began to place more of an emphasis on carrier operations. The much publicized Fleet Problem IX in January 1929 dramatically demonstrated the capability of an aircraft carrier to launch a surprise attack against a shore installation, in this case the Panama Canal. During later exercises, similar raids were conducted against Pearl Harbor, foreshadowing the Japanese attack of 1941. As more carriers entered service during the 1930s, carrier vs. carrier engagements appeared more often during the annual fleet exercises, but aviators were increasingly frustrated by the fact that the flat-tops were continually tied to the battle line. During Fleet Problem XVIII in 1937, the premise of the exercises was the occupation of Lahaina, French Frigate Shoals, and Midway by the Black Fleet, while the White Fleet attempted to disrupt the landings. Although the Black Fleet held a three-to-one superiority in carriers, umpires ruled *Langley* sunk, *Lexington* heavily damaged, and

Saratoga partially damaged. Some of the damage was caused by the aircraft from the White Fleet's sole carrier, USS *Ranger* (CV-4).[9]

In his assessment of the air operations of Fleet Problem XVIII, the air commander of the Black Fleet stated that energy and strength of naval aviation and its ability to establish control of the air was reduced if it was burdened with multiple defensive missions. "Once an enemy carrier is within striking distance of our fleet, no security remains until it—its squadrons—or both, are destroyed, and our carriers, if with the main body are at a tremendous initial disadvantage in conducting necessary operations." Fleet Problem XVIII thus reaffirmed the airmen's belief in the necessity of freedom of operation for the aircraft carrier and its primary mission of destroying the enemy's air assets. Providing defensive air cover for an amphibious landing, as aptly demonstrated during the exercises, placed the carrier at risk.[10]

In addition to the annual fleet problems, during the period 1935–1941 the Navy conducted a series of Fleet Landing Exercises, mostly in Puerto Rico. Though these operations demonstrated that a successful amphibious landing required control of the air in the landing area, these exercises did not incorporate aircraft carriers, but generally employed Marine Corps aircraft and occasionally Navy patrol planes. Only within the context of some of the fleet problems would carrier aircraft practice support of landing operations, and only as a secondary aspect of the exercises.[11]

Thus, it is apparent that whether operating at sea or formulating war plans for future operations, the proponents of the aircraft carrier chose to focus more on establishing it as an effective offensive weapon at sea. At the same time, they relegated any defensive role for the carrier to secondary status, or in many cases, ignored it altogether.

The concept of a small deck carrier in the U.S. Navy appeared in 1927, the same year that the giant aircraft carriers *Lexington* and *Saratoga* joined the fleet. In May, Lt. Comdr. Bruce G. Leighton, who in 1919 had commanded the first formal aviation organization attached to the U.S. Fleet, wrote a paper outlining the potential employment of "light aircraft carriers." Viewing them as substitutes for cruisers, he envisioned them operating in the roles of antisubmarine warfare, scouting, reconnaissance, attacks against enemy shipping, and reduction of enemy shore bases.[12] In addition, carrier tonnage limitations imposed on the United States Navy under the provisions of the Washington Naval Treaty of 1922 affected thoughts about carrier design. In a letter to the General Board on 20 June 1927, Moffett stated that "aircraft can be handled far more expeditiously from a large number of small carriers than from a small number of large carriers."[13]

However, it would not be until the eve of U.S. entry into World War II that the construction of small deck carriers became an urgent necessity. In December 1940, Vice Adm. William F. Halsey, Commander Aircraft, Battle Force, expressed concern over the fact that large deck carriers were being employed in the aircraft ferrying role, and proposed that merchant ships be converted into auxiliary aircraft carriers capable of carrying out this mission.[14] Though Halsey's point was a valid one, it was the increasing U-boat threat in the Atlantic and President Franklin D. Roosevelt's pledged support of Great Britain that brought about construction of the escort carrier. In December 1940, Roosevelt received a disturbing message from British Prime Minister Winston Churchill that included an attachment containing statistics on merchant ship losses to submarines. The President read with dismay that Nazi wolf packs were sending an average of ninety merchantmen to the bottom each month, and determined that the United States must find some way to assist in protecting these convoys, which were vital to the survival of the United Kingdom. Through his naval aide, Capt. Daniel J. Callaghan, Roosevelt sent a note to Chief of Naval Operations Adm. Harold J. Stark proposing the conversion of a 6,000–8,000 ton merchant ship into an aircraft carrier. Capable of making at least fifteen knots, the ship would be designed to operate either ten small autogyros or ten aircraft with low landing speeds. The following month, despite the feeling of some officers within the Navy Department that the project had limited chances for success, Roosevelt issued a veritable presidential mandate, telling Stark in so many words that he expected the project to be completed within three months.[15]

The resulting carrier was USS *Long Island* (AVG-1), commissioned at Newport News, Virginia, on 2 June 1941 with Comdr. Donald B. "Wu" Duncan commanding. Converted from the merchantman *Mormacland*, the new carrier was 492 ft. long, 69 ft., 6 in. by the beam, and displaced 13,500 tons. Additionally, she could make 16½ knots. For flight operations, the diminutive carrier was fitted with a flight deck measuring 362 ft. in length, with the ship's bridge located just below its level on the forward end of the ship.[16] Following commissioning, *Long Island* conducted a series of short cruises designed to evaluate the effectiveness of the ship. Of particular interest to this study is her participation in an amphibious landing exercise at New River, North Carolina, during August 1941, in which the carrier's aircraft performed gunfire spotting for the pre-landing bombardment and provided air support for the landing force. In this first use of the escort carrier in an operation of this nature, the results were not favorable in the minds of the senior officers governing the exercise. The main criticism was that a ship of *Long Island*'s size could simply not provide the necessary degree of air support for an amphibious operation. Duncan understood his command's limitations, but nevertheless reiterated the importance of air cover in an assault from the sea, concluding, "Without sufficient fighter protection, transports and troops would undoubtedly be easy prey to even a small number of bombers."[17]

The Japanese attack on Pearl Harbor and the subsequent entry of the United States into World War II spurred the development of the escort carrier. While ships still smoldered along Battleship Row, the Navy approved conversion of twenty-four C-3-S-A1 merchant ship hulls to aircraft carriers. Called the *Bogue*-class escort carriers after the maiden ship of the line, the 8,390-ton (13,890 tons fully loaded) ships featured a slightly larger flight deck than *Long Island* (436 ft., 8 in., by 80 ft.), as well as a more extensive hangar deck accessible with two midship elevators. Unlike "Wu" Duncan in *Long Island*, skippers of the *Bogues* were blessed with a small starboard island that allowed for better navigation, a flight deck closer to the hull that improved overall stability at sea, and an overall much stronger ship with the addition of more transverse bulkheads. Armament included 5-inch guns, supplemented by ten

40mm and twenty-seven 20mm mounts, a veritable fortress compared to *Long Island*. Able to carry twice the oil of their predecessor, the *Bogues'* steam turbine propulsion plant allowed a maximum speed of eighteen knots.[18]

All told, forty-four *Bogue*-class escort carriers rolled down the ways at Todd Shipyard in Tacoma, Washington, all but eleven of them being transferred to the Royal Navy. The remainder established quite a reputation during their service, mainly in the Atlantic. *Bogue* and her embarked squadrons were credited with twelve U-boat sinkings during the war, the most of any escort carrier, and sister ships *Card*, *Croatan*, and *Block Island* accounted for twenty-five more between them.[19] Just as these ships revolutionized the role of the aircraft carrier in antisubmarine warfare, another of their sisters was destined for a pioneering role on the opposite side of the globe. Her name was *Nassau*.

In June 1942, Comdr. Austin K. Doyle approached Capt. Arthur W. Radford to request a transfer. The news from the Pacific brought reports of great carrier battles at Coral Sea and Midway, and the veteran pilot wanted to trade his desk in the Training Division of the Bureau of Aeronautics for a carrier bridge. In fact, the commanding officer of USS *Saratoga* (CV-3) had already asked him to take the post of executive officer, which in Doyle's mind would provide him with the opportunity to gain some much needed experience before taking command of his own ship. To his surprise, Radford denied the request. There was still much work to be done in building the establishment that would be responsible for training the thousands of cadets and sailors who would man the aircraft and carriers springing forth from the nation's industry. Only when Doyle received a command would Radford release his valuable assistant.[20]

At forty-three years old, Austin K. Doyle had spent all of his adult life in the Navy. A native of Staten Island, New York, and the son of a state legislator, he graduated from the United States Naval Academy with the Class of 1920, whose members received their commissions in June 1919 because of World War I. A natural competitor, in part the result of having two older brothers, he played baseball at Annapolis, and in later years would liken service aboard the carriers *Lexington* and *Saratoga* as being in the "big leagues."

Following the typical path of newly commissioned officers during that time period, Ensign Doyle went to sea, eventually serving aboard the battleship *Utah*, one of the mighty ships of the battle line that was the backbone of the Navy. However, during a port visit in Tunisia, an event occurred that changed his future—an airplane ride. Requesting assignment to aviation, Doyle reported to Naval Air Station Pensacola, Florida, earning his wings in December 1922. Aside from an initial tour flying World War I–vintage F-5L flying boats and later duty as a scouting pilot aboard a cruiser, Doyle spent his entire prewar flying days in fighters. This included duty in the famed "Fighting Chiefs" of VF-2B, a squadron composed mainly of enlisted pilots, and command of VF-3, the "Felix the Cat" squadron. All culminated with command of the air group aboard *Saratoga* during 1939–1940. Interspersed with sea duty were shore assignments as a flight instructor, baseball coach at Annapolis, a stint as the tactical officer on the staff of Aircraft Squadrons, Battle Force, and a tour in the Bureau of Aeronautics, where he held down the fighter desk. When he approached Radford he was nearing completion of his second tour in the bureau.[21]

"He was chunky, full of life, very outgoing, acting on things at once . . . I suppose that he had an Irish fire in him," was how one officer described his first meeting with Artie Doyle.[22] To be sure, he was a gregarious character, inclined towards practical jokes, and more often than not wearing a wry smile beneath his narrow eyes. However, behind this outward demeanor there existed a certain seriousness of purpose in Austin K. Doyle. He was the type of man who did not shrink from the responsibility of acting upon his convictions, a fact he demonstrated later in the war when he made some disparaging comments in his action reports while serving as skipper of USS *Hornet* (CV-12). "I'm doing my darndest (*sic*) not to make a normal mistake, but I run on the border line every minute by action report criticisms," he wrote his wife in March 1945. "I haven't yet compromised with my conscience."[23]

He could also be innovative, as demonstrated in December 1941 when an artist named Robert Osborn appeared at his desk in the Bureau of Aeronautics bearing three books on shooting and fishing that he had illustrated. Remembering a trip to England the previous year in which he had seen how the Royal Air Force used a cartoon character as an effective instruction method in educating pilots about the hazards of flying, Doyle arranged orders for Osborn that day. Within weeks the two had developed "Dilbert," the bumbling pilot who never did anything right, who eventually appeared in hundreds of posters and pamphlets and certainly saved the lives of many a fledgling aviator.[24]

Both of these attributes—the strength of his convictions and his innovative mind—would serve him well when an opportunity for command arrived. It did not take long. In August 1942 orders came down detaching Doyle from his duties in Washington, D.C., and directing him to report to the Puget Sound Navy Yard in Bremerton, Washington, to take command of *Nassau* (AVG-16). Having been a participant in the evolution of the aircraft carrier by flying in the famous Fleet Problem IX carrier raid against the Panama Canal in January 1929 and logging traps aboard the Navy's first three flattops, Doyle certainly relished his first seagoing command. However, given the fact that he had on occasion teased his fellow aviator "Wu" Duncan about commanding a "merchant man," the ex-ball player may have regarded his new ship as being part of the "bush leagues." As he winged his way westward on a commercial aircraft after bidding farewell to his family in Pensacola, little did he know that his little "baby flattop" would help lead the aircraft carrier down a new path of naval warfare.[25]

Comdr. Austin K. Doyle arrived at the Puget Sound Navy Yard late in the evening of August 15th, and the next day revived his sea legs by sailing aboard USS *Copahee* (AVG-12) for her Builder's Trials. That night he wrote to his old boss back in Washington, putting in a plug for the new ships and the special role he envisioned for them.

> These ships are the finest that I have ever seen, handle beautifully, with minor exceptions are well arranged, and are invaluable as our only expendible

(*sic*) carriers. They must not be used for anything but combatant ships, pushed close to beach heads (*sic*). I have never been so pleased in my life. . . . Please tell Wu that I apologize about my crack about "Merchant Men," these are the finest ships that I have ever seen and are going to prove to be the work-horse of this war.[26]

His comments regarding the future employment of the escort carriers proved timely given recent events off Guadalcanal.

With the great victory at the Battle of Midway in June 1942, in which four Japanese carriers were sunk by U.S. Navy carrier-based aircraft, Adm. Ernest J. King sought to exploit the opportunity and assume the offensive in the Pacific. He met with objections from the Army in the form of Gen. George C. Marshall, whose interests lay in Europe, and Gen. Douglas MacArthur, who proposed an invasion of the Japanese bastion at Rabaul, naturally, under his overall command. To King, it was an aberration to place Navy ships and Marines under Army command. Deciding to force the issue, he instructed Adm. Chester W. Nimitz, his commander in the Pacific, to prepare for an amphibious assault against the small island of Tulagi in the Solomons using only naval assets. This came despite the fact that Tulagi lay in the Southwest Pacific zone that by Joint Chiefs of Staff agreement was under MacArthur's command. The resulting imbroglio lasted until the last day in June, when Marshall and King reached a compromise that shifted Nimitz's command zone to the west to include the lower Solomons. The invasion, expanded to include Guadalcanal and code-named Operation *Watchtower*, was set for August.[27]

Within the minimal time allowed for planning of the operation, one of the central focuses was air support. With the loss of *Yorktown* (CV-5) at Midway, only four carriers remained in the Pacific, and three of them were earmarked for participation in *Watchtower* under the command of Vice Adm. Frank Jack Fletcher, a veteran of the carrier battles at Coral Sea and Midway. Meetings between Fletcher and Rear Adm. Richmond Kelly Turner, slated to command the amphibious forces for the invasion, produced a consensus that the key to the success of the operation was the ability of MacArthur's Southwest Pacific air forces to neutralize Japanese air assets, particularly at the giant base at Rabaul. If this did not occur, planners did not rule out the possibility of losing a carrier.[28]

Nevertheless, the plan that emerged from the meetings called for Fletcher's carriers to provide close air support for the invasion force two days prior to August 7th landings and throughout the entire course of D-Day. A later discussion between Fletcher and Turner aboard the former's flagship *Saratoga* on 27 July 1942 extended the time the carriers would spend in close support of the amphibious forces by two days until August 9th. Turner also expected that his transports could unload and be withdrawn within that time frame.[29]

Unlike the heavily defended beaches of Tarawa and Iwo Jima that would confront Marines later in World War II, the leathernecks of the First Marine Division met minimal resistance going ashore at Guadalcanal. However, such was not the case in the air. A total of fifty-three aircraft, a mixture of A6M2 Model 21 and A6M3 Model 32 Zeros, Aichi D3A dive-bombers, and G4M1 twin-engine bombers, appeared over the landing area from Rabaul at 1315, just over four hours after the first troops hit the beach. In the air ready to meet them were eighteen carrier-based F4F-4 *Wildcat* fighters and a handful of SBD-3 *Dauntless* dive-bombers. The ferocious air battle that ensued succeeded in thwarting the Japanese attempts to bomb the transports—they scored only one hit on a destroyer—but cost the defenders half the fighters engaged. This initial raid was followed by one more at 1400 and another the morning of August 8th. This strike encompassed thirty-eight G4M1s and escorting Zeros, and was decimated by a combination of antiaircraft fire from the ships of the amphibious force and carrier fighters. They did, however, manage to severely damage one transport and a destroyer.[30]

Two days of combat thus shrunk Fletcher's precious fighter strength from ninety-nine to seventy-eight aircraft, and convinced the admiral of the continued strength of Japanese land-based air power on Rabaul. Still believing that Turner planned to withdraw the ships of the amphibious force by that day, he requested and received permission to withdraw the valuable carriers to a position southeast of Guadalcanal. The ships of his task force remained in a position from which they could support the assault forces the following day. Unbeknownst to Fletcher, who due to faulty communications did not receive the message, Turner had changed his mind. His transports had not unloaded as quickly as expected and he desired to remain off Guadalcanal until all supplies were put ashore.[31]

The subsequent night engagement in the early morning hours of August 9th, in which a Japanese surface force sank four heavy cruisers, and Turner's decision later that day to withdraw his ships because of lack of carrier air support proved damning to Fletcher. Marines never forgave him and the Navy in general for abandoning them and historian Samuel Eliot Morison lambasted this decision in his landmark history of naval operations during World War II. Fletcher's defenders criticize Turner for not unloading the transports on schedule and highlight the fact that Fletcher's command represented seventy-five percent of all carriers available to the U.S. Navy in the Pacific. His top priority was preservation of this valuable asset, particularly given the fact that Japanese carriers could be lurking in the vicinity.[32]

The experience at Guadalcanal confirmed the need for aircraft carrier support for invasions and Fletcher's decision illuminated the fact that until greater numbers of fleet carriers were commissioned, another alternative was necessary. Fortunately, the Marines fighting on Guadalcanal held Henderson Field, a veritable unsinkable carrier, in the face of numerous Japanese attacks. Landbased aircraft, ferried to Guadalcanal in large part on the flight decks of escort carriers, were thus able to provide a certain degree of air support. However, future operations might not present the same situation of having an airfield in close proximity to the engaged ground forces.

On 20 August 1942, Artie Doyle stepped to the microphone to read his orders on the flight deck of *Nassau*. Perhaps he was aware of the recent events at Guadalcanal, especially in light of his letter to Radford four days earlier. However, it would be many weeks before his new command could do anything to assist in the operations on that far flung island. He couldn't even live aboard his ship yet, and once the brief ceremony ended, 2,000 yard workers resumed the work of getting the ship ready for sea, with blow torches glowing and the clanging sounds of jackhammers and other tools reverberating throughout the small carrier's hull.[33]

Obtaining qualified personnel was the new captain's first priority. On his first full day as skipper, Doyle wrote to Capt. Ralph E. Davison, Assistant Chief of the Bureau of Aeronautics, expressing his dismay at the numbers and quality of personnel being assigned to the escort carriers. Although now in commission and expected to conduct sea trials within weeks, *Nassau*'s complement included no officer qualified to stand a deck watch at sea. Additionally, the ship lacked a Communication Officer and no officer on board had ever fired a gun or served in the Gunnery Department of a combatant ship.[34] "We are definitely going to be in the front lines, we are your only expendable carriers and we haven't had our proper cut on what experienced Officers there are in the Navy," he concluded. As far as Bupers (*sic*) is concerned we are 'BEEF BOATS,' and unless we get our share of experienced officers our performance of missions will be commensurate."[35]

In early September, Vice Adm. William F. Halsey passed through the area and called a conference of all escort carrier skippers at Naval Air Station Sand Point, Washington, at which they attempted to persuade him of the necessity of assigning one escort carrier to training in order to allow qualified personnel to keep pace with the mass production of the ships. "We all, of course recognize the urgent need for CV's (*sic*), but in the long run training can be done so much more efficiently under training conditions than under war conditions," Doyle wrote Rear Adm. John H. Towers of Halsey's negative response to the suggestion.[36]

The personnel situation would plague *Nassau* during her first months of operations. As Ludlow Baldwin, a lieutenant assigned to the ship in December, recalled half a century later, "Captain Doyle had plenty to write home about the inexperience of the crew aboard, . . . of which I, though a so-called 'Senior Officer of the Watch' on the bridge, [was] a prime example. That we had no collision while I had the deck is simply an example of my good luck at all times during my wartime career."[37] As for the crew, *Nassau* benefited to a certain degree from having over 100 survivors from the sunken *Lexington* (CV-2) assigned to her. However, for one sailor assigned to her later after his carrier was sunk off Guadalcanal, her crew left much to be desired. "We were naval snobs, used to the big ships and the smartness of the prewar navy, and everything about this little tub, manned with reserves, and some dregs of the regular navy, offended our sense of propriety."[38]

In addition to personnel issues, tactics were very much on Doyle's mind as he prepared to take his new command out for her sea trials. In another letter to Towers, he envisioned operating escort carriers in divisions of four, with two carrying only fighters and the other pair operating dive-bombers and torpedo-planes. Coupled with the support of a battleship, Doyle concluded, "they provide a force that can back up a beach head (sic) more effectively and with more flexibility of operation than could a larger carrier. The enemy would have a difficult time putting four of these out of commission when 60VF s (sic) are available for protection." And the escort carrier had another advantage in Doyle's mind, especially in light of the recent events off Guadalcanal. "These are so cheap and are so easily constructed that they are bound to be our shock troops in the Pacific."[39]

Nassau put to sea for the first time on September 19th and conducted trial runs and equipment checks into October. "We don't know when we are going to leave but we hope that it is soon and that we stay in the Pacific," Doyle wrote to old friend Spig Wead. Their wish came true with receipt of orders to Naval Air Station Alameda, California, in early October. After loading nine F4F *Wildcat* fighters of VGS-16 at Port Angeles, Washington, *Nassau* was underway for California on October 7th, arriving three days later. Taking aboard an additional twelve aircraft, TBF *Avenger* torpedo-bombers assigned to VGS-16, the ship departed Alameda bound for Pearl Harbor. *Nassau* was off to war.[40]

Though *Nassau*'s ultimate destination was the South Pacific, where fighting on Guadalcanal continued until February 1943, her role was as an auxiliary vessel devoted primarily to the ferrying of aircraft. Nevertheless, it was an eventful first cruise for the ship, which at Pearl Harbor offloaded the aircraft of VGS-16 in exchange for twelve TBFs, twenty SBD *Dauntless* dive-bombers, and five Army Air Forces P-40 *Warhawk* fighters for transport to Guadalcanal. Departing Pearl Harbor on 27 October, she arrived at Palmyra Island three days later and then sailed to Nouméa, New Caledonia, without the benefit of a destroyer escort, a risk in waters where Japanese submarines operated. After only one day at anchor, the *Nassau* was again underway, this time bound for Espiritu Santo, New Hebrides, the staging area for aircraft being sent to Henderson Field on Guadalacanal. The aircraft she carried arrived on the embattled island on the eve of the Naval Battle of Guadalcanal, and helped hammer Japanese surface forces making a last ditch effort to take the island.[41]

It was the closest *Nassau* would get to the action, as she would spend the next four months cruising between Pearl Harbor and the South Pacific. Vice Adm. John H. Towers, Commander, Air Forces, Pacific Fleet, debated employing *Nassau* and her sisters *Altamaha* (ACV-18) and *Copahee* (ACV-12) in direct support of operations in the Solomons. However, the arrival in theater of the *Sangamon*-class aircraft carriers in January 1943 ended any notions of this. Having recently participated in the invasion of North Africa, the new arrivals were combat ready, and it thus made more sense to employ them in direct support of fleet operations in the area. To this end, *Chenango* (ACV-28) and *Suwanee* (ACV-27) were assigned to Task Force 18 under Rear Adm. Robert C. Giffen, which engaged Japanese forces in the Battle of Rennell Island on 29–30 January 1943.[42]

Though his command was not on the firing line, Doyle certainly appreciated the time at sea, for it provided an opportunity for his crew to gain much needed experience and learn the nuances of their ship. Writing to old friend Capt. Cato Glover, prospective commanding officer of an escort carrier, Doyle lamented about everything from a bower that was too light to keep the ship from dragging in certain anchorages to leaky dampers on the exhaust stack to an aircraft elevator that stuck because of a loose pin in the control shaft. As for the crew, the old baseball coach in the skipper bred competence by employing competitions between the gun crews in firing exercises and pitting Officers of the Deck against one another in reading signal flags. Having served under Adm. Ernest J. King and witnessed firsthand some of his legendary tirades, Doyle added a touch of humor to the latter contest by having the signal officer run up flag hoists spelling out orders in King's unique vernacular, which usually contained a fair amount of expletives.[43] Additionally, with four lieutenant commanders on board with no recent time at sea and a navigator who had never served in that capacity before, the new skipper had his hands full.[44]

Realizing that the effectiveness of *Nassau* lay in how quickly she operated aircraft, Doyle took every opportunity to drill his crew in that area of operations. In one instance, when the wind had died down to four-to-five knots, he decided to make use of his catapult, achieving positive results.

> Two TBF's (*sic*) cut No. 5 wire and almost hit the barrier, but otherwise it was successful. We know we can operate fighters, and in an emergency, TBF's (*sic*) in light winds. We have made 80 catapult shots so far and the pilots prefer it. The best time to date is a minute and a half between shots. Landing intervals are not good because the seas give us a bad pitch at times and we played safe. These ships have got a quick pitch in certain weather.[45]

Having observed how his ship handled flight operations, Doyle also took advantage of his time at sea by revisiting the issue of how escort carriers should be employed in combat, forwarding his opinions to Pacific Fleet headquarters at Pearl Harbor.

"The physical limitations of this class ACV . . . will dictate employment and tactics to which large and fast carriers are not necessarily bound," Doyle began a 5 January 1943 memorandum. To this end, he recommended that carriers of the *Suwanee*-class, converted oilers with their increased speed and longer flight decks, be devoted to operating dive-bombers and torpedo planes, while *Bogue*-class carriers like *Nassau* be designated to carry fighters.

Configured in this manner, a tactical group of six escort carriers would form a potent offensive force capable of fielding its own combat air patrol, scouting for an enemy force, and launching strike groups. Though Doyle considered a four-carrier group quite feasible, he concluded the reduction of the task force from six to four ACVs gives a disproportionate drop in striking strength. It appears, therefore, the economy of force dictates the use of six ACVs in a task force."[46]

The *Nassau*'s skipper defended the escort carriers in a memorandum to Towers the following month. Admitting deficiencies in speed and defensive firepower, as well as a dependence on catapult launches that detracted from their ability to operate a mixed group of aircraft efficiently, Doyle nevertheless indicted fellow naval aviators who had submitted negative recommendations regarding the employment of escort carriers in combat. "These recommendations have been based upon insufficient operational experience with the class," he concluded, "and upon failure to give consideration to their value when used in a manner designed to exploit their favorable characteristics."[47]

Continuing, Doyle reiterated the point of his earlier letter in stating that escort carriers had never been operated together in large enough numbers to assess their capabilities. "An individual ACV does not operate with the efficiency of the more expensive CV, nor is it as fast and well protected," he wrote. "But four ACV[s] operating together can carry more airplanes and operate them more efficiently than one large CV." With increased service tests on catapults and a shoring up of defensive armament, the *Nassau* skipper believed in the potential of the ships to do good work, the limited expense and ease of their construction enabling them to be built in great numbers. "The Commanding Officer is convinced that these are splendid ships and urges a service test of a division . . .," he concluded. "This test should include combatant operations."[48]

To be sure, Doyle had selfish reasons for advancing the cause of the escort carrier. A born fighter, he tired of reading magazine accounts lauding the accomplishments of the large deck carriers, and speaking of "a large number of completed merchantmen, which while not good for combatant duty, are useful for transport work."[49] Having been on the periphery at Guadalcanal and heard the stories of combat from friends who fought in the battle, he wanted the same opportunity for himself and his crew, and for his ship and those like her, which he had believed in from the start. "It's got past the stage of saying that Doyle's just enthusiastic," he wrote a friend in the Bureau of Aeronautics. "These are good ships . . . and when we get enough of them they'll do a great deal to win the war."[50]

The official response to Doyle's memorandums came from Towers, who believed that a six-ship division was too unwieldy, and came down on the side of divisions of four escort carriers. As for their use as combatants, the admiral concluded "the greatest use of the NASSAU class ACV as a combatant carrier in the Pacific will lie in its use as a fighter carrier supporting the operations of other types of ships and of amphibious forces."[51] It was a prophetic statement for far to the north, in the frigid waters surrounding the Aleutians, events were unfolding that would eventually give Doyle and the men of Nassau their crack at the enemy.

As part of Adm. Isoroku Yamamoto's elaborate plan to seize Midway Island and destroy the surviving American carriers in June 1942, the Japanese staged a diversionary carrier strike against Dutch Harbor and landed troops on the islands of Attu and Kiska. Rather than use their new conquests as stepping stones for an advance against Alaska, the Japanese were content with the fact that they held two pieces of American soil. With operations in the South Pacific draining the limited resources in the Pacific, the Army and Navy were similarly content to let them stay there as long as the Japanese did not show any signs of a military build-up on either of the two islands. However, this did not mean that they left the enemy alone. To the contrary, American planes conducted periodic bombing missions against the garrisons and also staged a pair of bombardments with cruisers and destroyers.[52]

By late-1942, however, reconnaissance confirmed the fact that the Japanese were expanding the garrison on Attu and had their eyes on invading Amchitka Island, located just east of Kiska, for the purpose of building an airfield there. This news spurred interest in the Aleutians area of operations on the part of the high command, and Adm. Chester W. Nimitz, Commander-in-Chief, Pacific Fleet and Pacific Ocean Areas, ordered planning to commence for landings at both Amchitka and Kiska.[53] "It seems probable that convoys now en route to the western ALEUTIANS are bringing in reinforcements and replacements," the CINCPAC Command Summary noted on 30 November 1942. "Photos show that the enemy is there to stay until ousted by troops."[54]

Army forces seized Amchitka without opposition on 12 January 1943, and once an airstrip on the island was completed, air strikes against Attu and Kiska intensified, forming a veritable blockade of the islands because Japanese cargo ships dared not approach the area lest they be sunk. With the target date for the invasion of Kiska approaching, Rear Adm. Thomas C. Kinkaid, who had relieved Rear Adm. Robert A. Theobold as Commander North Pacific Force in January 1943, proposed that his forces first invade Attu, which boasted a smaller garrison than Kiska. Foremost in his mind was the fact that resources for Aleutian operations were still limited, and were not adequate for taking an objective on the order of Kiska. Nimitz agreed and obtained the consent of the Joint Chiefs of Staff, with D-Day for Operation LANDCRAB set for 7 May.[55]

LANDCRAB was planned as a joint operation. The Seventh Infantry Division had been shifted from training in the Nevada desert for action in North Africa to Fort Ord on the Monterey Peninsula to prepare for the assault against Kiska. There they received amphibious training under the guidance of MGEN Holland M. Smith, USMC, who was destined to make a name for himself during future assaults against Japanese strongholds in the Central Pacific. As estimates of Japanese troop strength on Attu increased, from 500 to between 1,600 and 1,800 men, the assault force and floating reserve grew to a force totaling around 11,000 troops under the command of Maj. Gen. Albert F. Brown, a veteran of combat in World War I.[56]

To support the landings on Attu, the Navy assembled a force of some 115 ships including PT-boats, submarines, oilers, transports, and minesweepers. Task Force 51, the Assault Force, included the main batteries of the veteran battleships *Idaho*, *Pennsylvania*, and *Nevada*, the latter two veterans of the Pearl Harbor attack seeking to avenge the "day of infamy." Though land-based heavy and medium bombers and fighters of the Army Air Forces and Royal Canadian Air Force were assigned to participate in the assault, the only close-in air support would be provided by *Nassau*. Thus, she became the first escort carrier ever assigned to provide close air support for an amphibious landing in the Pacific Theater.[57]

Nassau arrived at Pearl Harbor from the South Pacific in mid-March 1943. Taking aboard cargo and passengers, she departed for San Francisco on 21 March and a week later was moored to Pier #20 at the United Engineering Company in San Francisco undergoing repairs and alterations.[58] She would remain there for seventeen days, receiving some 385 modifications ranging from repair of piping and upkeep of the ship's main turbine to replacing a urinal in the island structure with a toilet. Still, the delayed arrival of material and shortage of time precluded installation of a modification of the Type H, Mark 2 catapult, YE homing device, and TBM-7 and TAS radio transmitters. Thus, the ship possessed only a TDA transmitter, which was not normally used with aircraft. The ship also departed the yard with inoperative electric generators, no adequate provision for pumping flooded compartments, and a shortage of spare parts. Doyle could only hope that his ship would hold up in the harsh environs of the Northern Pacific.[59]

To make matters worse, the time spent in the yard limited the number of days that the ship could conduct flight operations with her new squadron complement. For the Attu operation, *Nassau* would field twenty-six F4F-4 *Wildcat* fighters of VC-21, three F4F-3P photoreconnaissance aircraft of VMO-155, and an SOC-3A utility aircraft. Under the command of Lt. Comdr. Lloyd K. Greenamyer, USNA Class of 1929, VC-21 fielded an experienced group of lieutenants and lieutenants junior grade appropriated from VF-3, which was under the command of Lt. Comdr. Edward H. "Butch" O'Hare, the Navy's first fighter ace and a Medal of Honor recipient. Some were veterans of combat over Guadalcanal, including Francis R. "Cash" Register, an ace with six kills while flying with VF-5. VMO-155's three-plane detachment consisting of six pilots and nine enlisted men were the first Marines assigned to a carrier for a combat operation. They were not the Corps' only contribution to the operation as Lt. Col. Peter P. Schrider, who helped train VC-21 pilots in close air support, was assigned to the ship as air support operations officer.[60]

Such was the brevity of work-ups with the squadrons that spare parts for the *Wildcats* were in short supply aboard *Nassau* as she prepared to sail for northern climes. Deciding it was easier to ask for forgiveness that permission, *Nassau* crewmen stripped two aircraft damaged in accidents of all usable parts before turning them in to Overhaul and Repair at NAS San Diego. By the time the Commander, Fleet Air, West Coast, sent a letter of protest to Doyle, *Nassau* was on her way to Attu.[61] Though the crashes were of benefit to those assigned to aircraft maintenance, they worried one VC-21 pilot, Lt. Richards "Dix" Loesch. "In the last five days we've lost from one squadron three pilots seriously injured; one pilot minorly (*sic*) injured; an enlisted man killed while watching carrier landings; 7 planes almost completely wrecked . . .," he wrote his father on 22 April 1943. You can't do much when every day finds you flying with a new man."[62]

"To the soldiers who had to fight not only the Japanese but the weather and terrain of the island," an official Army historian wrote, "it must have seemed that the Creator of the universe was an unskilled apprentice when He brought Attu into existence."[63] The approaching forces found an island about forty miles long and twenty miles across at its widest point, crowned by mountain ranges rising to 3,000 ft. Though Attu presented a number of sand beaches suitable for landing craft, the valleys leading to the base of the mountains consisted of soggy tundra, black mud intermixed with lichens and moss. The tangled muck would prove to be a second enemy for the grunts of the assault force. For Army Air Forces fliers and the aviators manning their *Wildcats* on *Nassau*'s flight deck, the skies above the island were equally inhospitable, with thick fog oftentimes enveloping the area and dangerous williwaws gusting between the mountain ranges. In fact, during the six weeks leading up to the invasion, aircraft of the Eleventh Air

Force logged 1,175 sorties against Kiska and Attu, but the weather allowed only about thirty to drop on the latter island.[64]

Though the pilots aboard *Nassau* had the benefit of a large relief map of Attu, detailed information about the topography of the island was scarce, necessitating the formulation of five different assault plans. By D-Day, which was delayed from 8 May to 11 May because of weather and the rumored approach of a powerful Japanese surface force, the invasion plan adopted by the high command called for two landings, the main one in Massacre Bay on the southern end of the island and a secondary assault at Holtz Bay to the north. Driving inland, the two forces would converge upon an enemy airfield at the southern tip of Holtz Bay, and then clear out remaining Japanese resistance in the area. Commanders expected the action to be over in three days.[65]

From an air standpoint, *Nassau*'s planes were tasked with the primary mission of providing air coverage for the ships of the assault force, with a secondary mission of providing air support. Army Air Forces aircraft based at Umnak, Adak, and Amchitka, were tasked as the primary instrument of close-air support. P-38 *Lightnings* of the 54th Pursuit Squadron would orbit Attu during daylight hours in concert with a B-24 *Liberator* liaison aircraft that maintained radio communications with troops on the ground and the naval forces operating around the island.[66] Nevertheless, the *Nassau* fliers fully expected to play an important role in supporting the landings directly. "The Army and the Navy operating from our nearest Aleutian base (250 miles away) have about 150 planes (*sic*) of all types that are supposed to support during the attack," Loesch recorded in his ongoing letter, "but in the kind of weather we're expecting, I doubt we'll see much of them."[67]

The first troops ashore in the early morning hours of May 11th consisted of the 7th Scout Company, landed by submarine north of Holtz Bay via rubber rafts. After a reconnaissance party found a suitable landing site in the bay, elements of the 17th Infantry came ashore beginning at 1615. Meanwhile, on the opposite side of the island, the main assault force, having been floating around in their landing craft waiting for a break in the foggy weather, finally put their feet on firm ground. The forces encountered little enemy

The Evolution of Carrier-Based Close Air Support 239

resistance.⁶⁸ *Nassau* launched her first ever strikes against the enemy at 0623, sending two four-plane sections of VC-21 *Wildcats* off the deck to bomb and strafe pre-briefed targets. During the long transit from California to the Aleutians, ordnance men aboard the ship had fashioned weapons to make the *Wildcats* more potent ground attack aircraft. They adjusted the fuses on standard 100 lb. bombs to trigger just above the ground, creating a "daisy cutter" that was deadly to enemy personnel. In addition, they filled empty casings obtained in San Diego with rubber and gasoline, to create "oil bombs," incendiaries that were designed to ignite and flush enemy troops out of concealed emplacements. In company with the six .50-caliber machine guns in the wings, the daisy cutters and oil bombs made the F4F-4s potent weapons.⁶⁹

The weather on D-Day proved Mother Nature's dominion over any man-made weaponry. Returning pilots reported heavy fog and cloud cover that in some cases precluded delivering ordnance, and made observation of targets difficult. Additionally, five *Wildcats* either crashed during recovery on *Nassau*'s tiny flight deck or were ditched in the vicinity of the task force. The weather hampered the Army Air Forces strikes as well, preventing all but a few B-24s and B-25s from dropping their loads on Attu.⁷⁰ Nevertheless, by nightfall on 11 May, the Army forces ashore were well entrenched and had made sufficient headway in reaching most of their objectives.⁷¹

Events of the following day demonstrated that the Japanese were not going to relinquish Attu without a fight. From concealed positions dug into the ridges rising up behind the invasion beaches, enemy machine guns guarded the rugged passes leading into the interior and proved difficult to knock out. The ever-present mud also reduced the number of troops that could be committed to the advance, relegating them to carrying supplies forward in lieu of trucks that could not negotiate the terrain.⁷²

In addition to shelling by destroyers and battleships, *Nassau* operated off Holtz Bay to northeast of Attu, dodging in and out of fog and cloudbanks. Never more than forty miles off the coast, she sometimes approached to within ten miles of shore, enabling her to provide almost instantaneous air support to the forces on the ground. This marked a significant departure from the accepted doctrine that a carrier was vulnerable when tied to the beachhead. As Doyle had stated previously, escort carriers were ideal for supporting an amphibious operation because they were expendable. Despite the fact that Japanese submarines were active in the area, firing torpedoes at the battleship USS *Pennsylvania* on two occasions, *Nassau* plied the waters close to Attu.[73]

Under the guidance of the troops on the ground, who radioed range adjustments to the pilots via *Nassau*, Wildcats executed repeated glide bombing and strafing runs through fog to attack enemy positions on a ridge near Holtz Bay.[74] Loesch recounted:

> We proceeded in starting over a ridge between Holtz and Chicago harbor when suddenly everything seemed to go off at once. All around us at very close range AA guns opened up. . . . But we managed to strafe and bomb so well that when we were through there was almost no opposing fire. I think we nearly cleaned them out and reports from the Army confirmed this. . . . Many of them [AA bursts] hit all around me, jouncing the plane around and making it damned uncomfortable. But we pressed home our attacks to within 50 feet of the ground and don't think the ground troops didn't appreciate it.[75]

The VC-21 action report confirmed his recollections, stating that bombing and strafing hits on enemy positions "enabled ground troop (*sic*) advance and to establish artillery positions."[76]

The ensuing days continued the maddening routine of the first two with flight operations and ground support missions hampered not only by enemy fire, but also by the harsh Aleutians weather. On 14 May, three aircraft, including the *Wildcat* flown by the VC-21 skipper either crashed into the mountains of Attu or simply disappeared. Two days later, another aircraft crashed into Holtz Bay after a strafing run and a second plunged into the water about three miles from the ship. In addition, the consistently low ceilings made it extremely difficult for pilots to see panels placed by ground troops to guide the aircraft to the target. In one instance, *Wildcats* began strafing friendly lines before personnel on the ground were able to get word to them that they were off target.[77]

Nevertheless, the limited number of planes *Nassau* was able to put on target brought results, especially given the nature of the Japanese defenses, which were aptly described by the assault commander, Maj. Gen. Albert E. Brown.

> Japanese tactics comprise fighting with machine guns and snipers concealed in rain washes or in holes or trenches dug in each side and at varying heights of hill[s] along narrow passes leading through mountain masses. These positions are difficult to locate and almost impossible to shoot out with artillery.[78]

On 13 May ground troops directed attacks against a hill impeding their advance and eight F4F-4s of VC-21 braved enemy antiaircraft fire in an 800 ft. ceiling, each section making five-to-seven runs against the target. Their determined efforts allowed the Army troops to move through the target to a new position, where they could set up an artillery battery. Three days later, fifteen *Wildcats* launched from *Nassau* at 0738 to attack seven separate target areas with success. "I guess the big thing is that we're doing our job, and doing it right," "Dix" Loesch wrote on May 16th, "because the boys on the ground say it really helps and is most effective."[79] By May 20th, Army ground forces had bottled up the remaining Japanese troops in the vicinity of Chicago Harbor, and VC-21 pilots took advantage of a break in the clouds to hit revetments and foxholes scattered across the ridges overlooking the harbor. "Positions were clearly visible and shots were well placed after looking over the area and getting oriented," the VC-21 action report noted. An orbiting OS2U *Kingfisher* observation plane radioed the message "Good shooting, Right in Middle of Target," which certainly buoyed the pilots' spirits after losing so many of their comrades.[80]

It marked *Nassau*'s last day on the line in Attu and that evening she set course for Adak. The fighting on Attu continued for nine more days, culminating in a final *banzai* charge by nearly 1,000 Japanese soldiers on the night of May 29th. Of the more than 15,000 Army troops who went ashore, 3,797 had either been killed, wounded, or removed from the front lines due to illness or exposure. A total of 2,350 Japanese died attempting to hold the island, and only 209 of the enemy were taken prisoner. In terms of the ratio of casualties, Attu would rank second only to Iwo Jima in its bloodiness. For every hundred Japanese killed, seventy-one American soldiers were either killed or wounded.[81]

"Value of the Navy's auxiliary aircraft carriers–'baby flat-tops' — was proved (*sic*) in the Aleutians Campaign, where one of them ... played a vital part in the taking of Attu," an official Navy press release trumpeted on 10 July 1943. Citing the fact that land-based aircraft in Amchitka were oftentimes unable to get over the target because of bad weather, the public relations officer went on to state the fact that on occasion the tiny carrier "single-handedly provided our aerial offensive against the Japs." Though the unnamed officer may have been a bit fervent in his effort to downplay the contributions of the rival Army Air Forces, the Navy deserved to feel good about *Nassau*'s work off Attu.[82]

Even before filing his official report of the ship's operations, Artie Doyle sent dispatches detailing the operations to both Pearl Harbor and Washington. Writing to Capt. Forrest P. Sherman, Chief of Staff to Jack Towers, he acknowledged the relatively minor role of *Nassau* in the operation, but pointed to the operation as a giant step for the escort carrier.

> As to the broader question of ACV potentialities as combatant ships. (*sic*) <u>The fact remains that for ten days under "no wind" conditions, the *Nassau* delivered air support and air cover whenever required.</u> The proponents of the "Escort Carrier" can't laugh that off. ... These ships are ideal for amphibious operations. A division can carry as many planes as a big CV and with greater flexibility.[83]

To Rear Adm. John S. McCain, Chief of the Bureau of Aeronautics, he echoed these sentiments.

> Everybody was hollering for air support. The Army Air Corps (*sic*) couldn't get over [the target], or when they did, couldn't get under [the overcast]. Their effort was negligible during the ten days we were there I think the ACV is ideally suited for amphibious operations due to their flexibility and availability in numbers. We could have operated 36 VF [fighters] easily so that very few ACV[s] can maintain an imposing number of VF over an area. We operated in all kinds of weather — usually "no wind" though — and had no trouble.[84]

Submitted on 5 June 1943, Doyle's official report provided a more detailed commentary on the air support element of an amphibious assault. The weather conditions plagued the operation from the start, only once permitting air support for the engaged ground forces before noon and never permitting an "all-out air attack." Material deficiencies on the aircraft, namely the inability of external fuel tanks to withstand a catapult launch and still function, were countered by the success of the home grown "daisy cutters" and oil bombs.[85]

Problems did arise in the area of communications. Due to a breakdown in the fleet's radio network, *Nassau* for many days served as a relay station between the Task Force Commander, airborne units, and the forces ashore, which placed a great strain on the tiny carrier's small communications department. Additionally, since the carrier's primary mission heading into the operation was combat air patrol for the fleet, *Nassau* was provided her own fighter direction frequency. When enemy air opposition failed to materialize, her aircraft shifted to close air support, continuing to rely upon this particular frequency for communication. Ground troops would transmit messages to *Nassau*'s air pilot, which would then relay it to orbiting *Wildcats*, an arrangement that caused some delay in getting the aircraft over the target. In Doyle's mind, it would have been more desirable to have the planes on the Army Air Forces Air Support Radio Net, which would have made for more effective and timely support for the troops.[86]

> Where enemy and our own front lines are separated by as little as 10 yards, very close coordination between air and ground units is mandatory. If attacks had been made with the NASSAU out of communication range of the island, with planes on the combat frequency, there would have been no coordination.[87]

The intangible factor that countered any deficiency was the skill and determination of the aviators. *Nassau* made 179 catapult launches during her time off Attu, and each mission was a hazardous undertaking, particularly when Japanese antiaircraft fire gave the pilots something else to think about in addition to the consistently poor weather. "Pilots were well aware of the difficulties confronting them. The losses . . . were low considering difficulties of terrain and weather and the determination with which pilots made the repeated attacks," Doyle concluded. "Numerous messages over voice radio from ground observation parties ashore attest [to] the valuable aid given at critical moments."[88]

Doyle realized that the experience of his ship in Operation LANDCRAB was special, a sentiment echoed by amphibious commander Rear Adm. Francis W. Rockwell, who strongly advocated the assignment of baby flattops to future assaults. The *Nassau's* skipper concluded his official report of the action by recommending that more time be devoted to training under the tutelage of personnel experienced in amphibious operations. He went so far as to recommend that an escort carrier be permanently assigned to the Commander Amphibious Force to develop proper tactics for close air support. In order to avoid confusion in operations, he also suggested that in future invasions when two or more escort carriers were involved, there be a clear delineation in the missions of air defense, air surface support, and air ground support. Ideally suited for amphibious work, escort carriers were best employed when operating only one type aircraft. Finally, Doyle advocated that air assets assigned to close air support should be under the direct authority of the commander of the troops on the ground, concluding that "no responsible officer charged with execution of a mission ashore should ever be placed in a position where he must ask for air support."[89]

The Attu operation marked the apex of *Nassau*'s short time as a combat carrier. Drawing upon the experience gained in her operations and those of her sisters, more capable escort carriers were arriving in the Pacific, relegating *Nassau* to duty as an aircraft transport despite the appeals of her skipper. "The invaluable experience of the NASSAU in amphibious operations has been wasted due to her pending conversion...." Doyle wrote in June 1943. "The Commanding Officer... recommends that the honor of being designated as a combatant ACV be given this ACV which, from the beginning, has consistently, despite many contrary opinions, advocated combatant use of her class."[90] Though his words fell on deaf ears, the *Nassau* skipper's future proved much brighter than that of his ship. "Doyle was an excellent captain at sea, [but] he was not particularly well fitted for desk duties," Towers recorded in his diary on 26 September 1943.[91] Reflecting this opinion, after a stint on Adm. Ernest J. King's staff, the feisty aviator returned to sea in August 1944 as skipper of *Hornet* (CV-12), receiving two awards of the Navy Cross during his ten months in command. When he retired in 1958, he wore the stars of a vice admiral.

During Artie Doyle's eight months in command of *Nassau*, she experienced exactly ten days of combat, a fraction of the time he spent in action on the bridge of *Hornet* later in the war. Yet, it was aboard *Nassau* that he made his greatest contribution in shaping the course of warfare in the Pacific. Before ever going to sea in the baby flattop that was his first command, Doyle recognized the potential of ships like her. Some of his insights—namely the flexibility of operating escort carriers in divisions (though he alternated between four and six ships) and the realization that close air support was a specialty that required coordination—proved quite accurate.

One needs only to examine the capture of Mindoro in the Philippines during December 1944. Situated in constricted waters, surrounded by enemy airfields and nearly 300 miles distant from Allied land-based air assets on the island of Leyte, the success of the operation depended heavily on escort carriers. During the approach to the objective and while operating off the beach, a group of six escort carriers fended off repeated *kamikaze* attacks against the landing force and at the same time supported the troops ashore.

Among the observations recorded in the action report of Capt. Fitzhugh Lee, in command of USS *Manila Bay* (CVE-61), was the successful marriage of the escort carrier and older battleships in the prosecution of an amphibious assault.[92] In addition, he concluded the following about the employment of escort carriers:

> All in all, it is considered that the Task Group, within its limits, formed an excellent tactical unit as a striking or covering force. As a defensive force it is to be noted that 144 fighters were carried. Since the FM-2 [*Wildcat* fighter] has a higher rate of climb than the F6F [*Hellcat* fighter], and since there were six launching decks available, it is probable that a greater number of effective defensive fighters could get into action against an attacking enemy more quickly from this "Slow Carrier Task Group" than from a "Fast Carrier Task Group."[93]

The compatibility of operating prewar battleships and escort carriers in amphibious assaults and the inherent flexibility that multiple carrier decks provided on both the offensive and defensive echoed Doyle's arguments of 1942–1943. Though, it never reached the point where aircraft came under control of the commander on the ground, a measure Doyle proposed after the Attu operation, air-ground coordination developed during the course of the Pacific War. By the time of the invasions of Iwo Jima and Okinawa in 1945, a workable system of Air Liaison Parties and Landing Force Air Support Control Units existed to relay air support requests from ground commanders. Additionally, target coordination aircraft oftentimes carried Army or Marine Corps officers as aerial spotters.[94]

Speaking of his career shortly before his death in 1970, Doyle recalled a talk given to a group of midshipmen by Naval Academy superintendent Capt. Edward W. Eberle. "Don't forget, gentlemen," Doyle remembered him saying, "the Navy's mission is to put the man with the bayonet on the other fellow's beach and to keep him there."[95] Sitting in his study that day he must have thought fondly of *Nassau* and the difficult days off Attu, when he and his crew not only fulfilled this mission, but also forever changed how it was accomplished.

NOTES

[1] Rear Adm. William A. Moffett, Testimony before Naval Affairs Committee, U.S. House of Representatives, 21 February 1922. Quoted in William F. Trimble, *Admiral William A. Moffett: Architect of Naval Aviation* (Washington: Smithsonian Institution Press, 1994), 99.

[2] Comdr. John H. Towers, Testimony before the President's Aircraft Board, 16 October 1925. Quoted in Clark G. Reynolds, *Admiral John H. Towers: The Struggle for Naval Air Supremacy* (Annapolis: Naval Institute Press, 1991), 189.

[3] Lt. Logan C. Ramsey, "Aircraft and the Naval Engagement," *United States Naval Institute Proceedings*, vol. 56, no. 8, August 1930, 679.

[4] Comdr. P. N. L. Bellinger's thesis *Tactics*, submitted to the Naval War College, Newport, RI, on 9 May 1925, highlighted fourteen missions for aircraft. Only one, "Attack on enemy naval bases and naval establishments," involved a land target. See also Lt. Comdr. Logan C. Ramsey, "Aerial Attacks on Fleets At Anchor," *United States Naval Institute Proceedings*, vol. 63, no. 8, August 1937, 1126-1132.

[5] Comdr. P. N. L. Bellinger, *Aviation*, Lecture delivered at Naval War College, Newport, RI, 1 August 1924, 12.

[6] *War Instructions, United States Navy, 1924* (Washington: Government Printing Office, 1924), 4.

[7] *War Instructions, United States Navy, 1934* (Reprint) (Washington: Government Printing Office, 1942), 12.

[8] Edward S. Miller, *War Plan Orange: The U.S. Strategy to Defeat Japan, 1897-1945* (Annapolis: Naval Institute Press, 1991), 184, 197-199.

[9] *United States Naval Administrative History*, vol. 16, *Aviation in the Fleet Exercises, 1911-1939*, 157-165.

[10] Ibid.; Clark G. Reynolds, *The Fast Carriers: The Forging of an Air Navy* (Annapolis: Naval Institute Press, 1992), 18.

[11] *United States Naval Administrative History*, vol. 16, *Aviation in the Fleet Exercises, 1911-1939*, 218.

[12] Scot MacDonald, "Evolution of the Aircraft Carriers: Emergence of the Escort Carriers," *Naval Aviation News*, December 1962, 15.

[13] Rear Adm. William A. Moffett to General Board, 20 June 1927. Quoted in Trimble, 205.

[14] MacDonald, 16; James O. Richardson, *On the Treadmill to Pearl Harbor: The*

Memoirs of Admiral James O. Richardson (Washington: Naval History Division, Department of the Navy, 1973), 213.

[15] Robert J. Cressman, "The President's Escort Carrier: A History of USS Long Island (CVE-1)," *The Hook*, vol. 12, no. 1, Spring 1984, 21.

[16] William T. Y'Blood, *Hunter-Killer: U.S. Escort Carriers in the Battle of the Atlantic* (Annapolis: Naval Institute Press, 1983), 4.

[17] Cressman, 24.

[18] William T. Y'Blood, *The Little Giants: U.S Escort Carriers Against Japan* (Annapolis: Naval Institute Press, 1987), 17; Y'Blood, *Hunter-Killer*, 280.

[19] Y'Blood, *Hunter-Killer*, 282-283.

[20] Stephen Jurika, ed., *From Pearl Harbor to Vietnam: The Memoirs of Arthur W. Radford* (Stanford, CA: Hoover Institution Press, 1980), 9.

[21] Rear Adm. Austin K. Doyle, Transcript Record of Service, 6 April 1954; Doyle taped recollections, undated, in Papers of Adm. Austin K. Doyle in possession of the author (hereafter cited as Doyle Papers).

[22] Robert Osborn to author, 11 December 1993.

[23] Capt. Austin K. Doyle to Mrs. Austin K. Doyle, 5 March 1945, Doyle Papers.

[24] Osborn to author, 11 December 1993; Robert Osborn, *Osborn on Osborn* (New York: Ticknor and Fields, 1982), 78.

[25] Doyle taped recollections; Comdr. Austin K. Doyle to Capt. Arthur W. Radford, 16 August 1942, Doyle Papers.

[26] Third Endorsement of Orders, Commandant, Puget Sound Navy Yard to Comdr. Austin K. Doyle, 16 August 1942; Doyle to Radford, 16 August 1942, Doyle Papers.

[27] Thomas B. Buell, *Master of Sea Power: A Biography of Ernest J. King* (Boston: Little, Brown, and Company, 1980), 214-217.

[28] John B. Lundstrom, "Frank Jack Fletcher Got a Bum Rap," *Naval History*, vol. 6, no. 3, Fall 1992, 23-28.

[29] Ibid.

[30] Richard B. Frank, *Guadalcanal* (New York: Random House, 1990), 62, 64-69; John B. Lundstrom, *The First Team and the Guadalcanal Campaign* (Annapolis: Naval Institute Press, 1994), 62, 64, 74-79.

[31] Lundstrom, "Frank Jack Fletcher," 25-26.

[32] Lundstrom, "Frank Jack Fletcher," 22-27; Frank, *Guadalcanal*, 93-94.

[33] Ship's History, USS *Nassau* (CVE-16), Narrative Section, 2.

[34] Comdr. Austin K. Doyle to Capt. Ralph E. Davison, 21 August 1942, Doyle Papers.

[35] Ibid.

[36] Capt. Austin K. Doyle to Rear Adm. John H. Towers, 14 September 1942, Doyle Papers.

[37] Mr. Ludlow Baldwin, letter to the author, 15 January 1995.

[38] Y'Blood, *The Little Giants*, 27; Alvin Kernan, *Crossing the Line: A Bluejacket's World War Odyssey* (Annapolis: Naval Institute Press, 1994), 83.

[39] Capt. Austin K. Doyle to Rear Adm. John H. Towers, 14 September 1942, Doyle Papers.

[40] Ship's History, USS *Nassau* (CVE-16), Chronology Section, 1; Capt. Austin K. Doyle to Lt. Comdr. Frank W. Wead, 23 September 1942.

[41] Ship's History, USS *Nassau* (CVE-16), Chronology Section, 1; Lundstrom, *The First Team and the Guadalcanal Campaign*, 474.

[42] Y'Blood, *The Little Giants*, 18-23.

[43] Capt. Austin K. Doyle to Capt. Cato Glover, 6 November and 23 November 1942, Doyle Papers.

[44] Capt. Austin K. Doyle to Rear Adm. Ralph Davison, 26 November 1942, Doyle Papers.

[45] Capt. Austin K. Doyle to Capt. Cato Glover, 23 November 1942, Doyle Papers.

[46] Memorandum, Commanding Officer, USS *Nassau*, to Commander-in-Chief,

U.S. Pacific Fleet, 5 January 1943, Subject: Operations of Carrier Task Forces, Doyle Papers.

[47]Memorandum, Commanding Officer, USS *Nassau*, to Commander Air Force, U.S. Pacific Fleet, 12 February 1943, Subject: USS *Nassau* type ACV-Comments and recommendations in regard to, Doyle Papers.

[48]Ibid.

[49]Capt. Austin K. Doyle to Lt. Comdr. D. P. Caulkins, 12 March 1943, Doyle Papers.

[50]Ibid.

[51]Memorandum from Commander Air Force, Pacific Fleet, to Commander-in-Chief, Pacific Fleet, 16 February 1943, Doyle Papers.

[52]Samuel Eliot Morison, *History of United States Naval Operations in World War II*, vol. 7, *Aleutians, Gilberts and Marshalls, June 1942–April 1944* (Boston: Little, Brown, and Company, 1962), 4-21.

[53]Gerald E. Wheeler, *Kinkaid of the Seventh Fleet* (Washington: Naval Historical Center, 1995), 299.

[54]Quoted in Wheeler, 303.

[55]Morison, 20-21; Wheeler, 307-308.

[56]Morison, 38; Wheeler, 318; Stetson Conn, et al., *The United States Army in World War II*, vol. 12, *The Western Hemisphere: Guarding the United States and Its Outposts* (Washington: Department of the Army, 1964), 278, 282-283.

[57]Morison, 38, 333-335.

[58]Ship's History, USS *Nassau* (CVE-16), Chronology Section, 3.

[59]United Engineering Company, Specifications for Repairs on USS *Nassau* (ACV-16); Memorandum, Commanding Officer, USS *Nassau* (ACV-16) to Commander, Fleet Air, West Coast, 22 April 1943, Doyle Papers.

[60]*The Aleutians Campaign, June 1942–August 1943* (Washington: Naval Historical Center, 1943), 82; Steve Ewing and John B. Lundstrom, *Fateful Rendezvous: The Life of Butch O'Hare* (Annapolis: Naval Institute Press, 1997), 188; Lundstrom, *The First Team and the Guadalcanal Campaign*, 538-545; Robert Sherrod, *History of Marine Corps Aviation in World War II* (Washington: Combat Forces Press, 1952), 319.

[61]Memorandum, Commanding Officer, USS *Nassau* (ACV-16), to Commander, Fleet Air, West Coast, 15 June 1943, Doyle Papers.

[62]Lt. Richards Loesch to his father, 22 April 1943, Copy in Doyle Papers (Hereafter cited as Loesch letter). Loesch wrote a running letter during the entire cruise aboard *Nassau* with plans to share it with his father later. Without having to worry about censorship restrictions, he could be very frank and detailed in his opinions and descriptions.

[63]Conn, 281.

[64]Conn, 280; Wesley Frank Craven and James Lea Cate, eds., *The Army Air Forces in World War II*, vol. 4, *The Pacific: Guadalcanal to Saipan, August 1942 to July 1944* (Washington: Office of Air Force History, 1983), 379.

[65]Conn, 283-284; Morison, 45.

[66]USS *Nassau* (ACV-16), Action Report, Attu Island, May 11 to May 20, 1943, 4; Craven and Cate, 381-382.

[67]Loesch Letter, Doyle Papers, 4.

[68]Conn, 285-287.

[69]VC-21, Reports of U.S. Aircraft Action With Enemy, 11 May 1943; Captain Austin K. Doyle to Rear Adm. John S. McCain, 28 May 1943, Doyle Papers; Lt. Comdr. Howard A. MacDonald, USN (Ret), interview with the author, 15 July 1999.

[70]VC-21, Reports of U.S. Aircraft Action With Enemy, 11 May 1943; USS *Nassau* (ACV-16), Action Report, Attu Island, May 11 to May 20, 1943; Craven and Conn, 382.

[71]Conn, 291.

[72]Ibid.; *The Aleutians Campaign*, 103.

[73]*The Aleutians Campaign*, 103-104; Morison, 44-45.

74. VC-21, Reports of U.S. Aircraft Action with the Enemy, 12 May 1943.
75. Loesch Letter, Doyle Papers, 21.
76. VC-21, Reports of U.S. Aircraft Action with the Enemy, 12 May 1943.
77. USS *Nassau* (ACV-16), Action Report, Attu Island, May 11 to May 20, 1943; VC-21, Reports of U.S. Aircraft Action with the Enemy,16 May 1943.
78. Maj. Gen. Albert E. Brown to Commander Task Force 51, 14 May 1943, quoted in Conn, 292.
79. VC-21, Reports of U.S. Aircraft Action with the Enemy, 14, 16 May 1943; Loesch Letter, Doyle Papers, 27.
80. VC-21, Reports of U.S. Aircraft Action with the Enemy, 20 May 1943.
81. USS *Nassau* (ACV-16), Action Report, Attu Island, May 11 to May 20, 1943; Conn, 295.
82. Navy Department News Release, 10 July 1943, Doyle Papers.
83. Capt. Austin K. Doyle to Capt. Forrest P. Sherman, 21 May 1943, Doyle Papers.
84. Capt. Austin K. Doyle to Rear Adm. John S. McCain, 28 May 1943, Doyle Papers.
85. USS *Nassau* (ACV-16), Action Report, Attu Island, May 11 to May 20, 1943.
86. Ibid.; Memorandum, Executive Officer to Commanding Officer, USS *Nassau* (ACV-16), Subject: Preparations for and Operations in Support of Occupation of Attu Island, May 11-20, 1943, 20 May 1943, Doyle Papers.
87. USS *Nassau* (ACV-16), Action Report, Attu Island, May 11 to May 20, 1943.
88. Ibid.
89. Ibid.
90. Ibid.; Y'Blood, *The Little Giants*, 33.
91. Diary of Vice Adm. John H. Towers, 23 September 1943. Copy in Emil Buehler Naval Aviation Library, National Museum of Naval Aviation.
92. Y'Blood, *The Little Giants*, 250-266.
93. Quoted in Y'Blood, *The Little Giants*, 266.
94. Benis M. Frank, Jr., and Henry I. Shaw, Jr., *History of U.S. Marine Corps Operations in World War II*, vol. 5, *Victory and Occupation* (Washington: Headquarters, U.S. Marine Corps, 1968), 672; VC-21 Squadron History, Narrative Section.
95. Doyle taped recollections, undated, Doyle Papers.

Military Missionary:
The Riddle Wrapped in a Mystery inside an Enigma that Was Evans F. Carlson

Phyllis A. Zimmerman

> In many ways, Evans Fordyce Carlson (1896-1947) was a traditional professional soldier. After six years in the Army, he joined the Marine Corps in 1922 and served with distinction in Nicaragua and China. During the Pacific War he led the 2nd Raider Battalion at Makin and Guadalcanal, earning the adulation of a grateful nation. In equally significant ways, however, Carlson was also a maverick Marine. He trained his raiders using many of the "gung ho" (work in harmony) practices he had learned from the Chinese Communists while an observer with the Eighth Route Army in the late 1930s, and in 1946, *Time* magazine charged that he was "an apostle of Communist causes."[1] In this essay, Phyllis Zimmerman reconciles these two seemingly contradictory strains in Carlson's life. She concludes that Carlson remains controversial in part because his life mirrored two sometimes conflicting impulses in American history: the martial and the humanitarian.

When First Lieutenant Evans Carlson, USMC, first arrived in Nicaragua in 1930, he gave little evidence that he was anything but a traditional, patriotic, and dedicated U.S. Marine who shared the prevailing values of his fellow Marines. He believed that the United States generally, and the U.S. Marine Corps in particular, must bring stability and order to a lawless and contentious society. Carlson was convinced that "some people are superior and others inferior," and had no doubt which the Americans were.[2]

In Nicaragua he encountered his first peasant-based guerrilla resistance movement, led by Augusto Sandino. First Lieutenant Carlson trained the Nicaraguan security force—the Guardia National—who went after the elusive Sandino, and led them on

Phyllis Zimmerman is Associate Professor of History at Ball State University in Muncie, Indiana.

"search and destroy" missions to disrupt insurgent concentrations and end resistance. He was forced into bush warfare: no battle front, no decisive engagements, only an endless, frustrating cycle of patrols and minor skirmishes against guerrillas who often skillfully sidestepped impending attacks, ducking and weaving with an amazing ability to vanish across neutral borders.

Gradually, Carlson learned the rudiments of guerrilla warfare: special tactics to outflank; how to live, move and operate in the jungle; never to fight from a fixed position; how to move faster than the guerrillas. He introduced night-fighting tactics, shattering the complacency of the guerrillas who had never encountered the Guardia after dark. He earned a Navy Cross for leading a Marine-Guardia force of twelve against several dozen of Sandino's men at Pasmata, "resulting in their complete demoralization and routing," the citation read.[3]

Originally Carlson viewed Sandino as a "bandit," a "mule thief," who sought only personal glory. But, before leaving the country in 1933, he began to understand "the viewpoint of the Sandino group."[4] Many Nicaraguans resented a political system serving only the local politicians and narrow commercial interests. He began to regard Sandino as a revolutionary, and believed it was essential to solve the pressing economic issues of inequality and grinding poverty. A solution imposed by the military would solve nothing. Carlson also learned why the guerrillas had better intelligence information than the Marines.

It was the "boomerang" effect.[5] Destroying towns or crops to flush out the enemy served only to inflame the countryside and dry up Marine intelligence sources. He concluded that any successful counterinsurgency campaign must involve winning over important segments of support.

At this time, Carlson's thinking was only in its formative stage. This first experience with guerrilla fighting began a process of education, evaluation and reformulation of ideas, which would stretch over several more years; he would take its lessons to heart. Carlson was a man who, "once he had thought his way through experience to an opinion, suited his actions to his words."[6] In China his re-education took a giant leap, plunging him into one of the most exhilarating yet controversial periods of his life. The political machinations in China would make those in Nicaragua look like child's play. And Carlson found himself sucked into their vortex.

Carlson arrived for his second tour in China in March 1933. During his earlier experience (1927-1929), he had brought to China the usual imperial conceits. He had assumed that the only effective way to teach the Chinese order and efficiency was for the Marines to occupy places like Shanghai and trounce those who objected; otherwise the people would lose respect for foreigners.[7] He had spent thirty months studying Chinese language and culture, writing articles on the current Chinese political situation, and completing a detailed map of the international settlement. But he hungered for more exposure to China, and in 1933 he happily returned to his old job as Intelligence Officer with the 4th Marines. Seeking a deeper understanding of China, he requested a transfer from Shanghai to Peiping and duty with the Legation Guard.

Life in Peiping was good. There were the endless rounds of garden parties, teas, and receptions. Carlson continued to study Chinese ceramics, art, and architecture. Each Monday he dined with renowned American intellectuals—a heady experience for a high school dropout—and held his own in freewheeling discussions on politics and philosophy. He began a Legation Guard Language School that included a year-long course on Chinese language and history. He saw the attitude of the fifty Marines in that course change. They began to fraternize with the Chinese, practicing their language skills and boxing with them. He later noted that "The number of altercations involving Marines with townspeople dropped markedly."[8] Carlson also was changing his own opinion of the Chinese. Not until his third tour, however, did his changing beliefs force him to act.

Before Carlson left Washington for his third China tour in 1937, he met with President Franklin D. Roosevelt. He had developed a personal relationship with FDR when Carlson was second-in-command to the Marine Corps' guard detachment at Roosevelt's Warm Springs, Georgia, retreat. The president proposed a secret correspondence, by-passing the Marine and State Department chains of command. Carlson would tell FDR what was going on in China with letters sent directly to the White House addressed to the president's secretary, Marguerite "Missy" LeHand. Carlson promised to write regularly and to keep the correspondence a secret.[9] The captain found radically changed China. Japan had conquered Manchuria and by 1937 controlled over one-fifth of China's territory. The Chinese Nationalists had driven the Communists during the "Long March" into Yan'an in the northwest province of Shaanxi, but then, in 1937, both had joined in a United Front against the Japanese following the Marco Polo Bridge incident in July.

As a naval intelligence officer and neutral observer in the Shanghai area, Carlson (now a Captain) had a "front row seat, often watching from a rooftop, hotel window or shop doorway as the Chinese and Japanese fought a war within the city, across parks and streets, within temples and market places."[10] When reports filtered in during the fall of 1937 that the Eighth Route Army was doing a remarkable job fighting the Japanese, far superior to the Nationalists, Carlson requested that he be the first foreign military observer to visit the northwest. He had heard that the Communist general Zhu De invited criticism from his troops and even severely criticized himself in an attempt to circumvent the Chinese habit of "saving face." By December Carlson had received permission from American and Chinese officials and found himself at Zhu De's headquarters. The general and his army impressed him. He saw that Zhu De lived no better than a cook and welcomed the men to come directly to him with their complaints. No distinctions were made between officers and men at meals or socially. Before battle, leaders met with troops to explain the tactics and reasons for the battle. Afterwards, another meeting dealt with mistakes and how to correct them. No one was above criticism. The theory behind this approach was that "men who know most fight best."[11]

Zhu De reluctantly gave Carlson permission to go to one of the most dangerous sections of the front where eight Japanese columns were trying to smash through. In fifty-one days, Carlson traveled a thousand miles, many on foot, observing the Eighth Route Army and the Nationalists against the Japanese. It was his "toughest marching in twenty years" he wrote Roosevelt.[12] While the forces of Zhu De had high morale and a spirit of self-sacrifice, the Nationalists were often listless, sullen and indifferent. The Eighth Route Army mobilized the peasants for resistance by giving them civil rights and social equality; the Nationalist Army treated the peasants with contempt. Carlson saw groups of soldiers chained together as they walked and was shocked to discover that they were not POWs but rather Chinese Nationalist soldiers.

When Carlson returned to Hankou, he was anxious to share what he had witnessed. He wrote to his navy superiors and sent several letters to Roosevelt, outlining why he believed that Zhu De's army was the real military hope of China. Carlson even met with Jiang Jieshi, hoping to get the medicine, bandages, food and ammunition the Eighth Route Army desperately needed and which the Nationalists withheld. The generalissimo responded with stony silence. Despite Jiang's indifference, Carlson remained undaunted and used every method he could think of to raise funds for the Communist army, including a lottery and cajoling money from his friends. Within a month, medical supplies reached the front.

In the spring of 1938, the captain returned to Yan'an, this time to observe Mao Zedong's organization; and then to travel to Mongolia, to see how much organized resistance existed against the Japanese. First he met Mao Zedong, whom he later described to President Roosevelt as "a dreamer, a genius."[13] Carlson sized up Mao as a disciplined seeker of honest government and equality of opportunity for all Chinese. Mao complained to the captain that while the United States and the Soviet Union helped China the most, it disturbed him that America provided over half the war materials Japan purchased abroad. An indignant Carlson immediately wrote to Roosevelt to ask: "Is it true?"

Carlson began his seventy-seven day trek in May, crossing three Japanese blockade lines under heavy bombing and gunfire. The Marine captain conversed with peasants, observed military school training, interviewed Japanese POWs, and shared observations with missionaries from several countries. One of these, Episcopalian John Burt Foster, later described how proud he was that Carlson represented Americans in China and went on to say:

"Though not a Christian when he visited the Eighth Route Army, Carlson took a Bible with him and read the New Testament cover to cover, marking all statements that applied to the Eighth Route Army and its work."[14] Carlson confided to Foster that he was surprised at how many marks he had made.

In fact both Foster and Carlson saw similarities between Christianity and Communism and believed that China might produce a synthesis of both. It would be a kind of "Revolutionary Christianity" characterized by truth, honesty, selflessness, love and working for the betterment of people. They believed that some form of economic communism would almost certainly be the solution for China's blatant inequality and abject poverty. While the Nationalists appeared to be motivated by self-interest and narrow class ambitions, the Communists seemed to represent democratic forces wanting a voice in government denied to them. The only pure democracy in China was being worked out in the northwest. Of that, Carlson was convinced. And he was not alone in that rosy assessment. Colonel Joseph Fegan, commander of the 4th Marines, wrote in 1938 to Commandant of the Marine Corps, Major General Thomas Holcomb: "Communist leaders are honest and selfless men who inspire the confidence of the people and consequently constitute the strongest and most vital group in the Chinese pattern of resistance."[15]

On August 7, Carlson arrived back in Hankou. Convinced of the righteousness of the Communist cause, he spoke to reporters, effusively praising their efforts. His friends warned him that he would get in trouble with the brass as he seemed to be endorsing the Communists while the U.S. Government was officially neutral. As a Marine officer, Carlson was accustomed to discipline and ambitious to win the approval of senior officers, but he believed he had a greater obligation to inform the American people.

Some of his fellow intelligence officers took issue with Carlson's stance. Major James Marshall McHugh was among the most critical. A Naval Academy graduate and an "Old China Hand" who had authored a textbook for beginning students of Chinese, McHugh was also well connected, having married American minister Jacob Gould Schurman's daughter. McHugh's background contrasted sharply with that of high school drop-out Carlson, who had learned Chinese on his own.[16] While Carlson was observing and cultivating his Eighth Route Army sources, McHugh observed Nationalist military operations and became "an important conduit for informal communications between the Chinese and American governments."[17] He played golf almost daily with Australian journalist, W. H. Donald, a confidant of the Jiangs. McHugh regularly lunched with the Jiangs, helped them get economic aid from the American government and enjoyed such direct access to them that rumors circulated that he was Madame Jiang's lover.

McHugh also frequently dined with his fellow Marine, Carlson, and they corresponded when travel took them away to other parts of China. McHugh complimented Carlson in a letter to Commandant Holcomb, in April 1938: "Carlson has been doing a swell job up at the front and I think our work dovetails very well."[18] But by October 1938, McHugh had distanced himself from Carlson. He tried to dissuade Carlson from public pronouncements in early winter, arguing that only the navy attaché could give out publicity, and that he should remain incognito. When Carlson refused, explaining that he had to correct the unfair popular view of the Communists, McHugh admitted in a letter to Holcomb that he had pressured the Hankou Publicity bureau not to invite Carlson to speak anymore.

McHugh had no illusions about Jiang whom he called a dictator who ruled by fear. But he believed Jiang was the only unifying force in China against Japanese aggression. While he acknowledged the remarkable feats of the Eighth Route Army, he dismissed the Communist leadership's claim to honesty and integrity by saying, "I cannot forget that they still are Chinese." Arguing that Carlson had been soft-soaped by "liberals," people not entirely rational, McHugh feared that he had been misled by a cause which had "a false bottom to it." McHugh saw his role as a Marine in China as looking out for American interests, not working for the regeneration of China.

McHugh wrote Holcomb a stinging rebuke of Carlson, accusing his fellow officer of having "primarily selfish motives" for his public statements—to build up a background for a literary career. "I have always," McHugh wrote, "resented the efforts of anyone in our service to publicize himself for I feel that in the majority of instances it is done at the expense of brother officers."[19] McHugh even took a swipe at Carlson's language skills, telling Holcomb that while Carlson was publicizing himself as a language expert, "what he knew could have been put in your eye."

In the fall of 1938, the Navy took steps to silence Carlson, ordering him to give no more interviews on the situation in north China. Carlson was hurt and angry. He believed that he could no longer trust his superiors, and that the military life was incompatible with his own personal growth. He was sure China could check Japan's will to power if the Western democracies stopped supplying Japan with iron, steel and oil and instead offered support for the Eighth Route Army. Carlson felt that a "pressing sense of duty" left him no alternative but to resign. General Stilwell, among many, told him he was throwing too much away. He had twenty-five years in the armed forces and could expect to be promoted to major soon. Many of those devoted to him, including his wife, Etelle, tried to reason with him, reminding him of his love for the Corps, his past regret over leaving the Army, and how much he would lose financially. In one more year he could receive a pension! But Carlson would not be dissuaded.

Convinced that war with Japan was likely, Carlson rejoined the Marine Corps in May 1941. He had written two books on China and spent a year travelling 4,000 miles in China studying the industrial cooperative movement Indusco, established to substitute small-scale rural for urban industries lost to the Japanese. He and Eleanor Roosevelt had worked unsuccessfully to get a portion of an American loan of $500 million to China earmarked for the cooperatives. Carlson learned that the slogan of the cooperatives was "gung ho" which in Chinese (gonghe) means "work in harmony," or "work in accord." He would use this idea in training the 2nd Raider Battalion in the Pacific War.

Carlson commanded the 2nd Raider Battalion's hit-and-run raid on Makin Island in August 1942, followed by a month-long patrol, in November 1942, during the battle of Guadalcanal. His six-month training period proceeded along parallel lines. One stressed physical fitness, weapons of proficiency, drill and infantry tactics. The other Carlson called "ethical indoctrination," it emphasized cooperation, individual initiative, decentralized decision making, lack of rank distinctions and total, open communication of goals. He was trying out what he had absorbed from the Eighth Route Army.

He held weekly Friday night open forums, called "Gung Ho" meetings. Carlson would first call out "Ahoy, Raider." The resounding response would be "Hi, Raider." He'd give a brief talk about whatever was on his mind, and then any of the men could speak his mind on any subject. Part of each meeting was devoted to discussing their environment, the enemy, what they were fighting for. Regularly, they analyzed current political events. Before battle, a similar system was followed. Each man knew what his part in the plan would be. An after-action meeting gave free rein to all to discuss "what went right" and "what went wrong." Carlson invited criticism and suggestions.

The men responded to this "ethical indoctrination" in various ways. Richard T. Washburn, one of Carlson's company commanders, thought it was an excellent technique. "Probably one of the most valuable things I learned from the whole experience with The Second Raider Battalion," he wrote "was the need for people to know as much as they could about their total environment [and] about what they were doing in particular."[20] Some thought the "ahoy raider" call was adolescent, but in view of the enthusiasm around them, they kept those feelings to themselves. A few never went back after their first "gung ho" meeting. One such critic was Second Lieutenant Charles Lamb who "could not understand or digest Carlson's double talk" and who viewed his egalitarian approach as "strange talk from a Marine officer."[21]

Companies A and B of the 2nd Raider Battalion launched a hit-and-run raid on Makin in the Gilbert Islands, August 17–18, 1942. It garnered seven columns in the *New York Times*, and Hollywood subsequently immortalized the raiders in a 1944 movie, *Gung Ho*. The only landing raid ever made by Marines in rubber boats launched by two submarines, it captured the public imagination;

"The Carlson Raiders" were catapulted to instant fame. But in reality the Makin Raid was a tactically muddled operation. Nothing went as planned: from the landing when the element of surprise was lost after a raider accidentally fired his rifle, to the departure from the island a day late because of an unsuccessful bout with the surf the first night of the operation. The public was told 350 Japanese died and that raider losses were "moderate." In reality only eighty-seven Japanese held the island; eighty-three died, many from accidental strafing by Japanese planes. Of the 221 Marines in the raid, thirty died: fourteen were killed in action; seven were drowned; nine were left behind and became prisoners of war. In October 1942, they were beheaded by the Japanese. The Marine hierarchy found this ratio very disturbing and unacceptable, and the raider concept was soon to be shelved. Lingering questions remain: Did Carlson try to surrender? Why were nine Marines left behind? Were raiders necessary—"an elite within an elite?"

Fewer questions remained following the 2nd Raiders monthlong epic patrol at Guadalcanal in November 1942. Pursuing remnants of a Japanese force, which had eluded Marine envelopment, the raiders operated over 150 miles of rough terrain. They survived mainly on rice, sugar, raisins, biscuits, and bacon, sharing these provisions with native guides and scouts. Carlson's bravery was not disputed. On patrol, Carlson was "way out ahead of the point squad, imperturbable."[22] When the "Long Patrol" ended, the raiders had lost sixteen men and were credited with killing 488 Japanese. "Of 1,000 men, the Carlson raiders had only one psychiatric case," *Fortune* magazine reported, in contrast to the "group neurosis" which psychiatrists encountered for the first time after Guadalcanal.[23] The magazine questioned why, in view of the success of Carlson's methods, they weren't tried elsewhere in the Corps, and why he was kicked upstairs to a desk job as a planning staff officer.

Carlson never got another field command, though he would be an observer at the battles of Tarawa, Kwajalein and Saipan, where he was seriously wounded attempting to rescue an enlisted man. Wounds that did not heal properly forced his retirement. The 2nd raiders were combined with three other raider units in 1943 but used strictly as crack assault troops. In 1944, raider units were disbanded entirely. One explanation for this is that America had enough conventional military strength that a reliance on unconventional methods was not necessary. But another possibility is that Carlson's bold departure from ancient and tested ideas of command, discipline and organization could no longer be tolerated, particularly when they came from "Reds" in China. Finally, some suggest that his special relationship to President Roosevelt and the perks that came with it were a source of jealousy and resentment. Certainly negative attitudes toward Carlson helped to seal the fate of the Raiders.

Though in constant pain after the battle of Saipan, Carlson took up the cause of peace with fervor and became a tireless military missionary. The discipline of reason and knowledge, the encouragement of initiative and resourcefulness, which he had tried to develop in his men—these qualities would prepare men for postwar problems and be an effective check on abuse of power. Carlson urged veterans at their meetings to participate in government: vote; hold office; study current events. He joined a newly formed veterans' organization, the American Veterans' Committee (AVC), whose objective was to create a postwar America that lived up to the ideals men had fought and died for, specifically the "four freedoms" announced by President Roosevelt in his 1941 State of the Union Message as the pillars of American democracy: not only freedom *of* speech and press but also freedom *from* want and fear.

The AVC, composed solely of World War II veterans, opened its chapters to all races, both sexes, and fought for full employment, affordable housing for all Americans and an end to racial discrimination. The AVC wanted reform in the military as well: an end to racial segregation, promotion based on merit not seniority and equal treatment for officers and enlisted. Nor did international affairs escape the committee's attention. It supported civilian control of atomic energy within the U.S. and United Nations international control. Finally, it argued that the Chinese should determine their own fate without American involvement.

Carlson was comfortable with these ideas, and he elaborated on them in a letter that appeared in the AVC *Bulletin*. With missionary zeal he wrote about the objective "to achieve a more democratic and prosperous America and a more stable world" and called for vigilance against home-grown fascism.[24] Ronald Reagan, a fellow AVC member and Air Corps Captain in the Motion Picture Unit, read his letter and recommended it to cartoonist Bill Mauldin as doing "a pretty good job of explaining the whole idea" behind the AVC.[25] The organization was to combine education with activism. The veteran must know his rights and demand them. The Veterans Administration recognized sixty-three separate organizations dealing with veterans' problems. Servicemen and women consequently often got the run-around and were confused, bitter and disillusioned. Carlson believed that "men are disposed to live and work together harmoniously when their fundamental material needs are satisfied."[26]

Carlson literally wore himself down speaking all over the country, sometimes making several speeches in a week. He addressed labor unions, exhorting members to clean house in a democratic manner and get rid of the many racketeers among the leaders of organized labor or, he warned, "You won't get more than the cow's hind tit."[27] He spoke to tenants in a Federal Housing Project of the necessity of placing human needs on a par with profits. He crisscrossed the country, speaking in New York on atomic energy politics, and later the same week in San Francisco at a fundraiser for Chinese cooperatives.

California friends urged Carlson to enter the 1946 Democratic primary for the U.S. Senate nomination. He seriously considered it, and a "Stop Carlson" campaign even got going to block him. But by December 1945, any thought of a political career was dashed when Carlson had his first heart attack and doctors ordered bedrest for at least six months. He never regained his health. Four months after a February 1947 cerebral thrombosis attack, which paralyzed his right arm and leg, Carlson died at age fifty-one.

In his lifetime Carlson was deified and vilified. Likewise in death. But on the centenary anniversary commemoration of Carlson's birth, February 26, 1996, the Commandant of the Marine

Corps, General Charles Krulak, sent a "Message" eulogizing Carlson as "a man of intense moral as well as physical courage" whom Marines will be privileged to follow and who will "always be remembered and revered as a leader, hero and a visionary." Perhaps being posthumously rehabilitated is the next best thing to rising from the dead!

NOTES

1"Win the Peace for Whom?" *Time*, 16 September 1946, 21–22.

2Helen Foster Snow, ed., "Carlson of (the 'Gung Ho') Carlson's Raiders: His Own Sketch" (Baguio, Philippines: unpublished, 1940), 50. For Carlson's entire fifty-six-page autobiography, see P.C. 56, Evans F. Carlson Papers, Marine Corps Historical Center (MCHC), Washington, D.C.

3Walter G. Sheard to the Carlson Patrol, 18 July 1930, Nationale Guardia Officer File, box 1, Record Group 127, National Archives, Washington, D.C.

4Snow, "Carlson," 49.

5Samuel B. Griffith II, "Guerrilla!" II, *Marine Corps Gazette* 34 (August 1950): 45.

6Israel Epstein, "Some Memories of Evans Carlson," Centenary Birthday Anniversary Message, 26 February 1996, Portland State University, Portland, Oregon.

7Michael Blankfort, *The Big Yankee: The Life of Evans F. Carlson of the Raiders* (New York: Little Brown, 1947), 145.

8Snow, "Carlson," 38–39.

9Captain Evans F. Carlson to Marguerite Le Hand, 17 June 1937; and 14 August 1937, Presidential Personal File 4951 (hereafter PPF), Franklin D. Roosevelt Personal Papers, Franklin D. Roosevelt Library, Hyde Park, New York.

10Carlson to Le Hand, 20 August 1937, PPF 4951, Roosevelt Papers.

11Evans F. Carlson, *Twin Stars of China: A Behind-the-Scenes Story of China's Valiant Struggle for Existence By a U.S. Marine Who Lived and Moved With the People* (New York: Dodd Mead, 1941), 80.

12Carlson to LeHand, 4 March 1938, PPF 4951, Roosevelt Papers.

13Carlson to LeHand, 6 May 1938, PPF 4951, ibid.

14John Burt Foster to his parents, 14 September 1938, box 1, John Burt Foster Papers, Minnesota Historical Society Research Center, St. Paul.

15Thomas Fegan to Thomas Holcomb, 25 October 1938, box 2, PC 107, Thomas Holcomb Papers, MCHC.

16"Memoir" (draft), box 10, James H. McHugh Papers, Cornell University Library, Ithaca, New York.

17William M. Leary, "Portrait of An Intelligence Officer: James McHugh in China, 1937–42," *Naval History: Seventh Symposium of U.S. Naval Academy* (Wilmington, Delaware: Scholarly Resources, 1988), 252.

18McHugh to Holcomb, 12 April 1938, box 2, PC 107, Holcomb Papers.

19McHugh to Holcomb, 6 October 1938, ibid.

20Richard T. Washburn, telephone interview with Michael J. Zak, January 1980, in Michael J. Zak, "Evans Carlson and The Carlson Raiders: A Case Study" (MBA unpublished course paper, Harvard Business School, 1981), 9.

21Charles Lamb, "Comments on the Raid on Makin," PC 1338, Charles Lamb Papers, MCHC.

22Virgil S. Leeman, personal letter to author, 6 September 1996.

[23]"The Psychiatric Toll of Warfare," *Fortune*, XXVIII (December 1943): 278-280.
[24]Evans F. Carlson, "Gung Ho," *Bulletin* of American Veterans Committee, 15 June 1945, box 6, William H. Mauldin Papers, Manuscript Division, Library of Congress, Washington, D.C.
[25]Ronald Reagan to William H. Mauldin, 27 June 1945, box 6, Mauldin Papers.
[26]Charles G. Bolte, *The New Veteran* (New York: Penguin, 1945), 90.
[27]*Los Angeles Times Daily News*, 27 August 1945.

Admiral Henry Kent Hewitt: The Powerless Expert

Adrian Lewis

> Before the western allies attempted the massive cross-channel invasion of northern Europe in 1944, they teamed up to carry out a number of amphibious operations in the Mediterranean Theater: in North Africa, Sicily and Italy. U.S. Navy Admiral H. Kent Hewitt was a major player in all these operations. But Hewitt was frustrated during most of this time by his inability to convince his British partners, or even his U.S. Army counterparts, of the weaknesses in Anglo-American amphibious doctrine, especially the tendency to disparage the importance of naval gunfire support. In this article, Adrian Lewis relies heavily on Hewitt's own words to demonstrate that Hewitt was, in effect, a "powerless expert."

In World War II the Anglo-American Allies never achieved complete synergy in the conduct of combined, joint amphibious operations.[1] The operations in North Africa, Sicily, Italy, and Normandy failed to maximize the combat power available. Instead, when faced with strong opposition, the Allies improvised the necessary combat power under emergency conditions. This was the case at Sicily, Salerno, and again at Omaha Beach. The Anglo-American Allies failed to maximize the combat power of their resources for a variety of reasons, including the following:

First, doctrine for the conduct of amphibious operations was in its infancy when World War II began. Many lessons had to be learned at places such as Dieppe and Tarawa, and the Anglo-American Armies and Navies did not always agree on the lessons learned from such operations.

Second, the Armed Forces of the United States possessed no joint doctrine. No body of experience and knowledge existed in the conduct of joint operations in 1942.

Third, the cultures of the U.S. Army and Navy were

Adrian Lewis is Assistant Professor of History at the University of North Texas in Denton, Texas, and a retired major, U.S. Army, infantry.

significantly different, and each service was unwilling to yield to the superior knowledge of a sister service in a particular field. Thus, the U.S. Army for example, began in 1942 to construct its own amphibious training centers, and to build its own small-boat navy.

Fourth, operations in the Mediterranean were not simply joint operations, they were also combined operations. British practices and traditions of war did not merge well with those of the United States.

Fifth, unity of command was never established at the important operational level of war. The presence of a supreme commander at the strategic level of war did not guarantee unity of command in campaigns and battles. The resources of the Army, Navy, and Air Force of both nations were never under the command of a single operational commander.

And sixth, nationalism and egos damaged the ability of the Allies to generate the quality and quantity of combat power that was possible.

In spite of these circumstances, however, one might have expected a more steeply sloped learning curve after two years of planning, training, and fighting together.

Admiral H. Kent Hewitt was the man most responsible for the development and evolution of joint, combined amphibious doctrine. He advanced an amphibious doctrine that was different in significant ways from that employed in the Mediterranean by the Anglo-American armies. Alas, he was unsuccessful in convincing the commanding generals of the correctness of his vision, and this failure cost many lives.

Hewitt was one of the most highly regarded American naval officers in the Mediterranean and European theaters in World War II.

By training, experience, study, and accomplishments he was the most knowledgeable and accomplished officer in the Anglo-American navies in the conduct of amphibious operations. He commanded in every major landing in the Mediterranean, including Operations TORCH (the landings in North Africa), Operation HUSKY (the landings in Sicily), Operation AVALANCHE (the landings in Italy), and ANVIL/DRAGOON (the landings in the south of France). Hewitt put more men ashore on hostile ground than any other commander—army, navy, or marine—in World War II. And, while he did not command during the Normandy Invasion, he trained both senior naval commanders, Admirals Allan G. Kirk, commander of Western Naval Task Force, and John Leslie Hall, commander of Force "O," who landed the 1st Infantry Division at Omaha Beach. Both men had served under Hewitt in the Mediterranean. Yet, Hewitt is largely unknown to most Americans and neglected by historians; no book length biography of his life and accomplishments exists.

The evolution of Anglo-American combined amphibious doctrine commenced when Hewitt took command of the Amphibious Force, Atlantic Fleet. In August 1941 Admiral Ernest J. King ordered Hewitt and other flag officers to New River, North Carolina, to witness an amphibious training exercise. Hewitt watched the exercise from the observation plane of his cruiser. He later stated:

> After the beach landing was completed, I joined General Smith in his headquarters ashore to observe the purely military part of the exercise. It was all most interesting and rewarding. And while I was certain of the future probability of such operations, I little realized what was to be my own close connection with them.[2]

In April 1942 Hewitt assumed command of the Amphibious Force, Atlantic Fleet from Admiral Roland E. Brainard. The Amphibious Force, Atlantic Fleet (AFAF) was a newly created command, activated in February. Hewitt outlined the mission of his command as follows:

> Our mission was the preparation of training and also planning. The amphibious training involved not only the training of the transports and the landing craft that had already been assigned to us but training of officers and crews for large numbers of large

> landing ships and craft—the LSTs and the LCTs and the LCILs. That was the naval training end of it. Then we had to carry out military training of troops in amphibious landings and all the necessary joint training of shore parties—involving, for instance, navy beach battalions, naval beach master units, . . . army engineer units, . . . [and] also army and naval communication [units].[3]

Despite more than thirty years of service, this naval officer (like the vast majority of other Navy officers) had not conducted any joint exercises with the U.S. Army. Indeed, Hewitt had no experience in working with the Army. Yet now he was charged with producing combat ready Army and Navy amphibious forces for deployment in an operation of considerable strategic importance to the Allied nations.

Hewitt possessed several character traits that helped him to succeed in his new position for which he had no training or experience. He was a fast learner and willing to listen, and his ego did not preclude him from learning from subordinates, or anyone else who had knowledge or expertise. He was mission oriented, and possessed an unusual ability to get along and to make things work. Finally, Hewitt was also a teacher. He knew how to get his ideas across in ways that maximized understanding. These abilities helped Hewitt succeed and effectively communicate with the Army.

Hewitt also had the advantage of having worked with General Holland M. Smith, USMC, for a brief period before Smith departed for the Pacific. Smith commanded the Amphibious Corps, a training command that consisted of an Army and a Marine division. Smith provided Hewitt with principles that would serve him well in the years to come. Hewitt wrote:

> I was very happy to have the initial assistance of General Smith and his staff with all their knowledge of the amphibious work they'd done, and the general principles they had laid out from their previous ex-

perience were something I followed throughout after that.⁴

Hewitt was one of the few Admirals that made a positive impression on the irascible Marine General, and for whom the General had a positive word:

> Rear Admiral Hewitt was outstanding as directing head of the new enterprise. While he came to us with little background in amphibious training, he applied himself earnestly to our particular problems and made rapid progress. He was intelligent, sympathetic and willing to accept recommendations. Our relationship was pleasant and "all hands" were happy.⁵

Upon taking command, Hewitt established a joint staff. He appealed to the War Department and got Army personnel assigned to his staff. He then reorganized his staff to ensure effective communication with the Army, adopting the Army's staff system of functional area specialties, that is, G1, Personnel; G2, Intelligence; G3, Operations, Plans, and Training; and G4, Supply and Logistics. Hewitt's staff was designated N1, N2, N3, and N4, respectively.

Early in June 1942, Admiral King ordered Hewitt to report to him immediately. At the meeting King introduced Hewitt to Admiral Lord Louis Mountbatten, Commander of the British Combined Operations Command. Mountbatten was seeking a talented officer who could return to England with him and receive an education in the British way of war. Mountbatten recorded his initial impressions of Hewitt:

> I came into the room followed closely by a fat, bedraggled figure in kauki, with a shirt covered with dust that I saw to my astonishment had two stars on his collar. He [Admiral King] turned around and said, "Here you are Admiral, take him with you." This was Admiral Hewitt.⁶

Mountbatten soon developed a great respect for this bedraggled figure. In reference to Admiral Hewitt's trip to the United Kingdom Mountbatten stated:

> Well of course when he came over, he immediately enchanted everybody by his enthusiasm, his desire to fit in with us, he listened to everything.... They'd [Admiral Hewitt and his staff] come over to learn in 3 weeks how to set up a counterpart to my organization to train [the] American Navy. Admiral Hewitt went back to the states where he in fact did miracles in setting up his organization. He made history and he saved the honor of the American Navy.

Hewitt was the man most responsible for producing combined, joint amphibious doctrine for the conduct of operations against Nazi-occupied Europe. His vision, however, had to compete with that of the British, which the U.S. Army under the leadership of Eisenhower tended to favor. Hewitt quickly grasped the problems inherent in amphibious warfare, but until he gained experience in actual operations he could not refine his vision, nor argue for a particular doctrine.

With the decision to invade North Africa, Hewitt obtained command of the Western Naval Task Force that was to land an all American Corps in French Morocco. Its mission was not to destroy the enemy; rather it was hoped that the French would come over to the Allied side without the exchange of fire. If force was required, the Allies wanted to do as little damage as possible to French forces and French pride. American forces received strict orders not to fire until fired upon. To achieve surprise, there would be no pre-invasion bombardment. The French, however, decided to fight, and not until 11 November, three days after the landing, did the French agree to an armistice. During this period, naval gunfire knocked out enemy artillery batteries, armored vehicles, fixed positions, and French warships. Nevertheless, some Army commanders resisted the use of naval gunfire. In his report,

"TORCH Operation, Comments and Recommendations," "Naval Gunfire Support in the Port LYAUTEY AREA," Hewitt wrote:

> The fire of the U.S.S. SAVANNAH and fire support destroyers was effectively used against tanks, shore batteries and personnel. If some Army commanders had failed to appreciate the capabilities of Naval gunfire in supporting landing operations, their doubts were dispelled in this operation. The Army plan called for taking the KASBA Fort "by the bayonet", and naval gunfire on this objective was not requested. The delay incident to capture of the KASBA Fort and the coastal defense guns at MEHDIA might have been avoided by having the early support of naval gunfire on these targets.[7]

Hewitt was mistaken in his belief that Army commanders gained an appreciation for the capabilities of naval gunfire in the North Africa campaign.

Though the landing in North Africa was not a serious test of Anglo–American amphibious doctrine, the Army nevertheless formed an opinion about the conduct of amphibious operations, the usefulness of naval gunfire, and the proficiency of the navy in amphibious warfare. A report entitled "Lessons from Operation TORCH," prepared by Patton's headquarters, offered numerous negative comments about the ship-to-shore movement.[8] Ship navigation was faulty, boat and ship crews did not know their jobs, assault boats were landed on the wrong beaches, equipment broke down, and various other problems were identified. In regard to the tenets on which the landing was based, he offered the following comment:

> Daylight landings are too costly and will be successful only against weak or no opposition, although landings before daylight entail much difficulty in loading landing boats and navigation to beaches, it assures surprise and reduces casualties.

> Naval gunfire should not be fired on pre-arranged time schedules except as a shore barrage previous to any troops landing. Naval gunfire missions should be "on call" from naval gunfire support parties.

The landings in North Africa established a pattern of night landing based on tactical surprise that was followed until 1944.

The landings in North Africa did not build trust between the Army and Navy. In fact, trust between the two services sank to a wartime low. The Army did not trust the Navy to get its forces to the assault beaches at the right time and place, lacked confidence in naval gunfire, and tended to depend on its own means in an assault.[9] The Navy tended to believe the Army was naive, overstepping its jurisdiction in joint operations, and too involved in business that was exclusively in the realm of Navy responsibility. By July 1943, the time of the invasion of Sicily, Admiral Hewitt had concluded that the doctrine employed by the Anglo–American armies was flawed. In his oral history he stated:

> The Army was still sticking to night landings in spite of experience in Sicily. They had decided in Sicily that naval bombardment was unsuitable to support troops, and the big defenses had to be knocked out as much as possible by air and that the landing had to be carried out during darkness so that troops would have the cover of darkness, using machine gun fire and things like that. Then the naval bombardment might be used after that.[10]

Hewitt tried to change the Army's views on this subject. In his action report following the operation in Sicily, Hewitt took pains to explain the flaws in Army doctrine. He quoted the Army's operation orders and underlined certain passages to point out the fallacies in Army thinking. He went step-by-step through the problem as if he were explaining a mathematical word problem to a young midshipman at the academy. Hewitt then launched into an

The Powerless Expert

extensive lecture on errors in Army thinking. First, he highlighted the following from the "Appreciation of Force 141" prepared by Eisenhower's headquarters [the emphasis here is Hewitt's]:

> *Section VI – D Day: H Hour: Surprise.* The Appreciation of Force 141, (SSO 17/3(FINAL)), the document upon which the Highest Echelon Outline Plan was based stated:
> 72. To ensure the success of the seaborne assaults, it will be necessary first to neutralize the beach defenses, whether the assault is carried out in darkness, smoke or daylight. There are three possible methods of neutralization:
>   (a) Naval bombardment.
>   (b) Air bombardment.
>   (c) Action by airborne troops.
> It is considered that the number of ships available and the fact that *naval gun power is not designed for land bombardment make the use of (a) unsuitable.* The primary role of the air forces will be the destruction of enemy air power and therefore (b) will not be available. *Therefore it is essential that airborne troops be used to soften the defenses against which seaborne assaults will be made.*
> 76. (a) *Airborne troops are necessary to neutralize the beach defenses*, and their maximum employment is required.
>   (b) Seaborne assault should take place some two hours before first light.[11]

To Hewitt it seemed almost inconceivable that the Army would seek to neutralize a beach defense with airborne soldiers. He pointed out that to facilitate the airborne drop, a date for the landing had to be selected that provided significant moonlight for the paratroopers, but moonlight negated the whole purpose of a night landing:

> It will [be] noted in the Appreciation that the se-

lected date would "afford approach to the coastline the cover of darkness." An examination of the Astronomical Data above will reveal no such darkness. On the contrary the assault forces were required to make the approach in a brilliant waxing moon which would not set until the vessels had hove-to in the Initial Transport Areas immediately under the coast defense guns of the enemy. These facts were well known to the naval planners who pointed out the fact that the moon phase selected was most unfavorable from naval considerations. The date, however, was not changed because it was reiterated that this phase was most favorable to dropping of the paratroops who were the only means available to "neutralize the beach defenses opposing the seaborne assault" — "the most vital part of the whole plan."

Hewitt volunteered the Navy to soften up the beach defenses:

Since the softening of the beach defenses prior to the landing was so vital to the success of the whole plan, naval planners then proposed the employment of naval gunfire against the beach defenses. This was not acceptable to the Army because it was stated "surprise" was to be achieved in the assault.

Hewitt then outlined eleven reasons why "surprise" probably would not be achieved. He noted the increased tempo of Allied air attacks, the concentration of Allied landing craft in Tunisian ports, the fact that H-hour required naval forces to approach within twenty-five miles of the Sicilian coast at evening twilight, and numerous other factors that militated against achieving tactical surprise. Hewitt then concluded his analysis of the problems inherent in operations based on surprise by stating that:

The preservation of surprise was illusory. Under the circumstance existing, it was the naval viewpoint that surprise on the assault beaches was not feasible. It was, in fact, not necessary providing a proper employment were made to exploit the means available to us.

He concluded his lecture to the Army by emphasizing the awesome power and flexibility of naval gunfire:

> The old-fashioned military concept that naval guns are unsuitable for shore bombardment needs revision. Modern naval guns in cruisers and destroyers are high angle guns capable of ranging on reverse slope targets far in the interior in support of seaborne landings. The firepower in the vessels assigned to gunfire support exceeded that of all the artillery landed in the 7th Army assault. Due to the mobility of these ships, it is possible to bring about a concentration of gunfire on a shore target with greater firepower than is possible with Army artillery.... Thus there is available to the Army a mobile artillery concentration of tremendous power capable of being exploited to the advantage of the ground forces.

The Allies did not achieve tactical surprise at Sicily. The convoys were spotted enroute and attacked by enemy aircraft. Still the landing went well. In June the coast of Sicily was defended by the Italian Sixth Army, which consisted of seven static divisions of poor quality and low morale. Their mission was not so much to prevent a landing as to hold the advance until the main attack was revealed. Once that was evident, six mobile divisions—two high quality German divisions and four Italian divisions—were to counterattack the landing force and push it back into the sea. At Gela the U.S. 1st Infantry Division received the counterattack of the highly regarded Hermann Göring Division, and naval gunfire took part in the battle. Hewitt wrote:

> It was here that the Seventh Army began to appreciate the true effectiveness of naval gunfire. In this, probably the first cruiser-tank battle, many tanks were destroyed by direct hits, and many others were put out of action by near misses. Dazed survivors, from the famed Herman Goering Division, taken prisoner, wondered what terrible new anti-tank weapon the Americans had. They had never experienced anything like the rapid fire of a 15-gun battery 6" cruiser, and they had no idea that what had hit them came from the sea.[12]

This demonstration of the capabilities of naval gunfire did not change the Army's assessment on the correct employment of this weapon. In fact, it reinforced the Army's thinking. The 1st Infantry Division fought the battle, the Navy provided fire support on-call, and the battle was won. Army leaders paid little, or no, attention to Admiral Hewitt's strongly worded report.

In Operation AVALANCHE, the invasion at Salerno, Italy, the Anglo–American generals again decided on a night landing to achieve tactical surprise with naval gunfire in support on-call. On 9 September the U.S. 5th Army under the command of General Mark Clark invaded the continent of Europe. Hewitt commanded the landing force. Two corps made the initial landing at 0330. The assaults were based on the same tenets as the campaigns in Sicily and North Africa, and once again the Allies failed to achieve surprise. Hewitt wrote:

> By the same process of reasoning that led to the Allied selection of Salerno, the Germans deduced that was where the attack would come. Consequently, they were ready—and Salerno became the toughest of Mediterranean operations.[13]

At Salerno the battle began at the water's edge. The enemy opposition exceeded that encountered in North Africa and Sicily. In the American sector, there was no preliminary bombardment at all in order to maximize surprise. Indeed, the first four hours of the battle were fought without naval gunfire, artillery, or tank support. It was a battle fought at close range by men with bazookas, grenades, machine guns, bayonets, antiaircraft guns, and a few artillery pieces that made it ashore. Hewitt again outlined all the factors that had militated against large convoys reaching assault beaches undetected. He pointed out the existence of enemy radar stations, the concentration of enemy submarines, the concentration of Allied landing craft, the phase of the moon which offered significant light, and numerous other factors. He concluded with another stern lecture for the Army:

> The lesson learned in Sicily regarding the proper utilization of naval gunfire support in pre-H hour bombardments was reemphasized at Salerno. One is led to the invariable conclusion that there exists within the Army a considerable lack of appreciation of the effectiveness of the naval gun and its proper employment in amphibious operations. The margin of success in the Salerno landing was carried by the naval gun. This undertaking had forcefully demonstrated that future operations against strongly defended coasts must scrap the outmoded concept of surprise. The coast defenses commanding the assault beaches must be selected as heavy bombing targets for several days in advance of the landing. Any plan envisaging less than this is unsound.[14]

Hewitt well understood that some level of surprise was necessary in an amphibious assault. He probably overstated his case in order to convince the Army to change its doctrine, and perhaps out of frustration.

The failure of the Armed Forces of the United States to establish an effective joint doctrine, or to build up a reservoir of trust and respect cost the nation lives and resources in World War II. In 1942 and 1943 the British were the senior partners in the Anglo-

American alliance. In those years the British dominated planning. The campaigns in North Africa, Sicily, and Italy were primarily a function of the British strategic and operational thinking. The British were able to attain all senior operational command positions, and effectively block communication between the Supreme commander, Eisenhower, and senior American operational commanders, such as Hewitt and Patton, both of whom had different views on the Sicily campaign.[15]

Hewitt succeeded as an operational commander, and he deserves great credit for America's accomplishments in the Mediterranean. He failed, however, to convince his superiors of the correctness of his vision, and there is no indication that he took his concerns to Admiral King or General Marshall. It is unfortunate that he did not, for the result was higher casualties at Salerno and Normandy.

NOTES

[1]Adrian R. Lewis, "The Failure of Allied Planning and Doctrine for Operation Overlord: The Case of Minefield and Obstacle Clearance," *The Journal of Military History*, Vol. 62, No. 4, October 1998, 787–807. See also "The Navy Falls Short at Normandy," *U.S. Naval Institute Naval History*, Vol. 12, No. 6, December 1998, 34–39.

[2]John H. Clagett, "Admiral H. Kent Hewitt, U.S. Navy Part II—High Command," *Naval War College Review*, 1975, 64.

[3]H. Kent Hewitt, "The Reminiscences of Admiral H. Kent Hewitt," Naval History Project, Oral History Research Office, Columbia University, 1962.

[4]Hewitt, "The Reminiscences of Admiral H. Kent Hewitt," 15–10.

[5]Holland M. Smith, *Coral and Brass* (New York: Charles Scriber's Sons, 1949), 84.

[6]Admiral Lord Louis Mountbatten, Interview, Papers of Admiral H. Kent Hewitt, Box 2, NHC, Washington Navy Yard.

[7]H. Kent Hewitt, Commander Amphibious Force, Atlantic Fleet, Report: TORCH Operation, Comments and Recommendations, Dec 22, 1942, 1, RG 38, Box 530, Archive II.

[8]George S. Patton, Major General, U.S. Army Commanding, Subject: Lessons from Operation TORCH, 30 Dec 1942, 52, RG 38, Box 1696, Archive II.

[9] H. Kent Hewitt, "The Reminiscences of Admiral H. Kent Hewitt," 10–12, 21–3, and 22-7.

[10]H. Kent Hewitt, "The Reminiscence of Admiral H. Kent Hewitt," 22-7.

[11]H. K. Hewitt, Vice Admiral, Naval Commander, Western Naval Task Force, Action Report Western Naval Task Force, The Sicilian Campaign, Operation "HUSKY," July–August 1943, Papers of Walter Beddell Smith, Files Op Husky 1, 2, 3, 4, Box 40, 41, Dwight D. Eisenhower Library, Abilene, Kansas, 42–44.

[12]H. Kent Hewitt, "U.S. Naval Operations in the Northwestern African-Mediterranean Theater," March–July 1943, Hewitt Papers, Box 2, NHC, 26.

[13] H. Kent Hewitt, "The Strategic Employment of the Allied Forces in the Mediterranean in World War II," 1952, Hewitt Papers, Naval War College, Newport, R.I., 11.

[14] H. Kent Hewitt, Vice Admiral U.S. Navy, Commander Western Naval Task Force, Action Report the Italian Campaign, The Salerno Landings, September–October, 1943, 129, 130, Paper of Admiral H. Kent Hewitt, Box 2, NHC,

[15] Hewitt, "The Navy in the European Theater of Operations," 13.

Intelligence Test: Evaluating Ultra in the Battle of the Atlantic

W. J. R. Gardner

> The impact of intelligence decrypts on the progress and outcome of the Battle of the Atlantic has been a central topic of scholarship on World War II at least since the publication of F. W. Winterbotham's *The Ultra Secret* in 1974. In this essay, British historian W. J. R. Gardner reviews the historiography of Ultra, notes some of the defects that have crept into the literature on this subject, and proposes a new approach for assessing the ultimate impact that Ultra had on the shipping battles in the North Atlantic.

This paper is historiographical rather than historical, although the necessary shorthand may be a little difficult to follow for those with little background in that great misnomer: the series of campaigns (each comprising many battles) which is usually called the Battle of the Atlantic. A good working definition of this long, wide-ranging and often hard-fought struggle involving the effort of many people at sea and ashore would be: "The largely-German war-long attack on Allied (and neutral) shipping taking place world-wide (but predominantly in the Atlantic) and conducted by naval and air forces (but principally by submarines) and the allied response to that attack."[1]

It is not possible in this short paper to take in the full scope of the historical literature on this complex issue, but what follows is a short sketch.[2] One initial classification might be near chronological:

- **To mid–1950s** Staff and official histories
- **From 1950s** Memoirs and early-researched works
- **From mid–1970s** Post-Winterbotham[3]

W. J. R. Gardner is an Historian at the Naval Historical Branch, Ministry of Defence, United Kingdom.

The works in the first category were those commissioned officially with the aim of immediate publication in the public domain, known in the United Kingdom as official histories. A distinction here is drawn with staff histories, which are those works that were produced for internal consumption, by Admiralties, Navy Departments and other relevant offices of state. These latter volumes may often contain information not included directly in the official histories, but even they may have limits on the degree of knowledge that they may either draw on or use explicitly—this is an important distinction.[4] Examples of official histories are Samuel Eliot Morison's two volumes dealing with the Battle of the Atlantic in the United States and Stephen W. Roskill's *War at Sea* series in the United Kingdom, although the submarine war forms only part of the latter. Leading examples of staff histories are Freddie Barley and D. W. Waters's *The Defeat of the Enemy Attack on Shipping* and Gunther Hessler's *The U-boat war in the Atlantic*, both in Britain.[5] Also in Britain were a series of other monographic official histories dealing with various subjects relevant to the Battle of the Atlantic. These included such subjects as oil, war production and—most importantly for the Battle of the Atlantic— merchant shipping.[6] Many, if not most, of these works had been published openly or otherwise by the mid-1950s. Then, two new types of work started to appear. One was based on personal experience and, on the whole, these tended to be produced by the more senior participants. Examples include works by Daniel Gallery, Peter Gretton, and Donald Macintyre.[7] In addition a further category emerged: early examples of secondary works which were not written by participants.[8] These tended to be limited in their research for two reasons. The first was that both bibliographic and archival notation were subject to different standards then, especially in books intended for a popular audience. As a result virtually none of these works were referenced, few had bibliographies, and many lacked even an index. The second problem was one of access to the relevant records.

Nevertheless it would be proper to say that there was a general view of the Battle of the Atlantic, though little of this was very deep or analytical. The "what" of the Battle of the Atlantic had been addressed. But, the "how" was less well covered, and the question of "why" was virtually untouched. There was a further and perhaps less obvious deficiency in the corpus of literature. What, almost without exception, had been looked at was the action—the exciting bits. The humdrum but vital flow of untouched, or at least unscathed, shipping which delivered tens of millions upon tens of millions of tons of vital food, raw materials and the essentials of war was almost entirely unchronicled. This it can be argued was a case of a dog doing nothing in the night.[9] Whether these problems were even recognized is doubtful, but it mattered little since 1974 produced a seismic shock to the system with the publication of F. W. Winterbotham's *The Ultra Secret*, an event perhaps best perceived in theatrical, even melodramatic, terms.[10]

Winterbotham's work was of limited application to the Battle of the Atlantic for a number of reasons: the author was not involved in that field, and his work was largely a memoir which naturally emphasized his own contribution which was, in fact, slight or nonexistent.[11] Its importance lay in different directions altogether. Firstly, it made the subject of codebreaking intelligence, thenceforth to be titled popularly as "Ultra," known to an enormous audience, both within the historical profession and outside it. Secondly, it gave rise to a whole area of study in its own right, that of the production and use of Ultra. Thirdly, it made it virtually impossible for any future work to be written that did not at least make passing obeisance at the altar of codebreaking.

Having quickly surveyed the field, it is now necessary to turn to the treatment of Ultra itself. Again a threefold division can be suggested:

- Pre-Winterbotham
- The great revelation and subsequent work
- The coming of wisdom

The first of these may seem surprising. Surely the preceding section and the general perception of the subject suggest very strongly that there was no Ultra in history before Winterbotham. In one sense this is true, but there is a surprising amount of prehistory and prior hinting, if not outright revelation, of the subject. This ranges from passages that are clear only to insiders, to descriptions which must have tested secrecy legislation. The first category is best illustrated by Roskill's fairly well known remark published as early as 1956: "Though it runs ahead of the stage now reached in our story, it is relevant to mention that it was not until May 1943 that the discomfiture of the highly skilled German cipher-breakers was made complete and final. *The reader should not, of course, assume that we British were meanwhile idle in achieving the opposite purpose.*"[12] This, arguably, was a very English piece of prose, cleverly meaning one thing to one audience and a different one to another. But this was not the only suggestion that might be available to the alert reader, although it was certainly one of the first. Ladislas Farrago's *The Tenth Fleet* (1962) sailed pretty close to the wind and Ronald Seth's *The Fiercest Battle* (1961) also gave a single indication.[13] The latter is worth quoting:

> A great deal of the credit for these successes [the convoy battles of February 1943] Dönitz ascribes to the German "B" Service which, with great skill, managed to break the Allies' ciphers, with the result that the U-boat Command received British signals and routing instructions sent to convoys. Lest this should be thought a fantastic achievement, it must be noted that on our side *our experts were able to read the U-boat ciphers*, and since Dönitz required every U-boat at sea to report to him at least once a day, the whereabouts of the enemy were known, and convoy escorts could be warned.[14]

But perhaps the closest brush with Ultra reality prior to the publication of Winterbotham's work was in Donald McLachlan's *Room 39: Naval Intelligence in Action* (1968).[15] It has to be said that McLachlan, like Beesly a member of the wartime Naval Intelligence Division (NID), did not content himself with the odd veiled hint, but actually discussed such subjects as cryptanalysis and Station

X—one of the names for Bletchley Park—at some length. Further, McLachlan had access to certain official papers although Beesly writing over ten years after him was to be denied a view of them while writing his biography of Admiral John Godfrey, *Very Special Admiral*.[16] The strange thing is that McLachlan appeared to be paid little heed, and the truth of Ultra—he did not use the word itself — remained hidden.[17]

The great watershed of the Winterbotham book has already been mentioned but its significance is such that it bears repetition. There was, however, a difficulty for any historians who might wish to follow this important lead: the time it took for material to become available, a vast and largely unexplored subject in its own right. This was by no means an instantaneous process and is still incomplete. It is not intended here to detail the chronology of material becoming available. Little was to become usable in the immediate post-Winterbotham years and much was still not in the public domain by the time that the main volumes of the British official history were published in 1988.[18] Despite the paucity of material, there was obviously great demand to take account of this new factor in the conduct of the war: how could this difficulty be dealt with? One fairly obvious way was to deal with the subject in broad terms: if Ultra was available, then clearly there had been an influence on operations. But the mere presence of a factor does not automatically imbue it with significance. Further, the brilliant effort of *obtaining* this particular intelligence product does not necessarily prove that it had any practical utility. Such basic tests were occasionally ignored in the rush to publish. There was some sound work done, and due recognition ought to be given to the work of Jürgen Rohwer and Ralph Bennett, the latter drawing attention to the difficulties of assessing significance to a single source of intelligence at operational and strategic levels of decision-making.[19] However, the burden of comment tended towards the magical and mythical rather than cool analysis, such as this comment from Noel Annan: "In 1941 Ultra had enabled the Navy almost to drive the U-boats back to their bases, such were their losses."[20] This was wrong in several important particulars:

submarine losses were not especially high, "almost driving U-boats back to their bases" was not even remotely approached, the undoubted Allied success in that year was not solely attributable to the Royal Navy, and lastly Ultra's part was only one of many factors.[21] Another example was the comment by two American scholars that "Ultra made its greatest contribution in the winning of the Battle of the Atlantic and at least in 1941 played a decisive role by itself in protecting British convoys. . . . The results speak for themselves."[22]

Perhaps, the most pervasive and corrosive case however, was that of the million-ton myth. This is stated in a number of places.[23] The essence of the claim is that the improvement wrought by Ultra in the latter half of 1941 was responsible for the saving of 1.5–2 million tons of Allied shipping. The fullest apparent explanation of this was given by the late F. H. Hinsley and is based on projecting the achievements of the *U-bootwaffe* in the four months up to June 1941 (pre-Ultra) into the latter six months of the year post-Ultra. This putative figure takes the earlier totals and factors them up for the increased number of submarines. It then compares actual losses with projected and credits the improvement entirely to Ultra.[24] This is superficially plausible, but fails to take into effect a number of other factors, which also reduced the theoretical potential of the U-boats. These include:

- A progressive shifting of submarine operating areas to the west, increasing passage times and thus reducing productivity.

- The considerable difficulties of locating convoys in open ocean—even without the further intervention of Ultra's contribution to evasive routing.[25]

- The growing competence of escort forces.

- The bringing back into convoy of ships of speeds of 13–15 knots which had suffered significant losses when routed independently.[26]

However, viewing the genre as a whole it would be right to say that ten to fifteen years after Winterbotham that "the Ultra myth" was established and flourishing. What should have been at least the British antidote to this was the official history of intelligence, obviously much behind the comparable volumes on the war at sea because of the later revelation of Ultra. This appeared in three volumes between 1979 and 1988.[27] Such timing was rather late to stop the juggernaut of the Ultra myth, although the schedule was probably unavoidable. The plan of each volume was also one which did not make systematic study of any particular warfare area or campaign easy: it is unlikely that many readers, other than reviewers, have read these books from cover to cover. Lastly the style of the series, often resorting to layers of antithesis, sometimes made it difficult to extract unambiguous judgements from the work. More than one writer was to fall into traps that might have been avoided by a more meticulous reading of Hinsley.[28] Perhaps publication of the official history marked a turning of the corner, but the combination of the improper use made of it, and its accessibility, limited its impact. Its capacity to affect a sea change was also curbed by its emphasis on strategic and operational levels. These terms were not used in the work, but both its subtitle and content indicate this point strongly. As a result, the tactical level was hardly addressed. Yet the Ultra myth literature was quite strong in this field.

Some fifteen years after Winterbotham, it finally became possible to see the emergence of more balanced judgements on the subject, although the mythological interpretation was far from dead. There were several strands to this: practitioner's experience, journalistic instinct and academic effort both conceptually and at the coal face of the record offices. In one way, this may have begun as early as 1977 with Patrick Beesly and the publication of his *Very Special Intelligence* as well as other works including a paper given at the Third Naval History Symposium at the U.S. Naval Academy in 1979.[29]

Beesly had spent the war in the Admiralty's Operational Intelligence Centre as deputy in the Submarine Tracking Room to the redoubtable Rodger Winn. Thus, he was a user rather than a creator of Ultra. He suggested a number of things which should have been self-evident to those studying the subject:

- That bringing together more than one source of intelligence led to considerable added value.
- That Ultra by itself was subject to marked limitations.
- A workable initial criterion of tactical utility for Ultra was provided by the forty-eight-hour rule, that is had the signal been decrypted within forty-eight hours of transmission.

These were three useful rubrics that should have been engraved on the mind of any historian attempting to evaluate the role of Ultra in the Battle of the Atlantic. A further broad hint came from the writings of Dan van der Vat. He devoted a considerable part of his preface to suggesting that the significance of Ultra had been overplayed.[30] His argument was reasoned but unrigorous, and he quite correctly exposed the fallacy that extent of effort automatically implies significance. He was also right to point out that there were times during the Battle of the Atlantic when Ultra was either unavailable or of little relevance, or indeed both. This short piece of text could hardly be expected to destroy the Ultra myth all by itself, but it should at the very least have inspired more to follow his lead than did, or at least for a greater degree of scepticism to be exercised.

Also important was the work of Marc Milner. In his 1990 work on the Battle, he considered that the significance of Ultra lay in its ability to avoid convoy action, in other words, the evasive routing of convoys.[31] In making clear the importance of non-action, three further points arise: the attribution of enabling resource for this submarine countermeasure, to what extent submarine reconnaissance was effective with and without evasive routing and the further extension of Milner's non-action finding beyond his stated conclusion. Although there is little specific detail, it is clear that evasive routing was practiced successfully even before reliable and timely Ultra became available. It is thus difficult to attribute precise value to Ultra for this measure.[32] Further, it is clear that by early 1943 the sheer size of the deployed submarine force made practical evasive routing very difficult if not entirely impossible. This consideration did not apply, however, in mid-1941, that is around the time that Ultra first became available. Then, a quite marked improvement in Allied fortunes appeared, on first examination, to coincide with Ultra availability. But this attractive conjunction has been demonstrated to be illusory.[33] The situation was the result of a complex variety of reasons, of which the most important were British pressure forcing submarines westward into the open Atlantic and consequent reconnaissance problems.

Extending Milner's point on non-action brought about by evasion, another aspect, which deserves closer examination, is that of the German capacity to interdict Allied convoys. At no stage in the Battle of the Atlantic did it appear even likely that all convoys on all routes were likely to be engaged by submarines. Even at the peak of German submarine deployment, this was quite impossible. As a result, there were at any given time convoys which were likely to complete their voyages without molestation, *not* because their escorts had fought off determined enemy opposition, *not* because of cleverly inspired evasion, but simply as a result of never being targeted either specifically or generally. The vast majority of convoys never saw any form of enemy attention. Studies on this topic perhaps belong in the field of economics or operational research. It might even be argued that such subjects are not for historians, but the appropriate exercise of these other disciplines not only enhance historical study but is sometimes an essential prerequisite to a proper understanding of the subject.[34]

Another type of study which has aided comprehension of the proper significance of Ultra is the method adopted in the convoy monographs of David Syrett.³⁵ These related the action at sea to the availability of signals intelligence and, in particular, to the time that it became available in decrypted form. He is the only historian so far to have taken this vital point on board. Clearly if a relevant piece of intelligence was not available within reasonable time to decision-makers then it could not possibly have influenced any significant decisions. The corollary does not hold: mere timeliness does not automatically imbue influence. In any case, it is unlikely that any surviving papers can properly illuminate this dark corner. However, the power of the negative postulate is important in attempting to assess the significance of Ultra.

Lastly, it is worth noting the point well made by David Kahn. He notes intelligence as a secondary factor in war, quite correctly making the point that it is an adjunct to military strength, not a substitute for it. The point, all the more telling for being made by a cryptographic historian, is reinforced by the example of the Poles whose considerable cryptographic skill did nothing to save them from the German army in 1939.[36]

It should be evident from the preceding discussion that study of Ultra has been somewhat patchy, sometimes adequate but more often deficient and occasionally grossly so. The problems fall into two areas, which at first examination appear to be mutually contradictory: not looking closely enough at Ultra, and considering it too narrowly. Nevertheless these flaws not only are examples of bad historical method, but they also obscure the true strengths and merits of Ultra, both of which are significant.

There are certain key questions that need to be answered. Largely these concern the central arena of convoy warfare. Attacks carried out on independent shipping are largely free of interest to the study of Ultra for a number of reasons. Firstly, such shipping was rarely subject to full—and what would now be called interactive—routing.[37] Secondly, such attacks were usually carried out by single submarines whereas it was group operations that generated the large amounts of signal traffic which might allow Ultra full scope. There are other areas where some useful study of Ultra related to the anti-submarine war might be made, but convoy must remain at the heart of any useful study.[38]

Many studies of convoy actions concentrate on the last phase of operations: the attack. This is understandable because of the conjunction of high drama and the high intensity of action, but by doing so one of the two essential properties of convoy is ignored. Convoy's two most useful characteristics are the location of escort forces at the place where the enemy can do most harm, and the concentration of the target, thereby making the problem of reconnaissance very much more difficult for the submarine. This is of paramount importance in studying the impact of Ultra on operations.[39]

Apart from this unhelpful emphasis away from considering convoy warfare fully, there are certain tests that ought to be applied to Ultra decrypts when relating them to specific convoy actions: timeliness, relevance and criticality. These may seem self-evident but as precepts they are also less evident in historical practice. Take timeliness for example. Beesly has already suggested that it required not more than forty-eight hours between transmission and decryption, but there has rarely been any sign that even this rough precept has been considered in historical study.[40] In addition, timeliness has also to be examined in tandem with such factors as tactical geometry and the progress of the action as a whole. To illustrate this briefly, there is little point in a decrypt being obtained in twenty-four hours if the convoy and submarine group are but eighteen hours away from each other. Similarly, if attacks have already started on the convoy, even a virtually instantaneous decrypt is unusable in practice.[41] This suggests that other tests such as relevancy and criticality should also be applied. The second general problem evident in the past has been that Ultra has been considered too narrowly in the sometimes dazzling (or more often sea-gray dull) kaleidoscope that is the Battle of the Atlantic. Some aspects of convoy warfare co-exist independently of one another, sometimes they inter-reacted. Thus to attempt to assess the significance of Ultra without taking these other contexts into at least some kind of consideration is rather like a scientist attempting to discuss the Gaia hypothesis purely in terms of the behavior of subatomic particles. Reverting to the Atlantic, a number of further relevant fields might be suggested:

- The strategic background
- The economic dimension
- A German perspective
- Technology in a broad sense
- The full spectrum of intelligence

All of these have a bearing on the Battle of the Atlantic and all have connections with the assessment of Ultra, although the link is not always immediately obvious. In the field of technology, for example, two key questions that ought to be answered are: did Ultra have any significant effect on the development of Allied technology, and was Ultra an important source of information on German technical advances.[42] The writings of Donald McLachlan and Patrick Beesly make it very clear that Ultra was but one contributor to the multi-faceted world of intelligence. Another operative, Commander Kenneth Knowles, USN, argued that direction finding was more significant than Ultra, although Rodger Winn did not entirely agree.[43] But such disputes are to some extent sterile and, in any case, tend to conceal a larger truth — the importance of process in adding value to raw intelligence. Without that, intelligence as a product would only have been the sum of its seventeen or so parts, not rather more as it was in practice.[44] Turning to the economic dimension, several points might be made. This aspect has been touched on already but the sparseness of its coverage is striking. A small amount of literature deals with the organization of shipping and merchant shipbuilding, important matters both. What is even less evident is comment on the clear economic rationales informing much of Admiral Dönitz's strategy and operational deployments. Indeed, the justification deployed for the post–mid-1943 continuing deployment of submarines is almost entirely economic in concept, even if flawed in its detail.[45] The connection of all these subjects with Ultra might seem obscure, but they are important for a thorough and rounded examination of the significance of codebreaking intelligence. The shipping balance debited on one side by U-boats and credited on the other by the huge shipbuilding capacity of the United States makes both a contrast and a backdrop to the simultaneous tactical and operational level struggle in the Atlantic. It is surely historically unsound to attribute criticality to a month of losses at sea — actual as well as realistically potential—when a much larger tonnage was completed far away from the action. By adopting these perspectives and methods it is also easier to realize the significance of non-action rather than merely the dramatic episodes. In such ways, among others, the economic story has to be considered alongside operational activities.

These represent just a few examples of the ways in which Battle of the Atlantic subjects not always considered to be relevant to the full assessment of Ultra are nevertheless not merely appropriate, but also absolutely necessary adjuncts to the investigation of codebreaking alone.

Having been led into the maze that is the Battle of the Atlantic, how in the midst of all this complication, all this material, can a solution be found to the question of the significance of one type of intelligence in a six-year series of campaigns? Two general solutions have been implied. These share two characteristics: simplicity and a demand for large amounts of work in research and application but, perhaps, most of all in comprehension. If there ever was a good example of a "system of systems," then this is surely it. But while this is good conceptual stuff, it hardly suffices as a practical prescription for future work. All that can be profitably put forward is a further iteration of the points made earlier: greater rigor in the analysis of convoy actions and signals intelligence, and taking account of perspectives other than the one immediately surrounding convoy actions.

One example of techniques that might be used in assessing convoy actions is to look at the process of dealing with convoys from the dual perspectives of the sail of a storm-tossed U-boat and that of the *Befehlshaber der U-Boote*—also known as BdU or Admiral Dönitz. Here finding and attacking convoys is considered a four-phase process.[46]

This can be represented using the ORCA model which considers the processes as those in the Outer zone before groups are formed for search; Reconnaissance, which is the group searching until at least one makes convoy contact; Closure, the process when the rest of the group maneuvers to also gain convoy contact; and, finally, Attack proper. It should be noted that the diagram is systematic, not scalar, although in the cases of individual convoy actions, both distances and — almost more importantly — times can be applied to it. From this an approximate calculus can be derived relating the significance of Ultra to the progress of a convoy action. (See Figure 1 on page 294.)

This process is clearly indicative rather than one of extreme accuracy. Nevertheless, despite its undoubted roughness, it does suggest where the utility or otherwise of Ultra might lie. This is just one test that might be applied to convoy warfare. What is clear is that little of this sort of technique, either explicit or implicit, has been applied to the analysis of the subject in the past. Progressing up from the tactical level, the paucity of sound analyses is even more striking, and the isolation of the Ultra factor even more complete: opening this up to the other contexts can only benefit historical understanding of the subject.

It might be thought that this paper has dwelt unduly on the defects of past analyses without proposing a fully worked-out alternative interpretation. On one hand this is certainly true, as an implicit object has been to encourage further work rather than merely substitute a failed dogma with another doctrine which is no more satisfactory than its predecessor. As Henry Ward Beecher proclaimed, "Doctrine is nothing but the skin of truth set up and stuffed."[47] That said, a tentative conclusion about the overall significance of Ultra in the Battle of the Atlantic can be attempted. It was clearly a significant contribution to the war effort; often, but not always, it could be considered as important. However, it would be very difficult to represent its contribution as either constant or critical to the outcome as a whole.

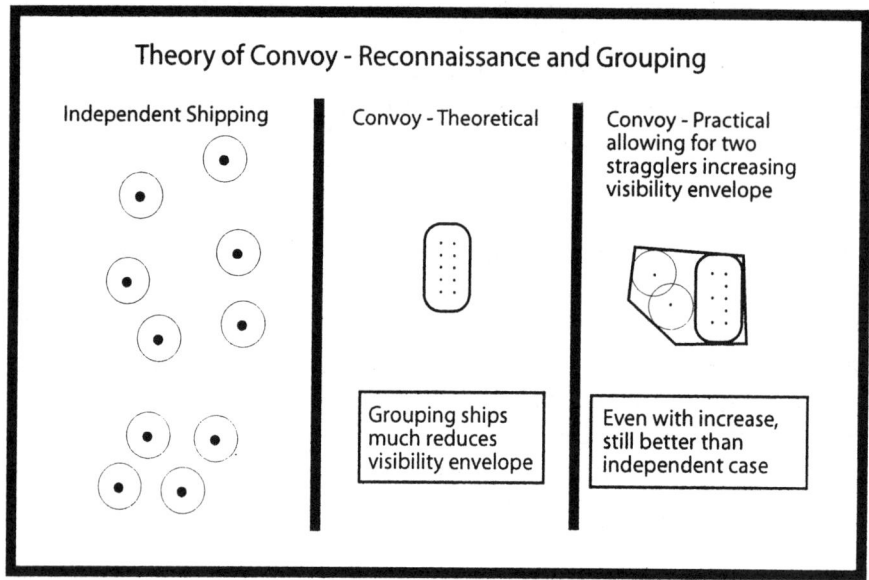

Figure 1

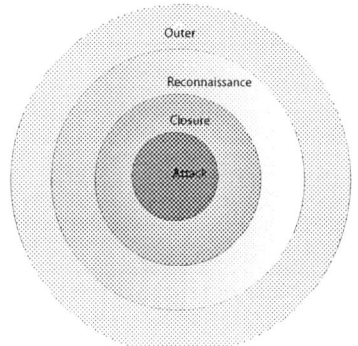

Figure 2

NOTES

[1] The author owes a debt to Kathleen Broome Williams, who noted the need for the last seven words of this definition.

[2] A fuller account adopting the same broad classification can be found in Stephen Howarth and Derek Law, (eds), *The Battle of the Atlantic 1939-1945: the 50th Anniversary International Naval Conference* (Annapolis, Md.: Naval Institute Press, 1994), Chapters 29 and 35.

[3] Rarely can such a mediocre work have established a valid claim to defining a whole genre of historical literature, but F. W. Winterbotham's *The Ultra Secret* (London: Weidenfeld and Nicholson, 1974) can do so legitimately. The flaws in the work largely concern lack of research (or even checking) and a tendency to attribute roles and actions to the author whose involvement in Ultra was much less than he implied.

[4] See the discussion on knowledge, implicit use and revelation in the discussion of Ultra in Battle of the Atlantic literature below.

[5] Samuel Eliot Morison, *History of United States Naval Operations in World War II: The Battle of the Atlantic, September 1939–May 1943* and *The Atlantic Battle Won, May 1943–May 1945* (Boston: Little, Brown, 1947 and 1956); S. W. Roskill, *The War at Sea, 1939-1945* (London: HMS, 3 volumes in 4 parts, 1954-1961); Freddie Barley and David Waters, *The Defeat of the Enemy Attack on Shipping: a Study of Policy and Operations* (London: Historical Section, Admiralty; 1957) 2 Vols; also (London: Navy Records Society, 1998). See also PRO ADM 234/578 and /579 and Gunther Hessler, *The U-Boat War in the Atlantic* (London: HMSO, 1989). See also PRO ADM 186/802. ADM 234/67 and /68.

[6] D. J. Payton Smith, *Oil* (London: HMSO, 1971); M. M. Postan, *British War Production* (London: HMSO, 1952); and C. B. A. Behrens, *Merchant Shipping and the Demands of War* (London: HMSO, 1955). The paucity of works on shipping is both notable and regrettable. A recent and honorable exception is Kevin Smith, *Conflict over Convoys: Anglo-American Logistics Diplomacy in the Second World War* (Cambridge, UK: Cambridge University Press, 1996).

[7] Daniel Gallery, *We Captured a U-boat* (London: Sidgwick and Jackson, 1957); Peter Gretton, *Convoy Escort Commander* (London: Cassell, 1964); Donald Macintyre, *U-boat Killer* (London: Weidenfeld and Nicholson, 1956). It is also worth mentioning two fictional works which drew on their authors' experiences and convey the *zeitgeist* well: Nicholas Monsarrat, *The Cruel Sea* (London: Penguin, 1951) and Lothar-Günther Bucheim, *U-Boat* (London: Collins, 1974) (published in German as *Das Boot*).

[8] C. S. Forester, *Hunting the Bismarck* (London: Michael Joseph, 1959) and Ronald Seth, *The Fiercest Battle: the Story of North Atlantic Convoy ONS5, 22 April–7 May 1943* (London: Hutchinson, 1961). Paul Lund and Harry Ludlam; *Night of the U-boats* (London: Foulsham, 1973) is a later example of the same type.

[9] Arthur Conan Doyle, *Memoirs of Sherlock Holmes* (1894), "Silver Blaze." Often misquoted as the dog that did not *bark* in the night.

[10] The thespian metaphor is explored at greater length in W. J. R. Gardner, *Decoding History: the Battle of the Atlantic and Ultra* (Annapolis, Md.: Naval Institute Press, 1999), 210–11.

[11] A further criticism, not directly relevant to this paper, was made by those who had worked in the field. While they had rightly maintained tight silence over decades, they felt it wrong that Winterbotham should not only publish but also be rewarded handsomely. See new introduction to Patrick Beesly, *Very Special Intelligence: the Story of the Admiralty's Operational Intelligence Centre* (London: Greenhill Books, 2000).

[12] Roskill, *The War at Sea*, 2:208 (emphasis added). Roskill's wartime knowledge was indisputable, as he had served as a Deputy Director of Naval Intelligence.

[13] Ladislas Farrago, *The Tenth Fleet* (New York: Ivan Obolensky, 1962).

[14] Ronald Seth, *The Fiercest Battle*, 64 (emphasis added). Although there are resonances to Roskill's passage, this is very much more explicit. Seth's war service, as far as is known was as a field operative in the Special Operations Executive (the British equivalent of OSS), so contemporary knowledge of Ultra was extremely unlikely. Telephone conversation with SOE historian, Professor M. R. D. Foot, 13 August 1999.

[15] Donald McLachlan, *Room 39: Naval Intelligence in Action 1939–1945* (London: Weidenfeld and Nicolson, 1968).

[16] Patrick Beesly, *Very Special Admiral: the Life of Admiral J H Godfrey, CB*; (London: Hamish Hamilton, 1980).

[17] It is interesting to speculate on reasons for the official inaction. Not only would a prosecution have drawn premature attention to Ultra, but McLachlan had held several prominent posts in the national press and any action against him would have attracted much publicity.

[18] F. H. Hinsley, E. E. Thomas et al., *British Intelligence in the Second World War: Its Influence on Strategy and Operations*; three volumes in four (London: HMSO, 1979–88).

[19] Jürgen Rohwer, *The Critical Convoy Battles of March 1943: the Battle for HX229/SC122* (Shepperton, Surrey: Ian Allan, 1977); Ralph Bennett, *Behind the Battle: Intelligence in the War with Germany* (London: Sinclair-Stevenson, 1994).

[20] Noel Annan, *Changing Enemies: the Defeat and Regeneration of Germany* (London: Harper Collins, 1995), 52. This is a late example of the judgment by an authority normally considered to be magisterial. It is quoted to illustrate the pervasiveness of the fallacy.

[21] For a full analysis of 1941 see W. J. R. Gardner, "The Battle of the Atlantic, 1941—the First Turning Point?" in Geoffrey Till (ed), *Seapower: Theory and Practice* (Ilford, Essex: Frank Cass, 1994) and the same author's *Decoding History*, Chapter 8. These make it clear that the reasons for the outcome were complex and included such factors as air surveillance west of UK, German reaction to this, the robust action of the United States in the western hemisphere, German high command reaction to this and the difficulties of ocean surveillance for the Germans. In most of this, Ultra played little or no part.

[22] Allan R. Millet and Williamson Murray (eds), *Military Effectiveness*, (Boston: Allen and Unwin, 1988), Volume III: the Second World War, 116–7. The data referred to is Roskill's tabular enumeration of monthly losses.

[23] Specifically Christopher Andrew and David Dilks (eds), *The Missing Dimension: Governments and Intelligence Communities in the Twentieth Century* (London: Macmillan, 1984), 165; David A. Charters, Marc Milner and J. Brent Wilson (eds), *Military History and the Military Profession* (Westport, Conn.: Greenwood Publishing Group, 1992), 83. In none of these instances is the working revealed.

[24] Harry Hinsley; "The Enigma of Ultra" in *History Today*, September 1993, 19.

[25] See also below, page [... Although there is little specific detail, it is clear that evasive routing was practiced successfully even before reliable and timely Ultra became available. ...]

[26] A fuller discussion of these points is in *The Battle of the Atlantic, 1941* and *Decoding History*, Chapter 8.

[27] Hinsley, *British Intelligence in the Second World War*. There were two subsequent volumes covering security and counterintelligence, and strategic deception respectively: neither of these are directly relevant to the present paper.

[28] For an example of this see, Gardner, *The Battle of the Atlantic, 1941*, 118.

[29] Patrick Beesly, *Very Special Intelligence: The Story of the Admiralty's Operational Intelligence Centre, 1939–1945* (London: Hamish Hamilton, 1977) and Patrick Beesly, "Special Intelligence and the Battle of the Atlantic: the British View" in Robert W. Love Jr. (ed.), *Changing Interpretations and New Sources in Naval History: Papers from the Third United States Naval Academy History Symposium* (New York: Garland Publishing, 1980), 416.

30Dan van der Vat, *The Atlantic Campaign: the Great Struggle at Sea 1939–1945* (London: Hodder and Stoughton, 1988).

31Marc Milner; "The Battle of the Atlantic," *The Journal of Strategic Studies*, (March 1990), 45–66.

32Gardner, *Decoding History*, 171.

33Gardner, *The Battle of the Atlantic*, 1941, also *Decoding History*, Chapter 8. See also this paper on the million-ton myth.

34Both of these are neglected areas of study but they are crucial to understanding systemic and holistic aspects of the battle.

35David Syrett, "Prelude to Victory: the Battle for Convoy HX231, 4–7 April 1943," *Historical Research*, Vol 70 No 171 (February 1997), 99–109; "The Battle for Convoy ONS-154, 26–31 December 1942," *The Northern Mariner/Le Marin du Nord*, (April 1997), 41–50; "The Sinking of HMS *Firedrake* and the Battle for Convoy ON153," *The American Neptune*, No 51, (Spring 1991), 105–111 are examples.

36David Kahn, *Seizing the Enigma: the Race to Break the German U-Boat Codes 1939–1943* (London: Souvenir Press, 1991), 91.

37A significant exception was made for the "Monsters," large and usually fast liners such as the Queens. See Beesly, *Very Special Intelligence*, 147–8.

38A most interesting area for work—as far as is known largely unstudied—is the mining campaign carried out in the Baltic which had major effects on the German submarine trials and training program. It is thought that much of the direction of this was Ultra-informed. Similarly the disruption of the industrial effort of building the new generation Type XXI and XXIII submarines would repay the interest of historians. In both cases the skills of both economic history and operational research would be useful.

39It can be argued that the significance of submarine groups as a reconnaissance device is at least as important as the subsequent concentration for attack, a point often missed by those facilely using the term "wolf-pack tactics." The other point worth making is that the geometry of the group for reconnaissance is radically different from that used for attack. See also discussion of ORCA below.

40A marked exception is the work of David Syrett whose decrypt references provide such information. See Note 35 above.

41Such points are discussed in greater detail below. See the ORCA concept.

42These points are discussed in Gardner, *Decoding History*, Chapter 6. Here, too, the normal definitions of technology are stretched somewhat but justifiably to include such matters as production engineering and the efficiency of organizations.

43United Kingdom Public Record Office, ADM 223/286 Operational Intelligence Centres: formation and history; paper "The Americans, the Navy Department and U/Boat tracking" (by Barrett) unnumbered fourth page including marginal note by Rodger Winn. I am grateful to Ralph Erskine for drawing my attention to this passage.

44The figure of seventeen comes from McLachlan's *Room 39* (not apparently including Ultra). It is this feature which goes a long way to explaining the paradox—usually unaddressed—of German codebreaking dominance for much of the Battle. See letter *The Mariner's Mirror*, Volume 85, No. 1 (February 1999), 94; letter from Dr. Peter Coy, "Sailors v. Codebreakers, Authors v. Reviewers" and response "Sailors v. Codebreakers" in Volume 85, No. 2 (August 1999).

45W. J. R. Gardner, "ASW Victory: Resources or Intelligence," *Les Marines de Guerre du Dreadnought au Nucléaire* (Chateau de Vincennes, France; Service historique de la Marine, 1988) for a fuller explanation of this point. See also *Decoding History*, Chapter 3.

46Some time after formulating this approach it was discovered that a very similar classification, but of three steps, was used by Professor Blackett, the British operational researcher.

47Henry Ward Beecher, *Proverbs from Plymouth Pulpit* (1887).

F-21 and F-211:
A Fresh Look into the "Secret Room"

David Kohnen

At the Third Naval History Symposium in 1977, a panel devoted to the question of how the allies exploited Ultra intelligence sources in the Battle of the Atlantic featured Patrick Beesly, the British author of *Very Special Intelligence* (1977), the German scholar Jürgen Rohwer, and U.S. Navy Capt. Kenneth A. Knowles who as a commander in World War II ran the submarine tracking program (F-21) at Navy headquarters in Washington, D.C. At the time of the 1977 panel, security restrictions prevented Captain Knowles from discussing key aspects of submarine tracking operations, in particular of a "secret room" (F-211) on U-boat intelligence. In this essay, David Kohnen uses recently declassified material to take a "fresh look" at the submarine tracking program, and at the broader issue of Anglo–American cooperation in the Battle of the Atlantic.

During World War II the Anglo–American Allies pioneered new methods for gathering and exploiting operational intelligence at a tactical level. In the Battle of the Atlantic, the Allies used intelligence first to safeguard merchant shipping and then as a means of deploying limited offensive assets to engage enemy naval forces with extreme precision. At the strategic core of the Allied naval effort in the Battle of the Atlantic were Royal Navy Volunteer Reserve Comdr. Rodger Winn of the Admiralty Operational Intelligence Center (OIC) and U.S. Navy Comdr. Kenneth Alward "K. A." Knowles of the U.S. Navy "F-21 Atlantic Section." Together, Winn and Knowles influenced the most pivotal decisions and operations in the Atlantic, Indian Ocean, and other naval theaters as well. Commanding the "submarine tracking rooms" of their respective services, Winn and Knowles fostered an atmosphere of Anglo–American cooperation that Patrick Beesly, former deputy chief of the Admiralty tracking room, once described as "probably closer than between any other British and American organizations in any [s]ervice and in any theater."[1]

David Kohnen was Curator and Project Manager for the battleship USS Wisconsin (BB-64). He currently serves as Curator of the U-505 exhibit at Chicago's Museum of Science and Industry.

The Winn-Knowles connection was essential in facilitating Anglo–American cooperation after 1942. Freely sharing information and opinions, Winn and Knowles created a forum where British and American strategists unified the Allied naval command, which was decisive in the overall Allied victory in the Battle of the Atlantic. To perform their missions, Winn and Knowles correlated information from all sources with highly classified signals intelligence (SIGINT) material—including information originating from cryptologic special intelligence. Such information was commonly classified under the covernames ULTRA and MAGIC, though other classification markings were also used. With victory secured in 1945, Winn and Knowles, along with their tracking room subordinates, were recognized with awards and commendations, though the details of their wartime contributions were not cited in these accolades in order to safeguard the secrets of their work. As a result, Winn and Knowles were largely obscured by postwar secrecy in the Cold War era. Always security conscious, Knowles himself wrote in a memo of 30 April 1945 that "[i]n order to protect sources of information it is strongly recommended that these F-21 and OIC serials either be destroyed or their security classification raised" to a level of secrecy precluding access" . . . to various officers and civilian historians who may examine these files."[2] Fortunately, the records were mostly preserved intact and eventually housed in sequestered storage facilities in the United States and Britain. Though their secrets were safely secured, the fundamental role of Winn and Knowles in determining Allied naval strategy nevertheless appeared in Battle of the Atlantic literature.

During the 1950s and 1960s, information about the Winn and Knowles tracking rooms trickled into the unclassified histories. Authors like retired Royal Navy Rear Adm. W. S. Chalmers alluded to the success of the British OIC and the submarine tracking room under Rodger Winn. In his 1954 work *Max Horton and the Western Approaches*, Chalmers provided a relatively candid account of Winn and the role of the OIC in Royal Navy operations. He portrayed Winn as a highly influential figure in determining the course of Allied convoy routing operations.[3] Among authors like Chalmers who were familiar with such details, the race to publish highly sanitized references to the contributions of Winn and Knowles steadily intensified in the 1950s; often assuming the dimensions of an Anglo-American rivalry at interpreting the history of the Battle of the Atlantic. This point can be observed in the text of official histories. For example, Royal Navy Capt. Stephen Roskill released the first of four volumes in the *War at Sea* series beginning in 1954. Within the next eighteen months, U.S. Navy Adm. Samuel Eliot Morison published the twenty volume *History of United States Naval Operations in World War II*. Both histories are important historiographic foundations in Battle of the Atlantic literature. Yet, security considerations precluded these authors from writing much about Winn and Knowles and their tracking room operations.

Though they provided remarkably detailed assessments on the role of operational intelligence, the official histories of Roskill and Morison only hinted about the more sensitive aspects of Allied strategy and tactics employed in the Battle of the Atlantic. Thus, Winn and Knowles appear as background characters in the grand scheme of Allied naval operations within the official histories. Reading their works in hindsight, Roskill and Morison implied that Winn and Knowles had an important role in defeating Axis submarines. In 1956, Morison referred to "Kenneth A. Knowles" directly in describing the role of his submarine tracking room in U.S. Navy operations. Morison explained that Knowles and his staff provided U.S. Navy strategists with a "clearinghouse for U-boat intelligence, including the high-frequency radio direction-finder network."[4] Without referring to Winn, Morison also provided a footnote reference to a "similar control center . . . with which Commander Knowles freely and constantly exchanged information" at the Admiralty.[5] Morison's reference to "high-frequency radio direction finding" (HF/DF or "huff-duff") is consistent with other Battle of the Atlantic literature in the 1950s and 1960s. For those authors who knew otherwise, HF/DF was commonly used as an umbrella reference to obscure the role of Allied successes in special intelligence.

Like Morison, Stephen Roskill referred to HF/DF extensively while describing the role of the submarine tracking rooms in supporting the Allied naval effort. Nearly four years after Morison's account appeared on the bookshelves, Roskill published Part I of Volume III from the *War at Sea*. In this study, Roskill referred to the role of Roger Winn in supporting Admiralty decision-makers. Like Morison, Roskill avoids making direct connections between the Allied submarine tracking rooms under Winn and Knowles. He primarily focuses on Winn's operation, but also describes the "equivalent organizations, built to the British model, on the other side of the Atlantic. . . ."[6] Devoting less than a page of text to his analysis, Roskill was somewhat more explicit than Morison in describing the role of the Allied submarine tracking rooms and, more importantly, the developing role of operational intelligence in modern naval warfare. For example, Roskill states, "[t]hough no details of the methods employed can be given, a large share of our success can confidently be attributed to the intuition of certain experienced individuals with the most modern technical resources."[7] He further pays homage to Winn specifically, again without reference to Knowles.

As semi-official historians, Roskill and Morison were likely constrained by the censors in providing the most detailed accounts of Winn and Knowles and their tracking rooms. Yet, the veil of Cold War secrecy was progressively eroding by the early 1960s. For example, Ladislas Farago provided a surprisingly detailed account of the Winn and Knowles tracking rooms in his 1963 work *The Tenth Fleet*. During the war, Farago served as the chief of research and planning for the U.S. Navy Office of Naval Intelligence (ONI). In the postwar era, Farago earned a reputation as a writer of novels and narrative histories about the war. With very limited access to primary materials, Farago nevertheless provides a balanced survey of Anglo-American intelligence operations in general. Given the amount of detail in *The Tenth Fleet* text, Farago was apparently familiar with the Allied submarine tracking rooms as a result of his wartime service. He capitalized on wartime recollections and postwar social connections to write works such as *The Tenth Fleet*. Moreover, Farago was largely beyond the control of the censors. Arguably, he was most able to expand upon the works of others to provide details about the wartime production and dissemination of operational intelligence within the Anglo-American Alliance. As a result, Farago's *The Tenth Fleet* brought greater resolution to the tracking rooms of Winn and, to an even greater degree, Knowles.[8]

Maintaining their wartime vows of secrecy throughout the 1950s and 1960s, Winn and Knowles remained publicly silent about their role in defeating Axis naval forces. Like many other Allied intelligence veterans, Winn and Knowles avoided drawing attention to themselves even as their names appeared in the histories of the war. In broad terms, authors who referred to Winn and Knowles essentially based their perspectives and conclusions in patriotic terms. British authors largely concentrated on describing the role of the Admiralty OIC by making passing references to Winn. Likewise, American authors generally followed Farago's earlier work by focusing on the Anti-Submarine Warfare (ASW) operations of the U.S. Navy Tenth Fleet, without referring to the "F-21" designator for the Knowles tracking room upon which the Tenth Fleet was centered.[9] Generally appearing separately in the various histories of the Battle of the Atlantic, the Winn and Knowles stories progressively merged in the literature, once British and American authorities began to review the declassification of records relating to Allied codebreaking successes during World War II—though access to these records was initially limited to a select number of researchers.

A new contingent of official historians were granted access to the cryptologic records of World War II in the 1970s. Within many scholarly circles, rumors about Allied codebreaking successes had been common.[10] Yet, official histories documenting the role of Allied codebreaking were not immediately forthcoming in the early 1970s. Cold War secrecy precluded declassification when, in 1974, former Royal Air Force Group F. W. Winterbotham released his memoir *The Ultra Secret*. The work was an immediate bestseller. Despite many inaccuracies, *The Ultra Secret* effectively exposed the general public and many scholars to previously obscured aspects of British codebreaking. Though widely disregarded as an unreliable reference by many contemporary scholars, *The Ultra Secret* had a lasting impact.

During the war, Winterbotham was assigned to the Government Code & Cypher School (GC&CS). He served on the grounds of the main British codebreaking facility at Bletchley Park, located in Milton Keynes in England.[11] When writing *The Ultra Secret*, Winterbotham admitted that he had little access to the official records and, thus, qualified his account by stating that "[s]ince virtually all the signals quoted or referred to in this book were in the Enigma Cypher I have thought it necessary to label each one and have therefore included them all under the 'umbrella' of the code name *Ultra* which was given to this particular intelligence."[12] Without full access to the records relating to Allied codebreaking, many authors and scholars accepted Winterbotham's simplified use of the covername ULTRA, and a flood of scholarly and popular works focused on the "ULTRA secret" aspects of the war. As authors and scholars reinterpreted the Battle of the Atlantic "in the light of Ultra," the covername itself evolved into a generic term for describing Allied cryptographic intelligence.[13]

Allied naval intelligence veterans who worked directly with the material that the codebreakers produced knew that Winterbotham's use of the covername ULTRA was technically incorrect. Some were extremely frustrated that these scholars were using the term so freely to evaluate the information in the primary documents, which were steadily becoming accessible through declassification programs and initiatives. In his 1977 memoir entitled *Very Special Intelligence*, Patrick Beesly was determined to clarify and properly redefine the covername ULTRA. From his standpoint as the former assistant to Roger Winn in the Admiralty OIC, Beesly observed that [t]he word Ultra has now come to be used in a generic sense for all information available to the British in the last war derived from cryptanalysis, whatever the nation of origin and whatever form it took. This usage is incorrect and in the Navy, at least, it was only applied to outgoing signals and documents as a security grading and the actual information itself was always referred to as "Special Intelligence."[14]

Unlike the codebreakers who primarily produced *cryptographic* SIGINT, Beesly had access to a wide range of intelligence sources. He correlated cryptographic material with other sources to produce *operational* intelligence. The reports produced by Beesly and others were always marked with the classification of the most sensitive source cited—including ULTRA but not excluding other covername categories such as Z, SHARK, CIROPEARL, PEARL, and THUMB.[15] Each of the aforementioned classifications indicated the sensitivity and reliability of the intelligence information for the operational consumers who used the material to escort convoys and attack Axis naval forces efficiently.

With declassification, Beesly's revised definition of ULTRA was largely substantiated. In the submarine tracking rooms of Winn and Knowles, Allied trackers generally used the phrase "special intelligence" to describe information derived from intercepted Axis radio transmissions. SIGINT derived from cryptanalysis often featured precise information about Axis operations. Therefore, this highly sensitive intelligence was generally known as *"very* special intelligence." Such material was further designated with specific covername references delineating the various forms of SIGINT used in reporting Axis naval activity.[16] Under Winn, Admiralty submarine tracking room personnel pioneered methods of using special intelligence to *forecast,* rather than simply report, Axis movements and initiatives. By anticipating the possible locations of Axis attackers, Winn hoped to divert Allied vessels away from danger.[17] After 1941, American intelligence personnel visited the Admiralty tracking room to work with Winn and study his methods. Such visits enabled the Americans to develop further the techniques employed at the Admiralty. After 1943, Knowles and the U.S. Navy F-21 tracking room began using special intelligence to target Axis naval forces for attack, much to the chagrin of Winn and many others at the Admiralty. As a result, the various covernames used to classify the sources of special intelligence became especially important at the tactical level.

Though Beesly attempted to explain the idiosyncrasies involved with classifying SIGINT, authors and scholars largely continued using Winterbotham's colloquial definition for the ULTRA covername. Beesly essentially failed to readjust the contemporary definition of the ULTRA covername to its wartime significance. Nevertheless, he succeeded in providing a well-balanced survey of British successes in developing a viable OIC organization through the experience of World War I and during the Spanish Civil War. Beesly also described the innovations of Winn in pioneering new methods for using operational intelligence in naval strategy and tactics. Most importantly, Beesly emphasized the significance of the Winn and Knowles team by describing their personal friendship as an important cornerstone in the broader Anglo-American coalition.[18]

Beesly was an influential figure in the new wave of literature examining the Battle of the Atlantic in the 1970s and 1980s. Commonly cited by authors reexamining the role of intelligence in the Allied victory, he continued the crusade to redefine the popular definition of ULTRA. In this quest, Beesly assisted researchers through articles, correspondence, and personal interviews. He regularly attended conferences and symposia, including the Third Naval History Symposium held at the United States Naval Academy on 27 and 28 October 1977. During this gathering, Beesly evaluated the role of special intelligence in the Battle of the Atlantic from the "British View" by expanding upon his work *Very Special Intelligence*.[19] Beesly appeared with distinguished German scholar Jürgen Rohwer who presented the "German View." Building from the text of his work *The Critical Convoy Battles of March 1943*, Rohwer demonstrated with charts and graphics the importance of radio communications in German Navy strategy and tactics.[20] He also provided a definitive evaluation of the *Spruchschlüssel-maschine-M*, best known by its commercial name "Enigma." Rohwer emphasized the significance of Allied codebreaking successes in solving the expanded four rotor (M4) models of the Enigma machine cypher, which was used on a standard basis aboard U-boats after February 1942. Highlighting Allied cryptographic successes in solving the M4 Enigma, he also recognized the essential role of HF/DF and RADAR in the Anglo–American SIGINT victory over Axis forces during the war.[21]

The Beesly and Rohwer presentations were complimented by Kenneth A. Knowles who examined the Battle of the Atlantic from the "American View." For the first time since the war, Knowles publicly described the role of operational intelligence from the perspective of the F-21 submarine tracking room and U.S. Navy Tenth Fleet. In his talk, Knowles reaffirmed the importance of Anglo–American cooperation in defeating Axis forces. However, he also drew some key distinctions between British and American views on using special intelligence for targeting purposes. Knowles explained that American trackers generally used intelligence "more directly than the British." He admitted that, on occasion, "we [in F-21] skated on some pretty thin ice" when tactical precautions about using special intelligence for targeting was considered less important than the potential strategic dividends. Knowles justified the aggressive use of special intelligence by describing a point in the war when American decision makers were willing to accept "the calculated risk" to defeat the Germans before they could exploit a growing technological advantage in submarine snorkel propulsion, acoustic homing torpedoes, and radio burst transmissions. Burst transmissions, in particular, may have undermined the Allied advantage in SIGINT. Had the Germans succeeded in using newly developed technologies to regain a tactical initiative in the Battle of the Atlantic, Knowles observed that "it would [have been] touch-and-go all over again."[22]

Reflecting upon the problems inherent with using cryptologically derived SIGINT, Knowles emphasized the decisive role of HF/DF in tracking room operations. He observed that Allied codebreakers were "frequently" unable to solve Axis codes and cyphers on a timely tactical basis. Sometimes, the Winn and Knowles tracking rooms were deprived from reading the text of intercepted Axis radio messages for prolonged periods.[23] As a result, HF/DF and RADAR fixes were often the main sources used in the Allied tracking rooms. Moreover, during periods when cryptologic intelligence *was* available, Knowles explained that the information was only deemed fully reliable when corroborated against other sources such as HF/DF. He reinforced Beesly's account by emphasizing that cryptologic intelligence was essential to tracking room operations. In general terms, however, cryptologic intelligence represented only one of many types of intelligence sources available to Winn and Knowles. In concluding his presentation, Knowles also criticized the new wave of literature reexamining the war through the revelations of ULTRA. He suggested that many new works seemed overly focused on the codebreaking aspects of the war. Knowles further observed that many new works were somewhat unobjective by stating:

> I gather the impression from existing books and articles . . . that the British not only succeeded in breaking the German U-boat cipher, with the acquisition of an 'Enigma' machine and the capture of the U-boat location chart, but continued to break the cipher and sort of spoon feed the Americans with its tremendous benefits throughout the Battle of the Atlantic. Not having played any part in the cryptographic wizardry, I can only speak indirectly, but it is my distinct impression that, once we got into the war, the American contribution to "Ultra" was at least equal to the British effort.[24]

Indeed, recently declassified material substantiated the recollections offered by Knowles in 1977. Documents released as late as 1996 reveal the vital role of OP-20-G, the U.S. Navy cryptologic section, which had a leading role in creating a machine capable of solving the four rotor M4 Enigma. These documents even suggest that the U.S. Navy, rather than the British, largely controlled the production and dissemination of cryptologically derived special intelligence on U-boat operations after 1943.[25]

Though many of the wartime records produced by Knowles and his F-21 staff were still classified at the time of the Third Naval History Symposium, he provided a balanced and detailed description of the F-21 submarine tracking room. Until recently, the original and uncensored photographic and documentary records, produced by this submarine tracking organization, remained largely inaccessible. In the 1980s, many of these records were finally declassified. Soon thereafter, a number of studies were published examining the role of Allied codebreaking and operational intelligence in the Battle of the Atlantic. Authors and scholars were immediately drawn to examine newly accessible document collections, which were compiled by the National Security Agency and released as Record Group (RG) 457. These records were eventually transferred to the National Archives and Records Administration. A favorite document among those reexamining the Battle of the Atlantic remains RG 457, SRMN 038, "Functions of the 'Secret Room' (F-211) of COMINCH Combat Intelligence, Atlantic Section, Anti-Submarine Warfare, WWII, UNDATED." This highly detailed study describes the most secret aspects of submarine tracking in the Knowles organization. Outlining the various methods of compiling and assessing cryptographic and other forms of SIGINT, SRMN 038 yielded much previously classified information about the American submarine tracking room. However, this document was too detailed to provide a broader and more comprehensive appreciation of the F-21 organization.

In September 1998, more files from the F-21 organization were made accessible at an unclassified level to researchers. These records were previously stored at the U.S. Navy storage facility at Crane, Indiana, and many documents in this collection remain untapped. Some of the newly released files include a report submitted in 1945 by Knowles to the wartime Commander in Chief of the Navy (COMINCH), Adm. Ernest J. King. This report features previously unreleased photographs of the F-21 submarine tracking room along with a detailed diagram outlining the ways in which SIGINT was disseminated within the COMINCH command and out to other Allied commands. The report provides a broader understanding of F-21, showing clearly the aforementioned F-211 "Secret Room" as a smaller subsidiary of the submarine tracking room where only the most secret compartmentalized information on Axis naval activity was processed. SRMN 38 only revealed a minor portion of the overall F-21 operation to previous researchers. Documents newly released from Crane, Indiana, now allow contemporary researchers unprecedented access to Knowles and the U.S. Navy submarine tracking room.

Though they had different philosophies on using special intelligence at a tactical level, Winn and Knowles were a fine example of Anglo–American cooperation. Together, their staffs orchestrated the events that ensured the Allied victory in the Battle of the Atlantic. However, the Winn and Knowles team was only possible after British and American leaders had successfully negotiated solutions to many contentious issues, which hampered Allied collaboration in the early months of the war. Shocked by the crippling Japanese attacks in the Pacific in December 1941, the United States formally joined the British in fighting Axis aggression. Initially unprepared to wage a two-front war against the Japanese in the Pacific along with German and Italian forces in the Atlantic, American naval leaders were unable to mount a credible defense. Meanwhile, small waves of U-boats inflicted severe damage on Allied shipping along the eastern seaboard of the United States during spring and summer 1942 during operation *Paukenschlag* (Drumbeat), causing great tension within the Anglo–American Alliance. As a result, British and American leaders were compelled to balance national pride with the necessity for establishing a lasting and "very special" relationship.

Throughout 1942, U.S. Navy Adm. King worked hard to reorganize the American fleets to fight simultaneously on many fronts against various and different enemy forces. As one of the oldest active sailors in the American naval service, King was arguably more innovative and flexible than many of his contemporaries, especially at identifying and finding long-term solutions to problems inherent with coordinating a global naval strategy and maintaining the Allied coalition. Although many local area commanders opposed King, centralization became a priority within the COMINCH organization.[26] Alleviating many British concerns about operational security, King reorganized and consolidated the COMINCH staff. By adopting many small, but well-planned measures aimed at streamlining the COMINCH organization, King eventually created an OIC similar to the Admiralty model. In comparison with the Admiralty OIC, King's OIC would arguably have a greater role in *decisively* defeating the U-boats in the Battle of the Atlantic.

Unlike the Admiralty tracking room under Winn, the U.S. Navy lacked a viable organization capable of producing useful operational intelligence on Axis naval forces. In the main U.S. Navy tracking room known as "F-35," Comdr. George C. Dyer and his staff toiled at tracking U-boats and enemy surface vessels throughout the *Paukenschlag* crisis in summer 1942. Yet, most of his staff was not allowed to see information recorded on the plot boards of the separate COMINCH Atlantic Section (F-11), under Lt. George H. Laird. With information filtering in from ONI, OP-20-G, and the Admiralty, Laird and his staff were often overwhelmed with conflicting information about enemy locations and activities—though they performed remarkably well under pressure during the *Paukenschlag* crisis.[27] As a command chartroom for Adm. King, the F-11 plots often illustrated the highly classified details of planned future operations. Access to F-11 was, therefore, limited to a restricted list of officers, making it impossible to provide adequate support to the F-35 war room staff.[28] Laird and his F-11 staff were also unpracticed in the art of creating "Working Fiction," or forecasting enemy activity.[29] The Americans were simply unfamiliar with the innovative methods of Rodger Winn in the Admiralty OIC. As a result, the operational intelligence available in F-35 and F-11 was inadequate to support the needs of the U.S. Navy and King, in particular.

Nevertheless, King was in an excellent position to overhaul the U.S. Navy's ASW intelligence structure within a very short period. As OP-20-G and GC&CS negotiators made arrangements to cooperate in SIGINT, a key ingredient to obtain the clearest operational intelligence picture, King received a recommendation from President Franklin D. Roosevelt's "Special Observer" to the Admiralty in London, Rear Adm. Robert Ghormley. For nearly two years, Ghormley had worked as the president's personal envoy to the Admiralty. Earning the trust of many ranking and influential British leaders, Ghormley was eventually given a tour of the heavily fortified "Citadel" complex where he observed Winn and his tracking room staff in the Admiralty OIC.[30] Ghormley informed King about the highly unorthodox operational intelligence methods of Winn. He wrote that Winn's operation was so secret that "only about twenty-five officers of the British navy are admitted" into the OIC tracking room.[31] Shortly after King received this correspondence from Ghormley, the Admiralty OIC became a topic of discussion at a high-level meeting between OP-20-G and GC&CS. When asked, the British representatives explained how the Admiralty was developing further the OIC network and expanding the operation in Newfoundland. Piquing American interests in the Admiralty OIC concept, arrangements were made to bring Winn to the United States. During his visit to America, Winn also toured the Royal Canadian Navy (RCN) OIC tracking room under Lt. Comdr. John B. McDiarmid, RCNVR, in Ottawa.[32]

Numerous authors have characterized Winn's visit to the United States in spring 1942 as yet another British attempt at tutoring King and his band of hard-headed Yankees on the COMINCH staff. In many accounts, ranking American naval leaders are portrayed as being disinterested or even abrasive in meetings with Winn.[33] Clearly, some tension existed between the British and American commands. Unquestionably, Winn was subjected to a gauntlet of questions from skeptical American officers, unconvinced of using operational intelligence to predict where the enemy *might* attack. It also seems likely that the COMINCH staff may have been preparing Winn to meet with the most senior Admiral in the U.S. Navy. King, and his predecessor Stark, had already begun centralizing U.S. Navy operational intelligence before Winn arrived in Washington on 20 April. Therefore, to suggest that Winn had "sold" the OIC concept to King and other American leaders, seems an oversimplification.[34] King was continuing to improve the COMINCH tracking organizations by building upon the foundations initially created under Stark.

To this end King was better prepared to act decisively once a basic framework for cooperation between OP-20-G and GC&CS was solidified in April 1942. His meeting with Winn is generally portrayed as being "surprisingly" cordial. One British author even observed that King uncharacteristically "gave Winn a friendly hearing" and then, following the meeting, "moved with a speed and efficiency that was surprising to anyone accustomed to the ways of the Admiralty" in creating an American OIC.[35] After meeting with Winn, King directed Adm. Russell Willson, Chief of Staff to COMINCH, to select an officer who could study under Winn and learn about British intelligence in general. Willson's assistant, Adm. Francis F. "Frog" Low, immediately recommended a nearsighted reservist, who had nearly six years experience aboard destroyers and battleships, named Lt. Comdr. Kenneth "K. A." Knowles, USNR.[36]

Knowles seemed an unlikely candidate for such an important intelligence assignment. Although he had graduated near the top of the U.S. Naval Academy Class of 1927 and had finished some postgraduate work at Annapolis in 1934, Knowles suffered from physical disabilities that ultimately forced him out of the active navy as a lieutenant in 1936.[37] Nevertheless, Knowles maintained close ties with the navy by serving as an editor for the journal *Our Navy* and, for the next three years, worked in the journal's offices on the tenth story of the Brooklyn National Bank overlooking the Brooklyn Navy Yard.[38] Meeting frequently with ranking naval officers and covering many important events at the navy yard, Knowles gained some notoriety as an intellectual and writer among many actively serving naval officers.[39] When Knowles rejoined the active navy, his reputation was an important factor in his assignment to the COMINCH staff.[40]

Since the beginning of his naval career, Knowles was recognized by his peers as a hard working and serious officer who set the highest standards for achieving excellence.[41] One naval academy classmate described Knowles as quiet and unassuming, but [he] has a fine sense of humor and is always ready to give a helping hand. As a worker, he is *par excellence*. . . . If work makes a naval officer, then Ken is due to fly that two-starred flag some day, for he believes in getting results. He makes friends rather slowly, but when one is taken into his confidence there is nothing that Kenny wouldn't do for him.[42]

After joining the regular navy, Knowles served under Capt. Russell Willson aboard the USS *Pennsylvania* (BB-38). Later, Knowles proved himself to be an excellent gunnery officer serving under then Comdr. "Frog" Low aboard the USS *Paul Jones* (DD-230).[43] Periodically serving together in the small and often intimate peacetime American navy, Low and Knowles maintained a strong relationship even when Knowles was cashiered and sent into the USNR.[44] Working for *Our Navy*, Knowles was grateful to his employers for giving him a good civilian job, which allowed him to concentrate on naval affairs. Yet, as American naval forces began participating more directly in the Battle of the Atlantic, Knowles yearned to rejoin the active ranks of the navy. In spring 1941, he seized an opportunity to restart his naval career by assuming command over the newly organized Naval Reserve Officer Training Command (NROTC) detachment at the University of Texas. Knowles was glad to be back in uniform and teaching navigation as an NROTC instructor, but he desperately wanted to command a destroyer. Due to the physical disabilities, however, the U.S. Navy Bureau of Medicine rejected Knowles' application for assignment to a combat command. After Pearl Harbor, Knowles believed he was destined to "linger" for the rest of the war as an NROTC instructor in Texas.[45]

Knowles exploited some very powerful connections at the highest levels of U.S. Navy command in hopes of securing a better wartime billet. In spring 1942, his former skipper "Frog" Low asked Knowles if he would be willing to work in Washington, D.C. Knowles remembered accepting the offer by saying "anything that's closer to the front would be most enjoyable for me."[46] Low, therefore, arranged Knowles' assignment to the F-35 section of the COMINCH staff. While Knowles lacked experience as a naval intelligence officer, Low was confident in his former shipmate's ability to organize, analyze, and comprehend vast quantities of information, and then submit clear and concise recommendations.[47] Excited by the opportunity to serve again under Low and Willson, Knowles also knew that his assignment would be tough. He later remembered both of his former skippers as "SOB's, and as far as operations went, they were pretty strict on performance and so was I, so we fitted together pretty well."[48] Therefore, when King decided to send a member of his COMINCH staff to visit the Admiralty OIC in April 1942, Low and Willson quickly selected Knowles for the job.

Knowles proved to be the perfect choice as the future American counterpart to Winn. The two struck an immediate and lasting friendship during summer 1942. Although their personalities and professional backgrounds were somewhat different, Knowles and Winn shared many similarities in their life experiences. Arriving in Britain in July, Knowles met with Winn and his assistant in the OIC tracking room, Lt. Patrick Beesly, RN, for the first time in the war. Soon after his arrival, Knowles was brought into the OIC where he witnessed Winn and his tracking room staff gleaning operational intelligence from all sources. For example, the Admiralty OIC received a continuous flow of updates from various land-based RADAR and RDF sites. Using these rough bearings, OIC trackers plotted azimuths between a given intercept point and a possible enemy position. The enemy was then pinpointed by bringing various azimuths together on a converging point in a process known as "resection." Tracking room personnel also used the RDF plots to perform "traffic analysis." In other words, British trackers could usually identify the more important enemy targets by evaluating the number of transmissions sent to and received by an enemy radio. Through this method, they deduced which targets might be an enemy resupply vessel or, perhaps, the lead U-boat in a wolfpack patrol line.

Admiralty submarine trackers augmented their RADAR and RDF plots with information derived from other intelligence sources like POW interrogation summaries. While POWs customarily falsified information to mislead Allied interrogators, tracking room analysts used the summaries to confirm or discount their operational and technical assumptions about the enemy. Similarly, aerial reconnaissance and spy reports brought greater resolution to the intelligence picture of Axis activity.

Gaining some practical experience working with Winn and his staff, Knowles assisted for several weeks in OIC operations and planning. He remembered "spen[ding] a good ten hours every day in the tracking room [where he] absorbed, by osmosis at least, a great deal of [British] experience in tracking."[49] During his time in the Admiralty OIC, Knowles was also exposed to "special intelligence" derived from cryptographic sources.[50] Prior to his visit, Knowles was *not* given detailed information on enemy codes and cyphers and he *never* toured the center of British codebreaking at Bletchley Park.[51] Though the British codebreakers were, at that time, experiencing problems with the M4 Enigma and TRITON, Winn demonstrated for Knowles the full potential of using special intelligence to fight U-boats.[52] Highly impressed with the apparent extent and sophistication of British codebreaking, Knowles learned how all the information was first collected in the OIC, and then distilled and sanitized before it was transmitted over a teletype to the Headquarters of the Western Approaches at Derby House in Liverpool. At Derby House, the operational intelligence was replotted on a massive greenish-blue chart of the Atlantic where Admiralty strategists could then consider Winn's guestimates and determine a proper course of action. By the time Knowles returned to the United States, he was fully initiated into the small society of those who were familiar with the most secret aspects of ULTRA special intelligence. Moreover, Knowles was also experienced in all aspects of Admiralty OIC operations and fully understood Winn's techniques in the art of tracking the enemy.[53]

Knowles established fundamental bonds at a tactical level with his counterparts during this initial visit to Britain. After returning to the United States in August 1942, Knowles formally replaced Laird as chief of the F-11 Atlantic Section. As F-11, he placed a high priority on maintaining a "close personal relationship" with Winn and his tracking room staff in the Admiralty OIC.[54] Now familiar with the operational intelligence methods of Winn, Knowles started transforming F-11 into a bonafide OIC tracking room. Meanwhile, King and his staff were also planning a complete strategic overhaul within the American naval command. By fall 1942, the COMINCH organization was poised to shift from a defensive to an offensive strategy in the Battle of the Atlantic. Manning the COMINCH F-11 Atlantic Section, Knowles and his staff were already key players in the planned reorganization.

Based upon his experience working with Winn in the Admiralty OIC, Knowles quickly established the foundation for developing a highly efficient tracking room, which complimented similar facilities in Canada and Britain. While Knowles was initially a novice at collecting and evaluating operational intelligence, Winn trained Knowles to think of tracking room operations as simply using "available intelligence to reproduce as nearly as possible the operations room of the enemy."[55] Yet, in fall 1942, Allied codebreakers were mostly unable to provide enough information to the Allied OICs to achieve such an ideal tracking situation. During this time, however, Knowles assembled the core of his submarine tracking team. Primarily drawing from members of F-35 and the F-11 Atlantic Section staff, Knowles began teaching them Winn's methods in tracking U-boats.[56]

Focusing primarily on tracking U-boats in the Atlantic and Indian Ocean, Knowles and his staff initially worked in the former spaces of the OP-38-W "war room," located across the hall from the main COMINCH plotting room in the Main Navy Building on Constitution Avenue in Washington, D.C. For security reasons, Knowles moved his operation into a compartmentalized office adjoining the main COMINCH plotting room. On 27 December 1942, F-11 was redesignated as F-21 in the COMINCH table of organization. Although the administrative changes were not fully enacted until July 1943, F-21 fell under the COMINCH Combat Intelligence Division (F-2).[57] As the scope and mission of F-21 increased in spring 1943, Knowles was reinforced with seven WAVES officers and four enlisted WAVES, all of whom were reservists.[58] Once Knowles assembled his tracking room team, he jealously observed that "it is of utmost importance that the personnel of the [F-21] Tracking Room be permanently assigned there." He justified this statement by arguing that "familiarity with enemy thought processes as applied to his operations and the characteristics of individual U/Boat commanders can only be developed with long practice."[59] By the end of the war, up to fifteen officers and five enlisted personnel were working under Knowles in the tracking room.[60]

Keeping a continuous four-section watch, F-21 personnel maintained the most current tracking information on enemy activity by updating four large wall charts of the major fronts in the Battle of the Atlantic. These charts were the focal point of the F-21 tracking operation. The two main charts illustrated the primary U-boat operations areas in the North and South Atlantic while two auxiliary charts depicted other areas where Axis naval forces threatened Allied shipping. These included a chart of the Pacific between the longitudes 60E and 70W and a global world chart, which was used to record a continuous fifteen-day plot of U-boat activity in general. The global chart was convenient for making quick references to past trends and estimating possible future enemy activity. Data used in creating all the main F-21 plots were kept in a chronological written log and on smaller file charts, used in creating a more detailed analysis of Axis naval activity.[61]

Beginning at 0900 every morning, Knowles or an F-21 representative presented a fifteen-minute briefing in front of the main charts in the tracking room. Recounting the key events that transpired over the course of the previous day, the F-21 briefings were usually given for ranking Allied officers like Adm. Richard S. Edwards, COMINCH Chief of Staff, and Adm. Martin Kellog Metcalf, COMINCH Director of Convoys and Routing. Roughly half a dozen other key officers who were involved with ASW strategy also attended the F-21 briefing on a regular basis.[62] Knowles later remembered that King would occasionally attend these briefings. Originally, Knowles and his staff only recorded U-boat activity and locations on the main F-21 charts for briefing purposes. Eventually, they also plotted the locations and activities of Allied forces as well. This produced a more comprehensive operational and strategic situation estimate for Allied decision-makers.

Although they were still perfecting the techniques pioneered in the Admiralty OIC, Knowles and his F-21 staff devised a very simple and efficient system for tracking enemy forces. Like their counterparts in the Admiralty OIC, F-21 trackers used a number of methods to create clear, concise, and graphic illustrations of U-boat activity. Akin to basic library research and archival registration, the F-21 trackers compiled raw intelligence and then organized the material into a usable form by following two basic procedures. First, newly acquired intelligence was recorded on the plotting charts to show the paths of individual enemy vessels or wolfpack formations. Allied decision-makers could then consult the F-21 plot and quickly review their tactical and strategic options. Second, F-21 personnel correlated new data with information that was already available. Then, written estimates and graphic templates illustrating possible enemy courses of action were compiled for future reference.[63]

One of the major functions of F-21 was maintaining a current and accurate record of the number of U-boats at sea and those in port. This information appeared on a "port board" display adjacent to the main F-21 plotting charts.[64] By moving pins from the wall plots to the port boards, F-21 trackers maintained a graphic record of U-boat movements in and out of port. The main port boards recorded information about the major U-boat bases along the coast of occupied France in the Bay of Biscay. Smaller displays illustrated the U-boat bases in Norway, the Mediterranean, and East Asian bases like Penang in Malaya.[65] All the graphic displays were updated on a daily basis.

Much of the information processed in F-21 was based upon HF/DF and RADAR fixes. In many histories describing the tracking organizations of Winn and Knowles, this point is often obscured by the generic term "ULTRA." While this covername and others were used extensively by Winn and Knowles when referring to special intelligence, it is important to recognize that the term ULTRA implies only cryptologic intelligence to many contemporary readers. Yet, it was impossible for Allied codebreakers to furnish information derived from cryptologic sources for many months of the war. During these periods, Winn and Knowles devised a standard system for denoting the accuracy or inaccuracy of HF/DF and RADAR fixes on enemy locations.[66] Highlighting the point that cryptologic intelligence on U-boat activity was mostly unavailable on a timely basis until 1943, Knowles noted that "[e]ven when the enemy's cipher is broken, there are many times when the navigational positions are still unreadable."[67] Of course, tracking the enemy was much easier when cryptologic intelligence was available.

All U-boat tracking information was originally recorded on the main wall charts in the F-21 plotting room. Once Allied codebreakers began experiencing greater success at solving M4 Enigma and TRITON, however, Knowles decided that further compartmentalization was necessary within F-21. To limit access to raw cryptologic intelligence, he created a separate compartmentalized section within the F-21 tracking room known as F-211. Sealed off, the space occupied by F-211 was widely referred to as the "Secret

Room" among the F-21 trackers and those outsiders who were familiar with Knowles and his operation.[68] Housed in a space that was always secured from personnel who had no need to know detailed knowledge of ULTRA, the F-211 Secret Room was manned by Knowles, an executive officer named Lt. John E. Parsons, USNR, Lt. (j.g.) John V. Boland, USNR, and Yeoman First Class Samuel P. Livecci, USN—the only "regular navy" enlisted sailor who served in the F-21 organization during the war.[69] Later, Ens. René B. Chevalier, USN, also joined the Secret Room staff.

While Knowles concentrated on running the overall F-21 operation, Parsons gradually assumed control over the day-to-day operations in the F-211 Secret Room. In spring 1943, Knowles sent Parsons to the Admiralty OIC to become familiar with the tracking methods of Winn.[70] After Parsons returned from Britain, he worked closely with Knowles running the Secret Room. By summer 1943, the most significant tracking work was performed in the security of the Secret Room. Once the operational intelligence was sufficiently condensed, the data were moved outside and transferred onto the main charts in the adjacent F-21 plotting room. Secret Room trackers also drafted a highly sanitized digest of information on enemy movements known as the U-boat "location list."[71] Every morning, F-21 yeoman used the location list to update the main wall plots and other tracking information.

Inside the Secret Room, F-21 trackers maintained three wall charts, which were smaller copies of those in the main F-21 plotting room. One chart illustrated the North Atlantic from 73N to 05S and from 100W to 60E. Another chart depicted the South Atlantic from 35N to 60S and 100W to 52E while the third and smaller chart illustrated the Indian Ocean.[72] Since an adequate chart of the Capetown area was unavailable, Secret Room trackers taped the Atlantic chart together with the Indian Ocean chart to illustrate the courses and activities of U-boats or other blockade runners cruising from Europe to East Asia.[73] Individual U-boat positions were recorded with color-coded pins on the Secret Room wall charts. These pins were labeled with tabs indicating the type and tonnage of a given U-boat along with the names of known U-boat commanders. The U-boat commanders were also identified by their two character Enigma "bigram" signatures.[74] All the pins included a date and time group indicating the age of a given plot marker. Other labels indicated whether U-boats had been damaged or destroyed in a reported attack. Colored string also marked the routes and operational areas of individual U-boats and wolfpack groups. Overall, this pin and string array included information on friendly forces, enemy surface and air forces, blockade runners, neutral shipping, and U-boat cruises of particular interest.[75]

The information compiled in the F-211 Secret Room was derived from all sources on a daily basis, but the most significant information was derived from the text of decyphered enemy radio messages. After summer 1943, the vast majority of these intercepts was sent directly to the Secret Room over a scrambled teletype by the OP-20-G codebreaking and translation specialists in the naval annex at Mount Vernon Station on Nebraska Avenue in Washington, D.C.[76] Other sources of cryptologic intelligence included the "ULTRA serials," which became available from the Admiralty after the Wenger-Travis arrangements of October 1942.[77] The raw data listed on these serials were largely based on material collected at Bletchley Park and then compiled by Winn and his OIC tracking room staff. These were not circulated outside the Secret Room and were often annotated with observations and personal notes between Winn and Knowles. Every morning, commissioned U.S. naval officers delivered the "ULTRA serials" in double sealed pouches to the Secret Room directly. The information was then processed and condensed. Listed alphabetically and by date and time reference, Secret Room trackers used the ULTRA serials to update bigram signatures and to create the location list. This chronological list also served as an excellent index for evaluating the activities and histories of individual enemy commanders, their U-boats, and the various U-boat wolfpack groups.[78]

Arguably, the most important function performed in the Secret Room was compiling and condensing intelligence derived from GC&CS and OP-20-G sources. Almost daily, Lieutenants Parsons and Boland processed the Admiralty information for comparison with information derived from American sources. After Commander Knowles reviewed all of the intelligence, Yeoman Livecci organized the material in a small archive. He then updated a wall calendar recording the number of days that U-boat communications had been successfully intercepted. Livecci also organized all the U-boat intelligence by three categories. First, by U-boat hull number, then by an intercept's date and time group, and finally by subject matter. Once the Secret Room staff updated all the wall plots and port boards with the U-boat location lists, duplicate sets were created for use in the main F-21 plotting room, OP-20-G, and the Admiralty OIC.

Altogether, the accumulated information was transposed onto 5x7 index cards, which were stored in the Secret Room archive.[79] Each individual U-boat had its history carefully recorded on these "sub cards."[80] Information indicating the number of patrols undertaken, the geographic areas visited, and the wolfpack groups with which a given U-boat had operated was carefully typed onto the sub cards. Similar cards were created for Italian submarines (U-It), *Yanagi* ships, U-boat supply vessels, and blockade running Japanese submarines in the Atlantic and Indian Oceans.[81] For quick and easy reference, sub cards were also generated for each U-boat group operation and then arranged alphabetically by the German cover-name for the given wolfpack. The individual bigrams of U-boat skippers were listed on the wolfpack sub cards to record their participation in various group operations. Information on the wolfpack sub cards was also color coded to indicate the source of the U-boat intelligence. For example, information derived from Admiralty sources was typed in red ink while U.S. Navy information appeared in black ink.[82]

These various methods of filing and indexing made it possible to access all the traffic concerning any particular U-boat for a given period quickly and efficiently. With this information, Allied trackers could review the full text of past messages when forecasting future U-boat activity. By late 1943, when the "high speed" American *Bombes* were available on a grand scale, OP-20-G essentially controlled cryptologic ULTRA.[83] Nevertheless, the Admiralty OIC was kept abreast with the most current U-boat intelligence in a publication known as the "F-211 serial."[84] Once Secret Room personnel completed the process of evaluating and organizing the material, the F-211 serial was retransmitted back to the Admiralty OIC and, to a lesser extent, the Canadian OIC in Ottawa.

Through various serial dispatches, therefore, all the Allied OICs maintained a uniform strategic picture of enemy activity. To avoid any duplication of effort, Knowles personally edited the F-211 serial. For simplicity and greater security, he and Parsons devised a code of symbols to convey all the various aspects of U-boat intelligence before retransmission.[85] In general, the F-211 serials updated Admiralty trackers of changes in bigram signatures, decyphered U-boat grid square locations, and newly identified U-boats and skippers. Since the serials were not circulated outside the Secret Room and the tracking room in the Admiralty OIC, Knowles and Winn often sent extremely candid messages and observations to each other in the F-211 serial.[86] The system was so efficient and secure that Adm. King sometimes used the F-211 serial as a means of corresponding with the First Sea Lord.[87] Occasionally, these highly classified exchanges between COMINCH and the First Sea Lord were surprisingly terse.[88]

Communication between F-21 and the tracking room in the Admiralty OIC was essential in maintaining an accurate tally on the number of enemy vessels in service and at sea. Along with the ULTRA and F-211 serials, Winn sent Knowles a weekly "special" serial recording his estimate on the number of operational U-boats in service.[89] F-21 trackers reviewed the special serial and other reports to confirm or discount reported U-boat "kills" and "liquidations."[90] With this in mind, the women of F-21 perhaps shared some of the stress of participating in ASW combat. Each time F-21 trackers updated the pin and string plotting information on the various charts and files, an Allied vessel might be saved or a U-boat destroyed. With access to the most detailed information leading to and following ASW operations, F-21 trackers were usually better informed about the full brutality of a given attack than those who were actually on the scene. In the antiseptic atmosphere of F-21, Knowles and his staff reviewed evidence such as intercepted enemy signals, attack reports and photographs, or accounts obtained from POW interrogations.

All this evidence was compiled and reexamined to determine whether or not an enemy vessel had been destroyed or only damaged. Knowles submitted his findings to senior ranking COMINCH officers who served on the "F-21 Liquidated U/B Assessment Committee."[91] Sometimes, the Assessment Committee denied "credit" for a reported "kill" because evidence was found that the enemy vessel had actually escaped. This often occurred in cases when kills were reported after a depth charge attack and little physical evidence was retrieved. By reviewing all the data collected in F-21, Knowles could usually assess the true results of a reported attack with great accuracy.[92] When the Assessment Committee determined that an enemy vessel had in fact been sunk, the results of the attack were noted on the daily summery of events. F-21 trackers then placed all the plotting information which had been used in sinking an enemy vessel into a file known as the "morgue," which was located in the main F-21 plotting room.[93]

Assessment Committee findings were published in a highly sanitized biweekly U-boat intelligence summery for circulation within COMINCH and the Admiralty. These were known as the "Radio Intelligence Summaries" (RI), which were generally classified as "TOP SECRET-ULTRA." Even with the ULTRA classification, the RI summaries were edited for use in other sections, for Allied intelligence personnel with lower security clearances, but who also "needed to know" the information.[94] For example, the U.S. Navy Special Warfare Branch, Intelligence Division (OP-16-W), used the RI summaries to wage psychological warfare against U-boat sailors. Based on POW interrogations, OP-16-W personnel knew that U-boat crews often preferred listening to the entertaining swing music and radio programs that were found on Allied radio broadcasts.[95] OP-16-W used the RI summaries to draft a well-orchestrated radio transcript. Information about U-boat liquidations and other adverse news regarding the war was then broadcast in German to the U-boats at sea.

Working with other Allied intelligence sections like OP-16-W was extremely useful for tracking room operations. For example, one of the most difficult problems with reading decyphered Enigma messages was determining the exact identity of the U-boat that was sending or receiving signals. Dönitz and his command staff usually addressed a given message by using U-boat hull numbers and skipper's names interchangeably, but never together.[96] Likewise, U-boat commanders either signed their messages with a "trigram," denoting the hull number for short signals while using their last names for longer signals and attack reports. As a result, F-21 and Admiralty trackers experienced extreme difficulty in determining who was sending what signals to which receiving station. Further complicating Allied tracking, newly commissioned U-boats, newly appointed skippers, or previously identified skippers recently assigned to new U-boats constantly appeared in the radio traffic.

F-21 trackers thus relied on information from other sections to maintain a current fix on new variations in enemy radio traffic. For example, POW interrogation summaries compiled by OP-16-Z were used to confirm intelligence information on U-boat commanders and officers, enemy operations, bases, and U-boat flotillas. Based on such information, F-21 trackers maintained three separate lists.[97] One alphabetically listed confirmed bigram signatures; another depicted known commander's names; and a third indexed U-boat hull numbers. These tables were kept on three separate desks in the main F-21 plotting room. The information was then cross-referenced, often revealing the identity of a given U-boat.[98] When cryptographic intelligence was unavailable in the F-211 Secret Room, it was still possible to identify and track targets by monitoring the Morse key "fist" signatures of enemy radio operators. OP-20-G SIGINT specialists kept oscillograph recordings of past enemy transmissions known as TINA. Essentially, individual radio operators touched the Morse key differently when transmitting signals. Thus, OP-20-G analysts could usually determine the identity of an enemy vessel by using TINA to "finger-print" and track individual enemy radio operators.[99]

When cryptographic intelligence was available, Allied trackers used references in enemy messages to identify targets. Working closely with F-21, Winn and his tracking room staff specifically focused on "passage report" signals sent from departing U-boats back to their command.[100] U-boat commanders customarily used their hull number as a signature for their passage report to BdU. With this in mind, Winn watched for signals signed by the skipper's name. Comparing these separate signals with radar and RDF bearings, Winn was often able to determine who belonged to which U-boat. He recorded these findings and wrote his identifications as margin notes in the ULTRA summaries that he sent to Knowles and the F-21 staff.[101] Sometimes, the Germans simplified the identification process for Winn. For example, after a given U-boat commander signed a message by his hull number, BdU often acknowledged the message by the skipper's name, or *vice versa*.[102] Other times, BdU requested fuel and location reports from U-boats at sea by addressing the signals by hull number. U-boat commanders often replied to these inquiries by using their name. As a result, with German assistance, the Allies generally identified individual U-boats within about three weeks.[103]

F-21 and OIC tracking room personnel used decyphered U-boat position reports to plot the locations on acetate overlays of captured copies of the *U-Bootseekarten Quadratkarten Kriegsmarine* (U-boat Grid Chart or German Naval Grid). Designed for use with the Enigma cypher machine, the Naval Grid simplified position plotting by a system of artificial squares superimposed onto the globe. The squares were drawn to Mercator's projection and each covered approximately 900 kilometers, or about 486 nautical miles (nm). Each square was then assigned a two-letter grid reference. The grids were subdivided by smaller numerical references.[104] For example, if a U-boat was operating in the eastern part of the Gulf of Aden, the location reference of the U-boat might read MQ 5971. After 1943, Allied cryptanalysts were usually able to decypher U-boat messages and read the encyphered Naval Grid references. Allied trackers then used this intelligence to pinpoint the exact locations of targeted U-boats on the Naval Grid by using the very radio signals that the BdU staff relied upon to maneuver their U-boat forces at sea.[105] Therefore, a correct and consistent solution to the Naval Grid was vital to F-21 and Admiralty OIC operations.

The Germans were not amateurs, however, and often disguised the two letter grid references by designating a color code to U-boat patrolling areas on the Naval Grid. Although the system was designed to thwart the Allied trackers, F-21 and OIC tracking room personnel used this color code system as yet another means of tracking U-boats. One method of solving the color code references was comparing RADAR and RDF bearings with the last known locations of targeted U-boats, which were already illustrated on the wall plots from the previous day. Every morning, Knowles and his Secret Room staff studied these plots and compared new data with previously identified location references on the Naval Grid.[106] Allied trackers worked together to update their old copies of captured charts with new alterations in the grid location system; thereby maintaining a constant portrait of enemy locations, plans, and initiatives.

The color code was also used as a means of ascertaining the missions and objectives of U-boats already at sea. Secret Room personnel first used the U-boat histories to figure the tonnage of a given U-boat. Then comparing a targeted U-boat's tonnage with certain trends in German submarine strategy, they noticed that Dönitz and his staff usually dispatched 500 ton Type VII U-boats to patrolling areas in the North Atlantic or Mediterranean while the 740 ton Type IX U-boats generally operated in distant or remote patrolling areas.[107] Secret Room trackers then monitored the transmissions between BdU and the U-boats at sea. For example, if a Type VII sailing in 47N 18W was ordered to sail on a heading of "Green XM," the solution of the disguised grid reference might be a patrolling area in the North Atlantic.[108] Through comparative analysis, Secret Room and Admiralty OIC trackers could usually forecast U-boat destinations and identify the disguised grid references with great accuracy.

During spring 1943, the F-21 staff gained priceless experience working with the Admiralty OIC and using all the various methods of tracking U-boats. Although TRITON still complicated Allied tracking operations, Winn and Knowles worked closely together to maintain current and uniform plots on U-boat locations and dispositions. Yet, the F-211 Secret Room was only in the early stages of development in spring 1943. Unauthorized to use the U-boat plotting information to maneuver Allied convoys and escort forces directly, F-21 trackers worked through the COMINCH organization to dispatch information to the fleet. While COMINCH was the higher command, the sea frontier commands primarily controlled convoy routing up to the MOMP. The Admiralty OIC, therefore, continued performing the primary tactical functions of maneuvering convoys away from danger during the first months of 1943. In March, however, the Allies began to reorganize the divisions of labor between the Admiralty and the U.S. Navy. Consequently, the relationship between F-21 and the Admiralty OIC evolved in conjunction with the changes in the Allied war effort in the Atlantic.

By spring 1943, Adm. King was preparing to launch an offensive against the U-boats. On the other side of the hill, Dönitz and his staff were also planning an all-out U-boat offensive in the North Atlantic. Encouraged by the U-boat successes of January and February, Dönitz was confident that a suitable number of operational U-boats was now available to initiate a decisive battle with the Allied convoys.[109] Yet, after nearly a year of war, King held the strategic advantage over Dönitz. Finally controlling enough air and sea escorts to cover many vulnerable points in American waters and with the Interlocking Convoy System, Germans were forced to shift their main U-boat effort back into the North Atlantic "black pit" where Allied air and sea escort strength was still restricted.[110] However, this reshifting of the U-boat offensive was a mixed blessing for the Allies. During the last months of 1942 and early 1943, U-boats operating in the black pit inflicted serious losses on Allied shipping.

The early springtime success in the U-boat offensive influenced President Roosevelt to commit the United States to a drastic wartime strategy. In January 1943, the president surprised many in the Allied hierarchy when he demanded an unconditional surrender from the Axis powers, while meeting with other Allied leaders at the Casablanca Conference. Prior to the president's ultimatum, the other Allied powers were generally unprepared to constrain themselves to such a unilateral war strategy. The Allied coalition had essentially been one of convenience, but when the United States assumed a more assertive role in the war, the other Allied powers of Britain and the Soviet Union were compelled to join the Americans and work more diligently at securing a final victory.

The new Allied commitment to an unconditional total war greatly enhanced Adm. King's status as *the* preeminent naval commander in the Allied coalition. After Casablanca, King was uniquely positioned to assert certain tactical, strategic, and political ideas more forcefully among his fellow Allied commanders. The United States had become the dominant power in the Allied coalition and King was prepared to assume more control over strategy and tactics on the grandest scale. In March, King met with British and Canadian naval leaders in Washington for the Atlantic Convoy Conference. King's primary objective in calling the conference was to devise a new Allied strategy for fighting the U-boats and to clarify political issues with the Admiralty, which had been lingering since the United States formally entered the war in 1941. In the conference, King introduced a new Allied ASW strategy in the Battle of the Atlantic by changing the relationship between the U.S. Navy and the Royal Navy.

Although King personally had much to gain by affirming American seapower over that of the British, his motives were also very pragmatic. Many Allied leaders had already recognized the need for clarifying naval command and control in the Atlantic. As early as fall 1942, Royal Air Force Marshal Philip Joubert de LaFerté proposed a supreme naval command in the Atlantic. He envisioned a command structure similar to that of the Supreme Headquarters Allied Expeditionary Force (SHAEF) under General Dwight Eisenhower in Europe. However, inflated egos and Anglo–American politics impeded the creation of a supreme Atlantic command. During the Atlantic Convoy Conference, King strongly criticized de LaFerté's concept and offered an alternate solution. King simply proposed a realignment of authority, whereby the British, Canadians, and Americans controlled their own forces in the Atlantic. After some deliberation, the idea was endorsed by the British and Canadian delegations. According to the arrangement, the British and Canadians shared the responsibility of controlling the North Atlantic seaways, while the U.S. Navy assumed almost total control over the Central and South Atlantic.[111]

However, King was unwilling to allow the British to assume direct command over American naval forces and he withdrew American naval forces from most convoy escort missions in the North Atlantic. Shortly after the March conference, King formally assumed direct strategic control over U.S. Navy ASW and convoy escort operations on 6 April 1943. He also instructed Adm. Low to study the problem of protecting Allied shipping in the American sectors of operation, which were outside the operational range of land-based aircraft. Low soon submitted a series of recommendations aimed at establishing the maximum escort presence in the American sectors.[112] Based upon Low's report, King created the Tenth Fleet (F-X) in May 1943.[113] Vessels were not specifically assigned to the Tenth Fleet, and the organization essentially served as an administrative body. Nevertheless, Tenth Fleet quickly evolved into a first-rate strategic ASW organization.

The Tenth Fleet was unique and was truly one of King's most brilliant strategic moves during the war. It allowed him to shift Allied ASW strategy away from the defense to the offense. While Adm. Low primarily controlled the daily operations of Tenth Fleet, King symbolically provided all of the authority of COMINCH by assuming direct command over the organization. At the heart of Tenth Fleet operations, King relied on Knowles and his F-21 staff to provide the most current and reliable operational intelligence data for COMINCH and the rest of the fleet. With this in mind, it is interesting to note that King seemed an ominous and distant figure from the F-21 perspective. Knowles remembered King as "a very exclusive person. He wasn't one to be familiar with in any way, a very stern person."[114] Working through Adm. Low, however, Knowles always had direct access to King whenever it was necessary.[115]

Technically speaking, Low's Tenth Fleet had no direct authority to dispatch convoys or escorts. Instead, King preferred an informal relationship between the Tenth Fleet and the tactical commands. Standing as a testament to his remarkable leadership and management ability, King avoided using Tenth Fleet as a omnipotent command with overriding authority. By fostering a corporate atmosphere among his subordinate leaders, King established the Tenth Fleet as an information clearinghouse in support of American fighting forces in the Atlantic. Passing messages through the preexisting sea frontier and fleet commands, Low and the Tenth Fleet staff provided accurate intelligence to Allied tactical commanders in a secure and timely manner.[116] Eventually, the Americans began reshuffling tactical assets and using ULTRA as a means of maneuvering escort forces against U-boats. In the Atlantic, Low's Tenth Fleet served as the brains, while Adm. Royal E. Ingersoll's Atlantic Fleet provided the brawn in the U.S. Navy's ASW offensive against the U-boats after 1943.[117]

With the formation of Tenth Fleet, F-21 increasingly became the most important Allied tactical center for hunting down and destroying enemy forces. Knowles and Low were usually in "hourly" contact, working together at keeping the fleet updated on the latest enemy locations and activities.[118] Knowles himself met regularly with escort commanders before they departed for sea; providing them with detailed estimates of enemy trends in their planned operations area. Gradually, Knowles and his F-21 staff developed great rapport with the tactical commanders themselves, especially when the U.S. Navy began using offensive "hunter-killer" ASW tactics in the Atlantic in summer 1943.[119] For security reasons, it was unnecessary for the hunter-killer task group commanders to have direct knowledge of ULTRA and other forms of SIGINT. However, Knowles remembered that they regarded F-21 information as "more right than wrong and, therefore, they listened very carefully to everything we sent out."[120] Confirming this assessment, one hunter-killer task group commander stated in a postwar report that:

> [t]here was a Commander Ken Knowles in Washington who ran this submarine estimate thing. He was a soothsayer. He could put himself in the position of a German skipper and just figure out what the guy was going to do, and where he would go. He was absolutely uncanny in his predictions.... I treated the COMINCH daily estimate as Bible truth every day, and we based our operations on it completely.[121]

With F-21 providing the means for locating and fixing the enemy, the hunter-killers chased the U-boats away from the convoy lanes. Hunter-killers also moved on F-21 information aggressively; thus, individual U-boats were destroyed and wolfpack concentrations were dissolved. In one case, F-21 had a key role in capturing a U-boat.[122] Most importantly, however, the hunter-killers obliterated the logistical network supporting the U-boats.

In summer 1943, Dönitz and his staff struggled to support those U-boats that had successfully penetrated the Allied air and sea blockade in the Bay of Biscay to reach the open sea. Therefore, F-21 trackers extensively used all the various forms of ULTRA to concentrate hunter-killer groups on attacking the U-tankers and in establishing a constant presence in U-boat resupply areas. Although cryptographic information on the U-tankers was often several days old when it reached the F-211 Secret Room, the Germans customarily designated U-boat rendezvous points up to three weeks in advance. As a result, Knowles and his staff usually had enough time and information to ambush U-boats during the most vulnerable phases of refueling and replenishment. In June 1943, for example, the Germans had a total of nine operational U-tankers. Between June and August, hunter-killer groups played a key role in sinking eight U-tankers and a number of combat U-boats during refueling operations. In a postwar assessment of the effectiveness of hunter-killer tactics in summer 1943, the U-tankers were described as "the pivots which, upon being dislodged, made of B.d.U.'s moving structure a disjointed frame, sagging here, hastily bolstered there, gradually crumbling to inevitable collapse."[123]

In general, the British condemned the Americans for using ULTRA offensively in coordinating hunter-killer attacks. Like many of his superiors at the Admiralty, Winn was paranoid about any operation that might possibly cause the Germans to realize that their codes and cyphers were compromised.[124] Knowles described the differences between the American and British concept of using ULTRA stating that:

> [t]o the British ULTRA was [a] lifesaving operation. I mean, it was the only thing that we had to save Britain from complete destruction.... But Roger had the feel of the British, naturally, of protecting ULTRA at all costs. So they were very cautious in utilizing ULTRA. They made very indirect moves in order to support it with an operational program so that it was completely submerged in this operation. Whereas, over in my area, being younger at the game and also being somewhat aggressive we were using ULTRA more aggressively. There's quite a difference in philosophy here.[125]

Although Winn had many reservations about using ULTRA offensively, the British did attempt hunter-killer tactics in areas like the Indian Ocean where the Eastern Fleet was frequently unequipped to support convoys and cope with Axis submarines. In such cases, however, the Admiralty only authorized ULTRA-based hunter-killer operations when other evidence such as a reconnaissance sighting or HF/DF bearing could also be attributed to an enemy sinking.

Admiralty leaders preferred to use ULTRA with extreme caution, primarily as a means of evading U-boat concentrations, while U.S. Navy leaders adopted a more direct ASW doctrine aimed at hastening the Allied victory in the Battle of the Atlantic.

Although the British and American strategies for fighting the war were very different, the Allies overcame these tensions with the strategic reorganization in spring 1943. In the primary North Atlantic sealanes, the overhaul generally allowed the British to provide greater escort support to the convoys. Meanwhile, Winn and his OIC tracking room staff deprived enemy attackers of clear targets by diverting Allied shipping away from danger, thus forcing the Germans to seek targets in other less decisive operations areas. Covering the more southerly convoy routes, U.S. Navy escort strength was enhanced because issues of command and control were clarified by the formation of Tenth Fleet.

Acting on intelligence collected by F-21 and the Admiralty OIC, Allied convoys traversed the Atlantic safely while American hunter-killer formations brought the overall U-boat offensive to a grinding halt. From summer 1943 to the end of the European war in 1945, F-21 and the Admiralty OIC were involved in destroying a decisive number of strategically important Axis surface vessels and submarines. In the end, the submarine tracking rooms under Winn and Knowles were decisive in sinking more than seventeen surface vessels (fifteen blockade runners and two U-boat refuelers).[126] Similarly, F-21 and the Admiralty OIC undermined Axis submarine operations in the Atlantic and Indian Ocean. By using SIGINT, the OICs guided Allied tactical assets to the exact locations of the enemy, resulting in the "liquidation" of more than ninety-three Axis submarines (fifty-four to U.S. Navy hunter-killer groups).[127] Stressing the importance of Allied operational intelligence, Adm. Low noted in a postwar report that:

> the stated mission for ASW, no matter what line of advance is taken, we always get back to the "hunt them down and kill them" statement which inspires the fire breathers, but to the basic fact that however the skin is taken off this particular cat, the basic accomplishment must be to "deprive the enemy of effective use of his submarines." Even with the discovery ranges of say 40,000 yards, we would still need information as to how to route our most vital shipping. I do not believe that there is any other way around the fact that the single most important

point which must be covered is the maintenance of a high degree of effective operational intelligence for use in combat. Combat intelligence multiplies our effective forces by factors which are impossible to achieve by simply building more units and training more men. Examples which are known to me are the German evaluation of the number of active hunter-killer groups we were operating in the Atlantic during the war. They estimated 200 operating groups at a time when, in actual fact, we had six operating groups plus a high degree of operational intelligence. . . . The Battle of the Atlantic was, in large measure, a battle of wits in which intelligence played the major role. Unfortunately this fact is fully understood only by a relatively small group of officers because of the highly classified nature of the subject.[128]

As Low implied, the Allied naval victory of World War II depended heavily on the contributions of F-21 and the Admiralty OIC. Working together, the Allies secured decisive victory before the Germans could turn the technological tide in the war at sea. Yet, the essential role of F-21 and the Admiralty OIC in defeating Axis naval forces was obscured by postwar secrecy and the Cold War. It is only with the recent declassification of much cryptologic material that we now can appreciate more fully the role of the F-21 organization, under Kenneth Knowles, and the Admiralty OIC tracking room under Rodger Winn, in securing the Allied victory in the Battle of the Atlantic.

NOTES

[1]Patrick Beesly, *Very Special Intelligence: The Story of the Admiralty's Operational Intelligence Center, 1939–1945* (London: Hamish Hamilton, 1977), 192.

[2]College Park, Maryland, National Archives and Records Administration—Archives II (NARA II). Record Group (RG) 38, Records of the Office of the Chief of Naval Operations, World War II Files of the Commander in Chief, Naval Operations (COMINCH), Crane Files, SSIC 3840/2, F-21 Memos Regarding U-boat Tracking and Operations, January 1943–June 1945, Memo of 30 April 1945.

[3]W. S. Chalmers, *Max Horton and the Western Approaches* (London: Hodder and Stoughton, 1954), 170–81.

[4]Samuel Eliot Morison, *History of United States Naval Operations in World War II: The Atlantic Battle Won, May 1943–May 1945* (Boston: Little, Brown and Company, 1956), Vol. X, 24.

[5] Ibid.

[6] Stephen W. Roskill, *The War at Sea, 1939–1945: The Offensive* (London: Her Majesty's Stationary Office, 1960), Vol. III, Part I, 16.

[7] Ibid.

[8] Ladislas Farago, *The Tenth Fleet: The Untold Story of the Submarine and Survival* (New York: Obolensky, 1963), 212-15.

[9] Formed in spring 1943, Tenth Fleet served as the central administrative command for U.S. Navy ASW operations and convoy routing. See ibid., and David Kohnen, *Commanders Winn and Knowles: Winning the U-boat War with Intelligence, 1939–1943* (Kraków, Poland: The Enigma Press, 1999), 120-38.

[10] Jürgen Rohwer explained that he and many other postwar historians suspected that the Allies solved German codes and cyphers during the war. Widely renowned for his tireless work in documenting the Battle of the Atlantic, Rohwer consistently tried to confirm Allied successes in codebreaking and operational intelligence during the 1950s and 1960s. Once described in Patrick Beesly's *Very Special Intelligence* as the historian "who probably knows more about the Battle of the Atlantic than anyone else alive," Rohwer explained how, at one point, he had almost succeeded in confirming his suspicions about wartime Allied intelligence successes. During interviews with British and American veterans who had been "in the know" during the war, Rohwer would make references to the possibility that the Allies had significantly compromised German codes. Then he would watch their reactions to his questions. Nevertheless, Cold War secrecy always hindered Rohwer's quest to substantiate the many rumors and assumptions about Allied codebreaking in World War II. Jürgen Rohwer interview by the author, Stuttgart, Germany, 22 May 1996; Jürgen Rohwer, "Hitler, Raeder, and Dönitz and Their Use of Naval Intelligence," manuscript for a paper presented at The Mariners' Museum, Newport News, Virginia, 25 January 1996; Beesly, *Very Special Intelligence*, 192.

[11] Located approximately sixty miles north of London, Bletchley Park was also known as "BP" or "Station X" among Allied cryptanalysts and intelligence officials during the war.

[12] F. W. Winterbotham, *The Ultra Secret* (New York: Harper & Row, 1974), vii.

[13] W. J. R. Gardner, "An Allied Perspective," in Stephen Howarth and Derek Law, eds., *The Battle of the Atlantic, 1939–1945: The 50th Anniversary International Naval Conference* (Annapolis, Md.: Naval Institute Press, 1994), 530-31.

[14] Beesly, *Very Special Intelligence*, 105.

[15] Patrick Beesly, "Special Intelligence and the Battle of the Atlantic: The British View," in Robert William Love, Jr., ed., *Changing Interpretations and New Sources in Naval History: Papers from the United States Naval Academy History Symposium* (New York: Garland, 1980), 413. See also NARA II, RG 38, COMINCH, Crane Files, "COMINCH F-21 (Atlantic Section of Combat Intell.) War Report on U-boat Tracking, 15 May 1945" (F-21 War Report), NARA Declassification 18 September 1998, 23; London (Kew), Public Record Office (PRO), Records of the Ministry of Defense (Naval), Admiralty Records (ADM), "The Role of Special Intelligence in the Battle of the Atlantic," Part 1 – Admiralty Control in Operations, ADM 223/88, 48-49.

[16] NARA II, RG 38, F-21 War Report, 23, and PRO, ADM 223/88, 48-49.

[17] Allied trackers commonly referred to reports forecasting Axis movements and operations as "guestimates" or "Working Fiction." See Beesly, *Very Special Intelligence*, 60, 172, and Kohnen, *Commanders Winn and Knowles*, 128-30.

[18] Beesly, *Very Special Intelligence*, 115, 265-66.

[19] Beesly, "Special Intelligence in the Battle of the Atlantic: The British View," 413-19.

[20] Jürgen Rohwer, *The Critical Convoy Battles of March 1943: The Battle for HX 229 and SC 122* (Annapolis, Md.: Naval Institute Press, 1977), 192-244.

21. Jürgen Rohwer, "Special Intelligence and the Battle of the Atlantic: The German View," in Robert William Love, Jr., ed., *Changing Interpretations and New Sources in Naval History: Papers from the United States Naval Academy History Symposium* (New York: Garland, 1980), 420–43.

22. Kenneth A. Knowles, "Special Intelligence and the Battle of the Atlantic: The American View," in Robert William Love, Jr., ed., *Changing Interpretations and New Sources in Naval History: Papers from the United States Naval Academy History Symposium* (New York: Garland, 1980), 444–49.

23. Ibid., 446–7.

24. Ibid., 448–49.

25. NARA II, Records of the National Security Agency (RG 457), "Bombe History," NR 1736, Box 705, formally declassified in 1996. See also Kohnen, *Commanders Winn and Knowles*, 63–74.

26. For example, King's former roommate at the Naval Academy Class of 1901, Adm. Adolphus Andrews, now Commander of the United States Eastern Sea Frontier, openly opposed plans for centralizing U-boat tracking activities. King tolerated some debate among his subordinates as long as they were working to achieve some sort of solution. Once King made a decision, however, he was less patient. See Love, "Ernest Joseph King," 137–79; Farago, *The Tenth Fleet*, 91–96; and Andrews' defiant remarks in the NHC, OA, "Eastern Sea Frontier War Diary, June–August 1942."

27. For more on the role of the *Paukenschlag* crisis in fostering Anglo-American cooperation, see Kohnen, *Commanders Winn and Knowles*, 33–53.

28. In summer 1942, Laird (F-11) was administratively detached from support for the F-35 section, and he reported directly to the Assistant Chief of War Plans (F-1). Wyman H. Packard, *A Century of U.S. Naval Intelligence* (Washington, D.C.: Naval Historical Center, 1996), 204.

29. Beesly, *Very Special Intelligence*, 172.

30. For more on Ghormley, the "Citadel," and the Admiralty tracking room, see Kohnen, *Commanders Winn and Knowles*, 8–20.

31. Washington, D.C., Naval Historical Center (NHC), Operational Archives (OA), COMINCH Correspondence, Ghormley to King, 6 April 1942.

32. For more on the GC&CS and OP-20-G negotiations and agreements of 1942, see Kohnen, *Commanders Winn and Knowles*, 53–75.

33. See Beesly, *Very Special Intelligence*, 114–16; Thomas Parrish, *The ULTRA Americans: The U.S. Role in Breaking the Nazi Codes* (New York: Stein and Day, 1986), 150–51; and Bradley F. Smith, *The Codebreakers War: ULTRA–MAGIC Deals* (Novato, Calif.: Presidio, 1993), 122–23.

34. Smith, *The ULTRA–MAGIC Deals*, 123.

35. Beesly, *Very Special Intelligence*, 115.

36. Farago, *The Tenth Fleet*, 214–15.

37. On 19 August 1986, NSA historian Thomas R. Johnson conducted an oral history interview with Knowles shortly before his death in November 1986. In September 1998, Johnson told the author in a telephone conversation that Knowles was "extremely lucid and sharp" throughout the interview in which Knowles discussed all aspects of his naval career. Describing the physical disabilities that initially put him out of the navy, Knowles stated that "[w]ithout radar in those early days, eyesight was very important for a naval officer and my glasses didn't correct the necessary . . . [pause] and I also had hearing disabilities which were eventually stabilized, but my eyesight never was." NSA, Center for Cryptologic History (CCH), Oral History Interview with Kenneth A. Knowles (NSA OH-22-86), Conducted by T. R. Johnson at Captain Knowles' Residence in Stuart, Florida, 19 August 1986, Declassified 21 July 1998, 2.

38. Ibid.

39. Farago, *The Tenth Fleet*, 215.

40. Ibid.

A Fresh Look into the "Secret Room" 335

⁴¹Annapolis, Md., U.S. Naval Academy Yearbook, *The Lucky Bag of 1927*, 252.
⁴²NSA, CCH, OH-22-86, 3.
⁴³Farago, *The Tenth Fleet*, 214–15.
⁴⁴Ibid.
⁴⁵NSA, CCH, OH-22-86, 3.
⁴⁶Ibid.
⁴⁷Ibid., and Farago, *The Tenth Fleet*, 214–15.
⁴⁸NSA, CCH, OH-22-86, 4.
⁴⁹Ibid.
⁵⁰NARA II, RG 38, F-21 War Report, 23, and Beesly, "Special Intelligence and the Battle of the Atlantic: The British View," 413.
⁵¹Ibid., 21.
⁵²For more on the M4 Enigma and the TRITON "blackout" of 1942, see Kohnen, *Commanders Winn and Knowles*, 64–71.
⁵³Chalmers, *Max Horton and the Western Approaches*, 124.
⁵⁴NARA II, RG 38, F-21 War Report, 4.
⁵⁵Ibid., 4.
⁵⁶Farrago, *The Tenth Fleet*, 216.
⁵⁷On 1 July 1943, the former F-35 "war room" organization was formally dissolved and replaced with the F-2 command, under Rear Adm. Roscoe E. Schuirmann, USN. The former "war room" sections were then assigned new designations to reflect a given area of interest under F-2. For example, F-21, under Knowles, focused on the Atlantic and Indian Ocean while F-22, under Lt. Comdr. William J. Sebald, concentrated on the Pacific. NARA II, RG 38, Crane Files, COMINCH Intelligence Organization—F-22, World War II, NARA declassification 9 September 1998, 1–5.
⁵⁸WAVES is the acronym for Women Accepted into Volunteer Emergency Service. The Admiralty OIC also relied heavily on women serving in the WRNS, Women's Royal Navy Service.
⁵⁹NARA II, RG 38, F-21 War Report, 14.
⁶⁰Ibid., 7.
⁶¹Ibid., 14.
⁶²NSA, CCH, OH-22-86, 30.
⁶³NARA II, RG 457, SRMN-038, 1–2. See also copies of the original estimates in NARA II, RG 457, SRMN-036, "COMINCH File of U-boat Situation Estimates 15 June 1942–21 May 1945."
⁶⁴Ibid.
⁶⁵Ibid.
⁶⁶NARA II, RG 38, F-21 War Report, 16.
⁶⁷Ibid., 13–14.
⁶⁸Ibid.
⁶⁹NARA II, RG 457, SRMN-038, "Functions of the 'Secret Room' (F-211) of COMINCH Combat Intelligence, Atlantic Section, Anti–Submarine Warfare, WWII," UNDATED, 1.
⁷⁰NARA II, RG 38, F-21 War Report, 20.
⁷¹Ibid. See also copies of the original locations lists in NARA II, RG 457, SRMN-034, "COMINCH Rough Notes on Daily U-boat Positions and Activities, 1943–1945."
⁷²F-21 and the Admiralty OIC used the same charts to plot U-boat locations. Therefore, F-21 used charts from the British Home Office (H.O.) Inside the F-211 Secret Room, the basic chart used in tracking U-boats in the Atlantic was number H.O. Misc. 9901. This chart was smaller in scale than the chart for the Indian Ocean, which was H.O. Misc. 9817. As a result, the two charts were slightly incompatible when they were taped together. NARA II, RG 457, SRMN-038, 2.
⁷³Ibid. See also the original charts produced by F-211 and COMINCH personnel in NARA II, RG 457.1.

⁷⁴As a means of identification, BdU assigned each U-boat skipper a "bigram" signature for use in Enigma communications. For example, the skipper of U.188 was Lt. Siegfried Lüdden. Between 1942 and 1944, his bigram was "HM." F-21 trackers used the HM signature as a means of cataloging and documenting the exact identification of who was commanding U.188 during the vessel's training cruises and three war patrols. NARA II, RG 457, SRMN-038, 2.

⁷⁵Ibid.

⁷⁶Knowles never visited the OP-20-G codebreaking facility on Nebraska Avenue. When asked about Nebraska Avenue, Knowles stated that in the Secret Room "[w]e weren't curious about their end of it, we were curious only in terms of what they were producing. Incidentally, the British were great pioneers in this whole breaking of the German cypher, and continued to be so, but eventually our own capabilities actually exceeded that of the British." He went on to describe the codebreakers as "a pretty exclusive society. . . a weird group." NSA, CCH, OH-22-86, 20-21.

⁷⁷For more on the arrangements for sharing intelligence secrets as negotiated by U.S. Navy Comdr. Joseph N. Wenger, OP-20-G, and Sir Edward Travis, Director of GC&CS, see Kohnen, *Commanders Winn and Knowles*, 69-74.

⁷⁸NARA II, RG 457, SRMN-038, 3-4.

⁷⁹Ibid., 4-5. Also see the original 5x7 index cards in NARA II, RG 38, Records of COMINCH, organized by hull number, date and time group, operational covernames, and Allied code names.

⁸⁰NARA II, RG 457, SRMN-038, 3-4.

⁸¹"*Yanagi*" was the Axis covername for blockade running operations between Europe and Asia and for the exchange of critical materials and technology. Initially, surface vessels performed the *Yanagi* missions. Later, submarines were used after the surface blockade runners became too vulnerable to Allied attack. Information derived from ULTRA and MAGIC enabled the Allies to locate, track, and attack the *Yanagi* vessels during their long east-west voyages. By late 1944, the *Yanagi* program was for all intents and purposes eliminated by superior, and precisely deployed, Allied naval power. See Carl Boyd's works *American Command of the Sea Through Carriers, Codes, and the Silent Service* (Newport News, VA: The Mariners' Museum, 1995), 22, and *Hitler's Japanese Confidant: General Ōshima Hiroshi and MAGIC Intelligence, 1941-1945* (Lawrence: University Press of Kansas, 1993), 48-49.

⁸²NARA II, RG 457, SRMN-038, 4.

⁸³Ibid., 5.

⁸⁴Ibid.

⁸⁵Ibid., 5-6.

⁸⁶Ibid.

⁸⁷Ibid., 6.

⁸⁸See copies of some of the messages in NARA II, RG 38, Crane Files, "Admiralty-COMINCH ULTRA Message Exchange, 25 June 1942-17 October 1944," an uncensored version of RG 457, SRMN-035, NARA declassification 18 September 1998.

⁸⁹NARA II, RG 457, SRMN-038, 6.

⁹⁰Ibid., 2-3, 9.

⁹¹"U/B" was commonly used by Allied trackers as an abbreviation for the word "U-boat." Ibid., 9.

⁹²For example, F-21 declared U.188, under Lieutenant Lüdden, as being sunk west of the Cape Verde Islands at 16N and 32W on 6 May 1944. F-21 trackers used ULTRA as a means of guiding a "hunter-killer" group of four destroyers and the USS *Block Island* (CVE 21) into position for an ambush. Since the northbound U.188 was out of torpedoes and returning to port, BdU directed Lüdden to provide fuel to the U.66, under the veteran skipper Lt. Gerhard Seehusen. The BdU message included the exact location of the rendezvous. Allied codebreakers provided that

information to the F-21 trackers who then monitored the progress of both U-boats as they sailed to the appointed position. U.66 was ultimately destroyed in a particularly violent attack by the USS *Buckley* (DE 51), under Lt. Comdr. Brent M. Abel, USNR. Caught on the surface, U.66 was rammed by *Buckley* and, as his crew fought a bitter hand to hand battle with the Americans, Seehusen sent a final desperate message to BdU stating *"Atlantikmitte schlimmer als Biskaya"* (Mid-Atlantic is worse than the Bay of Biscay). Submerged, Lüdden watched the attack at a distance through his periscope—later describing in his logbook *"Immernoch rollen Wabo-und Fliebodetonationen"* (constantly rolling waves of depth charge and depth bomb detonations). As Lüdden diverted U.188 away from the doomed U.66, he recorded that a feeling of great despair spread among his crew as their comrades were being cut down before their eyes, which for Lüdden was like a *"schlag ins Gesicht"* (a punch in the face). Following the sinking of U.66, no messages were intercepted from U.188. Their radio transmitter had failed and it was impossible to send messages. Consequently, both BdU and F-21 trackers declared both U-boats as being sunk in the same attack. In June 1944, F-21 discovered in German radio traffic that U.188 had surprisingly survived the battle of early May. As a result, U.188 was removed from the F-21 roster of "liquidated" U-boats. See Lüdden's account of the attack in TMM, Ktb. U.188, 6-7 May 1944, David Kohnen, comp. See also the BdU report on the sinking of U.188 in NARA II, RG 242, BdU/Ktb., May 1944, and the F-21 assessment committee report on "Case 6269" in NARA II, RG 457, SRMN-037, "COMINCH File of U-boat Intelligence Summaries, January 1943-May 1945," Entry of 22 June 1944, 407.

[93]NARA II, RG 457, SRMN-038, 6.
[94]Ibid.
[95]NSA, CCH, OH-22-86, 22-23; Farrago, *The Tenth Fleet*, 147-56; and Packard, *A Century of U.S. Naval Intelligence*, 124-29.
[96]NARA II, RG 457, SRMN-038, 6.
[97]Ibid., 7.
[98]Ibid.
[99]Kenneth A. Knowles, "ULTRA and the Battle of the Atlantic: The American View," in Love, ed., *Changing Interpretations*, 445.
[100]NARA II, RG 457, SRMN-038, 6.
[101]Ibid.
[102]Ibid.
[103]Ibid.
[104]Jak P. Mallman Showell, *The German Navy in World War II: A Reference Guide to the Kriegsmarine, 1935-1945* (Annapolis, Md.: Naval Institute Press, 1979), 216.
[105]F-211 Secret Room trackers possessed copies of the main grid for *Nordatlantischer Ozean Nr. 1870G* (North Atlantic Number 1870G), *Südatlantischer Ozean Nr. 3500* (South Atlantic Number 3500), *Ansatzblatt zu 1903G-Nordpolarmeer* (Arctic polar seas to the chart for 1903G), and finally for the *Indischer Ozean*.
[106]NARA II, RG 457, SRMN-038, 8.
[107]Ibid.
[108]Ibid.
[109]Rohwer, *Critical Convoy Battles*, 47-49.
[110]The "black pit" was an area south of Greenland that was beyond the operational range of convoy air escorts. The colloquialism was widely used among Allied merchant sailors.
[111]The Allies also expanded the number of vessels assigned to convoys after the Atlantic Convoy Conference. Based upon a study conducted as result of the conference, Allied analysts found that the Germans were rarely able to concentrate more than ten U-boats in a wolfpack against Allied convoys between 1941 and 1943. Therefore, vessels that had sailed with smaller convoys were found to have been in greater danger than those that sailed in larger convoys. The study effectively illustrated the most efficient way of using the finite number of escorts in

protecting a greater number of vessels in convoy. Farago, *The Tenth Fleet*, 157–66; Rohwer, *Critical Convoy Battles*, 187–88; and William T. Y'Blood, *Hunter-Killer: U.S. Escort Carriers in the Battle of the Atlantic* (Annapolis, Md.: Naval Institute Press, 1983), 31–32.

[112]Farago, *The Tenth Fleet*, 166, and Packard, *A Century of U.S. Naval Intelligence*, 206.

[113]According to one author, the Tenth Fleet designation was "picked out of the hat" by King. On 15 March 1943, King reassigned the numbers of U.S. Navy fleets according to their geographic operations areas. American fleets in the Pacific were given odd numbers while those assigned to the Atlantic had even numbers. Since the Tenth Fleet mainly focused on defeating U-boats in the Atlantic, the organization was assigned an even number. Farago, *The Tenth Fleet*, 167.

[114]NSA, CCH, OH-22-86, 14–15.

[115]Ibid., 31–32.

[116]Each sea frontier command maintained a plotting room similar to the main COMINCH plotting room in Washington, D.C. F-21 updated the frontier commands by sending sanitized dispatches over a scrambled teletype printer network. Fleet commands then dispatched plotting references and operations orders to the relevant tactical units. These dispatches often referenced F-21 as the original source of the information. Eventually, it was possible for Knowles to send routing dispatches to specific tactical units without first sending the information through another command. For some examples of dispatches sent from F-21 to the fleet commands and forwarded to the maneuver units, see NARA II, RG 38, "Dispatches and Records from Chart Room-COMINCH, 1941–46."

[117]Ingersoll was later replaced as CINCLANT by Adm. Jonas H. Ingram in 1944.

[118]NSA, CCH, OH-22-86, 9.

[119]By fall 1943, the Allies were using medium sized escort "jeep" carriers (CVEs) to establish an air umbrella over areas in the Atlantic which were beyond the operational range of land-based aircraft. With the formation of Tenth Fleet, the Americans began using information compiled in the Secret Room to support "hunter-killer" ASW tactics. Acting on information supplied by F-21, hunter-killer groups could often intercept and destroy enemy targets with extreme precision. A typical American hunter-killer formation usually included destroyers (DD) or destroyer escorts (DE) working with a CVE. For a comprehensive study on American hunter-killer tactics and operations in World War II, see Y'Blood, *Hunter-Killer*.

[120]NSA, CCH, OH-22-86, 7.

[121]NHC, OA, OH, "Reminiscences of Daniel V. Gallery, 26 May 1945," 88.

[122]On 4 June 1944, hunter-killer task group TG.22.3 used F-21 information to intercept and capture Lt. Harald Lange's U.505 (Type IXC) north of the cape Verde Islands, approximately 150nm off Cape Blanco along the western coast of Africa. Under the overall command of Capt. Daniel V. Gallery, USN, TG.22.3 included USS *Guadalcanal* (CVE 60), USS *Pillsbury* (DE 133), USS *Pope* (DE 134), USS *Flaherty* (DE 135), USS *Chatelain* (DE 149), and USS *Jenks* (DE 665). Before departing from Norfolk with TG.22.3 in May, Gallery visited the main COMINCH plotting room where he received a detailed briefing from Knowles (F-21) and Capt. Henri Smith-Hutton, USN, Assistant Chief of Staff, COMINCH Combat Intelligence (F-20). Known for what Smith-Hutton referred to as "having the tendency for exaggerating the extreme," Gallery wanted information from the COMINCH staff, which would be useful in capturing a U-boat. Although Gallery was not given direct access to cryptographic ULTRA, Knowles told him that he may face 500-ton Type VII U-boats, but to expect the longer range Type IX series in his planned operations area south of the Azores Islands. Knowles also showed Gallery the sailing routes most commonly used by U-boats in that area. Smith-Hutton then gave Gallery detailed drawings of Type VII and Type IX U-boats. Compiled by the

A Fresh Look into the "Secret Room" 339

ONI Technical Intelligence section (OP-16-PT), the drawings included references to the possible locations of key sea valves and the most likely places where scuttling charges might be situated. Sailors serving under Gallery then used this information to rehearse boarding party procedures. Following the capture, U.505 was towed to Bermuda where Knowles and Adm. Low examined the U-boat and participated in POW interrogations. The cryptographic material found aboard U.505 included an Enigma M4 and the latest edition of the Naval Grid. Yet, Knowles remembered that the most significant items found aboard U.505 were examples of the latest acoustic homing torpedo known as T-V *"Zaunkönig"* (wren). For the capture, TG.22.3 received the Presidential Unit Citation and individuals on the boarding party were decorated, including one Congressional Medal of Honor. Though they had a key role in each phase of the much-vaunted capture of U.505, American naval intelligence personnel only received a highly classified commendation from COMINCH. Due to cold war secrecy, Gallery was also unable to reveal the pivotal role of F-21 when he wrote his memoirs of the capture, though he did send Knowles a photograph of himself standing in the battered U.505 conning tower. In 1954, U.505 was placed on display at the Museum of Science and Industry in Chicago, Illinois. Ibid., 64–80; NSA, CCH, OH-22-86, 9–12, 32; and NHC, OA, OH, "U.S. Naval Institute Oral History with Capt. Henri H. Smith-Hutton, 1979," Vol. II, 394–402. Documents used by members of the American boarding party in seizing U.505 are available in Chicago, Illinois, The Museum of Science and Industry (MSI), Archives, U.505 Manuscript Collection, "Boarding and Sa[lv]age Bill," Used by Boatswain's Mate Second Class Wayne Pickels, USN, Box 1, Folder 1. See also the works of Daniel V. Gallery, *Clear the Decks!* (New York: William Morrow, 1951), and *Twenty Million Tons Under the Sea* (Chicago: Henry Regnery, 1956). Stephen W. Roskill accused Gallery of grandstanding and overstating the importance of capturing U.505 in his 1959 work *The Secret Capture*. Roskill also reviews the heroic exploits of British sailors in capturing a number of enemy vessels, including the U.110.

[123]NSA, CCH, GC&CS Naval History, Part 6, 344.

[124]NSA, CCH, OH-22-86, 5–6.

[125]Ibid., 6.

[126]See NARA II, RG 457, SRH 260, "OP-20-G File of Memoranda, Reports and Messages on German Blockade Runners (World War II) (1943–1944)." This study contains location reports and operational dispatches relating to blockade running Axis surface vessels and selected enemy submarines. SRH 260 also includes some detailed diagrams of the search and attack tactics employed by U.S. Navy attackers in sinking many of the blockade-runners.

[127]This figure only reflects the number of Axis submarines that were "liquidated" as a direct result of Allied SIGINT and the hunter-killer tactics used primarily by the Americans. F-21 and the Admiralty OIC were, nevertheless, involved in other sinkings not listed in NARA II, RG 457, SRMN-051A, Vol. II, "OP-20-GI Memoranda to COMINCH F21 on German U-boat Activities," Appendix I, "U-boats Sunk by U.S. Forces with the Aid of Radio Intelligence."

[128]NHC, OA, "United States Naval Administrative Histories of World War II, Appendices Collection," Command Files, Low Report, Francis F. Low, *A Study of Undersea Warfare*, TOP SECRET Annex, Draft submitted on 1 January 1946.

Part V

The U.S. Navy Since World War II

A New Cold War: U.S. Marines in Norway and the Search for a New Mission in NATO

David B. Crist

> Developments in naval and defense issues are seldom the result of one man's inspired vision. More often they result from the confluence of a variety of motives that coincide to produce change. In this essay, David Crist demonstrates how Norwegian concern about a Soviet buildup on the Kola Peninsula in the 1970s, and the eagerness of the U.S. Marine Corps in the post-Vietnam era to broaden its mission, led to the implementation of a new NATO strategy for the defense of Europe's northern flank. Despite political, diplomatic, and logistic difficulties, these twin concerns eventually led to the establishment of a new element in NATO's overall war plan and a new mission for U.S. Marines. Though the Cold War came to an end before the policy could be fully evaluated, this case study shows how the various elements of naval and defense planning interact to bring about change.

In the mid 1970s, the United States and Norway began new military planning about the defense of NATO's northern flank. Spurred by growing fears of increased Soviet military capabilities on the Kola Peninsula, which threatened the sea lines of communication into central Europe, both Washington and Oslo took a new look at the threat in the Arctic Circle. For Norway this marked a major change in her participation in NATO, overcoming historic resistance to allowing military equipment to be based in its territory. For the U.S. military, especially the Marine Corps, the threat to Norway initiated a new commitment to NATO. Norway offered the Marine Corps an opportunity to operate in Europe for the first time in decades with a mission that was tailor-made for the unique capabilities of the service. Its amphibious and closely integrated air-ground task forces fit perfectly into the challenges

David B. Crist is a historian at the Marine Corps Historical Center in Washington, D.C.

posed in defending the fjords and mountain passes of Norway. In the process, the Marines developed new innovative doctrine, which culminated with the prepositioning of equipment in "caves" which allowed for a rapid reinforcement of Norway in the event of war.

With a population less than Manhattan, Norway's strategic value lay primarily in its location. Other than Turkey, Norway was the only NATO country to share a common border (122 miles) with the Soviet Union. Its long 1,600-mile coastline is punctuated by deep, ice-free fjords, which had served the German surface and submarine forces well during World War II. Further, it lay along the shortest line of flight between the U.S. and the Soviet Union and was the likely route for strategic bombers destined for either country in the event of a major war. Additionally, the U.S. and Soviet Union viewed Norway's northern airfields as critical in any conflict. The large airbases at Bodo and Orland, in central Norway, were an important part in NATO's air defense scheme and contained all of Norway's fighter aircraft. Additionally, anti-submarine assets, both fixed-wing and helicopter, stationed in the far north at Bardufoss and Tromsö would be paramount in attacking Soviet submarines of the Northern Fleet.

If NATO controlled the northern Norwegian airfields, it could press forward toward the Soviet bases and bottle up the Soviet naval forces while simultaneously ensuring the safety of the main sea lines of communication (SLOCs) into Germany. These sat astride the route that would be used by 90% of the U.S. reinforcements to NATO's central front. NATO planners feared that if the Soviets seized the airfields in Norway, combined with their strong presence in the Norwegian Sea, they could literally cut the NATO supply line into the main front in Germany.[1] This would allow the Soviets to push an air umbrella well west toward the Greenland–Iceland–United Kingdom [G-I-UK] gap. This, coupled with their large number of attack submarines, could drive out NATO naval forces giving them unhindered access into the North Atlantic, especially for their ballistic missile submarines which would then be positioned to attack the United States. Further, controlling northern Norway safeguarded the Kola Peninsula, which was critical to the Soviet's air defense and early warning system as well as home to two-thirds of their ballistic missile submarines. In short, the war in Europe might not be won in the northern flank, but it could be lost there.

For the first two decades of the East-West rivalry in Europe, NATO viewed Norway, as one NATO official would later admit, "with benign neglect." This is not to say that NATO ignored the northern flank; one of the first major NATO naval exercises (MAIN BRACE) held off Norway in 1952, involved no fewer than six aircraft carriers in an operation designed to threaten Soviet naval bases.[2] However, the Soviets simply lacked the capacity to seriously threaten the U.S. Navy outside of their coastal waters. Vietnam took center-stage throughout the 1960s, and the Commander-in-Chief, Atlantic Fleet, devoted much of his time and effort to providing forces to Southeast Asia rather than dealing with a growing Soviet Northern Fleet.

By the 1970s, the Soviets had built up a considerable military presence in the Kola Peninsula providing them an offensive capability to threaten NATO and the U.S. Navy. Two motorized rifle divisions were permanently positioned on the Norwegian border, with ten other divisions designated as reinforcements.[3] In addition, an airborne division and two specialized brigades, naval infantry and a special forces (*Spetsnaz*) had been added to the Soviet forces and appeared to be positioned to strike quickly against Norway's northern airfields. The Soviet Northern Fleet Air Force alone had over 400 aircraft, with an additional 450 air defense and tactical aircraft.[4] Even more alarming for NATO was the rapid growth of Soviet northern naval forces. These nearly doubled from 1965–1980, with over 130 attack submarines and eighty major warships. At the same time, the number of ballistic missile submarines rose from eighteen to thirty-nine by 1980 and comprised nearly two-thirds of the Soviet ballistic missile fleet.

For Norway, the German invasion in 1940 had demonstrated the limitations of neutrality for a small country with limited defense resources—a mistake their government was determined not to repeat. Membership in NATO, in conjunction with Sweden's large regional force, provided Oslo security from its large Soviet neighbor. But Norway, with its strong pacifist and neutralist streak, brought its own twists to NATO. As the Norwegian Minister of Defense, Johan Jorgen Holst later described it: "In relation to the Soviet Union the posture reflects a trade-off between considerations of deterrence and reassurance . . . Unmitigated pursuit of deterrence could result in provocation, while maximizing reassurance could lead to appeasement."[5] Oslo had no intention of deliberately antagonizing her large neighbor. As a precondition to NATO membership, Norwegians had refused to allow foreign troops to be based on their soil and would not allow their territory to be used for offensive action, unless Norway itself were attacked.[6] In short, Norway wanted to keep NATO over the horizon, but close enough to come to its aid in the event of an attack. Over the next two decades, Norway reaffirmed the no basing policy and placed further restrictions on NATO forces to prevent them from operating near its border with the Soviet Union.

However, the build-up of Soviet forces on the Kola Peninsula alarmed the Norwegian government, since the Soviets forces now dwarfed the combined forces of all the Nordic countries. Whereas in 1949, the Soviet Union did not pose a serious threat to Norway, by the early 1970s Soviet submarines and aircraft threatened the very NATO reinforcements vital to Norway's survival. As Minster of Defense, Holst noted:

> Allied assistance was dependent on transportation by sea, and Soviet submarines and naval aircraft . . . emerged as a potential threat against real effectuation in an emergency . . . With the growing might of the Soviet Northern fleet based upon the Kola peninsula, the Soviet Union has been able to move her defense perimeter still further west and south into the Norwegian Sea, down to the G-I-UK gap. A bonus effect would be, of course, to separate Norway from the source of planned reinforcement.[7]

Within the Norwegian government, there was little enthusiasm for increased defense spending. However, as weapons and manpower costs rose, it became increasingly difficult for such a small expenditure to maintain a modern force.[8] As a 1974 U.S. State Department document observed, "most Norwegians preferred to allocate their national resources to social welfare, not for a war which seemed unlikely or unwinnable."[9]

In 1970 and 1971, the Norwegian government conducted several classified studies outlining the growing threat of the Soviet fleet and the danger of the decreased NATO naval presence in the northern waters. Released to the public in March 1972 by the Ministry of Defense, these reports concluded that "the Soviet defensive zone encompassed all of the Norwegian Sea and the approaches to the Atlantic coasts of Britain, Ireland, and Iceland."[10] Few missed the assertion that the whole of Norway lay behind the Soviet's defensive zone. As Norwegian Defense Minster Alf Jakob Fostervoll stated, "Norway would have to creep further under NATO's umbrella."[11]

While Oslo publicly voiced its concerns, it also quietly began lobbying the Pentagon about the Soviet threat. In a visit to Washington in November 1970, Foreign Minister Svenn Stray found little interest among U.S. officials, including Henry Kissinger. However, they found a more receptive ear in the Chief of Naval Operations (CNO), Adm. Elmo R. Zumwalt. Zumwalt had close contacts with Norwegian officials, especially the Chief of Defense, Adm. Folke Hauger Johanessen. Following a 1971 visit to Norway, Admiral Zumwalt noted, "Norway feels increasingly behind the Soviet line . . ." and added that the Norwegian's military position had weakened due to the increased Soviet military strength and the difficulty of NATO's ability to reinforce the northern flank.[12] Over the next few years, Washington and Oslo held formal and informal talks about how best to deal with the Soviets.

Norwegian concerns coincided with the U.S. Navy's re-examination of its own global strategy and development of what would later become known as the Forward Maritime Strategy (FMS). In the early 1970s, Navy planners concentrated on the second of Zumwalt's "Four Missions of the U.S. Navy" — control of the sea.[13] The Navy began studying a new aggressive war strategy which entailed advancing on the Soviets using submarines and carrier strike forces. The new strategy was designed to engage the enemy fleet as close to its bases as possible, bottle it up and destroy its offensive capability. Refined over the next decade, FMS came to fruition in the 1980s. The outgrowth of this new thinking was a greatly increased role in NATO for the U.S. Navy. In the late 1970s the CNO Adm. Thomas Bibb Hayward renewed this emphasis on Europe and outlined that any NATO-Warsaw Pact conflict would be worldwide, and the SLOCs would be extremely vulnerable without maritime superiority. Nowhere was this more apparent than the northern flank. As former Commanding Officer of 2d Fleet Adm. Henry C. Mustin noted: "The Norway defense was integral in the FMS, where both the land campaign and the Navy are integrally linked with the success of the central front rested on its success."[14] While Norwegian officials would later take credit for nudging the U.S. into addressing the northern flank issue, SACEUR, the CNO, and SACLANT had all arrived at the same conclusion, Norway's lobbying serving to reinforce their opinions.

While still maintaining their no basing stance, Norway quietly began pushing for an increased American presence. In May 1971, U.S. Navy and Royal Norwegian Air Force representatives negotiated an agreement in Oslo that permitted the storage of aviation fuel and ammunition at Bodo and two other airfields for use by Navy aircraft.[15] In May 1974, the Norwegians agreed to allow U.S. Air Force aircraft use of their airfields. This was part of the U.S. Consolidated Operating Bases (COB) which allowed for minimally essential airfields from which aircraft arriving from the U.S. could operate. In August 1975 the agreement was revised to include the airbases in northern Norway.

The immediate aftermath of Vietnam was not an especially happy time for the Marine Corps. Racial tensions, discipline problems, and drug use occupied much of the Marine Corps leadership's attention. Even more alarming to many within the Corps was the rising chorus from Washington that the service had become irrelevant. The Ford, and later Carter, Administrations focused their defense efforts on Europe and NATO. The Marine Corps, which had operated almost exclusively in the Pacific since 1941, had little presence in Europe, an area where few defense experts saw any real opportunity for amphibious operations. The

Secretary of Defense, James R. Schlesingner, even publicly doubted whether the Marines could conduct an amphibious operation in a high threat environment such as would occur in a European war.[16] Some argued that the Marine Corps should be reduced from its configuration of three divisions and three wings, which had been established for nearly three decades before. A 1976 Brookings Institute study advocated reducing the Corps's amphibious emphasis, drastically reducing its tactical aviation, and increasing its support of the Army in Europe.[17] Others, such as William Lind, argued that the Marine Corps was inadequately prepared to operate in heavily mechanized warfare, as would undoubtedly be the case in a war in central Europe and had recently occurred in the Middle East during the 1973 Arab-Israeli War.[18]

The Marine Corps responded to this criticism by pointing out the innovations currently underway within the service, chiefly the soon-to-be-introduced Vertical Takeoff and Landing (V/STOL) Harrier which would provide new capabilities. Further, what became known as the Haynes Report noted that the Marines' mission transcended the traditional maritime role by embracing "a multitude of global missions which the Marine Corps is uniquely qualified to fulfill because of its responsiveness, combined arms organization, and its ability to conduct operation on the land, sea, and in the air."[19]

But within the senior leadership of the Marine Corps, opinion grew that the service needed to tie itself to a NATO mission. In 1975, the Assistant Commandant, Lt. Gen. Samuel J. Jaskilka and others lobbied the new Commandant, Gen. Louis H. Wilson, for a stronger NATO mission.[20] They (including Wilson) believed this was a necessity if the Marine Corps wanted to compete for scarce defense dollars. These concerns seemed well-founded. President Carter's first defense budget increased NATO-specific accounts by five percent, or two and one-half times more than the defense budget as a whole was slated to grow. As the *Washington Post* pointed out, "Service leaders, acutely aware that NATO is the name of the game, are putting Vietnam out of their minds and concentrating on widening their roles in Europe."[21]

The Marine Corps had not completely ignored Europe, but it operated on the periphery. A reinforced battalion, in various forms, had continuously operated in the Mediterranean supporting the Seventh Fleet since 1948. Additionally, since 1950 two Marine Expeditionary Forces (MEFs) had been designated as theater reserves in the event of a large scale conflict with the Soviets. The Marine Corps exercised this plan in 1964 with Operation STEEL PIKE—a large scale operation by II MEF held in southern Spain. But in reality, the Fleet Marine Force Atlantic took a back seat to its counterpart based in Hawaii.

The question, therefore, was not if, but where in Europe could the Marine Corps increase its role. Central Europe had little appeal. The service lacked the mechanized assets to add any substantial capability to that of the Army's two corps, and might even work to the Marine Corps' detriment as critics could then charge that the nation had no need for two land armies. The flanks of NATO held the most promise, where the Corps could operate closely with the Navy and utilize its unique amphibious capabilities. While the Mediterranean held promise and the Marines remained committed to reinforcing the southern flank, General Wilson believed there was little "opportunity to use any combat troops for amphibious operations even in the case of a massive attack to the west."[22]

Norway, however, offered many opportunities. As the Navy began to reassess the threat to the northern flank, Marine Corps planners at FMFLant and Plans and Operations at Headquarters Marine Corps, examined how the Marine Corps could best support Navy plans to contain the Soviet fleet. Two areas in the north seemed to hold the most promise. One was northern Norway where Marines could secure valuable airfields. From these, Marine Corps, as well as Air Force and Navy aircraft, could operate as a land-based carrier.[23] This would provide a formidable integrated air defense by combining both sea-based and land-based aircraft in support of the U.S. Navy's campaign to contain the Soviet northern fleet. As General Wilson pointed out in 1977, "Without question, a ready amphibious force of U.S. Marines in full partnership with the U.S. Navy offers a powerful deterrent, a flexible asset for planners and a strong adjunct to total forces for use . . . weather in the air, on the land or sea."[24]

The other possible site for employing Marines was in Denmark and the Jutland Peninsula. The narrows north of Kiel in Schlewig-Hosltein offered a highly defensible position where Marine refinements could provide a secure "island" for NATO airbases, which could strike at the Soviet Baltic Fleet or ground troops pushing across the north German plain. As General Wilson summarized, the situation, "We could be a threat to their exposed flank from the Baltic, providing some 200 aircraft for support of the forces defending the North German plain, and then in a position to launch attacks . . . from the ground and from the air."[25]

While a coherent strategy for Norway came to fruition under Wilson's tenure, the origins date back at least four years. In September 1972, 3,000 Marines from 6th MAB stormed ashore near Tromsö north of the Arctic Circle in Exercise STRONG EXPRESS. While primarily designed to show that the Atlantic Fleet was doing more than providing ships for Vietnam, its major success lay in developing techniques for working Marine Corps aircraft into the Norwegian air defense scheme. It also left a strong impression on numerous Marine Corps officers who would later champion the cause for Marine deployments to NATO, among them Col. Philip D. Shutler who commanded the air component of the MAB.

In 1975, Shutler, now deputy commanding general FMFLant, served on a Marine Corps/Navy briefing team designed to convince NATO officials of the Marines' capabilities in the north, and to push for conducting an exercise the following year.[26] With the strong endorsements of Supreme Allied Commander Atlantic Adm. Isaac C. Kidd, and Shutler's boss, Lt. Gen. Robert L. Nichols, they outlined what capabilities the Marine MAGTF could bring to NATO, while educating NATO officers, most of whom had never trained with American Marines.

The Marine MAGTF, they argued, was flexible enough to meet almost any contingency. It could operate as a mechanized task force, which, with its air component, would be useful in attacking the Soviet flank in north Germany. Or it could be configured as an aviation heavy force. It could provide nearly 200 additional aircraft, with its own ground security, which could operate as a self-contained air enclave from which it could attack Soviet ground or naval forces. In addition, the MAFTF could operate amphibiously, from Navy shipping. This would allow for rapid reinforcement in the north, or the Marines could attack Soviets anywhere along the 2,500-mile front from Germany to the North Cape off Norway. Simply stated, no other force within NATO combined both the combat power and the flexibility of a Marine Corps MAGTF.

The briefings met with a warm reception within NATO. The Commander, Naval Forces Europe, Adm. David H. Bagley, endorsed the proposal, despite some initial concerns by the Navy about operating amphibious ships so close to the Soviet Union. Only two reinforcement options existed for Norway in NATO's war plans, and both involved two U.S.-based Army units, the 82d Airborne and 9th Infantry Divisions. In reality, neither were likely to ever make it to Norway, the former because of its global commitments and the latter because it would take over sixty days to arrive and was too heavy and cumbersome for Norway.

Only Alexander Haig, then Supreme Commander, Allied Forces Europe, raised any argument against using Marines on the northern flank. In talks with the Marine Commandant in Brussels in early 1976, Haig told Wilson that the two Marine MAFs assigned to Europe were his reserves. If he started earmarking them for a specific area, he lost the ability to employ them as he needed. In essence, he would lose his reserve. As Wilson later recalled:

> If one MAF were to be committed to the north, this would be of concern to the Greeks and Turks, because they would feel they were being slighted. Therefore he would prefer not to make the commitment or even earmark a MAF for the north.[27]

But Haig never voiced enough concern to stop the Marine deployment to the north, especially since the Marine Corps had the support of both the Navy and State Departments. No doubt Haig, too, saw the potential threat to his supply lines if the Soviets were successful in the north. His successor, Gen. Bernard Rodgers, USA, supported the Marine Corps initiative, and any resistance from SACEUR quickly disappeared.

In the autumn of 1976, after nearly a year of briefings and planning conferences, the stage was set for the Corps' largest deployment to Europe since World War I.[28] Six thousand Marines of the 4th MAB, commanded by Brig. Gen. Alfred M. Gray, loaded aboard Navy shipping in North Carolina for an exercise designed to test "the flexible employment and reinforcement capability of projecting a MAB ashore in the Northern European Command."[29] On 21 September, with the King Olav of Norway and numerous other dignitaries looking on, 1st Battalion, 8th Marines conducted an amphibious assault with the Royal Marines near Namsos, in central Norway, as part of a massive NATO naval exercise code named TEAMWORK 76.[30] While hundreds of Norwegian civilians watched, the Marines secured an air-bridgehead which allowed Marine aircraft to fly in and operate in support of the larger naval exercise of some 250 ships from ten countries. Other than a successful "tear gas raid" on the MAB headquarters by some Royal Marines who played the opposition, the exercise proved a success and greatly impressed the Norwegians, who noted particularly the Marines' use of aviation and their ability to use their amphibious assault vehicles to maneuver in the fjords.[31]

At the conclusion of TEAMWORK 76, the 4th MAB back-loaded and headed for rainy, foggy Jutland for a second and much larger exercise, called BONDED ITEM. In October, Gray's Marines conducted a traditional amphibious landing near the Danish town of Esbjerg. Now organized as a mechanized task force, they pushed south to occupy defensive positions in the narrow neck of Schleswig-Holstein, while Marine aircraft provided support from newly occupied Danish airfields.[32] In the mock wargames which followed with a German *panzergrenadier* brigade, the Marines performed well in the tank-heavy environment, pleasantly surprising many NATO observers.

Following the success of TEAMWORK/BONDED ITEM, the Marines and NATO immediately began planning additional exercises in northern Europe. In September 1977, a much smaller, company-sized, exercise was held north of the Arctic Circle. The following year, 4th MAB returned with an even larger force for NORTHERN WEDDING/BOLD GUARD—nearly 10,000 Marines, including all the tanks of 2d Marine Division. As in 1976, the bulk of the exercises occurred in Jutland, while smaller portions took place throughout Norway and the North Sea. The exercise included a two-battalion helicopter lift into the Shetland Islands.[33] Like north Norway or Jutland, the Shetlands provided a good air facility from which to operate Marine fixed-wing aircraft in support of the 2d Fleet's operations.

While these large, early exercises were successful, they convinced the Marine Corps that Germany was not really the optimal environment to deploy the MAFTF. A MAB, even with a battalion of tanks, would have a negligible impact in the northern plains of Europe. But the islands and waterways of the Norwegian coast were clearly an area where the Corps could have a great impact upon any conflict in Europe. Over time, the focus of the exercise shifted away from Denmark and entirely to Norway.[34]

Northern Norway was a difficult tactical environment for anyone. Wide north-south running fjords cut deep into coast. Most movement between towns traveled by ferry rather than overland. Roads, where they existed, were small and required constant snowplowing. The deep snow and potential for avalanches made off-road moment difficult and hazardous. Large mountain ranges forced movement into channelized valleys. The only real avenue of approach into northern Norway, other than by sea, was the "Finnish Wedge." This was a protrusion of relatively open Finnish territory that ended at the strategically important Norwegian port of Bardufoss. This approach appeared the likely avenue for a Soviet attack. It too could be defended, provided that the defender could maneuver around the mountains and in the deep snow.

Skiing was the preferred method to move forces in Norway, and both the British and Norwegians were adept at moving their battalions this way. But the Marine Corps lacked both the training and continuity in personnel to be effective, at least initially, on skis. However, the Marine Corps brought to Norway hardware possessed by neither the Norwegians nor the British in large numbers—helicopters. Infantry could be moved rapidly from point to point to counter any Soviet thrust. While it might take hours for Norwegian troops to navigate one of the ridgelines, the Marines could overcome it in a ten-minute helicopter ride.[35] In addition, the Amphibious Assault Vehicles (AAV) provided the Marines with a unique means of transportation. The AAV allowed the Marines to maneuver in and around the fjords, bypassing the snow covered roads entirely. While not eliminating the need for better training and equipment, the air element of the MAGTF provided a whole new dimension to fighting in Norway.

While amphibious operations had gone well, serious problems emerged from the early NORTHERN WEDDING and BOLD GUARD exercises. Most of these were directly attributable to the Marine Corps' inexperience in operating in cold weather. First, 4th MAB had conducted virtually no work-ups prior to deploying to Europe.[36] Marines were taken from the temperate climate of North Carolina and deployed to the wet and cold of northern Europe with minimal training. Further, the Korean War-vintage equipment was completely inadequate. The Marines had no effective over-the-snow vehicles.[37] Basic hygiene was nonexistent. Cold weather injuries forced the evacuation of an entire company, while Marines did not shave for days and emerged from their snow caves, faces soot-blackened from the candles used to keep them warm.[38]

Obviously, major work needed to be done. Over the next two years, smaller, carefully monitored, exercises were conducted in Norway. Studies were done on everything from diet to the need for a smaller Norwegian built Ahkio to pull equipment through the deep snow. In May 1981, the Commandant designated the Deputy Chief of Staff for Plans and Operations as the central coordinating authority for all cold weather issues, from training to procurement. In February 1982, the Marine Corps conducted a "Cold War Study" which made some forty specific recommendations and became the blueprint for procurement and training changes within the service. It observed:

> The most pressing cold weather problem facing the Marine Corps is its efforts to develop and maintain a satisfactory state of training readiness for cold

weather operations within the FMF. Present facilities and training programs are inadequate to keep Marines fully trained, conditioned and acclimatized to function effectively under the most severe conditions of weather, terrain, and enemy action.[39]

From 9 to 12 March 1982, a Joint Cold Weather Conference was conducted in Norway to provide additional input into refining the ability of U.S. forces to operate in Norway. While agreeing with the earlier study, it emphasized the need for better equipment, especially over-the-snow mobility:

> The helicopter is by far the fastest, has the greatest range, has a great load carrying capability and is extremely flexible . . . The helicopter is extremely vulnerable to the vagaries of weather . . . and should not be relied upon as the only means of tactical mobility or logistics support . . .[40]

The first issue addressed was training. The Marine Corps began adopting many of the Royal Marines' training procedures that had proved successful in preparing them for Norway. Critical in this was the need for all units to have an extensive two-month work-up prior to deploying to a cold weather environment.[41] The first major changes were felt at the Marine Corps Mountain Warfare Training Center at Bridgeport in California's Sierra Nevada Mountains. Founded in 1951 as a reaction to the cold weather casualties during the Chosin Reservoir, it was reopened in 1976 to train a small number of unit leaders in cold weather operations.[42]

In 1982, as a result of these studies, the staff was doubled to allow for an entire battalion to rotate through the facility for a month at a time. Almost immediately, individual Marines' skiing abilities improved dramatically, which had long been a major problem for the Marines trying to maneuver in the Norwegian snow. After Bridgeport, Marine units would go to Fort Drum, New York, for an additional month of training. Thus, by the time of an exercise in Norway, any Marine unit had already spent two months operating in cold weather conditions. Additionally, to facilitate institutional knowledge of cold weather operations, 4th MAB was designated as the sole Norway brigade, another item which came from the Royal Marines' experiences and was recommended in the 1982 study.[43]

New equipment, however, took longer. To enhance mobility in the snow, the Marine Corps had wanted a tracked vehicle, such as Swedish built BV206s commonly used by the Norwegian and UK forces, to support the ground forces. But it would be FY85 before the first of several hundred could be purchased. New clothing, such as advanced water repellent Gortex outerwear or Nomex underwear took even longer and would not be commonly issued until 1987.

Thus far, Marine reinforcements had arrived in Norway by traditional amphibious shipping. There was a major problem with this plan. It required several weeks for the Marines to embark in the U.S. and make their way across the Atlantic. In the event of hostilities with the Soviet Union, by the time they arrived, the Soviets would already be in control of the strategic northern airfields. If they could arrive by aircraft instead, with most of their heavy equipment already prestaged, Marines could rapidly reinforce Norway, eliminating the need for shipping and with an 80% reduction in the amount of airlift required. As a former chief of staff, FMFLant observed:

> The timeline simply was not there. The intelligence indicators would give us some advanced warning, but not enough to get there in time by ship. Flying them in and falling onto prepositioned equipment seemed to be the only way.[44]

As early as 1976, the Norwegian government pushed for negotiations on the pre-positioning of equipment in Norway, with the hard details to be worked out in a close-hold, classified, joint U.S.-Norwegian Study Group. The Norwegians had been impressed by the Marine Corps performance in TEAM-WORK/BONDED ITEM 76, and believed that the integral use of aircraft and amphibious forces were perfectly tailored to operate in the islands and waterways of northern Norway. That same year, General Wilson met with the study group and pledged Marine Corps support for the defense of northern Norway.

In 1978, discussions continued on Norway within the new Carter Administration. As Secretary of Defense, Harold Brown stated, "The United States would be able to contribute significantly to a forward defense in the Northern Region through the deployment of Marine Forces supported by sea-based and land-based tactical air forces. Such a contribution would help stabilize the situation in the north."[45] In July, the Deputy Secretary of Defense, Charles W. Duchan, Jr., instructed the Secretary of the Navy W. Graham Claytor, Jr., to initiate planning for the rapid reinforcement of Norway. By 1979, the Joint American-Norwegian Study Group concluded that NATO should pre-position a brigade's worth of equipment in north Norway near one of the airfields around Tromsö.

The Soviets reacted with typical anger and indignation. In December 1979, the Soviet ambassador made an informal threat to the Norwegian government, declaring "We know how to react, how to make trouble for you."[46] It had its desired effect. The next month the Labor Government in Oslo suspended talks with the U.S., pending an internal review of pre-positioning.

When talks resumed in the summer of 1980, Johan Jorgen Holst, now State Secretary of Foreign Affairs, went to Washington to work out a final agreement. But he proposed several major changes in the pre-positioning plan. The Marine brigade's equipment would now be stored near Trondheim, some 400 miles south. Holst informed both the U.S. government and NATO, that the Norwegian government and public opinion simply would not allow a more northern deployment. This, he said, was seen as simply too provocative towards the Soviets. Additionally, the Norwegians wanted to place restrictions on the use of Marine Corps A-6 aircraft, prohibiting them from being included as part of the air element of the MAB to be deployed to Norway. The Oslo government perceived the A-6 as having "offensive capabilities" and capable of carrying nuclear weapons.

The U.S. reaction was less than enthusiastic. The Marines now found themselves falling in on their equipment hundreds of miles south of where they wanted to defend. While solutions could be found to work around this, the A-6 was the Marine Corps' only all weather aircraft, "capable of providing any degree of close air support when weather conditions are at their worse."[47] When U.S. negotiators pointed out that a similar 1979 agreement with Canada and the UK had allowed for the pre-positioning of their equipment north of the Arctic Circle, the Norwegians countered that their forces were seen as less provocative to the Soviets.[48]

After much haggling, on 16 January 1981, the two governments signed a Memorandum of Understanding Governing Prestockages and Reinforcement of Norway that incorporated all the Norwegian conditions at a ceremony in the Pentagon. The Norwegian ambassador to the U.S., Knut Hedemann, described the agreement as "An expression of war prevention by joint action," noting that it was "purely an defense arrangement."[49] For the United States, as Robert W. Komer, Under Secretary of Defense for Policy, observed, it facilitated "reinforcement of NATO's defenses even if the seas around Norway are contested."[50]

In October 1982, the storage agreement was finalized, providing for thirty days supplies and enough equipment for a Marine brigade of 13,200 men and 155 aircraft—now designated the Norway Airlanded MAB. The equipment was tailor-made for operating in the confines of north Norway. No tanks were included, but it did have an artillery battalion, engineer equipment, and Swedish-built over-the-snow vehicles, and a large number of infantry antitank weapons. All the equipment needed to fight, except the men and communications gear, would be ready and waiting in climatically controlled caves, hollowed out into the sides of mountain. The first of the equipment began arriving in November and was placed in old World War II German bunkers until the first pre-positioning facility could be completed in 1985.[51]

The plan for airlifting in the Marines was simple in theory, but difficult to execute. In developing the pre-positioning plan, several important assumptions had to be made. First, the Marines had to arrive in a benign environment as they had no capacity for a forced entry. Thus intelligence had to provide enough warning — at least a week — for the Norway Airlanded MAB to deploy.[52] In the event of hostilities, the Marines would be flown in on charter aircraft into two airfields around Trondheim — Vaernes and Orland. There, they would head to nine different assembly areas, then on to three major pre-positioned storage sites where ammunition, food, and vehicles were stored. Once the men and material were united, they would drive to six different ports and embark on board twelve small Norwegian Ro/Ro ships to be ferried 400 miles north to the Norwegian port of Bardafuss.[53] From there they would deploy to the north and east into their battle positions. Simultaneously, Marine helicopters would be disassembled, loaded on to Air Force C-5 aircraft and flown to Norway, where they would be reassembled and flown north, with their support equipment coming from the pre-positioned sites. Fixed wing aircraft attached to the MAB could be flown in directly from the United States to airfields in central Norway. In all, it was estimated that it would take nearly a week to get the entire MEB in by air.

The Achilles heel of the entire plan was the timing for the incoming Marines. With thousands of personnel arriving at two airfields, all headed for a few pre-positioned sites and ports, and all on traveling over the same few roads, it was a recipe for complete chaos even without the Soviets firing a shot. Further, in the event of a crisis, there was no guarantee that Military Airlift Command could supply the required aircraft on time to deploy the MAB as intended. Units that the Marine commanding general might wish to arrive first may get delayed and actually arrive sometime in the middle of the "pack."

To help alleviate these problems, the pre-positioned caves were designed to facilitate rapid withdrawal of equipment. Circular, with two separate entrances, the vehicles were staged around the outside edge of the cave's interior, thus no matter what unit arrived first, it could access the equipment and retrieve it from the facility without having to wait for another unit which might have been delayed. The vehicles themselves were preloaded, including snow-chains and fuel, needed only a battery to install their radios. In the climate-controlled caves, they were as ready to go as any in the

FMF—in fact, most were in better condition than those used by the FMF.

However, more scientific methods were needed to develop a workable timetable for the deployment of the Marines around Trondheim. The Center for Naval Analysis (CNA), working in conjunction with Norwegian Defense and civil officials, developed a detailed model for the movement of the MAB from arrival to embarkation on Norwegian shipping. Two years in the making, it examined every aspect of the movement, from aircraft offload rates, to where hot food would be provided en route. It was detailed enough that at any specified time, the model could display the number of people, vehicles, and pallets at the specific staging area or on any stretch of road.[54] CNA tested the model repeatedly, beginning with the first exercise of the pre-positioned equipment in February 1985. Further, extensive refinements were made the following year when 4th MAB and Norwegian Defense forces conducted a logistical exercise to notionally flow the entire MAB through central Norway. As was later noted, based upon the model run, participants recommended changes to the arrival sequence of MAB units, airflow, ship embarkation plans, and the distribution of units to equipment storage sites.[55] Over the next few years, at least half of all of 4th MAB's exercises involved only the Airlanded MAB, continuing to try and refine its deployment and movements in Norway.

Ironically, the completion of the last of the pre-position caves coincided with the collapse of the Soviet Union. Nearly two decades of debate, planning, and expenditures came to naught as the threat from communism dissipated. Marine Corps' exercises in Norway continued, albeit with less urgency and importance than a decade before. In 1998, for the first time, the entire NORTHERN WEDDING exercise was manned and controlled by Marine reservists. In the post-Cold-War era, the debate is whether millions of dollars of pre-positioned hardware should remain in Norway in an era of diminishing resources.

While the entire debate over the defense of NATO's northern flank may be reduced to a footnote of the Cold War, it had some lasting effects on the Marine Corps. It established the Marines as the premier service within the DOD in cold weather operations, providing invaluable training for all the armed services in an area where few had looked since the early 1950s. In a purely parochial view, the Marines obtained an entire brigade's worth of equipment over and above what was required in the Fleet Marines; with the funding provided by supplemental appropriations. This does not include the additional money obtained to purchase new Gortex and other cold weather clothing, replacing those designed three decades earlier.

The use of the Marines in northern Europe provided valuable lessons on how the Marine Corps could be used to support the fleet, particularly in the littoral areas. Using the Marines to secure airfields to supplement carrier aircraft, while not a new concept, added a new dimension to considerations of how NATO could fight the Soviets in confined waters of the Norwegian Sea. The ability to alter the organization of the Marine MAB was instrumental in supporting the naval campaign, be it against the Soviet fleet or attacking the flank of the Soviet army in Germany.

The United States Marine Corps' commitment to NATO's northern flank developed as both the Unites States Marine Corps and Norway reached the same conclusions for different reasons. A worried Norwegian government needed greater support from the U.S. and its decision to allow pre-positioning of equipment marked a dramatic turn in its foreign policy. While the restrictions placed upon NATO's military operating in the north were not always popular with the United States, in doing so, Norway overcame strong neutralist instincts and allowed large numbers of foreign troops to train on her soil for the first time in the modern era.

For the U.S. military, the Soviet threat to the northern flank represented a grave challenge to NATO itself. A more robust presence in Norway facilitated a new, aggressive way of countering the threat from the Russian Bear. For the Marine Corps, specifically, deployments to Norway offered the chance offer a solution to a problem the other services were slow in seeing. In the process this afforded the Marine Corps the opportunity, once again, to provide an example of its ability to innovate and adapt to changing times and defense concerns.

NOTES

¹Strategic Studies Institute, "Soviet Strategy and NATO's Northern Flank" (Carlisle: U.S. Army War College, 1 May 1978), 7–8.

²Eric Grove, *Battle for the Fjords: NATO's Forward Maritime Strategy in Action* (Annapolis: Naval Institute Press, 1991), 9.

³Johan C. Haraldsen, "Nato Expansion and Norway" (MA Thesis, Indiana University, December 1997), 53.

⁴John Lund, *Don't Rock the Boat: Reinforcing Norway in Crisis and in War* (Santa Monica: The Rand Corporation, 1989), 45–49. Also Rodney Kennedy-Minott, U.S. Regional Force Application: *The Maritime Strategy and its Effect on Nordic Stability* (Stanford: Hoover Institute, 1988), 4–5.

⁵"Northern Security and Arms Control," An address by Johan Jorgen Holst to the 33d annual session of the North Atlantic Assembly, (22 September 1987), 4–5. Located in the unprocessed papers of Gen. Alfred M. Gray, Archives, Marine Corps Historical Center, History and Museums Division, HQMC, Washington, D.C.

⁶Lund, 13. Also Tim Greve, *Norway and NATO* (Press Department: Royal Ministry of Foreign Affairs), 2.

⁷ Holst address, 10.

⁸"Scandinavia: Defense Policies under Review," U.S. Department of State, Bureau of Intelligence and Research, 3 January 1974, 2. Located in Operational Archives, Naval Historical Center, Washington D.C., Political-Military Policy Division, Department of the Navy, Series XXXIV, Box 644.

⁹Ibid, 7.

¹⁰Rolf Tamnes, *The United States and the Cold War in the High North* (Aldershot, U.K.: Dartmouth Publishing Co., 1991), 235.

¹¹Ibid, 236.

¹²Elmo R. Zumwalt, *On Watch: A Memoir* (New York: New York Times Book Co., 1976), 467–468.

¹³Capt. Peter M. Swartz, USN, "The Maritime Strategy Debates: A Guide to the Renaissance of U.S. Maritime Strategic Thinking in the 1980s" (Monterey: Naval Post Graduate School, 24 February 1988), 1–2.

¹⁴Rodney Kennedy-Minott, *U.S. Regional Force Application: Maritime Strategy and its Effect on Nordic Stability* (Stanford: Hoover Institute, 1988), 13.

¹⁵CINCNAVEUR to CNO, Subj: INVICTUS Arrangement, 7 October 1971. Located in Operational Archives, Naval Historical Center, Washington, D.C., Political-Military Policy Division, Department of the Navy, Series XXXIV, Box 644.

¹⁶Martin Binkin and Jeffery Record, "Where Does the Marine Corps Go from Here?" (Washington, D.C.: The Brookings Institute, 1976), 1.

¹⁷Major Gen. Fred Haynes, "The Marines Through 1999," *U.S. Naval Institute Proceedings* (September 1978), 25.

¹⁸William S. Lind and Jeffrey Record, "Twilight for the Corps," *U.S. Naval Institute Proceedings* (July 1978), 39–43.

¹⁹Headquarters, United States Marine Corps, "Report on Marine Corps Manpower Quality and Force Structure," Report to the United States Senate Armed Services Committee on the Marine Corps Mission, Force Structure, Manpower Levels, and Personnel Quality (1 January 1976), Executive Summary, 2.

²⁰Col. John H. Ripley, USMC (Ret), Interview with Author, Washington, D.C., 8 September 1999.

²¹George C. Wilson, "Carter's NATO Budget Indicates Shift of Military Focus," *The Washington Post* (15 January 1978), A-6.

²²Gen. Louis H. Wilson, Oral History Collection, Marine Corps Historical Center, Washington, D.C., 1984, 166.

23Lt. Gen. Philip D. Shutler, USMC (Ret), Interview with author, Washington, D.C., 14 September 1999.

24Gen. Lewis H. Wilson, "The Marine Corps Role in NATO," *Marine Rundschau* (December 1978), 688. Also in Lewis H. Wilson Personal Papers, "Role of the Corps in NATO," Personal Correspondence (PC 562, Archives Section, Marine Corps Reach Center, Qunatico, Virginia).

25Wilson Oral History, 165.

26Along with Shutler, the team included the FMFLant Chief of Staff, Col. George B. Crist, and the Commander, Amphibious Group 2, Rear Adm. Frederick F. Palmer.

27Wilson Oral History, 165.

284th MAB Command Chronology, 1 January–30 June 1975 (Marine Corps Historical Center, Washington, D.C.), part II, 4.

294th MAB Command Chronology, 1 July–31 December 1976 (Marine Corps Historical Center, Washington, D.C.), part III, 1.

30Office of the Assistant Secretary of Defense (Public Affairs), Memorandum for Correspondences, dated 21 September 1976.

31Col. Jeremiah O Leary, "Bright Autumn Days in Foggy Northern Europe," *Marine Corps Gazette* (January 1977), 28.

324th MAB Command Chronology, 1 January–30 June 1976 (Marine Corps Historical Center, Washington, D.C), part III, 1.

334th MAB Command Chronology, 1 July–31 December 1978 (Marine Corps Historical Center, Washington, D.C.), part IIII, 1–2.

34In 1984 the TEAMWORK exercise was conducted almost exclusively north of the Arctic Circle and was the largest operation thus involving 11,500 Marines, not counting 3,000 Dutch and British Marines. 4th MAB Teamwork 1984 After Action Report, dated 5 June 1984, 12. Located in enclosure (1), 4th MAB Command Chronology, 1 January–30 June 1984 (Marine Corps Historical Center, Washington, D.C.).

35Interview with Major Gen. Harry W. Jenkins, USMC (Ret). Oral History Collection, (Marine Corps Historical Center, Washington, D.C., 23 June 1996).

364th Marine Amphibious Brigade, Post Deployment Report for Exercise Northern Wedding/Bold Guard, dated 2 November 1978 (Marine Corps Research Center, Quantico, Virginia), 3-1-3-15.

37Marine Corps Development and Education Command, "Marine Corps Cold Weather Combat Operations Study," dated 8 February 1982 (Marine Corps Research Center, Quantico, Virginia), 4-3.

38Ripley Interview.

39Marine Corps Development and Education Command, "Marine Corps Cold Weather Combat Operations Study," dated 8 February 1982 (Marine Corps Research Center, Quantico, Virginia), xviii.

40Ibid., 3–49.

41Ibid., 4–11.

42Speech by Lt. Col. William H. Osgood, USMC, Conference on Cold-Weather Operations Final Report, (Headquarters, Marine Corps, June 1982), 3–25. It was selected from as it located near the 38th parallel and approximated the weather found in Korea.

43"Marine Corps Cold Weather Combat Operations Study," dated 8 February 1982, 9-5–9-7.

44Gen. George B. Crist, USMC (Ret), Telephone interview with author, 5 September 1999.

45Report of Secretary Harold Brown to the Congress on the FY1980 Budget, FY 1981, Authorization Request and FY1980–1984 Defense Programs (Washington, D.C.: Government Printing Office, 25 January 1979), 103–104.

46Lund, 21.

47"Marine Corps Cold Weather Combat Operations Study," dated 8 February 1982, 9-6.

[48]Johan Jorgen Holst, Kenneth Hunt, and Anders Sjaastad, eds, *Deterrence and Defense in the North* (Oslo: Norwegian University Press, 1985), 219.
[49]Fred S. Hoffman, Associated Press, dated 16 January 1981.
[50] Ibid.
[51]Headquarters, United States Marine Corps, CMC ALMAR 105/85, Dated 16 May 1985.
[52]John F. Nance, USMC Norway Preposition Program (A Briefing Presented to CINCLANTFLT Staff)(Washington, D.C.: Center for Naval Analysis, 30 May 1985), 7.
[53]John F. Nance, USMC Norway Preposition Program (A Briefing Presented to the 4th Marine Amphibious Brigade and Brigade Service Support Group 4)(Washington, D.C.: Center for Naval Analysis, 10 September 1985), 12.
[54]Peter A. Beling and John F. Nance, "CNA Research Memorandum 87–112, Time-Motion Model Runs and Sensitivity Analysis" (Washington, D.C.: Center for Naval Analysis, 28 July 1987), 2.
[55]Ibid. Also John F. Nance, Interview with author, Falls Church, Virginia, 10 August 1999.

"Boulder Boys": Naval Japanese Language School Graduates

Pedro Loureiro

> Quite a bit has been written about the so-called "China Hands" who played such an important role in helping define America's policies toward the Far East in the years before and after World War II. Relatively little, however, has been published about what might be called the "Japan Hands," those men and women who lent their expertise in Japanese language and culture to the American war against Japan after Pearl Harbor. In this essay about the graduates of the Navy's intensive Japanese language program at Boulder, Colorado, Pedro Loureiro illuminates both the character of the Navy's program and the impact which that program had on many of those who participated in it.

By Pearl Harbor day, 7 December 1941, the Office of Naval Intelligence (ONI) had long realized the importance of providing language training to its officers. Navy officials wisely anticipated the need for capable linguists in the event of conflicts with foreign countries. In Asia, ONI focused on China because of the Navy's mission to protect American lives and interests there. The main emphasis, however, was on its traditional hypothetical enemy, Orange—Japan. Officers were assigned to Japan to study Japanese as early as 1910, and in 1922 the Director of Naval Intelligence authorized the naval attaché in Peking to initiate a similar Chinese language program which was staffed predominantly by Marine officers. Such assignments usually lasted three years. In addition to five days of classroom studies a week, officers were encouraged to familiarize themselves with the local culture and report on their travels within the country.[1] The program in Japan was particularly successful in producing a small group of officers who would play significant roles in ONI during the prewar and wartime years. Prominent figures included Ellis Zacharias, Arthur McCollum, William Sebald, Henri Smith-Hutton, Edwin Layton, Joseph Rochefort, Redfield Mason, Alwin Kramer, and Joseph Finnegan.

In 1940, while Capt. Arthur McCollum was the head of ONI's

Pedro Loureiro is Director of the Pacific Basin Institute at Pomona College.

Far East Desk, a reserve intelligence officer, Albert E. Hindmarsh approached him for a job. Unaware that Hindmarsh had been a confidential civilian agent during the tenure of Director of Naval Intelligence, Capt. William Puleston, McCollum informed him that there were no openings for a professor of international law from Harvard University.[2] Hindmarsh did not reveal his previous ties to ONI and instead tried to pass himself off as being able to understand Japanese from his one-year stint as an exchange professor at Tokyo Imperial University. When McCollum tried to explain that there was still no need for a person like him, the law professor pleaded that he was willing to do anything. At this point, McCollum agreed to find some sort of work for him, but he could not understand why a professor from Harvard, who did not like the climate in Washington, with a family of four which had to be relocated from Cambridge, would want to perform menial office chores for a living. McCollum later recalled that although the former law professor was "a tower of strength . . . he quickly learned that he didn't know much Japanese for the kind of thing we required, but he had a feel for it."[3] Hindmarsh's persistence paid off very shortly afterwards when in December 1940, he suggested that ONI should determine how many Japanese linguists were available in the event of a conflict.

The results of the initial findings helped to launch Hindmarsh's career in the Navy. McCollum and ONI were surprised that of the fifty-three officers who had been sent to Japan for language training over the years, only about twelve attained, and hopefully still retained, the level of fluency that would be necessary for translation, interpretation, and interrogation. These officers were not identified but they must have included the nine prominent figures mentioned earlier. Instead of questioning why the language program in Japan produced such meager results, McCollum, at the urging of Hindmarsh, approved a plan for a nationwide survey of available Japanese linguists. The study found that only five or six universities offered courses on Japanese and that only about 300 persons in the United States had any limited exposure to the language.[4] Anyone who had lived or traveled in East Asia was liberally included on the list.

The Navy and American academia had very little knowledge

about Japan and its people. The survey indicated how woefully unprepared the United States was on the eve of the Pacific War. The only place where Japanese was even taught on a regular basis was within the Japanese–American communities. Yet, the Navy did not use Japanese–Americans because these language schools and their teachers were thought to be subversive and had been placed under ONI surveillance for almost a decade.

By July 1941, Lt. Cmdr. Hindmarsh was put in charge of developing a Japanese language program for the Navy. It is quite amazing how rapidly the former professor moved up the ranks and Navy records describe him as the key figure behind the Japanese Language School. But the development of the program also owed much to ONI's top Japanese linguist, Glenn Shaw, who spent many years in Japan teaching at Kobe University and also working for the *Asahi* newspaper. Given Hindmarsh's limited experience with Japanese and language training, it is difficult to believe that Shaw did not play a more significant role. Actually, Shaw's daughter Daphne (a "BIJ" or born in Japan), later became a graduate of the Boulder school while he himself became Director of the school in June 1944. Together, both men designed a course that would provide the Navy with qualified interpreters and translators in fourteen months. The University of California, Berkeley, and Harvard University agreed to administer the program. In July 1941, fifty-six candidates from the list of 300 persons were selected as potential students for the first class of Japanese linguists. They were all white, male, between twenty and thirty years old, had either college training or had lived in China or Japan. On 1 October 1941, twenty-one enrolled at Berkeley and twenty-seven at Harvard.[5]

The programs at the two universities were short-lived. Personality conflicts between Hindmarsh and Professor Serge Elisséeff who ran the course with Edwin Reischauer and disagreements over the curriculum ended Harvard's role after a year. The course at Berkeley proceeded smoothly under the direction of Florence Walne—a BIJ herself, daughter of Baptist missionaries. She completed her Japanese studies at Radcliffe and became Chair of the Oriental Language Department at Berkeley. Although the June

1942 order to exclude all Japanese from the West Coast, did not affect the American students, it did apply to the instructors, most of whom were Japanese-American or Japanese nationals. Since these teachers were irreplaceable, the Navy quickly came up with a plan to move the entire Berkeley operation to the University of Colorado, Boulder. By July, 153 students, twenty instructors, and Florence Walne arrived in Boulder. In January 1944, the Japanese Language School was designated "The Navy School of Oriental Languages" when Chinese, Malay, and Russian were added to the curriculum.[6] To keep up with the demand for language officers, the Navy established an additional school at Oklahoma A&M College in Stillwater in June 1945.[7] Although the language program was based initially at Harvard and Berkeley, and although women were enrolled later, the phrase, "Boulder Boys" nevertheless stuck.

By October 1942, competition from local draft boards and the Army's own Japanese Language School (Camp Savage)[8] made it increasingly difficult to find quality candidates for the language program at Boulder. The Navy felt that it needed as least 500 more students for the next several years. So, instead of recruiting candidates with Chinese or Japanese language backgrounds, Hindmarsh and Shaw began to broaden their search by canvassing all the major universities looking for bright university students, especially those in Phi Beta Kappa and anyone who had taken courses in foreign languages, the classics, or expertise in shorthand. As one graduate explained about the shorthand criteria, "the technique for learning to read and write shorthand is the same as learning to read and write Japanese characters."[9] The extremely high standards of the selection process was one of the main factors that limited the number of eligible students. But there was no shortage of applicants. For many who wished to perform their patriotic duty, what better way than to study Japanese safely tucked away from the realities of war? Word about the Navy language school spread, and potential applicants overwhelmed Hindmarsh on his recruiting trips. He later recalled that when he arrived at Yale to interview the fifty students who had set up appointments, he was surprised to find that more than 250 turned up. From November 1942 until mid-December, Hindmarsh interviewed 1,500 candidates throughout the country but accepted 302. In fact, one Boulder graduate learned about the school when the *Gripsholm* that was repatriating him and other Americans stopped over in Rio De Janeiro.[10] By December 1942, 300 students were enrolled while three classes had graduated.

From September 1941 until June 1944, a total of 915 were accepted into the program out of 8,000 applicants. Until the summer of 1943, when women were admitted, the student body was, according to the Navy, "86% Caucasian and 14% Semitic." The average age was twenty-five. Almost half (46%) had undergraduate college degrees and 32% came from Phi Beta Kappa. Only 7% were enrolled or commissioned in the Navy when they entered. Geographically, the East Coast provided 44% of the students, while 33% came from the West Coast. Seventeen percent of them were BIJ's or BIC's (born in Japan or born in China). The background of the students was quite varied. Many (38%) were college students, but the rest came from all walks of life. They ranged from teachers to missionaries to executives to one who was the former secretary to the American ambassador to Japan. Despite the rigorous routine at Boulder, the dropout rate (physical and dismissal) was only 13%. In October 1943, a small number of British and Canadian officers entered the Boulder program—six British junior officers and two Canadian junior officers. Of the British, the most famous was W. (William) G. Beasley, the Japanologist, and most controversial was Sub Lieutenant John Catt because he was unwilling to shave his beard.[11]

The entire idea behind the Japanese Language School was to produce competent linguists and translators in fourteen months. Former language officers and academics had serious doubts about the project. This had never been carried out successfully before, especially on such a large scale and in such a short period. Despite the uncertainties, the Navy realized how few Japanese linguists were available and thus gave its complete support—even before hostilities began with Japan. Hindmarsh and Shaw decided to model their curriculum after the Navy's three-year residency program in Japan. They utilized the methods and textbooks of Naoe Naganuma who had taught many of the Navy, Army, and

State Department students in Japan. They believed that similar results could be achieved through an intensive program of total immersion into Japanese. Naval activities such as reviews and parades were eliminated. Even physical exercise was excluded during the first year because it would have been too distracting. Though after complaints from the senior resident, Navy officer students were required to have one hour of physical exercise a day. The environment at Boulder was intended to encourage serious studies and academic excellence. Libraries, study areas, and living quarters were purposely maintained to continue the college atmosphere. They reasoned that a pleasant environment would allow the students to concentrate fully on their language studies.[12]

Recruiting students was a difficult task, but locating Japanese instructors would not be easy either. The Japanese communities which stretched from Seattle to San Diego had always been a cause of concern for Naval Intelligence. For over twenty years, ONI had placed all the Japanese on the West Coast under close surveillance. By the late thirties, 5,000 names had been entered into a subversive list which would be used by the Federal Bureau of Investigation to round up dangerous suspects immediately after the air attack on Pearl Harbor. ONI had been very liberal in labeling potential suspects. A word of praise about Japan or activities such as going to a Buddhist or Shinto church would land one on the suspect list.[13] There was no reason to doubt the loyalty of the rest of the Japanese-American community. Yet the Navy was reluctant to open its doors to Japanese-Americans. But in the case of the Japanese Language School, the Navy was forced by necessity to utilize Japanese-Americans and even Japanese nationals. There simply were not enough non-Japanese instructors to staff the school. There was a handful of Caucasian teachers who had taught at the Universities and there was also a small group of missionaries who had lived in Japan. Thirty-two Japanese taught at Boulder during the first year. By 1943, the number increased to 140 (excluding two Koreans). The Navy never encountered any problems with the teachers except for one who was dismissed after being discovered that he had been teaching the students to write Japanese war slogans such as "Asia for the Asiatics!"[14] There were, of course, no Japanese-American or any Asian *students* at Boulder. The Navy's rationale for this was that "No students of oriental blood were admitted as it was felt that their presence aboard ship might be undesirable."[15]

This group of Japanese teachers had varied backgrounds. Most came from the West Coast and many from the internment camps. There were second-generation or *Niseis*; there were the Japanese who were born in the United States but went to Japan to live or work before returning, they were known as *Kibeis*; and then there were some Japanese nationals. The head instructor was Susumu Nakamura, who was a *Kibei*. Nakamura had attended Keio University in Japan and graduated from UC Berkeley. There were also four medical doctors and their wives, a Berkeley landscape artist, a voice student from Los Angeles, and so on. It was rough at first, but in time these Japanese-Americans felt comfortable in Boulder. The local people had never experienced such an influx of Asians. After a few unpleasant instances at the beginning, the newcomers were accepted by the locals. Groups of Japanese-Americans and their families strolling downtown became a common sight. They quickly became part of the community. They rented homes from locals, sent their children to local schools, and worshiped at the local churches on Sunday.[16]

The *Nisei* experience at Boulder sheds new light on the U.S. Navy's relations with Japanese-Americans. Unlike the Army, which accepted *Nisei*s into combat units in Europe and its intelligence service, the Navy has received much criticism for its unwillingness to utilize these loyal Americans. The Boulder project, however, provides at least one instance where Japanese-Americans and Japanese nationals were trusted to train the bulk of the Navy's intelligence officers in the war against Japan. This story has not received much attention because of the reluctance of the Navy and of the teachers openly to acknowledge their roles during the war. The Navy kept their identities confidential in order to protect them from retribution after the war; the teachers themselves wanted to avoid the publicity of having worked for Naval Intelligence. Even to this day, the few surviving Japanese instructors have been unwilling to talk about their experiences at Boulder. The issue of loyalty was an extremely sensitive subject. As a matter of fact, there were several riots between the pro-Japan and pro-American Japanese groups at several of the internment camps.[17]

While the U.S. Navy should receive credit for utilizing Japanese and Japanese-Americans at the language school, it did not do enough to acknowledge the important work of this group of loyal and dedicated employees. Although the program was funded by the Navy Department, all the *sensei* were hired as civilian employees of the university, first as employees of the University of California and later as employees of the University of Colorado. When the Pacific War ended, the teachers were simply dismissed without receiving any government pensions. Only a handful were recognized for their contributions to the war effort. This came simply in the form of a short letter of thanks signed in May 1946 by Capt. Al Hindmarsh, who was then a reserve officer in the Navy.[18]

School life at Boulder was rigorous. Classes were held five days a week and Saturday mornings were devoted to examinations. Instruction was almost one-on-one as there were no more than six students per class. The first four hours of the day were devoted to classes which covered conversation, new vocabulary, and dictation. Students were expected to spend the next eight to ten hours studying on their own. Longs hours of work were necessary to prepare for the tough translation exams on Saturday, though many pointed out that the daily dictations were the most difficult part of the program. Every six to eight weeks there was a comprehensive oral exam. Everyone knew how everyone else was doing as grades were posted weekly on the main bulletin board. Mediocre grades and marginal performance were often grounds for dismissal. As a result, long hours of study was the norm for all the students.[19]

Memorization was an important factor in attaining success in the program. Students memorized an average of sixty new words a week. They even had to recite the Japanese National Defense Act. Clarence Barbier, who had played football at Yale, had a tendency to talk in his sleep and he would actually carry on conversations. Barbier had failed an oral test one day when he had been unable to recite the National Defense Act. However, in his sleep, with a little prodding from his colleagues, he began to recite the act *verbatim*.

The Japanese instructor, John Sato was quickly brought to the room to witness this, and Sato immediately declared that Barbier had passed.[20]

The students were encouraged to use Japanese as frequently as possible, not only when speaking with the instructors, but also in casual conversation with each other. Japanese movies were shown once a week and attendance was mandatory. This was all part of the school's total immersion approach to studying Japanese which turned out to be quite effective.[21]

Part of the students' training came from their exposure to the Japanese they met at Boulder. For many, this was the first time that they had ever come in contact with a Japanese. The relations between the teachers and the students were very close. Some of the instructors who had little or no training in teaching were actually too polite at first even to correct the mispronunciation of some of their students. It was inevitable that a strong bond developed between many students and their teachers. Japanese teachers often invited students to their homes where they would eat Japanese food and learn about Japanese culture. For most of the students, this was the first time that they tried *sashimi* or *tempura*. One former graduate recalled that eating *sashimi* at Boulder was much like the first cigarette, something that "would be remembered for the rest of their lives as a step into the unknown."[22]

Many graduates recalled that one of the most important things that helped maintain their high standards and morale was competitive rivalry and bonding. It was an extraordinary group of talented young minds. These included the BIJs who spoke the language but had limited writing and reading abilities as well as many highly intelligent college students from the best of America's universities. The challenge was to be able to achieve the seemingly impossible task of mastering spoken and written Japanese in a short period of fourteen months. Thus, everyone put a maximum effort into the endeavor.[23]

In July 1943, the first detachment of eighty-six WAVES (Women Accepted for Volunteer Emergency Service) entered the language school. Lt. Rebecca W. Smith, who had a Ph.D. in English from Texas Christian, was the officer in charge. The Navy felt that by training a pool of women linguists for desk duty, more men from Boulder could be freed to be assigned outside of the continental United States. Advertisements and articles in major newspapers, in Phi Beta Kappa's own publication, the *Key Reporter*, attracted over 600 applicants. The selection process was much like that of the men, with Hindmarsh conducting the interviews. The caliber of the applicants was extremely high. A ninety-day evaluation report on the WAVES noted that, "Evidence of strain was not visible. The group of women is unusually personable and alert," and in those less sensitive days, the report noted, too, that there was a "notable absence of 'queers.'" Almost one third of them were born in Japan, coming from Navy, Army, diplomatic, or missionary families. Upon arriving in Boulder, the women were housed in three separate converted fraternity houses. Each house had its own "housemother." Ens. Tallulah Peckham Hinds was the housemother for the quarters on 1005 Broadway, Lt. Smith at the house on 1029 Broadway, and Laura Kroll presided over the third converted fraternity on 1111 College Avenue which was almost a mile away. On the average there were eighteen to twenty-five women in each house. The WAVES encountered the same regulations as their male counterparts. For instance, one of the General Rules stated that "no liquor or gambling is permitted on the station."[24] Women also ate and attended classes separately from the men. While Japanese was technically mandatory at the men's mess hall, the WAVEs were allowed to speak English when they dined.[25]

The women at Boulder underwent the same rigorous training as the men and that was characterized by similar concerns. Florence Walne and the President of the University of Colorado were concerned that the school was run more like "a military activity" than a language program. Walne felt that the extremely demanding curriculum required the full attention of the WAVES, who were being distracted from their intensive studies because of extracurricular activities such as "military ceremonies, detached housing . . . regimentation of individuals, and the like." Physical training or *Undo* was also part of the requirements. Lt. Dorothy Johnson was the officer-in-charge of *Undo*. As the local newspaper reported, "The women marched two days a week and reported to the gym two days."[26] A report on the situation stated that "the Director believes the Senior WR [Women's Reserve] officer and her staff of assistants have aggravated the situation by missing the point and being over-energetic in supervision of trainees."[27] As one former student recalled, "What got us all down was the endless swimming under oil (really useful when we couldn't even go overseas!) Inspections, lucky bags and all that nonsense!"[28] Walne cautioned that the language program would be affected adversely if such military requirements were not kept to a minimum.

In addition to the WAVES, the Marine Corps also tapped into the Boulder school for Japanese translators and interpreters. At the time of graduation, the men had an opportunity to elect to serve with the Marine Corps. The Marines desperately needed language officers because their Japanese language school, which was established at the University of Hawaii, had been forced to close before all twelve Marines had completed their courses in late 1941.[29] The Navy agreed to make some of its graduates from each class available to the Marines. Those interested in joining the Marine Corps volunteered and were commissioned as Marines at the time of graduation. By 1944, approximately 111 Boulder graduates had joined the Marine Corps.[30]

In March 1943, Capt. Ellis Zacharias contacted the school concerning the possibility of admitting Coast Guard personnel into the program. Commander Hindmarsh was open to the idea and it was agreed that the Coast Guard would not require more than five officers. No information is available as to whether any Coast Guard personnel entered the school or if any graduates were allowed to volunteer.[31]

Between June 1942 and July 1946, about 1,100 men and women graduated from the Navy Japanese Language School in Boulder. The rigorous curriculum at the language school did not expose the students to any military or naval indoctrination except for the occasional drills and exercises. A graduate of one of the earlier classes recalled that his total knowledge of the Navy occurred "when a student formally requested that we be given some naval indoctrination, the captain . . . solemnly read aloud all the offenses that were punishable by death, such as deliberately running one's ship aground on a reef. . . . Later on, when I was actually on a battleship, I at first did not know which was the front and which the rear of the ship . . ."[32] After the first three classes graduated without any knowledge of naval matters, the Navy required all graduates to attend a month and a half indoctrination program at the Advanced Navy Intelligence School at the Henry Hudson Hotel, on West 57th Street in New York. Through lectures and films, the language students were introduced to topics such as combat intelligence, ship and aircraft recognition, prisoner interrogation, and military etiquette. There were also field trips to the Brooklyn Navy Yard and to the anti-submarine warfare school on Staten Island.[33] A similar indoctrination program for the WAVES was established at Smith College.[34]

After the short introduction to the Navy, language students began their real work. All the women (sixty-nine graduated from the first class) ended up in Washington, D.C., where they worked either at ONI's top-secret Communications Annex or the Washington Document Center at Fourth and K Street. Initially, the men were assigned mainly to Washington, D.C., Pearl Harbor, or Australia. Later, others were detached to the Southwest Pacific, accompanied Army and Marine units to the front, and went to China. An interrogation camp at Byron Springs,[35] California, was staffed by several language officers. This center was closed down for six months in September 1943 and was reactivated at Tracy, California.[36]

The majority of the language officers ended up at Pearl Harbor with ICPOA (Intelligence Center Pacific Ocean Areas, redesignated JICPOA, Joint Intelligence Center Pacific Ocean Areas in September 1943) where there was the greatest demand for Japanese linguists. Other than highly classified intelligence from radio intercepts, very little information flowed through ICPOA the first eight months of the war. But the campaigns at Guadalcanal and the Solomon Islands began to produce a steady stream of captured documents and prisoners by the end of 1942. Pearl Harbor, however, had no interrogation or translation section until the first group of twenty graduates arrived from Boulder in February 1943.[37] The initial response to these language officers was skepticism. Regular Navy officers who had spent three years studying Japanese in Japan had a hard time believing that fourteen months of study could produce anyone with competent knowledge of Japanese. One Boulder graduate recalled:

> We reported first to an office in Pearl Harbor where Japanese documents were translated. We were welcomed by a lieutenant in the regular Navy (a graduate of the Naval Academy in Annapolis), who informed us that the work we were about to do was highly secret, and that any betrayal of this secret would unquestionably lead to the death penalty. He continued, "And I personally will see to it that you are hanged." This officer never changed his low opinion of us. He refused even to acknowledge that we too were officers, invariably referring to us as "you language students."[38]

Both parties at Pearl were initially unprepared for their tasks. No one at ICPOA had any experience in organizing a translation and interrogation center. The "Boulder Boys'" language training did not concentrate on specialized Japanese naval terminology and their knowledge of ships and the Navy was rudimentary. Since there were not that many documents to be translated or prisoners to interrogate at this early stage, much effort was spent on compiling key word lists and reference guides. The hard work and dedication of the Boulder Boys quickly dispelled any lingering doubts about their abilities. In fact, Capt. Jasper Holmes, who was officer in charge of the Combat Intelligence Unit at Pearl Harbor, commented after the war that: "Respect for language officers and appreciation of their value increased with each succeeding operation.... It was a privilege to serve with the Navy language officers. They contributed their fair share to the victory in the Pacific..."[39]

As captured Japanese documents began arriving at Pearl Harbor, the newly arrived language officers were given the tasks of translating them into English. The Boulder Boys referred to the

Translation Section as the "Salt Mines" or the "Zoo Section" because of its designation as the Z Section. Life in the Zoo was hectic. It operated in three shifts of eight hours each per day, seven days a week. The work was also extremely boring. Many of the officers found it very difficult to appreciate the significance of their tasks or the connection between their work and operations. Typical remarks made by translators included comments like: "Unfortunately, the material, almost without exception, was extremely boring and without any conceivable military value. There were detailed reports on the health of Japanese army units that had ceased to exist, charts of equipment down to the last nail and bottle of ink, and long lists of the names of soldiers in a battalion. At first we worked with great seriousness, wanting to believe that our translations were of the highest importance, but gradually the dullness of the material dampened our initial enthusiasm."[40] Similar sentiments were found among the graduates at the Washington Document Center. Mary Craig McCullough, who headed the Japanese Literature Department at Berkeley after the war, described her job as being "involved mostly [with] translating documents of dubious utility to the intelligence-gathering enterprise."[41]

On the other hand, there were those who found much satisfaction with their work. For instance, Sherwood Moran,[42] who served at Pearl Harbor's codebreaking unit, Station Hypo, from February 1943 to August 1944, recalled that he found his task very exciting and satisfying. Moran was proud that information that he provided on the movement of Japanese vessels enabled American submarines to successfully intercept and sink many of "their *marus*."[43]

An unexpected challenge that faced the translators was the steady flow of personal diaries that were captured or recovered from the bodies of Japanese soldiers and sailors on Guadalcanal. The inexperienced Boulder Boys had scant training in reading *sosho*, cursive writing. The language officers were used to reading printed characters or clearly written calligraphy. But the rapidly scrawled handwriting of a soldier or sailor under battle conditions made the diaries extremely difficult to read. However, a select few quickly took to the task of tackling diaries. One notable figure was Donald Keene who trained himself to decipher the script and eventually developed the skill as his specialty. At the end of war, he received a decoration from the Navy for his ability to read such documents.[44] Although many of these diaries were of a personal nature, in a few cases valuable intelligence was obtained. Jasper Holmes kept one diary that described the torturing of two American prisoners who tried to escape. A Japanese surgeon cut out their livers to see how long they would survive.[45]

As the American offensives in the Pacific intensified in 1943, the Translation Section had to be reorganized in order to handle the mass of documents that were flooding into JICPOA. Fifteen subsections were organized with each specializing in translating documents on a certain subject. For example, there was a section for Japanese aviation, one for the army, one for radar and sonar, one for ordnance, one for ships and shipbuilding, and so on. This new method allowed language officers to develop an expertise in Japanese terminology dealing with their special subject. Even then, it was impossible to translate every document that came to JICPOA. One shipment from Saipan contained fifty tons of Japanese documents. Items deemed to have little or no intelligence value were forwarded to the Washington Document Center. But identifying the useful materials required a group of highly skilled and experienced officers to sort and classify important documents when they first arrived at Pearl Harbor. These teams came to be known as Sparrows because of their unusual ability to pick out the few gems from amongst the boxes of paperwork that arrived daily.[46]

In addition to the flood of documents that was arriving at JICPOA, large numbers of prisoners were being captured. At first, few Japanese became prisoners because of the stigma of shame. But as the war lengthened more and more Japanese became involuntary prisoners because of factors like illness, serious wounds, or unconsciousness from explosions. In 1942, there were only forty-nine prisoners from the Pacific. By late 1943, there were 522 Japanese POWs from the Pacific and slightly over a thousand from the South West Pacific area. In order to cope with this increase in numbers, JICPOA, in early 1944, established a separate interrogation section. The Officer-in-Charge was Lt. Frank Huggins and the Executive Officer was Lt.(jg) Otis Cary.

The interrogators were a unique group of men. Not everyone was qualified for this job as it took a certain degree of fluency in Japanese to conduct interrogations. About a dozen language officers[47] worked in interrogation on a permanent basis and other officers were brought in when needed. At times, men from the Translation Section were sent to the POW stockade for interrogation duty in order to keep them from forgetting their conversational Japanese.[48] Most of the men in interrogation were BIJs, but there were others like Frank Gibney, Kermit Lansner, Lionel Casson, and George Romani whose mastery of spoken Japanese qualified them for work as interrogators. Gibney recalled amusingly that "Since I was good at spoken Japanese, or at least at mimicking its sound, I was taken into the bosom of the Interrogation Section quite readily."[49]

The job of the interrogators at JICPOA was to solicit strategic and tactical information from the prisoners. They were questioned about their background, morale, and details about their hometowns such as the locations of military or naval bases or military/naval factories—information that would prove useful in selecting targets for American bombers. Because of the shameful stigma attached to being taken prisoner, and also because of the good treatment by their captors, most Japanese prisoners at Pearl Harbor were quite willing to talk. They accepted the fact that they could not return to Japan because it would bring shame to the family if it were known that they had not carried out the proper procedure of committing ritual suicide. In fact, when asked whether they wished their names to be made known to the Japanese government, as required by the Geneva Convention, almost all said no or never.[50]

Of course, some stubborn Japanese refused to cooperate. In one instance, Frank Huggins dealt with a refusal by letting one of his Marine sergeants rough the fellow up in a small cell which the Japanese referred to as the *buta-bako* or pig box. Otis Cary, the Executive Officer, took a very different approach. He believed that he could convince the Japanese of the virtues of Christianity and democracy. Otis visited the prisoner whom Huggins had beaten and apologized profusely for the rough treatment. He brought the prisoner cigarettes and other goodies while explaining that such beatings were quite un-American. But as Gibney noted: "In actual practice, this combination of the hard and soft sell proved to be oddly effective. Nobody wanted to be in the *buta-bako* for very long. And the combination of slaps and shoves from Gunnie (for Gunnery Sergeant) Tropea followed up by exhortations from Lieutenant (j.g.) Cary about building the brave new world would be enough to confuse any recalcitrant boatswain's mate or leading private and make him amenable to spilling the most closely held secrets."[51]

By November 1944, JICPOA decided to send teams of specialists along on operations with the Marines and the Army. The team was made up of a language officer, an officer from the Enemy Bases section, a photo expert, a ground forces specialist, and an enlisted man. These teams carried out on-the-spot interrogations and also ensured that key prisoners and documents were sent back to JICPOA. However, souvenir hunting among the troops created a major problem for JICPOA. In one instance, an important Japanese code book was found in the possession of one of the men during an inspection. As a result, a new policy was instituted whereby all souvenirs had to be inspected and approved by the language officers who would stamp items to indicate that they had passed inspection.[52] Not only did Boulder graduates accompany army units on operations, but in some cases they headed teams of *Nisei* interpreters and translators. Although the Army could not produce enough Japanese language officers it was unwilling to give Japanese-Americans officer status. Adamant that only Caucasians should lead the *Nisei* units, the Army actually welcomed Navy officers instead of using *Niseis*.[53]

Officers of the Interrogation Section were invariably affected by their constant contact with prisoners. In Frank Capra's *Know Your Enemy: Japan*, a popular government propaganda film of the era, the Japanese were depicted as deceitful, cruel, fanatic, and militaristic. Despite whatever preconceived ideas they may have had, many interrogators began to view the prisoners as people like themselves.

Gibney described his initial reaction in the stockade: "My first experience in the prison camp was to be brought into a volleyball game, which shocked me a bit—weren't these people the enemy? But as I stayed there, we began to develop good relations and formed some friendships during that time which have remained over the years."[54]

Otis Cary felt an even stronger bond with the prisoners. When the war was over he actually brought back many letters that he had promised to deliver to the families of the POWs. Cary went out of his way to contact the families. He likened his job to that of a divine mission: "It turned out to be the closest thing to playing Jesus I would ever want to try." Many of the families he visited thought that their loved ones had died because the Japanese government had announced that many of the Pacific campaigns ended gloriously with the heroic death of every man. Though it was a tough job, Cary was the type of person who gained a lot of personal gratification for this type of work.[55]

Donald Keene was another whose views of the Japanese were changed by his work as an interrogator and translator. Questioning prisoners did not have as strong an impact on him as the reading of captured diaries. He recalled that "As I read the diaries of men who were suffering such hardships, it was impossible not to be moved. . . . By contrast, the letters of the American sailors I had to censor once a week revealed no ideals, and certainly no suffering, but only their reiterated desire to return to their former lives. Throughout the war this contrast haunted me."[56]

Without question World War II had a great impact on the men and women of that generation. The Pacific War, in particular, affected the lives of those who became Japanese language officers at Boulder. But the establishment of the Navy's Japanese Language School brought together some of the brightest minds whose seminal experience helped influence postwar American–Japanese relations. Most of them, however, did not realize where their postwar paths would lead them. Many simply went back to their old pursuits and never used their Japanese again. It was a logical decision because at the end of the war, there simply was no demand for Japanese either academically or in the business world. American companies regarded interpreting or translating as menial labor and in any case, it cost them much less to hire a Japanese national. Japan lay in ruins and everyone felt that it would be decades before recovery was possible.

Moreover, the Navy did little to retain the services of this large group of Japanese linguists. The immediate years after the war were some of the most difficult that the Navy had experienced. With the defeat of Japan, the American fleet and personnel were reduced drastically as a result of demobilization and budget cuts. Naval personnel shrank from 3.4 million men in the summer of 1945 to 375,000 by 1950. Japan no longer posed a threat and American attention was drawn increasingly to China where a major civil war was being waged between the Nationalists and the Communists. The small naval force in the North Pacific came under the command of Gen. Douglas MacArthur and its primary mission was to support the occupation of Japan. The bulk of the Navy's resources was allocated to Europe, especially to the Mediterranean.[57] There was little interest in Japan and even less in its former language officers. Without a viable enemy, the Navy quickly forgot the lessons of 1940 and 1941 when it was caught unprepared and had to hastily establish the Japanese Language School to correct the problem.

For those who might have contemplated staying in the Navy, there were no jobs. Many were assigned to the United States Strategic Bombing Survey; others joined SCAP (Supreme Command Allied Powers) as civilian employees during the occupation (economic section, censorship, etc.) since personnel from ATIS (Allied Translator and Interpreter Section) dominated the interpreting and translating. Some went into the CIA and a good number joined the foreign service. Because of their background, most returned to academia where they pursued advanced degrees or obtained teaching positions. Many of these Boulder graduates who persistently held on to their knowledge of Japanese went on to distinguished careers.

In the area of diplomacy, Marshall Green (who became Assistant Secretary of State), David Osborn, Philip Manhard, and William Sherman occupied senior positions at the U.S. embassy in

Tokyo. Except for Sherman, who became a deputy ambassador to the United Nations, all three ended their careers as ambassadors. In the field of journalism, Frank Gibney was a *Time* correspondent, the senior editor of *Newsweek* magazine, and is now president of the Pacific Basin Institute at Pomona College in Claremont, California. As a mater of fact, Gibney recently won the prestigious Japan Foundation award for his lifetime contribution of furthering mutual understanding between the United States and Japan. Kermit Lansner was the editor of *Newsweek* and then became senior editor of *Financial World*. Reed Irvine became CEO of Accuracy in Media. In business, Houghton Freeman took over the family insurance company and headed the American International Group (AIG). The Freeman family foundation frequently contributes not only to projects only connected with Japan, but also to a number of educational causes related to East Asia.

In the academic field, it is not an exaggeration to say that graduates of the Boulder program basically founded Japanese studies at America's institutions of higher learning. Some prominent figures include: Richard Beardsley, Theodore deBary, Donald Keene, John W. Hall, James Morley, Helen Craig McCullough, Robert Scalapino, Donald Shively, Ivan Morris, and Edward Seidensticker.

Within the Navy itself, fewer than a dozen Boulder Boys opted to remain after the war. Only six decided to make the Navy a career, and of those six, only two utilized their knowledge of Japanese. Hammond Rolph became an assistant naval attaché in Tokyo and Roger Pineau is best known for his collaborative work with Samuel Eliot Morison on the naval history of the Pacific War. Pineau should also be recognized for his role as the unofficial historian of the Japanese Navy Language Program. He devoted most of his life to this project. Pineau stayed in touch with many former graduates. He painstakingly compiled thousands of files containing biographies and correspondence. Unfortunately, Pineau passed away before he could finish his definitive history. Books have been written on America's China Hands but very little has ever been published on the Japan Hands. Their story is an important one that deserves to be recognized. Drawing loosely from the title of Gwen Terasaki's autobiography, these men and women were America's "Bridges to the Rising Sun."

NOTES

[1] Wyman H. Packard, *A Century of U.S. Naval Intelligence* (Washington, D.C.: Office of Naval Intelligence, Naval Historical Center, 1996), 365; Pedro Loureiro, "Intelligence Success," Ph.D. dissertation, University of Southern California, 1995, 26.

[2] Jeffery Dorwart, *Conflict of Duty: The U.S. Navy's Intelligence Dilemma, 1919–1945* (Annapolis, Md.: Naval Institute Press, 1983), 61, 63, 91; *The Reminiscences of Rear Admiral Arthur H. McCollum* (Annapolis, Md.: Naval Institute Press, 1973), Vol. 1, 260 (hereafter McCollum Oral History).

[3] McCollum Oral History, 259–260.

[4] Roger Pineau Papers, Japanese Language School 1-6, "The Navy School of Oriental Languages University of Colorado, Boulder, Colorado," undated manuscript, the University of Colorado at Boulder, Archives (hereafter Japanese Language School).

[5] Ibid.

[6] Ibid.

[7] The school at Boulder was closed on 1 September 1946 and operations at Stillwater ceased on 30 June 1946. *United States Naval Administration in WWII, The Office of Naval Intelligence* (Washington, D.C.: Naval Historical Center, nd), 715–716 (hereafter ONI History).

[8] The Military Intelligence Division of the War Department established the first Army Japanese language school under Lt. Col. John Weckerling at the Presidio of San Francisco on 1 November 1941. With the Japanese exclusion act, the school was moved to Camp Savage (near Minneapolis, Minnesota) in June 1942. In August 1944, it was relocated to Fort Snelling, Minnesota, where Chinese and Korean were included. A separate facility, the Army Intensive Japanese Language School was established at the University of Michigan, Ann Arbor. *The Pacific War and Peace: Americans of Japanese Ancestry in Military Intelligence Service 1941 to 1952* (San Francisco, Calif.: Military Intelligence Service Association of Northern California and the National Japanese American Historical Society, 1991), 16-19, 24.

[9] Larry Myers, "Language Training for War with Japan" essay from a publication by the U.S. Naval Cryptologic Veterans Association. Complete bibliographic information not available as photocopy of the article was provided to author by Hammond Rolph.

[10] Wendell Furnas interview Santa Monica, California, July 1999.

[11] Japanese Language School.

[12] Ibid.

[13] Pedro Loureiro, "Japanese Espionage and American Countermeasures in Pre-Pearl Harbor California," *The Journal of American-East Asian Relations* 3:3 (Fall 1994), 200.

[14] Donald Keene, *On Familiar Terms: A Journey Across Cultures* (New York: Kodansha, 1994), 16.

[15] ONI History, 713.

[16] Frank Gibney interview, July 1999, Pomona College, Claremont California.

[17] One *sensei* at Boulder, Fred Tayama, was hospitalized from being beaten for his pro-American views in December 1942 while he was interned in the Manzanar Relocation Center. Peter Irons, *Justice at War: The Story of the Japanese-American Internment Cases* (New York: Oxford University Press), 79–80. See also Brian Hayashi, *For the Sake of Our Bretheren: Assimilation, Nationalism, and Protestantism Among the Japanese of Los Angeles, 1895–1942* (Stanford: Stanford University Press,

1995), 155.

[18]Letter from Captain A. E. Hindmarsh, USNR, to Yuji Imai, 14 May 1946. Photocopy provided to author by Mrs. Yuji Imai.

[19]Frank Gibney interview, July 1999, Pomona College, Claremont, California; Japanese Language School.

[20]Frank Gibney Interview, July 1999, Pomona College, Claremont, California.

[21]Roger Pineau Papers, University of Colorado at Boulder, Archives, Frank Tucker Manuscript, 119.

[22] Keene, 17.

[23] Frank Tucker Manuscript, 113.

[24]*Sunday Camera*, 11 July 1993.

[25]Japanese Language School; Julia Rolph telephone interview, 21 November 1999.

[26]*Sunday Camera*, 11 July 1993.

[27]Japanese Language School.

[28]Julia Rolph letter to Pineau and Hudson, 10 May 1989.

[29]Capt. Nixon Ballard (USMC) was the Commanding Officer of the Marine Japanese Language School at the University of Hawaii. The instructors were Yukio Uehara, a certain Hayashida and a Buddhist priest. The students were: Eugene P. Boardman, Paul S. Dull, John C. Erskine, Richard A. Gard, Eugene E. Gregg, Gerald P. Holtom, John McLaughlin, John E. Merrill, Donald R. Nugent, John C. Pelzel, John H. Pierce, and William H. Shaw. "USMC Japanese Language School," Roger Pineau Papers; John C. Erskine, "Language Officers Recall Combat Roles in the Pacific," *Fortitudine* 15:4 (Spring 1986), 23–24.

[30]Japanese Language School; ONI History, 713-174.

[31]Ibid., 714.

[32]Keene, 18.

[33]Gibney Manuscript, 8; Tucker Manuscript, 126.

[34]Julia Rolph interview, San Gabriel, California, 23 November 1999.

[35]Stanley R. Townsend was one of the Boulder graduates who spent several months at this facility. Letter from Stanley Townsend to Roger Pineau, 5 June 1986, Roger Pineau Papers, File 28–3.

[36]John Prados, *Combined Fleet Decoded: The Secret History of American Intelligence and the Japanese Navy in World War II* (New York: Random House, 1995), 496.

[37]W. J. Holmes, *Double-Edged Secrets: U.S. Naval Intelligence Operations in the Pacific during World War II* (Annapolis, Md.: Naval Institute Press, 1979), 120.

[38]Keene, 21.

[39]Holmes, 169.

[40]Keene, 22.

[41]Helen Craig McCullough, reminiscences, 2.

[42]Moran was born and raised in Japan. His father Capt. "Pappy" Moran was a missionary who volunteered his services to the Marine Corps at the age of fifty-four. He was assigned to the First Marine Division and saw action at Guadalcanal. Moran became the chief interpreter/interrogator for Gen. Alexander A. Vandergrift. Letter, Sherwood Moran to author, 10 August 1999; Telephone interview, Sherwood Moran, 24 November 1999.

[43]Sherwood Moran, "Some War Reminiscences"; Telephone interview Sherwood Moran, 24 November 1999.

[44]Keene, 223; Holmes, 123.

[45]Holmes, 123.

[46]Holmes, 168.

[47]Members of the Interrogation Section included: Ed Buchannan, Otis Cary, Lionel Casson, Herbert Deane, Frank Gibney, William Gorham, Frank Huggins, Kenneth Church Lamott, Kermit Lansner, Scribner McCoy, Addison Parker, George Romani, Grover Sims, Arthur Szathmary, and (Tovy) Steingrimr Thorlaksson.

[48]Keene, 34.

[49] Gibney Manuscript, 2.
[50] Hiromichi Yahara, introduction and commentary by Frank B. Gibney, *The Battle for Okinawa* (New York: John Wiley & Sons, 1995), xxi–xxiii.
[51] Ibid., 6.
[52] Prados, 530–531.
[53] Keene, 50.
[54] Gibney Manuscript, 9.
[55] Otis Cary, ed., *War Wasted Asia: Letters, 1945–46* (Tokyo, New York: Kodansha, 1975), 217–227.
[56] Keene, 23.
[57] Dean C. Allard, "An Era of Transition, 1945–1953," in Kenneth J. Hagan, ed., *In Peace and War: Interpretations of American Naval History, 1775–1984* (Westport, Conn.: Greenwood Press, 1984), 290–303.

Protested Presence: The Nuclear Navy Comes To Japan, 1961–1968

Roger Dingman

> Visits of American warships to foreign ports are often freighted with issues of both local and international politics. During America's war with Vietnam, ship visits were frequently used as opportunities to protest U.S. policy, and when nuclear-powered warships made port calls in Japan, the stage was set for volatile protests. In this essay, Roger Dingman details the events surrounding the visits of four nuclear-powered U.S. warships to Japanese ports during the Vietnam War and shows how the American and Japanese response to these mini-crises helped strengthen and redefine both American-Japanese relations and civil-naval relations in America.

Technological change and adaptation to it are part and parcel of modern naval life. In the Twentieth Century two great changes in ship propulsion and weaponry have revolutionized navies. The first was singular—the shift from coal to oil propulsion—during the first two decades of this century. The second was twofold—the so-called "nuclear revolution" in both propulsion and munitions that swept over navies fifteen years after the end of the Second World War. As the 1950s turned into the 1960s, that second great change manifested itself in a series of vessels—the USS *Nautilus* (SSN 571), the world's first nuclear-powered submarine; the USS *Long Beach* (CGN 9) and the USS *Enterprise* (CVN 65), the world's first atomic-powered surface ships; and the USS *George Washington* (SSBN 598), the world's first nuclear-powered and atomic-armed submarine.[1]

The advent of these new tools of naval warfare was marked by great controversy, both within and beyond the United States Navy. Naval historians and biographers have detailed those battles and the personalities who fought them very well.[2] But neither they nor

---

Roger Dingman is Professor of History at the University of Southern California. Research for this essay was made possible by a generous Vice Admiral Edwin B. Hooper Research Grant from the Naval Historical Foundation.

those who write international history have paid much attention to the struggles that attended the deployment of these technologically revolutionary vessels far from American shores. This essay deals with one such fight: the struggle generated by U.S. Navy nuclear-powered and (presumably) nuclear-armed vessels' port visits in Japan.

That fight reached its peak while America was at war in Vietnam. That overlapping of events has obscured its significance and made it especially difficult for American historians to grasp its significance. The very few who have written about protests in Japan during the near decade between the 1964 Tonkin Gulf incident and the 1973 Paris peace agreement have depicted them as primarily a response to the Vietnam War. With but one important exception, they have also exaggerated their strength.[3]

This essay, however, rests on a different premise. It posits that the roots of Vietnam-era protests against American nuclear ship port visits to Japan are to be found in naval technological developments, the larger Cold War arms rivalry of which they were a part, and Japanese politics and psychology. The events that this essay will describe and analyze would have occurred even in the absence of war in Vietnam. And the significance of Japanese protests against American nuclear-powered vessels' visits to their ports transcends that unhappy conflict. For in what must surely be regarded as an irony of history, protests against an American nuclear naval presence in Japan in the 1960s helped guarantee its permanence in the decades that followed.

To see how and why that was so, it is essential to consider four basic questions about the protests that greeted the arrival of American nuclear-powered and (presumably) atomic-armed vessels in Japan between 1964 and 1973. First, why did the U.S. Navy send these ships to Japan? Second, who protested their arrival, and why did they do so? Third, how did the governments of Japan and the United States deal with the spectacular struggles that ensued? And, finally, what difference did this fight make for the future of the American naval presence in Japan and for Japanese-American naval and diplomatic relations?

Any answer to the first of those questions must begin by acknowledging a crucial fact: By the beginning of the 1960s, the naval nuclear revolution had reached a critical turning point. Washington had long since made the basic decision to "go nuclear," and prototypical vessels had begun to perform normal naval missions. The *Nautilus* had completed her pioneering voyages under the polar icecap and shed much of her celebrity as the world's first nuclear powered vessel.[4] From October 1958 onward, all newly laid down U.S. Navy submarines were powered by nuclear reactors, not diesel engines.[5] Within days of John F. Kennedy's election in November 1960, the USS *George Washington* put to sea on the first Polaris deterrent patrol. Less than a year after Kennedy's stirring call to Cold War combat in his Inaugural Address of January 1961, the world's first nuclear-powered surface Navy ships, the cruiser *Long Beach* and the carrier *Enterprise*, began operating with the fleet in the Atlantic.[6]

By that time no one doubted that a nuclear naval race was on between the United States and the Soviet Union. The Russians had completed their first nuclear submarine in 1958, and the ensuing competition to build more and better nuclear-powered naval vessels guaranteed that, sooner or later, these newest implements of naval warfare would show themselves in the Pacific.[7] Thoughtful observers could foresee the day when one of these vessels might need to put in to a Japanese port. American nuclear attack boats had taken over intelligence patrols in the Sea of Japan and along the shores of the Soviet Maritime Province once carried out by diesel-powered boats. Sub skippers' determination to get as close as possible to Soviet ports risked discovery, depth-charging, and, if not destruction, then the need to flee to the nearest port for repairs, replenishment, and the refreshment of their crews.[8] Japan, with two major American naval bases, both superbly equipped for ship repair work, was the closest place they could go. In retrospect, it is clear that a U.S. Navy nuclear ship port visit to Japan had become a question of when, not whether.

In prospect, however, things were not that simple. Secretary of State Dean Rusk first broached the possibility of a nuclear submarine port visit in conversation with Japanese Prime Minister

Ikeda Hayato in June 1961. The prime minister put off his American host by saying that at present there was "certain to be a great deal of opposition" to anything regarding atomic energy, "including a visit by nuclear-powered submarines." The Japanese public tended to relate "anything atomic to nuclear weapons and to the possibility of involvement in a nuclear war," and members of the Japan Science Council had "close ties to the left."[9] His words seemed prescient nine months later, when protests erupted in Tokyo over Washington's resumption of nuclear testing. But American diplomatic officials did not take them as the final word on port visits by ships of the new nuclear navy. In December 1962, while in Washington for consultations, Ambassador Edwin O. Reischauer told Navy officials and his diplomatic superiors that he thought the time had come to begin preparing for port visits by nuclear-powered, but not nuclear-armed, American submarines.[10]

The ambassador's suggestion represented his considered judgment about one of the most sensitive issues in Japanese-American relations. As America's pre-eminent Japanologist (a Harvard professor turned ambassador), Reischauer understood Japan's so-called "nuclear allergy." It was natural that the first nation to have suffered nuclear attack wanted nothing to do with anything atomic. More than that, Reischauer knew well how deeply the so-called *Lucky Dragon* incident of 1954, in which Japanese tuna fishermen had accidentally been irradiated by American thermonuclear weapons tests in the central Pacific, had scarred the Japanese psyche. Revulsion over the death of one of those men, together with pent up anger over the bombing of Hiroshima and Nagasaki had brought the Japanese Right, Left, and Center together in a strong national, anti-nuclear organization.[11] Opposition to the testing, deployment, or use of nuclear weapons seemed to have become a touchstone of Japan's national identity.

But Reischauer, much like physicians of that day, did not believe the allergy was permanent—or impervious to treatment. Controlled and limited exposure to things nuclear might, much in the fashion of an allergen periodically introduced into the body, eventually end the allergy or, at the very least, create a tolerance for the offending substance. To the ambassador and his aide responsible for politico-military matters, that was the lesson to be drawn from months of careful dialogue with Japanese opponents of nuclear testing.[12] Indeed, as 1962 turned into 1963, Reischauer was convinced that his patient diplomacy and openness to representatives of every point of view on the Japanese political and intellectual spectrum had restored the dialogue essential to good working of the Japanese-American alliance. Thus, in his view careful diplomatic and psychological preparation could prevent a recurrence of the political turmoil and rioting over ratification of a revised U.S.-Japan Security Treaty that in 1960 had toppled the government of Kishi Nobusuke and forced cancellation of President Dwight D. Eisenhower's planned visit to Tokyo. There was no need for "political excitement" or a "fracas" when that first nuclear boat arrived in Japan.[13]

In January 1963 Reischauer quietly raised the possibility of a nuclear sub visit in conversation with Foreign Minister Ohira Masayoshi, whom he trusted and admired. The American assured the Japanese that the boats in question would not carry nuclear missiles. He made it clear that, in Washington's view, the 1960 security treaty did not require "prior consultation" for the entry of such vessels, a position that Ohira accepted and eventually made the basis for his own explanation of why such visits were permissible.[14] But for the time being, the foreign minister suggested that it would be wise to proceed cautiously in view of "the complex sentiments of unease in Japan with respect to atomic energy."[15] Reischauer accepted that response and later praised Ohira and Prime Minister Ikeda for the "great caution" and political wisdom with which they dealt with the issue. Devoting "many months" to studying the potential dangers of radiation and giving "all sides . . . ample opportunity" to voice the pros and cons of American nuclear submarine visits had been the right thing to do.[16]

Those honeyed words concealed many a rough spot on the road to Japan's official acceptance of an American nuclear submarine's port visit. The Ikeda government began to walk down it by announcing, early in March 1963, the obvious: if an American nuclear boat came to Japan it would go to either Yokosuka, the largest American naval base in Japan, located on the southwest side of Tokyo Bay, or to Sasebo, a much smaller American facility more than six hundred miles south and west of the capital, on the island of Kyushu. A month later voters in the latter city elected a new mayor, Tsuji Ichizo, who defeated an incumbent willing to go along with whatever Tokyo said by promising not to agree to a nuclear ship's port visit until he was satisfied it would not be dangerous.[17] Then the *Thresher* (SSN 593) went down, raising fresh doubts about the safety of atomic-powered submarines.[18]

In Tokyo at almost the same time, Foreign Minister Ohira inadvertently complicated matters still further by implying in his answer to a Diet questioner that U.S. Navy nuclear submarines did not carry nuclear weapons and were not allowed to bring them into Japan. He "trusted the Americans." But his words alarmed both his political opponents and Ambassador Reischauer. The ambassador worried that Ohira had compromised the U.S. Navy's standard "neither confirm nor deny" policy on the presence of nuclear weapons aboard its vessels and contradicted a secret understanding about them in the 1960 security treaty revision negotiations. Reischauer eventually concluded that Ohira had fuzzed over a potentially explosive issue by saying that port visits by already nuclear-armed vessels did not constitute "introduction" of nuclear weapons into Japan.[19]

But the Japanese were not so sure. In August 1963, just when politicians and the public commemorated the horrors of Hiroshima and Nagasaki, the *Asahi shimbun*, perhaps the most prestigious of Japan's three major national newspapers, began running articles about the perils of possible nuclear submarine port visits.[20] That same month Foreign Minister Ohira acknowledged the U.S. Navy's impatience to have one of its nuclear subs visit Japan but added that it would be "politically wise" to wait until the head of Japan's Atomic Energy Commission could discuss technical matters with Admiral Hyman Rickover and present a favorable recommendation for such a port call.[21] On September 1, nearly one hundred thousand people went to Yokosuka and Sasebo to voice their opposition to Japan's becoming a base for American nuclear-powered vessels.[22] That same day, four thousand people gathered in Sasebo to discuss the issue, while fourteen ships, two aircraft, and a horde of zig-zagging demonstrators just outside the U.S. Navy base there proclaimed their opposition to any nuclear submarine visit. The next day Mayor Tsuji left for Tokyo to present their concerns to cabinet officials and responsible government agency heads.[23] The politicians there quieted him by promising to send Japan Atomic Energy Commission experts to participate in teach-ins. And to strengthen the arguments that those men would put forward, they invited Admiral Hyman Rickover to pay a secret visit to Tokyo to reassure them of the safety of nuclear propulsion for naval vessels.[24]

But no announcement of a decision on a port call by an American nuclear submarine followed. That made senior American naval officers in Japan restless, and some threatened to insist that the Navy must be allowed to come in its nuclear boats on its own terms, or it might not continue to come at all. Ambassador Reischauer calmed them down,[25] but he could not stem the growing impatience of their superiors in Washington. Finally, on August 3, 1964, twenty *months* after Ambassador Reischauer had broached the subject with Foreign Minister Ohira, Navy Secretary Paul Nitze, then on a visit to Tokyo, pointedly reminded his hosts that Washington was waiting for Japan's answer on the matter of a nuclear submarine port visit.[26]

His remarks may have forced the Ikeda Cabinet to speak its mind. Three and a half weeks later it formally approved such a visit—without setting a date for it.

Four days later, on September 1, 1964, members of the U.S.-Japan Security Consultative Committee (Reischauer, CincPac Admiral U.S. Grant Sharp, Foreign Minister Shiina Etsusaburo, and Defense Agency Chief Koizumi Junchi) held a press conference at which they sought to diffuse any lingering anxieties about a nuclear submarine port visit.[27] The very next day communist and socialist Diet members vowed to fight such to the bitter end. And in a *faux pas* that stirred "a hornet's nest of public excitement," the Defense Agency head "casually announced" that any sub that came would be armed solely with atomic warheads, not with conventional ones as Washington had promised nine months earlier. That error made

Sasebo Mayor Tsuji's visits to Prime Minister Ikeda and Ambassador Reischauer seem all the more urgent.[28]

But this flurry of concern quickly faded away. After initially surmising that protest demonstrations against an American nuclear submarine port visit would be "bigger than they otherwise would have been," Reischauer concluded, "on balance . . . the leftist effort to stir up a major incident over the submarines will fail." Indeed, the controversy might even prove beneficial in getting some Japanese to "think again" about what their nation's defense needs really were.[29] The Japanese public seemed to forget about nuclear issues—including China's explosion of its first nuclear device—as it enjoyed the pageantry and competition of the Tokyo Olympics. When they ended, public and media attention focused on the political drama caused by Prime Minister Ikeda's hospitalization for cancer and the ensuing struggle within the ruling Liberal Democratic Party over who would succeed him.[30]

By late October 1964, American embassy and Japanese officials alike had concluded that a nuclear submarine visit should come "the sooner the better."[31]

Japanese scientists had completed background checks of radioactivity at the two ports where it might occur. The boat chosen to make the visit, the USS *Seadragon* (SSN 584), was then in Hong Kong and could come to Naha, Okinawa, in a few days. Early in November, the embassy and Navy officials decided to let curious Japanese newsmen come aboard her to see for themselves how safe—and free of nuclear weapons—she was.[32] A week later, the new prime minister, Sato Eisaku, drew Ambassador Reischauer aside during an imperial garden party to reveal his preferred political tactics for managing the visit. While his government must be informed of the visit ahead of time, it preferred to remain ignorant of the boat's schedule until twenty-four hours prior to her arrival in Japan proper. That would prevent leaks that might allow "extremist elements" to mount big demonstrations.[33]

Reischauer readily concurred in that plan, for although the Navy ostensibly set a submarine's schedule, he had gotten authority to cancel any planned visit up to twenty four hours prior to a boat's scheduled arrival if he thought there was sufficient political reason to do so. But he saw none. The next morning Reischauer officially informed the Japanese Government that the *Seadragon* would enter Sasebo Harbor on the morning of November 12, 1964.[34] Then on that same evening, as if to celebrate the coming realization of a long-planned dream, the ambassador and his wife danced away the night at the embassy's Marine Corps birthday ball.[35]

Thus the stage was set for the first American nuclear submarine to enter a Japanese port. But in their preparations for that event over the preceding months and years, Ambassador Reischauer, Japanese government officials, and those who objected to their plans had changed the character of that event. What had ostensibly originated in naval need had become a political and diplomatic imperative. The *Seadragon* was coming to Japan so that other boats like her might someday rest their crews, replenish their stores, and, if non-nuclear needs arose, undergo repairs. But her visit had become, for Japanese, a political contest between their conservative government, which was firmly committed to alliance with America, and parties and groups on the Left who opposed that tie and objected to *any* American naval or military presence in their country. And for American naval and diplomatic officials the prospective visit had metamorphosed into an educational opportunity. They wanted it to help associate Japan "a little more closely" with America's Asia/Pacific defense system and "bring home responsibility" to an ally whose people were "strongly influenced by neutralism."[36] Would the *Seadragon* be able to accomplish all that during her visit to Sasebo?

On the morning of November 12, 1964, under leaden gray skies and with a cold wind following, the *Seadragon* threaded her way up the channel toward Sasebo.[37] Two hundred sixty-seventy feet long and twenty-five feet wide, the five-year-old boat carried eight twenty-one-inch torpedo tubes and eighty-four men eager for liberty in what was reputed to be the best liberty port in the Western Pacific. Barely ninety days earlier she had hurried west from the Washington coast in response to the Tonkin Gulf crisis on what would be her third Western Pacific cruise. After two months on patrol in the South China Sea in support of Vietnam operations, she had headed north for three days' stay in Hong Kong and then a week at Naha, Okinawa.[38] The Japanese reporters who had swarmed over her there put the *Seadragon*'s skipper, Commander Douglas B. Guthe, and his crew on notice: their visit to Sasebo would not be just an ordinary port call.

Those responsible for planning the visit had done everything they could, however, to make that visit appear ordinary. In Washington senior Navy officials overruled Admiral Rickover's attempts to shield the sub from public view.[39] In Tokyo, Japanese Foreign Ministry officials advised Ambassador Reischauer to get the Navy to have as many other non-nuclear vessels and ordinary sailors as possible present at Sasebo so as to deflect attention from the *Seadragon* and emphasize the economic value of American Navy port visits. The Navy complied by dispatching the USS *Columbus* (CG 12) to Sasebo. Liberal Democratic Party officials sought and got films and public information data on other American nuclear-powered vessels in order to combat the Left's anti-nuclear "propaganda."[40]

In Sasebo, the U.S. Navy base commander, Captain Arthur F. Farwell, Jr., a Chicago native and former PB4Y-2 pilot who had won a presidential unit commendation for sinking more than a hundred thousand tons of Japanese shipping in a mere five months during World War II, did everything possible to smooth the way for the *Seadragon*'s arrival. Familiar with the city since Korean War days, he had worked for months with Mayor Tsuji and local officials to prepare for a happy first nuclear submarine visit.[41] At Yokosuka, his superior, Rear Adm. John L. Chew, Commander U.S. Naval Forces, Japan, had at first been inclined to call out the Marines if demonstrators surrounded American bases. But wisely he deferred to the advice of local Japanese Maritime Self Defense Force admirals and decided to rely upon the Japanese police to handle them.[42] Farwell thus adopted for the Navy in Sasebo a non-provocative (but non-neutral) stance that the Japanese termed "a low posture."

That put the spotlight on Mayor Tsuji—and the protestors that had come to Sasebo from all over Japan. They and Tokyo television viewers watched the *Seadragon*'s arrival at Sasebo.[43] Just as the submarine drew near to her mooring alongside the USS *Ajax* (AR 6) in the inner harbor, two bursts of fireworks from the hillside headquarters of those opposing her visit went off. But a sudden shower hid the submarine from their view and prompted the mayor and Captain Farwell to hurry aboard her.[44] Tsuji had wanted to be the first Japanese official to board an American nuclear boat and to demonstrate, by that act, that the *Seadragon* was safe.[45] Commander Guthe welcomed him aboard, served him coffee, and then ushered his diminutive guest around the boat. Then the two men repaired to the *Ajax* for a joint press conference. None of the reporters asked them embarrassing questions about submarine-launched missiles or nuclear weapons. Instead, the emphasis was on safety and harmony. Commander Guthe reminded all within hearing that his boat had visited other ports in complete safety and that many other U.S. Navy ships had paid pleasant and memorable visits to Sasebo.[46] That was an appropriately indirect gesture of reassurance to his crew, to the city's population, and, by extension, to the Japanese people.

But an air of apprehension overhung these proceedings. Guthe would not let his men go ashore on liberty until later that afternoon, by which time Captain Farwell had seen to it that an adequate shore patrol was in place and Mayor Tsuji had taken first measure of the demonstrators.[47] They had come from all over Japan and reflected every color within the spectrum of leftist opposition to the ruling Liberal Democratic Party government of Prime Minister Sato Eisaku.

The so-called "Old Left" was split between the enigmatic Japan Communist Party, with factions that leaned either toward Moscow or Beijing, and the Japan Socialist Party and its allies in the giant labor union, Sohyo.[48] Members of the splinter Democratic Socialist Party, under whose banners Mayor Tsuji had been elected, were not prepared to condemn outright the American military and naval presence in Japan.[49] They were relatively few in number. The new Komeito, or Clean Government Party, which owed its allegiance and existence to the Soka Gakkai Buddhist sect, had an even smaller representation.[50] The most radical elements present, some of them veterans of the 1960 fight against renewal of the U.S.-Japan Security Treaty, were student protest groups, then loosely united as

Zengakuren, the All-Japan United Council of Student Self Government Associations.[51] On that cold and damp November afternoon, only the last, a relatively small group of two hundred fifty, stood ready to challenge the thousand police that had been mobilized and stationed around the base perimeter.[52]

Not much happened that first day. But on the next larger, but still peaceful, demonstrations, against the *Seadragon's* visit, continued in Sasebo—and elsewhere—with each group doing what it thought best. The local Diet member, a Socialist, toured the city by car exhorting citizens to oppose the nuclear presence in their midst. The communists distributed handbills and held a revival-like rally. The Zengakuren students resorted to "light summer rain" tactics, sending small groups rushing by the main gate of the navy base without trying to enter it. Honoring requests from labor union and Japan Socialist Party leaders, they kept apart from other protestors. Far to the east of Sasebo, in Osaka and Tokyo, an array of groups protested the submarine's visit. In the capital that day, twelve thousand people—the largest gathering of all—joined to show their opposition to it.[53]

Protests evoked counter-protests. In Sasebo, two Liberal Democratic Party Diet members and thirty-seven sound trucks drove around the city proclaiming the safety of nuclear submarines and citizens' responsibility to welcome them as warmly as people had in other countries. The even more conservative All-Japan Patriots' Party had its sound trucks blare the old Imperial Navy's *Warship March* as a sign of support for the *Seadragon's* visit. Japanese naval and military retirees drove around the city touting the submarine's safety, and a group of local notables—the Citizens Consultative Cooperative Association—expressed their views by touring the boat. And yet, despite the obvious strength of feeling on both sides, competing banners at Sasebo Station that urged citizens to welcome or oppose the nuclear submarine, continued to hang unmolested.[54]

That pleased Mayor Tsuji, for it suggested that the *Seadragon* would depart Sasebo with the city's reputation for naval hospitality and its public order intact. On the afternoon of November 14, he was on hand to bid her farewell. Captain Guthe and his crew left happy, (a mood shared by the city's merchants and owners of establishments in its pleasure quarter), for their liberty had proceeded without disruption. They and their boat simply slipped away down the long channel leading to the open sea while silent, cold demonstrators watched from their respective observation points atop the surrounding hills.[55] What in prospect had seemed ominous and potentially explosive, had in practice turned out to be peaceful.

That end to the first Japanese port visit by an American nuclear submarine prompted those who had planned and protested it to draw a great variety of conclusions about its significance. U.S. Navy officials could be proud that the visit had passed, as they later described it, "without incident;" that is, without confrontation between sailors and demonstrators or any untoward social behavior on the Americans' part.[56] Mayor Tsuji undoubtedly heaved a sigh of relief that ten demonstrations and thirteen lesser parades involving fifty-five thousand people had come to an end without unseemly clashes between them and the police. He reported to Tokyo on what his city had endured but took pride in having kept contending groups apart and Sasebo's citizens from harm. While some Komeito members came away from the protest opposed to cooperation with socialists and communists in any similar event in the future, "Old Left" leaders assured their followers that the *Seadragon* protests had given a firm warning to the unelected Sato government against excessive use of force to suppress the free expression of political ideas.[57]

Others more distant from the scene drew more sanguine conclusions about the first nuclear submarine's visit. Ambassador Reischauer praised the Navy for its contribution to the American and Japanese governments' "combined political-military effort" to get the Japanese people to accept the need for defense and the presence of the "best forces" the United States could provide.[58] He insisted that the *Seadragon*'s port call had gone even better than he had optimistically predicted. Indeed, it might work out as "a great triumph for forces of reasonableness [in Japan] . . . because the left did its best to stir up a major fuss and failed miserably." Only "the professional hard core" of demonstrators had turned out. Protests in the streets, he concluded, just wouldn't work as a means of political dialogue or an instrument for policy change.[59] Two of the three major national daily newspapers' editorial writers agreed with him. As the *Yomiuri* put it—in words more descriptive of what had happened in Tokyo than in Sasebo—"to defy public law and order, call out mobs into the streets, and to turn a goodwill visit by a foreign warship into a carnival of violence is an invitation only to anarchy."[60]

In retrospect, however, it is clear that all of these judgments on the significance of the first visit by an American nuclear vessel to a Japanese port were premature. The *Seadragon*'s visit marked the beginning of a period of change and struggle, not a decisive shift in attitudes or political behavior. The gap between Japanese and American officials' views on the utility of nuclear submarine visits remained considerable. Ambassador Takeuchi Ryuji, for example, betrayed at best lukewarm feelings when he told Undersecretary of State W. Averell Harriman that the first nuclear sub visit had turned out to be "not such a bad thing."[61] Perhaps the most that can be said is that the *Seadragon* established the feasibility of nuclear sub port visits in principle and the certainty that they would be met by vigorous protests.

That prospect prompted one American, a Fulbright scholar living in Fukuoka, not far from Sasebo, to pose the fundamental questions that the *Seadragon*'s visit raised: Given the strength of Japan's "nuclear allergy," were not American officials responsible for the nuclear boats' visits being "insensitive" and "arrogantly indifferent" to the damage to Japanese-American friendship that they appeared to be doing?[62] Were the nuclear submarine port calls not doing more harm than good?

The pattern of events over the next year suggested that the answer to those questions was no. Nuclear subs came, one after another, to Sasebo. The *Seadragon* returned barely ninety days after her first visit, and she was followed by *Snook, Permit* (SSN 594), *Plunger* (SSN 595), and *Sargo* (SSN 583). Late in 1965, three nuclear boats called at Sasebo within the space of a month.[63] Each port call elicited protests, but by years' end American diplomats in Kyushu reported that they had shrunk to the point of being "pro-forma" objections only.⁶⁴ American diplomatic and naval officials appeared to have succeeded in making the nuclear navy's visits to Japan routine.⁶⁵

Indeed, from their point of view the port calls had accomplished two very important objectives. On the one hand, once distant American naval and diplomatic officials and their Japanese counterparts were drawn into increasingly close cooperation in coordinating nuclear submarine visits to Sasebo. Late in December 1964, for example, Prime Minister Sato asked that the *Seadragon*'s second visit to Sasebo be postponed until an extraordinary Diet session had ended; that would deny his opponents a forum for attack. Ambassador Reischauer agreed and persuaded naval officials to modify the boat's schedule accordingly.⁶⁶ As 1965 grew older, American diplomats became aware of, and sensitive to, the possibility of Sasebo city officials coming down with "hospitality and protest fatigue;" they suggested modifying the pace and timing of nuclear sub visits accordingly.⁶⁷ By year's end, the Americans altered, at Prime Minister Sato's suggestion, the schedule of visits so as to keep his foes from rolling their opposition to nuclear submarines, the war in Vietnam, and establishment of full diplomatic relations into a club with which to beat him.⁶⁸

On the other hand, the Left weakened and fragmented. Socialists and communists split. Local "progressive groups" and unions opposed to anything nuclear fell into organizational disarray.⁶⁹ The numbers of protestors dropped dramatically by the fall of 1965.⁷⁰ And, most importantly, despite growing popular apprehension that Japan might be drawn into the Vietnam War, leaders on the Left failed to make that concern politically potent and to link nuclear submarine port visits to that conflict.⁷¹ By year's end, the Left appeared to have weakened to the point that nuclear submarine visits could recur "without serious political risks" so long as the boats were not armed with nuclear missiles.⁷²

Despite these developments, however, friends and foes of an American nuclear naval presence in Japan were simply biding their time and preparing for a more spectacular confrontation.

That clash came during the five days in late May and early June 1966 when the *Snook* came to Yokosuka, the biggest U.S. Navy base in Japan, and indeed the entire Western Pacific.[73] Everyone knew that the appearance of a nuclear submarine there—less than thirty miles from Tokyo, within easy reach by train for the capital's politicians, radical students, and media people—would be an event of a different order from anything that had happened in far-off Sasebo. Ambassador Reischauer worked hard with his naval and military counselors and with Seventh Fleet Commander Vice Admiral John J. Hyland to prepare for it.[74] The ambassador also felt that he made progress, within the U.S.-Japan Security Consultative Committee, toward "full . . . [and] frank] discussions of security issues with his Japanese colleagues."[75] His opponents—Socialist, Communist, Democratic Socialist, and Komeito party leaders—redoubled their efforts to refine their respective positions on the nuclear ship visit issue.[76] And, in an unusual gesture, Socialists and Communists who had worked along parallel but separate lines at Sasebo decided to develop a truly joint strategy to protest the arrival of an American nuclear sub at Yokosuka.[77]

Even Prime Minister Sato, whose government had insisted upon postponement of any nuclear sub visit to Yokosuka the preceding December, now looked forward to the *Snook*'s arrival there.[78] Sasebo, he confided to his diary, was "laden with experiences"—clashes and serious wounds—that he did not want to see repeated. To that end his party had given funds to the local Japanese-American Friendship Society in Yokosuka in hopes that it would quietly but effectively counter what his socialist and communist opponents might be planning. The locals showered the city with thirty thousand leaflets urging citizens to welcome the *Snook* and her crew. But, as Sato shrewdly sensed, what probably would make more of a difference on the local scene was the absence of Yokosuka's mayor, a socialist, who was hospitalized and the presence of a massive, thousand-man strong, police force.[79]

In anticipation of a great struggle, Tokyo's news organizations dispatched three hundred sixty reporters to Yokosuka. At first, they must have felt somewhat disappointed. On the eve of the *Snook*'s arrival, pro- and anti-visit spokesmen squared off as if to prepare for combat. Liberal Democratic Party secretary-general (and future prime minister) Tanaka Kakuei issued a statement proclaiming the government's and his party's firm conviction that nuclear powered ships had been proven safe and urging citizens to trust national policy and watch the situation calmly, "so as not to play into the hands of certain forces" trying to capitalize on the submarine's visit. A Japan Socialist Party spokesman countered by charging that the submarine heralded the arrival of "the whole U.S. nuclear fleet now taking part in the aggression against Vietnam." He proclaimed his party's determination to "resist the *Snook*'s entry into Yokosuka" because it would "imperil the safety of our land and people." That evening, six thousand demonstrators snake-danced around the base entrance shouting "Don't make Yokosuka a base for American aggression!" But only five people were arrested—and no one was injured.[80]

The fireworks, real and verbal, came the next day. It began with a prescient mixed message on the front page of the *Asahi shimbun*. While an article proclaimed just what U.S. Navy officials and Ambassador Reischauer wanted the Japanese public to hear—submarines of *Snook*'s class carried no nuclear weapons—the newspaper's cartoonist portrayed her rising from the sea shouting "War!" at Mount Fuji. Commander James D. Watkins, the sub's skipper and a future chief of naval operations, brought her alongside a Yokosuka pier precisely as scheduled.[81] But the seventy students who crashed the base's main gate shortly thereafter were quickly ejected. In Tokyo, government defenders and socialists traded arguments and insults in the Diet. The latter asserted that *Snook* was a rook for what Washington really wanted to bring to Japan, the nuclear-powered and presumably nuclear-armed *Enterprise*. She was just then completing a tour off Vietnam that had set records for numbers of sorties flown against the enemy. The former insisted that the government was "not even unofficially informed" of a planned visit by the mighty *E* and added, with a twist of sarcasm in his voice, that Japan had "of course, no reason whatsoever" to turn down a request for such if it was "duly made."[82]

That night the media people got a taste of what had been predicted. At Yokosuka police clashed with about two thousand students, some of them fatigue-clad, stone-throwing members of a radical anti-Japan Communist Party faction. They showed their opposition to the *Snook*'s presence by crashing through the main gate of the Yokosuka navy base. By the time they were thrown out by the Japanese police, ten were arrested and sixteen police and ten students had been injured. In Tokyo, one hundred determined Socialist Diet members decided to march in protest on the American Embassy. And in a move that carried ominous overtones of what had happened during the Security Treaty ratification crisis of 1960, they voted to raise the *Snook* visit issue in every Diet proceeding, paralyzing the legislature if necessary to make their point.[83]

Both of those gestures proved futile. The next day Foreign Minister Shiina Etsusaburo delivered a lecture on treaty obligations to the nation (and his opponents) in the Diet. He escalated the controversy still further by asserting that Article VI of the U.S.-Japan Security as revised six years earlier, created an obligation for Japan to welcome warships, like *Snook*, that had been or would soon engaged in operations in Vietnam, because *the latter were contributing to "peace and security in the Far East."*[84] His verbal escalation of conflict with opponents of the submarine's visit matched what his fellow conservatives did in Yokosuka. That same day, Funada Naka, Speaker of the Lower House of the Diet, his son, the governor of Tochigi Prefecture, and their aides, toured the *Snook*. What Mayor Tsuji and local notables in his distant provincial city had done, some of the most senior members of the Japanese Government and ruling Liberal Democratic Party were now repeating in the shadow of the capital. They put flesh on the concept of commitment to alliance with America.[85]

That most certainly pleased Ambassador Reischauer. He took a "low posture" during the *Snook*'s visit to Yokosuka, stealing away for some weekend rowing and relaxation at his seaside cottage at nearby Misaki. Then he flew to Morioka, far to the northeast, to give a university speech—and meet the press. What he told reporters there hinted at his optimism about the progress over the debate over an American nuclear presence in Japan. Reverting to his professorial role, he reminded them that submarines like the *Snook* patrolled the very seas through which Japan's life-giving oil and trade flowed. And when he returned to Tokyo and assessed the situation after Commander Watkins and his crew had departed Yokosuka, he once again drew an optimistic conclusion. The size and ferocity of the anti-nuclear submarine visit demonstrations had been much less than predicted. People were "just not that worked up," and the socialists had made "an extremely poor showing."[86] That, from his point of view, was progress.

But if the ambassador had scanned events and what was being written about them a bit more carefully, he might have drawn a somewhat less sanguine conclusion. When the *Seadragon* first came to Sasebo, editorial writers chastised the Left for its violent and distasteful display of opposition. Now, even though some criticized "foolish leftist demonstrations" that were "animated by political motives," there was a striking media consensus about the nuclear submarine visits that had triggered them.[87] The *Mainichi* noted that "only a few" would welcome an American nuclear submarine to Japan, and the *Yomiuri*, while backing the visit in principle, asked Washington clarify just why it was "essential" for the *Snook* to visit Yokosuka.[88] Even more remarkably, the normally conservative *Sankei shimbun* warned the Sato government to take careful stock of what the Socialists said was the real purpose of the submarine's visit: setting the stage for turning Yokosuka into "a U.S. nuclear fleet base."[89]

These subtle hints of uneasiness about American nuclear-powered ships entering Japanese ports contained the real messages of importance about the *Snook*'s visit. Japan's "nuclear allergy" had yet to clear up. The struggle to preserve it as *the* distinguishing national characteristic or to destroy it was far from over. The fight had simply shifted to center stage, where all of its bigger and more important contestants wanted it. And the U.S. Navy had yet to explain to the full satisfaction of the audience watching its performance precisely why its nuclear submarines had to come to Japan.

Six months after the *Snook* departed Yokosuka, Rear Admiral Eugene P. Wilkinson, first skipper of the world's first nuclear-powered submarine, the *Nautilus*, and first captain of the world's first atomic-driven surface ship, the USS *Long Beach*, reported for duty as chief of staff to Commander U.S. Forces, Japan.[90] By the time he arrived, there had been a change at the American Embassy in Tokyo, too. Edwin Reischauer had returned to Harvard, and his place had been taken by another "old Japan hand," the consummate foreign service professional, U. Alexis Johnson.[91] Together this new team of nuclear ship visit managers brought a new, cutting edge approach to the debate over their presence in Japan. They — and Prime Minister Sato — made the Left's nightmare come true. On January 19, 1968, the world's first nuclear-powered aircraft carrier, the USS *Enterprise* eased alongside her mooring buoys in Sasebo Harbor.[92] By the time she did so, nuclear submarines had called nine more times at Yokosuka and paid another four visits to Sasebo.[93] These port calls elicited protests of varying intensity, and all of those directly involved in managing them — U.S. Navy base officials, the mayors of Sasebo and Yokosuka, and the Japanese police — continued to work together so as to preserve public order.[94] What happened "on the ground," however, was much less significant than hardening attitudes much nearer the top of the American naval and diplomatic and the Japanese political hierarchies.

Ambassador Johnson, who lacked his predecessor's real affection for Japan, returned to Tokyo determined to sweep away the ambiguities in the U.S.-Japan security relationship even as he deliberately continued them in negotiations over the reversion of Okinawa and other American-administered islands to Japanese control. Although he acknowledged that the various Japanese political parties had irreconcilable differences over national defense policy, Johnson thought the time had come for Japan to take a more "mature" attitude in providing for its security. Tokyo should "openly and freely" acknowledge the American military and naval presence "out of a conviction that it served Japan's interest." Moreover, the Japanese should recognize a fact of Cold War life: nuclear weapons, as an essential element in the American arsenal, should not necessarily be removed from Okinawa before the island reverted to their control.[95]

Johnson's determination to make Japan's security posture clearer did not, in his view, run contrary to Prime Minister Sato's desires or the broad trend of Japanese atomic energy policy. After all, by 1967 thirteen nuclear power plants were operating in the country and Tokyo was building its own nuclear-powered merchant marine vessel, the *Mutsu*.[96] But Johnson's stance betrayed an appalling ignorance of the Japanese penchant for ambiguity when dealing with controversial matters. Moreover, his demand for clarity utterly contradicted the explicit obfuscation in the Navy's "neither confirm nor deny" policy regarding the presence of nuclear weapons aboard its ships. Nevertheless, by the time the first year of his embassy was nearing its close, Johnson, who had previously earned the sobriquet "admiral" for having pressed the Navy into sending a carrier task force into the Indian Ocean in 1964, stood ready to push for Japanese acceptance of a port visit by the *Enterprise*. Perhaps he hoped it would signal America's determination to maintain a nuclear naval presence in Japan, regardless of local opposition.[97]

Thus preparations for a visit by the big *E* moved ahead in the fall of 1967 with few of the precautions that Ambassador Reischauer and Prime Minister Ikeda had taken three years earlier in readying Sasebo for the *Seadragon*'s arrival. Early in September the American Embassy requested permission for a port visit and the Sato Cabinet approved it "at some point in the near future." That triggered press speculation, tensions between opposing groups in Sasebo, and police preparations for trouble. Late in October, the Sato Government revealed that Washington wanted the *Enterprise* to come to Japan and indicated that Sasebo would be her port of call.

Early in November, after his cabinet gave final approval to the visit, Sato departed for a summit meeting with President Johnson amidst unusually violent student protests at Haneda Airport. That untoward event should have sent up warning flags as to the storm that was brewing and prompted diversionary tactics on the part of Japanese government officials from Prime Minister Sato down to Mayor Tsuji. But instead, nearly six weeks before the *Enterprise* would reach Japan, the Foreign Ministry announced her probable arrival date.[98]

That gave all of the prospective antagonists ample time to

prepare for a fight. On January 6, 1968, only four days after the *Enterprise*, in company with the nuclear-powered *Truxtun* (CGN 35) and the guided missile frigate *Halsey* (DDG 23), departed California for the Western Pacific, the leader of the most radical Zengakuren faction announced that he would mobilize more than three thousand people. That same day, police spokesmen in Kyushu said they would send half again as many officers to Sasebo to deal with demonstrators. The Maritime Safety Board announced its intent to have fifteen observation vessels in the harbor, and a few days later Sasebo area school principals met to plan their response in the event that radical students invaded their campuses. By January eleventh, three days after the *Enterprise* and her accompanying ships left Pearl Harbor, Kyushu police announced they would nearly double their planned presence in Sasebo so as to prevent expected clashes between rival Zengakuren factions from getting out of hand.[99]

That news made it clear that the *Enterprise* was sailing toward a cauldron of trouble. Ambassador Johnson later claimed that he saw that and gave the Navy and Prime Minister Sato the chance to alter plans for the carrier to call at Sasebo.[100] But if he did, the prime minister left no record of such an offer in his diary.[101] Moreover, Johnson held fast to Navy policy and refused a request from Foreign Minister Miki Takeo, whose loyalty to Sato he doubted, to "state directly" that the *Enterprise* had no nuclear weapons aboard. Instead he suggested that Miki try to calm the situation in Sasebo by pointing out that the *Ticonderoga*, a carrier identical to the big E in everything save her conventional power plant, had just arrived at Yokosuka without incident. A week later, Johnson, in marked contrast to Reischauer, who had maintained a "low posture" during the first nuclear submarine visits to Sasebo and Yokosuka, flew with a group of Diet members and journalists to the *Enterprise* as she neared Sasebo.[102]

By the morning of January 19, 1968, when the carrier, *Truxtun*, and *Halsey* entered the harbor there, the fires of conflict had long since exploded. On the eve of their arrival, members of the Great Japan Patriotic Party stormed through Sasebo ripping down antinuclear ship port visit posters. The radical Sampa faction of

Zengakuren, armed with staves, hurled rocks at the police, who soaked them with fire hoses and injured sixty-five students.[103] That incident steeled Prime Minister Sato's spine, prompting him to wonder, sarcastically, if twenty years hence those protestors or the students about to set off on a goodwill cruise whom he had just seen off would be regarded as the defenders of Japan's national interest.[104] The next morning, just before the American ships were due to arrive, four hundred students charged police outside the Sasebo Navy Base gate, beating them back with tear gas, water jets, and truncheons.[105] That unhappy portent prompted the base commander and captains of the three ships to wait two hours before allowing crews eager for liberty to leave the base.[106]

They and those who followed them the next day had a good time, and only relatively few demonstrators protested visits by Mayor Tsuji, other political notables, and three hundred ordinary citizens to the *Enterprise*.[107] Prime Minister Sato took heart and surmised that the demonstrations might turn out to be nothing out of the ordinary.[108] What happened the following afternoon, January 21, however, proved him more than wrong. Around one, nearly ten thousand communists, socialists, and labor unionists rallied at a Sasebo park to protest the nuclear ships' visit. A half hour later the Sampa faction of Zengakuren students began their demonstration. After retreating briefly, the protestors rushed across the bridge that divided Sasebo's business district from the Navy base to confront its defenders. They seized one police armored vehicle. In an effort to restore law and order, the police then unleashed tear gas, water cannons, and truncheons against the students. The fighting continued for nearly five hours—in full view of a nationwide television audience. Before it finally subsided, one hundred sixty people had been injured.[109]

The "battle of Sasebo" stunned all who had been involved in planning the *Enterprise*'s visit. Captain R. E. Oliver politely thanked the police for protecting the base he commanded, and a numbed Mayor Tsuji proceeded stoically through ritual meetings with the leaders of various groups for and against the visit.[110] In Tokyo, Prime Minister Sato privately blamed "the messy affair" on the incompetence of local police; after all, simultaneous demonstrations at Yokosuka had proceeded without such violence.[111] But his senior spokesman, Chief Cabinet Secretary Kimura Toshio, issued a statement that put a very different take on the events in Sasebo. Noting that some local citizens, not just "outside elements" had participated in the clashes, he suggested that the government "must take serious note" of what had occurred. Kimura's remarks infuriated more conservative senior Liberal Democratic Party legislators who determined not to yield an inch in the face of leftist protests. Thus the *Enterprise* left in her wake a political crisis that was both domestic and international.[112]

By the time Prime Minister Sato responded to it, the *Enterprise*, *Truxtun*, and *Halsey* had departed Sasebo as scheduled. Their commanders and crews had enjoyed "a very pleasant visit" and did not think the "student demonstrations" had marred it.[113] They thought they were bound for combat in Vietnam. But North Korea's seizure of the USS *Pueblo* (AGER 2) in the Sea of Japan that same day forced them to turn north into the Sea of Japan for what turned out to be a futile effort to free the seized ship.[114] The ensuing crisis—together with the U.S. Air Force's announcement that it had accidentally dropped four nuclear bombs on Greenland—made it all the more difficult for Sato to calm the storm caused by the nuclear surface ships' visit.[115] On the Right, senior members of his own party wanted him to prosecute arrested demonstrators by invoking a special law that provided for harsh punishment of those who threatened the security of U.S. base facilities.[116] On the Left, Diet Socialists pilloried the government for allowing the *Enterprise* visit, saying that it was "obvious to the world" that she carried nuclear weapons.[117]

Prime Minister Sato tried to quiet the storm with a series of "clarifying remarks" and conciliatory actions. He distanced himself from his chief cabinet secretary's "soft" remarks and vowed to pay close attention to what his national chief of police said about the difficulties peace officers faced at Sasebo and elsewhere when dealing with demonstrators. He acknowledged that the state of affairs concerning visits by American navy ships was "not good," even as his foreign minister expressed Japan's support for the United States in its efforts to recover the *Pueblo*. Before the storm completely passed, he had to visit the palace to reassure the emperor, who was alarmed by the presence of so many American warships in the Sea of Japan and by the Tet offensive in Vietnam, that his government was "taking a calm posture."[118]

But in the long run what mattered most was what he said in the Diet about Japan's own nuclear policies and the movements of American naval vessels. It was the Government of Japan's policy not to manufacture, possess, or allow the introduction of nuclear weapons into the national territory. In the short term, that meant that, under the terms of the U.S.-Japan Security Treaty, Washington would have to consult with Tokyo prior to the entry of a nuclear-*armed* submarine. That in itself marked no departure from what had been standard practice for the nuclear-*powered* but not nuclear-armed vessels that had long since begun calling at Japanese ports. Moreover, Sato's refusal to engage in debate over whether prior consultation was required for port visits by U.S. Navy ships headed for combat in Vietnam indicated that he would not be drawn on the question of the supporting role bases in Japan played in that conflict.[119] But his enunciation of what subsequently became known as the "Three Non-Nuclear Principles" marked a major clarification of Japan's national security policy.[120]

That, surely, was not what Ambassador Johnson and Navy officials had hoped would result from the *Enterprise*'s visit to Sasebo. Her call there and the tumultuous events it triggered became, for Japanese, something like what the Kent State incident of 1970 became for Americans: a painful moment of domestic controversy that raised ongoing questions about the rights of protestors and the use of force against them.[121] What occurred in January 1968 at Sasebo prompted Nagasaki officials to rescind their invitation to the *Truxtun* to take part in their port festival later in the year; and two years passed before she returned to Sasebo.[122] Ten years would go by before American and Japanese officials agreed that the mighty *E* could return to Sasebo.[123] In the meantime, nuclear-powered but not atomic-armed submarines continued to visit both Sasebo and Yokosuka on a regular basis. By 1973 they had made one hundred Japanese port calls.[124] But although their size and intensity declined, anti-nuclear demonstrations continued to greet the nuclear boats.[125] Japan's "nuclear allergy" remained as strong as ever. Despite all the anger, turmoil, and anguish that the nuclear navy's visits to Japan had evoked, nothing appeared to have changed.

But surface appearances in Japan are not infrequently deceiving. When one peers beneath them, two things are clear. First, whether the nuclear navy's port visits to Japan were more costly than beneficial remains as difficult a question to answer now as it was when Ambassador Reischauer first posed it. But that these port calls had a significant effect on Navy policy, civil-naval relations in Japan and America, and on the function of an American naval presence in Japan on Japanese-American relations more generally is beyond doubt.

With regard to the first question, one could accept the verdict of earlier historians—Thomas R. H. Havens a dozen years ago, and Walter LaFeber and Michael Schaller more recently—and conclude that the negatives of nuclear ship port visits outweighed the positives.[126] But it is also possible to see why, as this essay has tried to demonstrate, American and Japanese officials then thought the *Seadragon, Snook,* and *Enterprise* would leave good things in the wakes of their Japanese port calls.

One can also draw different conclusions about the need for these nuclear ship port visits and the wisdom with which they were managed. The case for the necessity of nuclear-powered submarine visits was much stronger than that for the *Enterprise.* Because *all* American subs then built or building were nuclear-powered, it was reasonable to presume the need, present or prospective, for them to visit Japan. Their naval and intelligence functions were much more obviously related to preserving security in the seas surrounding Japan than were the Vietnam-related missions of the *Enterprise* and the ships accompanying her. The big *E* had turned in stellar performances in the South China Sea on two previous tours without ever nearing Japan, and she was, as yet, the only nuclear-powered carrier in the fleet—an anomaly rather than the assured norm for the future.[127]

Whether it was wise to raise, through the *Enterprise,* whose aircraft were nuclear-capable, the question of bringing nuclear weapons into Japan, and to stick to what Ambassador Johnson termed the Navy's "very rigid policy"[128] concerning acknowledgment or denial of their presence on a particular vessel, certainly remains open to question. One could argue that some verbal obfuscation like the words Ambassador Reischauer and Foreign Minister Ohira had used in the past, should have been devised so as to defuse the obvious tensions building up over that issue. Or, with equal force, one could point to the intensified leftist opposition to virtually everything Prime Minister Sato said or did with respect to relations with the United States as evidence either that the *Enterprise* visit should not have been attempted or that the opposition to it was simply not amenable to reason. The Japanese prime minister, the American ambassador, and the admirals who determined the ship's course may have been in a "damned if you do, damned if you don't" situation.

But once they decided to proceed with the nuclear carrier's visit, they should not have been surprised by the violence that greeted her arrival in Japan. Even if, as they most probably did, Sato and Johnson denied the principled concern and sincerity that motivated at least some of the anti-nuclear demonstrators, they should have been more attentive to signs pointing to a clash. Given the persistence of opposition demonstrations over the preceding years and the ferocity of leftist opposition in the fall of 1967 to Sato's defense and foreign policies, no one should have been surprised by the clash at Sasebo in January 1968. That that violence would be seen by a public, more than eighty percent of whom owned or had access to television,[129] that would react negatively to it and to its presumed nuclear naval cause, was not beyond the capability of the politicians, diplomats, and admirals of the day to imagine. But whether or not the turbulence that attended the visits of *Seadragon, Snook,* and *Enterprise and Truxtun* to Japan would have longer term consequences was not something they could see.

Today, more than thirty years after the last of those visits, their legacy seems clear. They most certainly helped transform a "very rigid" policy on nuclear weapons disclosure to dogma. Naval men, from ordinary seamen up to admirals, responded to protests at Sasebo and Yokosuka during the 1960s like proverbial ducks to water. They were determined not to let demonstrators spoil their plans for liberty or ships' deployments, and they continued to do what they felt they must.[130] What they saw and felt then may have strengthened their adherence to what they perceived as wise policy in the face of "crazy" anti-nuclear demonstrators. Indeed, it is possible that what happened to some of these men—then *Snook* skipper and later CNO James D. Watson, for one—in important and potentially powerful Japan preconditioned the Navy's response to tiny and insignificant New Zealand's challenge, two decades later, to the nuclear non-disclosure policy. If one weathered the big Japanese storm without compromise on essential principle, then surely lesser ones later and elsewhere could be survived.

In retrospect it is also clear that the nuclear navy's arrival in Japan altered the pattern of civil-naval relations both there and in the United States. As this essay has shown, the prospect of civil unrest demanded close cooperation between base commanders, ships' captains, and local officials as well as diplomats and political leaders. Challenges to the legitimacy and desirability of port visits by American vessels drew Japanese supporters of a U.S Navy presence out of the shadows and onto center stage. Commander U.S. Naval Forces Japan and his subordinate base commanders realized they had to cultivate these people as well as rely on local mayors, regardless of their political affiliation, for support and on local and national Japanese police for security. The U.S. Navy presence, nuclear and conventional alike, was, in the wake of the protests described in this essay, clearly dependent for its continuation on the support of its Japanese hosts.

What happened in Japan, however, also brought about changes in purely American civil-naval relations. Diplomats and admirals were drawn out of their isolation from and misapprehension about one another into truly cooperative endeavor. Ambassadors Reischauer and Johnson spent much more time on naval matters than either imagined before taking charge of the embassy in Tokyo. Reischauer went out of his way, in both the policy and the social spheres, to break down the barriers between diplomats and naval officers. Johnson discovered, to his surprise, that an inexperienced but quick-to-learn and skillful diplomatic assistant was at hand in the person of Rear Admiral Wilkinson.[131] The admirals, in turn, shed some of the Navy's prized autonomy to adjust ships' schedules and modify public relations plans to meet Japanese political leaders' partisan needs as well as American diplomats' desires. What these men did and experienced in dealing with nuclear ship port visit issues demonstrated, in microcosm, the macrocosmic changes in the character and responsibilities of naval officers that the Cold War brought about. American admirals and diplomats in Japan were learning how and why they must cooperate everywhere.[132]

Finally, the episodes described in this essay had a marked effect on the understanding, in Washington and Tokyo alike, of the Navy's reason for being in Japan and of its role in Japanese-American relations. The presence that had begun by virtue of Japan's defeat and occupation in 1945 had become something more than the protecting force envisaged when peace was formally concluded in 1951. What had proven a springboard for waging war in Korea and containing China in the 1950s had become, a decade later, the visible symbol of political commitment, on both sides, to alliance. Those nuclear-powered vessels came to Japan in the 1960s not simply to support war in Vietnam or gather intelligence from China and the Soviet Union. In the last analysis, they came to affirm the importance and vitality of the Cold War alliance between Japan and the United States. And by rising to the challenges that anti-naval nuclear protests presented, American and Japanese political, diplomatic and naval leaders reaffirmed their commitment to that bond. Their actions — good and bad, wise and unsound — demonstrated that, in the last analysis, the U.S. Navy's reason for being in Japan was as much political and diplomatic as it was naval.

That truth, made evident by the challenging events of the 1960s that this essay has described, would enable the United States Navy presence in Japan, nuclear and conventional alike, to survive the threats to its very existence that budget cutters in Washington and nationalists in Tokyo would present in the 1970s.

NOTES

[1] Sherry Sontag and Christopher Drew, *Blind Man's Bluff: The Untold Story of American Submarine Espionage* (New York: Public Affairs, 1998), 28, 43.

[2] Richard G. Hewlett and Francis Duncan, *Nuclear Navy 1946-1962* (Chicago: University of Chicago Press, 1974); Norman Polmar and Thomas B. Allen, *Rickover* (New York: Simon and Schuster, 1982), 115-265; Norman Friedman, *U.S. Submarines since 1945: An Illustrated Design History* (Annapolis: Naval Institute Press, 1994), 101-158.

[3] Thomas R. H. Havens, *Fire Across the Sea: The Vietnam War and Japan, 1965-1975* (Princeton, N.J.: Princeton University Press, 1987), especially 133-155; Walter LaFeber, *The Clash: A History of U.S. - Japan Relations* (New York: Norton, 1997), 339-347, *passim*; Michael Schaller, *Altered States: The United States and Japan since the Occupation* (New York: Oxford University Press, 1997), 184, 195, 203; Timothy P. Maga, *Hands Across the Sea? U.S.-Japan Relations, 1961-1981* (Athens: Ohio University Press, 1997), 70-72, 76. The exception is Akira Iriye, *Japan and the Wider World* (New York: St. Martin's Press, 1999), 153.

[4] Polmar, 165-176.

[5] Norman Friedman, *U.S. Submarines since 1945: An Illustrated Design History* (Annapolis: Naval Institute Press, 1994), 235.

[6] Polmar, 139-164, 542-547; Sontag and Drew, 45.

[7] Friedman, 64; George W. Baer, *One Hundred Years of Sea Power: The U.S. Navy, 1890-1990* (Stanford: Stanford University Press, 1990), 336-338.

[8] Sontag and Drew, 53.

[9] Edward C. Keefer, David W. Mabon, and Harriet D. Schwar, eds., *Foreign Relations of the United States, 1961-1963, Volume XXII: Northeast Asia* (Washington: Government Printing Office, 1996), 690-691; Tsuji Ichizo, *Chimmoku no minato [The Silent Harbor]* (Sasebo: Geibundo, 1972), 41 indicates that Japan's being the only state to have suffered nuclear attack was the reason for declining nuclear submarine visits at this point. Throughout this essay, Japanese names are given in the normal Japanese order, that is, surname followed by personal name.

[10] Edwin O. Reischauer, *My Life between Japan and America* (New York: Harper and Row, 1986), 239.

[11] Roger Dingman, "Alliance in Crisis: The *Lucky Dragon* Incident and Japanese-American Relations," in Warren I. Cohen and Akira Iriye, eds., *The Great Powers in East Asia, 1953-1960* (New York: Columbia University Press, 1990), 187-214.

[12] David Osborn 1989 interview, 10, Foreign Affairs Oral History Program, Lauinger Library, Georgetown University, Washington, D.C.

[13] Reischauer, 2-7, 41, 56-59, 113-121, 151-158; Edwin O. Reischauer family letters, August 28, November 15, 1964, Edwin O. Reischauer personal papers, Cambridge, Massachusetts. I am grateful to Mrs. Nancy Deptula, Reischauer's long time secretary and administrative assistant, for making copies of these letters in her possession available to me.

[14] Reischauer, 249-250.

[15] Sato Seizaburo, Koyama Ken'ichi, and Kumon Shunpei, *Postwar Politician: The Life of Former Prime Minister Masayoshi Ohira*, William R. Carter, transl. (Tokyo: Kodansha International, 1990), 205.

[16] Reischauer, 249-250.

[17] Tsuji, 42-43.

[18] Polmar, 428-430; Sontag and Drew, 48.

[19] Reischauer, 249-250.

[20] *Asahi shimbun*, August 12-31, 1963.

[21] Edward C. Keefer, David W. Mabon, and Harriet D. Schwar, eds. *Foreign Relations of the United States, 1961-1963, Volume XXII: Northeast Asia* (Washington: Government Printing Office, 1996), 789. This source will hereinafter be cited as *FRUS* with appropriate date, volume, and page citations.

²²*Japan Times*, September 2, 1963. I have used the Japanese National Police estimate of the number of demonstrators, as reported in this article. Protest organizers claimed 190,000 had participated in these demonstrations, but the American Embassy later reported they numbered no more than 82,000. See American Embassy Tokyo to American Embassy Manila, # 3609, June 4, 1964, file DEF 7 Japan-US, box 1648, Central Files of the Department of State, Record Group (RG) 59, United States National Archives, College Park, Maryland.

²³Tsuji, 53; Nakamoto Akio, *Sasebo minato no sengo shi [The Postwar History of Sasebo Harbor]* (Sasebo: Geibundo, 1984), 2:150.

²⁴Reischauer, 280. Behind the scenes, American and Japanese diplomats claimed to have "agreed in principle" on nuclear submarine visits but continued to disagree over the mode of prior communication concerning them and on technical issues such as indemnification in the case of a nuclear accident and the disposal of nuclear wastes. See *Japan Times*, September 23, 1963.

²⁵Rear Admiral George H. Miller Naval Institute oral history, 276.

²⁶Nakamoto, 2:149.

²⁷Reischauer family letter, September 5, 1964; Hayashi Shige and Tsuji Akira, eds., *Nihon naikaku shiroku 6 [The Historical Record of Japan's Cabinets, Volume 6]* (Tokyo: Dai ichi hokan shuppansha, 1981), 84-85.

²⁸Reischauer family letters, August 28, September 5, 1964; Tsuji, 62. Those who headed the Defense Agency in the 1960s were not military professionals but civil servants usually drawn from the ranks of the Home Ministry.

²⁹Reischauer family letter, September 5, 1964.

³⁰Nakamoto, 2:155-156; *Asahi shimbun*, November 3-10, 1964.

³¹Reischauer family letter, November 15, 1964.

³²Nakamoto, 2:157-158. My use of "she" in reference to naval vessels is not a manifestation of sexism, but rather deference to naval tradition.

³³Reischauer family letter, November 15, 1964; Reischauer, 280.

³⁴Ito Takashi, ed., *Sato Eisaku nikki [The Diary of Sato Eisaku]* (Tokyo: Asahi shimbun sha, 1998), 2:198. This source will hereinafter be cited as *Sato nikki* with appropriate volume and page indications.

³⁵Reischauer family letter, November 15, 1964.

³⁶*New York Times*, November 12, 1964.

³⁷*Asahi shimbun*, evening edition, November 12, 1964; Nakamoto, 2:160.

³⁸http://www.subnet.com/FLEET/ssn584.htm. In 1964, Okinawa was still governed by the United States and treated as a dependent territory, even though the 1951 Peace Treaty had acknowledged Japan's "residual sovereignty" over it.

³⁹Department of State to American Embassy Tokyo, and CincPac, August 28, 1964, folder DEF Japan-US 7, box 1648, RG 59.

⁴⁰American Embassy Tokyo to Department of State, # 1352, October 16, 1964; American Embassy Tokyo to Department of State, # 1362, October 19, 1964, box 1648, RG 59.

⁴¹Commander Fleet Activities Sasebo to Commander Naval Forces Japan, January 10, 1964, Command History, 1963, Classified Operational Archves, Naval Historical Center, Washington Navy Yard, Washington, D.C. This source location will hereinafter be cited as COA, NHC.

⁴²Vice Adm. John L. Chew Naval Institute oral history, 364-365.

⁴³American Embassy Tokyo to Department of State, # 1698, November 12, 1964, box 1648, RG 59.

⁴⁴Nakamoto, 2:160.

⁴⁵*Japan Times*, November 13, 1964; Nakamoto, 2:162.

⁴⁶American Embassy Tokyo to Department of State, # 1698, November 12, 1964, box 1648, RG 59; Nakamoto, 2:162.

⁴⁷*New York Times*, November 13, 1964. At Yokosuka, Capt. Charles C. Hartigan, Commander Fleet Activities, fearing possible trouble had initially indicated his intention to cancel liberty for all U.S. Navy personnel, then reversed that decision. *Japan Times*, November 13, 1964.

48*New York Times,* June 1, 1966; Paul J. Bailey, *Postwar Japan: 1945 to the Present* (Oxford: Blackwell Publishers, 1996), 103 indicates that socialists and communists within the Gensuikyo, the Japan Council Against Nuclear Weapons, were "hopelessly split" over Soviet nuclear weapons testing; Nakamoto, 2:158, 165.

49Commander Fleet Activities Sasebo to Chief of Naval Operations, April 13, 1967, Command History, 1966.

50*Kodansha Encyclopedia of Japan* (Tokyo: Kodansha, 1983), 4:266.

51cf Packard, *Protest in Tokyo* (Publication data) for Zengakuren background; also *Encyclopedia of Japan* 8:375.

52*Asahi shimbun,* November 12, *Japan Times,* November 13, 1964; Nakamoto, 2:162.

53Nakamoto, 2:165-160; American Embassy Tokyo to Department of State, # 1698, November 12, 1964, box 1648, RG 59.

54Nakamoto, 2:163, 168.

55Nakamoto, 2:169; *New York Times, Asahi shimbun,* November 14, 1964.

56Commander U.S. Naval Forces Japan to Chief of Naval Operations, 1964 command history, February 15, 1965, COA, NHC.

57Nakamoto, 2:170-171; Sato had succeeded Ikeda Hayato as prime minister in accordance with Liberal Democratic Party factional leaders' decision and subsequent Diet confirmation, not by popular election. See Hayashi and Tsuji, 6:105-109.

58American Embassy Tokyo to CinCPac, # 1812, November 24, 1964, box 1648, RG 59.

59Reischauer family letter, November 15, 1964.

60*New York Times,* November 15, 1964.

61Memorandum of Takeuchi-Harriman conversation, November 16, 1964, box 1648, RG 59.

62*New York Times,* February 15, 1965.

63Sasebo shi, *Kichi ni kansuru chosa,* 35.

64Nakamoto 2:178; *New York Times,* February 2, 4, 9, 11, August 23, 1965; American Embassy Tokyo to Department of State, # 1953, December 1, 1965, folder DEF 7 VISITS, box 1649, RG 59.

65Reischauer family letter, May 3, 1965.

66American Embassy Tokyo to Department of State, # 2030, December 30, 1964, box 1648; # 2236, January 19, 1965; Department of State to American Embassy Tokyo, # 1837, January 25, 1965. Similar requests for timing sub visits to suit the prime minister's political needs were presented and honored throughout the year. See American Embassy Tokyo to Department of State, # 3608, May 7; # 126, July 9; # 1063, September 22, 1965, box 1649, RG 59.

67American Embassy Tokyo to Department of State, # 2435, February 6; # 2243, December 25, 1965, box 1649, RG59.

68American Embassy Tokyo, # 1063, September 22, 1965, box 1649, RG 59.

69American Consulate Fukuoka to Department of State, # A-15, June 21; # 677, August 24, 1965, box 1649, RG 49. In 1965, socialists bolted Gensuikyo to form a separate anti-nuclear organization, Gensuikin [Japan Congress against Atomic and Hydrogen Bombs]. Bailey, 103.

70American Embassy Tokyo to Department of State, # 2435, February 6, # 5026, June 4; Naval Communications Intelligence Support Activity Sasebo to Naval Communications Intelligence Support Activity Japan, 280426Z, August 28, 1965, box 1649, RG 59.

71American Embassy Tokyo to Department of State, # 1063, September 22, 1965, box 1649, RG 59.

72American Embassy Tokyo to Department of State, # 1953, December 1, 1965, box 1649, RG 59.

73Jim Lewis, "U.S. Naval Forces, Japan," *All Hands* (April 1963), 58-59.

74Reischauer family letters, May 30, June 25, December 19, 1965, May 22, 1966.

75Reischauer family letter, September 5, 1965.

The Nuclear Navy Comes to Japan 421

⁷⁶Some of these definitions showed considerable verbal ingenuity. The Democratic Socialist Policy Foreign Policy Bureau chairman said his party opposed the nuclear boats' entry "unless the safety is proved beyond doubt." The Komeito attacked the government for "total lack of preparedness" for a possible nuclear accident. *Japan Times*, May 30, 1966.

⁷⁷*New York Times*, May 30, 1966.

⁷⁸American Embassy Tokyo to Department of State, # 2170, December 20, 1965, box 1649, RG 59. The *Plunger* had originally been scheduled to call at Yokosuka December 28-31, 1965.

⁷⁹*Sato nikki*, 2:431; *Japan Times*, May 30, June 1, 1966.

⁸⁰Commander U.S. Naval Forces Japan to Chief of Naval Operations, 1966 Command History, January 31, 1967; COA, NHC; *Japan Times*, May 30, 1966.

⁸¹*Asahi shimbun*, *Japan Times*, May 31, 1966. The *Snook*, a *Skipjack* class boat, displaced approximately 500 tons more than the Seadragon and had been commissioned two years after her, in 1961. Shorter and broader in beam, her chief distinguishing characteristic was speed while submerged. See http://www.subnet.com/fleet/ssn592.htm. Watkins, who had overseen construction of the *Snook*, was an obvious choice to command her during this pathbreaking port visit. He had been awarded the Legion of Merit for "a mission of great value" making the *Snook* the first nuclear submarine to visit the Republic of Korea in May 1965. See Rear Adm. James D. Watkins' 1973 biography, office biography files, COA, NHC; Gregg Easterbrook, "Watkins at Energy," *Washington Post Magazine*, February 18, 1990, 21.

⁸²*Asahi shimbun*, *Japan Times*, May 31, 1966; Edward J. Marolda, *By Sea, Air and Land: An Illustrated History of the U.S. Navy and the War in Southeast Asia* (Washington, D.C.: Naval Historical Center, Department of the Navy, 1994), 387; http://www.navy.mi/homepages/cvn65/facts.htm. In this instance, there was truth on both sides of the argument. Washington did see the nuclear sub visits as precursors to nuclear-powered surface ship port calls and had previously informed the Japanese Government of their assignment to the Seventh Fleet, as Tokyo had requested. See American Embassy Tokyo to Department of State, # 1317, October 8, # 1151, October 29, 1965, box 1649, RG 59.

⁸³*Asahi shimbun*, *Japan Times*, May 31, 1966.

⁸⁴*Japan Times*, June 1, 4; *New York Times*, June 1, 1966.

⁸⁵Funada Naka to Rear Admiral Frank L. Johnson (Commander U.S. Naval Forces, Japan), June 7, 1966, Masuoka Ichiro manuscripts collection, in possession of Nagao Hidemi, Civil and Media Affairs Liaison Officer, Commander U.S. Naval Forces, Japan, Yokosuka Japan. I am grateful to Mr. Nagao and to Mrs. Masuoka Yoko for allowing me to have access to this valuable collection. Funada's visit was but one of "numerous" tours of the *Snook* for Japanese political and industrial leaders. See Commander Fleet Activities Yokosuka to Chief of Naval Operations, 1966 Command History, February 16, 1967.

⁸⁶ Reischauer family letter, June 5, 1966; *Japan Times*, June 2, 1966.

⁸⁷ *Japan Times*, June 1, 1966.

⁸⁸*Mainichi shimbun*, *Yomiuri shimbun*, May 30, translations in *Japan Times*, June 1, 1966.

⁸⁹*Sankei shimbun*, May 31, translation in *Japan Times*, June 1, 1966.

⁹⁰Vice Admiral Eugene P. Wilkinson May 1972 biography, officer biography files, COA, NHC.

⁹¹Reischauer, 301-303, 307-308. U. Alexis Johnson, *The Right Hand of Power* (Englewood Cliffs, N.J.: Prentice-Hall, 1984), 1-90 richly details the new ambassador's Japan background.

⁹²*Asahi shimbun*, *New York Times*, January 20, 1968.

⁹³Yokosuka shi shi hensan iinkai, *Yokosuka shi shi [A History of Yokosuka City]* (Yokosuka: Yokosuka shi, 198), 1:189; *Kichi ni kansuru chosa*, 35.

⁹⁴Commander U.S. Naval Forces Japan to Chief of Naval Operations, 1966, 1967 command histories, January 3, 1967, June 6, 1968, COA, NHC.

[95] American Embassy Tokyo to Department of State, # A-647, November 14, 1966, file DEF 1 Japan, box 1647, RG 59; Johnson, 90, 452-453.
[96] Johnson, 490-491.
[97] Johnson, 367. The carrier in question may well have been the *Enterprise*. She circumnavigated the globe between August and October 1964. See Polmar, 250, 377, and *New York Times*, August 1, September 1, October 3-4, 1964.
[98] Nakamoto, 2:231-232.
[99] *Dictionary of American Naval Fighting Ships* 7:317-319; Nakamoto, 2:237-238.
[100] Johnson, 490.
[101] *Sato nikki*, 3:214-219.
[102] Johnson, 492; Commander Fleet Activities Sasebo 1968 Command History, [undated], COA, NHC.
[103] *New York Times*, January 20, 1968; *Sato nikki*, 3:218-219; Nakamoto 2:239-240.
[104] *Sato nikki*, 3:218.
[105] *Asahi shimbun*, evening edition, January 19, 1968; *New York Times*, January 20, 1968.
[106] *New York Times*, January 20, 1968; Nakamoto, 2:245-246.
[107] Nakamoto, 2:246-247.
[108] *Sato nikki*, 3:220.
[109] *New York Times*, January 22, 1968; *Asahi shimbun*, January 23, 1968; Nakamoto, 2:247.
[110] Nakamoto, 2:247-248.
[111] *Sato nikki*, 3:220.
[112] *New York Times*, January 25, 1968; *Sato nikki*, 3:220-221.
[113] Rear Admiral Horace H. Epes, Jr., to Masuoka Ichiro, January 22, 1968, Masuoka papers; *U.S.S. Enterprise 1968* [Nuclear powered attack aircraft carrier, CVAN-65 cruise book] (Marceline, Missouri: Walworth Publishers, 1969?), 54-56; *U.S.S. Truxtun DLG(N)-35) [Nuclear Powered, Guided Missile Armed, Destroyer Leader]* 1968 cruise book, (No place of publication: Pischer publishers, 1969), both in Nimitz Library, U.S. Naval Academy, Annapolis, Maryland.
[114] Nakamoto, 2:249; Commander U.S. Naval Forces Japan to Chief of Naval Operations, 1968 Command History; *New York Times*, January 23-24, 1968.
[115] *New York Times*, January 23, 1968.
[116] *Sato nikki*, 3:223.
[117] *New York Times*, January 31, 1968.
[118] *Sato nikki*, 3:222-228; *New York Times*, February 1, 1968.
[119] Havens, 146; *New York Times*, February 1, 1968.
[120] Sato was later awarded the Nobel Peace Prize for his enunciation of these policy principles. Bailey, 104.
[121] Havens, 150.
[122] Commander Fleet Activities Sasebo Command History, 1968, n.d., 1970, November 12, 1971, COA, NHC.
[123] *Kichi ni kansuru chosa*, 42-43; Havens, 151. *Truxtun* returned two years later, in March 1970. See Commander Fleet Activities Sasebo to Chief of Naval Operations, 1970 Command History, November 12, 1971, COA, NHC.
[124] Commander U.S. Naval Forces Japan Command History 1973, March 26, 1974, COA, NHC.
[125] *New York Times*, February 15, 18, 23, 27; May 15, June 3, December 18-19, 1968; Commander Fleet Activities Sasebo to Chief of Naval Operations, 1968, 1970, and 1972 Command Histories; Commander, U.S. Naval Forces Japan to Chief of Naval Operations, 1968 Command history, May 13, 1969; Commander U.S. Naval Forces Japan to Director of Naval History, 1969-1973 Command Histories, March 20, 1970; March 29, 1971; April 25, 1973.
[126] Havens, 155; LaFeber, 346-346; and Schaller, 207.
[127] Marolda, 386-387; Polmar, 389-391; http://www.navy.mil/homepages/-cvn65/facts.htm.
[128] Johnson, 490.

The Nuclear Navy Comes to Japan 423

[129] Handbook of Japan, 1968, 33.

[130] This generalization is based on my reading of senior officers' oral histories, command histories, and cruise books for ships, stations, and individuals involved in the nuclear ship visits to Japan during the 1960s.

[131] Johnson, 454.

[132] Admiral William J. Crowe, Jr., with David Chanoff, *The Line of Fire* (New York: Simon and Schuster, 1993), 24-25 and David Callahan, *Dangerous Capabilities: Paul Nitze and the Cold War* (New York: Harper Collins, 1990), 276-277, both identify the need for closer civil-naval cooperation as the chief Cold War "lesson" learned by the Navy and its leaders.

After The Gulf War: Operational History For The 21st Century

Charles D. Melson

> Navy and Marine Corps personnel not only make history, they also write it. Most services have branches whose purpose it is to maintain histories of the contributions of their service in both war and peace. But what is the purpose of this activity, and who is its proper audience? One use of operational histories is to pass on the lessons of recent (and not so recent) conflicts to future practitioners of war. Of course learning from operational histories is a skill itself. In this brief essay, the chief historian of the U.S. Marine Corps discusses some lessons from the Gulf War about compiling operational history, and some suggestions for using them.

The United States Marine Corps has written operational history since the conclusion of World War I in 1919. The ensuing eighty years offered numerous opportunities to develop this form of historical narrative. For the last twenty-five years the Marine Corps has used a tried and proven system of documenting and using operational history.

The most recent experience was during the decade following the 1990-91 Persian Gulf War. The Gulf War offered new lessons in the collection of records, oral history, and writing historical narratives. The question before us today is how were the demands for operational history met during the last conflict and what was learned that can be brought forward to enhance operational history in the future? Have the old ways survived and will they be up to the demands of a new millennium? These and other issues will be considered as the dust settles from the last conflict and preparations begin for the next.

First, what is "operational history?" It is defined by function, to provide in narrative form an account of military operations (who, what, where, and, as far as possible, why). Its purpose is to give commanders, staff officers, and students the essential facts of previous events for use in current or future military actions. It

---

Charles D. Melson is Chief Historian and Head of the Historical Branch at Headquarters, U.S. Marine Corps in Washington, D.C.

should be noted that this historical record allows contemporary "operators" to draw their own conclusions and lessons. As Marine Gen. Phil Shutler observed, the writers of your doctrine should not be the writers of your history, for this can lead to bad doctrine and bad history.[1] A secondary use of these accounts is to allow the people of the United States to see how the armed forces carry out their mandate by providing the basis for the institutional story of the Marine Corps. Finally, but no less importantly, it is to provide veterans and their families with the organizational outline of their individual service and its contributions.

Operational history is definitive as far as possible, but sometimes historians have to choose between being timely and being complete, and by nature some compromises will occur. If you write too soon in order to support prevailing needs, the work might be overcome by subsequent research. If you delay too long, the work can quickly become irrelevant. Thucydides' dictum still applies in this case: "I am not writing for the moment, but for all time." Another factor is that operational histories are produced by a staff agency of Headquarters U.S. Marine Corps and conform to legislative and institutional requirements.

At this writing, the History and Museums Division of Headquarters Marine Corps is completing its Gulf War series by publishing an account of the activities of the 3d Marine Aircraft Wing. The series began with the commencement of hostilities and has carried on to the final volume. In all, some eight titles were published between 1992 to date, all under the series title *U.S. Marines in the Persian Gulf, 1990-1991.* Six titles dealt with the operations of forces in the air, ashore, and afloat. Two were functional rather than operational monographs. Two others indirectly related accounts that cover the forces involved in humanitarian operations in Northern Iraq and Bangladesh. (See table)

The series relied heavily on the use of U.S. Marine Corps Reserve Mobilization training unit historians to collect and present the material. Not surprisingly, each used his own personal style. The authors included two civilian historians, two retired military writers, three active-duty writers, and five Marine Reservists—a mixed group to say the least. Their various backgrounds, included aviation, ground, logistics, and communications. Their educational level was also high, with several Ph.D.s and a National War College graduate. The professional staff of the History and Museums Division carried out production and distribution.

The process of preparing these monographs was a departure from that used during the Vietnam War, which in turn was based on the procedures for both Korea and World War II. An examination of this process leading up to the Gulf War series should indicate what steps might be needed in the future.

Perhaps the biggest problem identified with the "instant history" approach used for the Gulf War was that for smaller or more transitory conflicts (Somalia, Liberia, the Balkans, and Southwest Asia) it is harder to find a satisfactory "story line" within the service context of the operation. Post–Cold War narrative seems to be followed best at the joint headquarters level rather than the unit level—but this leads to a whole range of access, documentation, and inter-service sensitivities. Another problem is that "instant history" does not benefit from collegial debate, the impact of career or budget concerns, nor does it record what might be called "turbulence." Not every document is submitted in a timely manner, some are "short stopped" on their way to the historical division archives.

The Marine Corps produced Vietnam histories between 1974 and 1998. The Army, Navy, and Air Force are still working on their versions. In fairness to them, since the Marines see their role as making Marines and winning battles, this lends itself to a concentration on operational accounts while the other services focus more on broader strategic and policy issues. In addition, current personnel conditions prevent taking the long-term approach that produced the histories of World War II, Korea, and Vietnam; it is almost impossible to keep any one person assigned to a ten-to-twenty year project, even if getting the story right justifies the expense.

One possible solution is the adoption of a "thirty year" rule of records management. This would allow up to ten years to collect and document the actions (including declassification); another ten years to produce a definitive operational history; and a further ten years to work with the records before retiring them to the National Archives and Records Administration.

By way of summary, the historical division of the U.S. Marine Corps learned four main lessons from documenting the Gulf War: one, the importance of using previous historical references; two, the need to collect oral histories; three, the integration of production and collection of command chronologies; and four, the availability of field historians to enhance the process.

A review of the *Manual for the Marine Corps' Historical Programs* indicates three areas that would be useful to incorporate into the education of Marines at all levels in order to document operations in the future (the so-called lessons of the Gulf War). These are a progressive concentration on:

1) References
2) Oral History
3) Command Chronologies

While each of these ingredients can be approached separately, over time they combine to provide commanders and staff officers with an intimate knowledge of and experience in the historical process as it specifically affects individual Marines and Marine Corps commands and units. The issue of field historians will be dealt with separately.

References

While most Marines are taught historical research methods using primary and secondary sources, few have a mastery of the extensive Marine Corps publications that document Corps activities from the American Revolution to the present day. Fewer still understand how operational history can be used in academic or staff work, let alone the contribution such efforts make to the Marine Corps story. Some complain that operational histories are hard to read for pleasure, which is a little like saying that an encyclopedia should read like a Tom Clancy novel. The purpose of operational history is not to entertain, but to provide basic operational facts and narratives for a wide variety of practical uses. These users have to be taught the purpose of operational history starting at the Basic School, and taught again at Amphibious Warfare School, Command and Control Systems School, and finally at the Command and Staff College-level.

Oral Histories

Interview and documenting techniques are required in a variety of staff and problem-solving duties (operations, intelligence, legal, public affairs). What they have in common is the need to provide answers to who, what, where, when, and why, then to record this information in a useful, documented format for current and future use. This involves open-ended interviewing techniques, recording technology, transcription, and disposition. This is a basic skill that begins when one enters the service and should be developed throughout a career.

Command Chronologies

Early on in the Gulf War, the I Marine Expeditionary Force Commander suspended the monthly reporting requirement in lieu of a single submission at the end of hostilities. He also directed the quick declassification of operational records at the conclusion of the conflict. A number of journalists and commentators immediately took advantage of this to produce quick histories with commercial publishers.

Commanders and staff officers have many obligations of an immediate nature, to be sure. But they also have a responsibility to those who may succeed them. Because command chronologies do not move, pay, promote, or supply folks in the present, they are often neglected. This lack of immediacy should not obscure their greater impact over time. Without useful command chronologies, there can be no history of what a unit or command accomplished.

One way to strengthen command histories would be to have Marine students construct reports using historical data from reference books and oral histories to provide an example of the unique approach needed to make such histories useful to others. It would help improve historical and critical analysis (and contribute to better command chronologies). A necessary, but by no means critical, part of this is learning to write in a readable narrative style at odds with the jargon and acronyms of active military service. This is a more indirect benefit of the study of history.

Field Historians

One area that is currently under review is the organization and use of field historians who can be dispatched to conflict areas to improve the documentation of operations. During the Gulf War this was undertaken by reservists who contributed to both the collection and subsequent publication effort, along with the existing mobilization training unit. Both provided a pool of trained field historians who can deploy. Their ability to enhance the existing system, or engage in individual collection, or indeed in the writing effort itself, may vary, but having more individuals involved was still a plus.

The most immediate lessons from the Gulf War historical experience made full use of the existing historical program and structure. The existing publication, reference, and archival facilities allowed the field historians to follow up quickly so that the published products in most cases were "still warm" when delivered. There also was a staff of military and historical professionals to process the submissions as they came in from the field so that documentation was not lost because of indifference or lack of a destination for storage. Declassification began immediately and was completed in a timely manner.

A U.S. Army historian of the Gulf War recently commented that only about 10% of the Army units in the Gulf adequately documented their effort while 85% to 95% of Marine units did so.[2] The Gulf War experience for operational history did not make a revolutionary break with earlier procedures, rather it was successful because of an existing program, experienced personnel, and facilities. This in turn was a legacy of the Vietnam War (as is true of many other Gulf War initiatives). Alas, this same historic infrastructure has suffered in the subsequent Cold War draw-down.

Personal lessons that could be transformed into policy include the integration of civil servants (histories branch), active duty

(Headquarters Marine Corps current operations), and reserve (field history element) efforts to concentrate on the documentation of current events. This would ensure a focus on the process of collection, including the interaction with deployed units, Headquarters Marine Corps, and the transition from current budget and career concerns. There seems to be a natural thirty-year cycle in this process: ten years to collect and declassify documentation, interviews, and comment; ten years to write and review operational history; and ten years to exploit and transfer the records from the Marine Corps to the National Archive and Records Administration (including any final declassification).

While budget and resources are a continuing concern, for active duty Marines there is a continual need to practice the basic skills required to document and study history in a practical sense. The three areas of reference, oral history, and command chronology instruction are suitable for group or individual disciplines and can be brought together at the unit level to ensure continued adequate documentation to produce operational history. This effort can be aided, but not supplanted, by an active and knowledgeable field history unit at Headquarters Marine Corps. The purposes to which these are put will be the challenge for those in the present if they remember that history is an art to be cultivated and not a commodity to be ordered on demand.

Operational History Series Production Summary

Conflict & Dates	Total Volumes	Publishing Span	Average Production Time
World War I (1917–18)	1	1920	2 years
World War II (1941–45)	5	1958–1972	2.8 years@ total of 36 titles (1945–70)
Korean War (1950–53)	5	1954–1972	3.6 years@
Vietnam War (1965–73 or 1954–75)	13	1974–1998	1.8 years@
Gulf War (1990–91)	8	1992–1999	.87 years@

Table 1

NOTES

[1] Personal conversation, MGEN Shutler to the author, Quantico, Virginia, 14 Oct 1998.

[2] Bob Haskell, "Training Course Shows Importance of Keeping Records," *Pentagram* (19 Sept 1998), 11.

The Naval Institute Press is the book-publishing arm of the U.S. Naval Institute, a private, nonprofit, membership society for sea service professionals and others who share an interest in naval and maritime affairs. Established in 1873 at the U.S. Naval Academy in Annapolis, Maryland, where its offices remain today, the Naval Institute has members worldwide.

Members of the Naval Institute support the education programs of the society and receive the influential monthly magazine *Proceedings* and discounts on fine nautical prints and on ship and aircraft photos. They also have access to the transcripts of the Institute's Oral History Program and get discounted admission to any of the Institute-sponsored seminars offered around the country.

The Naval Institute also publishes *Naval History* magazine. This colorful bimonthly is filled with entertaining and thought-provoking articles, first-person reminiscences, and dramatic art and photography. Members receive a discount on *Naval History* subscriptions.

The Naval Institute's book-publishing program, begun in 1898 with basic guides to naval practices, has broadened its scope to include books of more general interest. Now the Naval Institute Press publishes about one hundred titles each year, ranging from how-to books on boating and navigation to battle histories, biographies, ship and aircraft guides, and novels. Institute members receive significant discounts on the Press's more than eight hundred books in print.

Full-time students are eligible for special half-price membership rates. Life memberships are also available.

For a free catalog describing Naval Institute Press books currently available, and for further information about subscribing to *Naval History* magazine or about joining the U.S. Naval Institute, please write to:

> Membership Department
> **U.S. Naval Institute**
> 291 Wood Road
> Annapolis, MD 21402-5034
> Telephone: (800) 233-8764
> Fax: (410) 269-7940
> Web address: www.navalinstitute.org